UP AND ABOUT

UP AND ABOUT

THE HARD ROAD TO EVEREST
DOUG SCOTT

Vertebrate Publishing, Sheffield
www.v-publishing.co.uk

UP AND ABOUT

THE HARD ROAD TO EVEREST

First published in 2015 by Vertebrate Publishing. This paperback edition first published in 2018.

 Vertebrate Publishing
Crescent House, 228 Psalter Lane, Sheffield S11 8UT, UK.
www.v-publishing.co.uk

Front cover: Dougal Haston on the south summit of Everest, 1975. Photo: Doug Scott.

Photography by Doug Scott unless otherwise credited.

This book is a work of non-fiction based on the life of Doug Scott. The author has stated to the publishers that, except in such minor respects not affecting the substantial accuracy of the work, the contents of the book are true.

A CIP catalogue record for this book is available from the British Library.

ISBN: 978-1-911342-82-3 (Paperback)
ISBN: 978-1-910240-42-7 (Ebook)

10 9 8 7 6 5 4 3 2 1

 Design and production by Nathan Ryder.
www.v-publishing.co.uk

Vertebrate Publishing is committed to printing on paper from sustainable sources.

MIX
Paper from responsible sources
FSC® C013056
FSC www.fsc.org

Printed and bound in the UK by T.J. International Ltd, Padstow, Cornwall.

CONTENTS

To Jan, Michael, Martha and Rosie.

All the world's a stage,
And all the men and women merely players;
They have their exits and their entrances,
And one man in his time plays many parts,
His acts being seven ages.

As You Like It, William Shakespeare

PREFACE

Here are a few observations about writing an autobiography starting with a chance remark I made to Dai Davidson, my local plumber, who had his head under the floorboards of my office as I passed by clutching a sheaf of papers. 'You're so lucky to be working with your hands, Dai.' He withdrew his head and looked up at me for a second or two. 'Are you telling me that I can't do your job and anyone could do mine? You are working with your hands, it's all the bloody same man.'

Dai's reply gave me pause for thought. Writers often come across as a pretentious lot but I could see there wasn't a huge difference between writers and tradesmen; both have to conceive what it is they want their hands to achieve. First the thought, then the action and the end result will depend on the clarity of that conception. A prerequisite seems to be intensity of experience – something that occurs regularly in the mountains.

This reminded me of when I was avalanched on Mazeno Peak in Pakistan. Rattling down a 500-metre gully, with time suspended, I found myself observing everything I experienced, as though from a bubble. There was no fear, just a series of impressions: tumbling down over rock and ice cliffs, wondering at how resilient the human body is and that I was still alive, turning this way and that, my whole weight bouncing off my right ankle. There was no pain, but I noted the situation was serious. I was then in space, clearing a step, sliding with the snow but unaware of the speed of my descent; I had time to register it was like being up with Leo Dickinson in his hot air balloon, not aware of the wind because we were moving at the same speed. I bumped gradually to a halt, partially buried on the glacier below but able to clear the snow away from my face, release the waist belt on my rucksack and breathe more easily.

There are other ways to have intense experiences. At an Edvard Munch art exhibition I was amazed to discover the lengths the artist would go to in order to generate creativity through denial and suffering. I was left wondering how valid it is to represent the manifestations of self-induced neuroses. I seemed to write best when I could forget myself, or at least go beyond myself, something I managed when I wrote stories for my children from the mountains, often about a character I called 'Warlock' – my alter ego, but a better version ruled by conscience. That, of course, was private stuff, like my diaries and letters written from the perilous mountains like a condemned man in his cell or a soldier sitting in the trenches.

What writing might climbers do at Base Camp, to friends and family, if such words were only to be read when dead? To communicate all that was good about their shared lives and make honest confessions that would otherwise be too awkward to face: parents taken for granted, wife abandoned or kids neglected. If we were aware of our mortality, if we remembered all the time that we are going to die, then we would deal with a huge amount we put to one side and write about it more honestly. This autobiography is a good chance for me to sort it all out even if everything is not included.

All I have to do now is overcome the disease of tomorrow and put pen to paper. The best antidote to that in the past has been naked ambition but at seventy-four that is starting to weaken. Hopefully, I will be able to keep the muse alive at the prospect of clearing more junk out of the way and creating more space for good things to happen. There is always the chance that others will find what I have to say of interest – I hope so.

I began climbing when I was a schoolboy. It feels like someone else started me off; he then turned into quite another person before changing again. Now I feel a need to turn full circle, certainly as far as my understanding of climbing is concerned. Children have something to show us, something that becomes obscured with the passage of time; anyone who came to climbing an innocent and of his own volition might benefit from looking back to those early years. I wonder now at the spontaneous antics of my youth.

It takes more than a cursory glance to see how it really was; only with a big effort am I right there, hands grazed and bloody from days on gritstone, my fingers smelling of lichen, my face wind-blasted and my limbs weary from storms on Kinder or cold, wet bivvies under boulders on Stanage with bacon and grit butties for breakfast and stews reeking of paraffin fumes for dinner, of singing in pubs and at the back of the bus back to Nottingham on Sunday nights. With these memories of smell, touch and taste of those distant times, like a film clip it starts to roll and I am right there, my memory sparked into life, seeing faces of who was there and a sense as well of who I was.

I see in the past the clues of who I am now.

That boy, who seemed like someone else, now seems like me again; I must just let these film clips run or I will get it all wrong. I must also admit I am lucky to have the carrot of this book to keep me at it through a million distractions. It is a real privilege to be paid to check myself out. I find I can't recall anything of my first three years and neither can I pinpoint any specific reason that led me to climb in the first place, so whether or not it was fate that I should have this 'rat' in my gut, or whether it was my destiny to wander the world's mountain ranges, I don't know, but perhaps something will emerge from what follows – so look out for clues!

Here is a warning to any young lad thinking of taking the mountain path: it's very hard to get off – I've tried but I'm happily resigned to walk and climb until I die as things are right now. The rational among you may shiver: 'My God, he's got a death wish.' My competitors might once have worried that I would be around forever, but now they can take satisfaction in my revelations of weakness. Admirers may feel let down – well, hard luck; my friends and kindred spirits will remain so, however close I get to the bone.

What am I letting myself in for? At one time, in the beginning, I would jump in feet first and ask questions later. Now I've got the bad habit of preparing the ground ahead – meaning reducing the risks by knowing what's coming. I've pulled a few books off my shelf to see what others have said, the book falling open at the apposite pages, as they do sometimes when you're really going for it. I got this from *Ascent* in 1976, where Tom Higgins responded to David Roberts' assertion that most autobiographies were somewhat banal and predictable. Tom found that Walter Bonatti at least could lift his spirits; I would like to do that, of course. On another shelf, another word of caution, this time from Alfred Richard Orage, socialist and editor of *The New Age*, about art as a means of power:

'To *express* himself is not enough; he wishes to *impress* himself. Readers feel towards him the repulsion as well as the attraction of the snake for the bird. Power they instinctively feel is there, and they are afraid of it. Style is only the device adopted by great writers to make their power more attractive. Style is power made gracious; we must write as if Homer and Demosthenes were to be our judges, as if our lives depended upon this approval ... All perfection is the fruit of sacrifice.'

That had me worried – immobilised and powerless for days. But I recall that I failed my English O level twice, so any style I have should be transparent at best and unlikely to pull the wool over any one's eyes. I turned to *Beelzebub's*

Tales to His Grandson, opened it at once at the page in the chapter 'The Arousing of Thought', where George Gurdjieff gives his opinion of professional writers: 'First of all, I am not young; I have already lived so much that I have been in my life, as it is said, "not only through the mill but through all the grindstones"; and secondly, I am in general not writing so as to make a career for myself, or so as to plant myself, as is said "firm-footedly", thanks to this profession, which, I must add, in my opinion provides many openings to become a candidate d-i-r-e-c-t for "Hell" … knowing nothing whatsoever themselves, they write all kinds of "claptrap" and thereby automatically acquiring authority … ' (Then again, Gurdjieff went out of his way to make his writings obscure. 'I bury the bone so deep that the dogs have to scratch for it.')

Though I have grasped the point, I hesitate and consult the *I Ching,* throwing hexagram 63. After completion, 'in principle, everything stands systematised, and it is only in regard to details that success is still to be achieved … everything proceeds as if of its own accord and this can too easily tempt us to relax and let things take their course without troubling over details. Symptoms of decay are bound to be the result; the need is for unremitting perseverance and caution.'

It is obviously no good just 'spitting it out'; I am going to have to remind myself to write from the heart to *express* the facts. Are you *impressed*? If not, try this from Tolstoy which is more encouraging: 'Art is a human activity having for its purpose the transmission to others of the highest and best feeling to which men have arisen.' And where do these 'highest and best feelings' arise? According to people living on the edge of existence, like the Caribou shaman Igjugarjuk: 'All true wisdom is only to be found far from the dwellings of men, in the great solitudes; and it can only be obtained through suffering. Suffering and privation are the only things that can open the mind of man to that which is hidden from his fellows.'

That must leave a familiar taste on the palate of anyone who has pushed themselves to the very limit on any weekend on our British hills or crags. As long as it was the limit, they will know what Igjugarjuk is talking about. They will have come back physically tired from their weekend's exertions, but inwardly glowing, enough to see themselves through the next week at work.

So, here I am, back at my desk, to live again the pain and pleasure, the heartache and happiness, though I doubt if you will be interested in all of it, and I wouldn't have the courage to tell you all of it anyway. This memoir is important, according to my Buddhist friends. They tell me that everything I have done will be 'up for review' on passing out of this life into the next, when I will have to pay for my sins by living again the pain I inflicted on others. I understand that it's a good idea to become aware of just how much my actions have affected others, not only to reduce the future shock but also to avoid thoughtless actions now: humility before senility, turning passion into compassion.

Just as I have committed to fight the disease of tomorrow and get down to this review of my climbing I was called away yet again, to Tierra del Fuego, where I read *Uttermost Part of the Earth* by E. Lucas Bridges. It includes a very perceptive observation made by the sculptor and Arabist Rom Landau: 'most of us cherish imaginary romantic notions about ourselves and only rarely succeed in breaking through the crust of self-deception … In books of an autobiographical background, an occasional word of self-criticism is usually outweighed by pages of self-praise, however cunningly disguised.'

Again, I hesitate, with this reminder to be honest, wondering if I am up to it, knowing the truth is relative to experience. Have I enough experience, for instance, to gauge the effect on those I write about? I know how I have been affected by what others have written about me in their autobiographies. I know there are many other climbing friends and acquaintances better equipped, far more honest than I, to write such a book about themselves – those of my friends who have passed on and never bothered, and those that live without much ego, living in the now, without the inclination to review their lives. And if they did, the tales they would tell would be as important and interesting as any of mine. They might well be told with better recall and more skill than I can muster.

For all these reasons, and more, I hesitate to write about the fact that from an early age I never felt so vital, more alive or spontaneously joyous, as when off with the gang, out into the countryside, the quiet of the forest, watching wildlife by the canal or lake, going a little further each time, learning to pace the journey and to find the way back home. One thing led to another; there was never any obvious plan: the country round my home, the Peak District, the mountains of Snowdonia, Scotland, the Alps and the Himalaya, always a little further, no turning back, hooked on steeper ground and higher summits, to the highest place, Everest, and beyond.

Beyond Everest? Yes, when I discovered there is more to be gained with less – fewer people, less equipment and less cost enabling more journeys, one after the other, twice a year or more, constantly prepared physiologically and psychologically for life in the thin cold air. I was driven to go where 'no one had gone before'. I came to know, as Don Munday did, hunting down *The Unknown Mountain*, that 'the joy of pioneering can be as transcendent as that of a composer of music is above one who is merely able to play it.'

Part of it was sheer curiosity, to know the lie of the land between peaks I'd climbed, putting another piece of the jigsaw into place, just as the old surveyors recorded details within the triangle of their calculations. I gained this knowledge, both inner and outer, among the most dramatic and beautiful landscapes in the world helped along by local people so attuned to life in the high Himal and elsewhere. Over the years I came to make a strong connection with these people who helped me climb their mountains and eventually responded to their request for help in improving conditions of labour in the climbing industry and the health and education in their villages. This was a good move, since it guaranteed me a continuing presence in their magnificent mountains and helped me know more about them and the nature of things, as if waking up now and again from a deep sleep, if only for a moment, to glimpse the infinite beauty and wonder of what is normally hidden, as Shakespeare explained it:

> Are not these woods
> More free from peril than the envious court?
> Here feel we but the penalty of Adam,
> The seasons' difference, as the icy fang
> And churlish chiding of the winter's wind,
> Which, when it bites and blows upon my body,
> Even till I shrink from cold, I smile and say
> "This is no flattery: these are counsellors
> That feelingly persuade me what I am."
> Sweet are the uses of adversity ...
> And this our life exempt from public haunt
> Finds tongues in trees, books in running brooks,
> Sermons in stones and good in everything.
> I would not change it.
>
> *As You Like It*

THE 1ST AGE

At first, the infant,
Mewling and puking in the nurse's arms.
Then the whining schoolboy, with his satchel
And shining morning face, creeping like snail
Unwillingly to school.

As You Like It, William Shakespeare

If he awakens hungry in the night he signals with
a soft grunt if he cannot find her breast; she will
then give it to him and again his well-being will
be re-established, without ever having come near
to straining the limits of his continuum. His life,
full of action, is consistent with the lives lived
by millions of his predecessors and meets
the expectations of his nature.

The Continuum Concept, Jean Liedloff

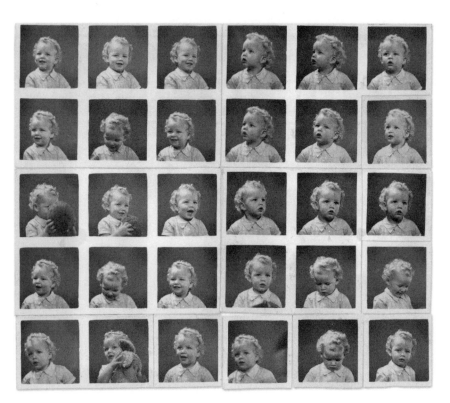

Douglas Keith Scott, aged just eighteen months in November 1942.

WARCHILD

In about the seventh year the changing of the teeth indicate
that the 'life forces of the body have completed their first task
– the building of a physical organism. The spiritual forces that
have been brought from the prenatal forces are still strong …
The child is mobile, spritely and unselfconscious.'
The Number Seven, A.E. Abbot

As a teenager my mother Joyce visited a fortune-teller who told her she would marry a man in uniform with shiny buttons and have three sons, the eldest of whom would be in trouble in a shelter, very high up – and that the whole world would be watching. Mum married a policeman, on 1 June 1940. I was born a year later, almost to the day. She had two more sons and many years later I survived a risky bivouac just below the summit of Everest. Thereafter Mum was much more relaxed when I went climbing. Later I discovered she'd been born at the same moment as Edmund Hillary. There may be something going on out there – a force propelling us down pre-determined lines, a hidden potential, much greater than outward appearances would suggest.

Mum was born in a terraced house that opened on to Queen's Grove, a cobbled street quite near to Nottingham's Midland railway station in an area called The Meadows. Grandma Gregory would scrub the front steps to keep them spotless. The front door, with its polished brass knob, led directly into the front room, the best in the house, where only the doctor seemed to be invited. The rest of the world entered from the backyard where there was an outside lavatory and a galvanised bath hanging between the back door and a sash window. Not much light came into the back; the yard was below street level and a few feet away from the high wall of the neighbouring timber merchant.

At the end of Queen's Grove was the Grove Tavern. Every evening, and lunchtime on Sundays, Gran would walk across with a large white jug and bring it back frothing over with stout. Grandad sat by the fire, wheezing and coughing into a pot. He wasn't a well man after years of smoking up to a hundred cigarettes a day, a habit he developed fighting in the Great War. Life in the trenches and years working as a coal miner and then in a slaughter-house had left him with arthritis. Once a week, the bath was brought in and filled with kettles and pots of boiling water from off the kitchen range. A clothes horse was arranged around it with towels and blankets to give Grandad some privacy while he took his bath.

With Grandad sick, Grandma did well to bring up three children on less than four pounds per week; there was very little state support. I remember visiting Gran and being treated to sugar butties, white bread and margarine with sugar sprinkled on. But despite the hardships, there was always something going on with my uncles Roy and Keith and all their friends milling about the house. Keith, seven years younger than Mum, was called up for National Service and he looked most dashing in his RAF uniform. Roy, always fit, swam and played water polo for Nottingham.

My father George came from a sporting family; his great-grandfather had been secretary of Notts County FC and his dad won many sporting trophies. My grandfather had died in 1938 from a burst peptic ulcer. Grandma Scott had stayed on in their comfortable bungalow in Wollaton Park until a woman latched on to her, offering her companionship in her loneliness. Grandma Scott was gradually swindled of all her money and with nothing left to pay the rent ended up in complete penury in a condemned house on Arthur Terrace in Radford, not far from my school. As an older boy I used to cycle round once a week to visit.

Dad was particularly annoyed Grandma had more or less given away the 'family silver' – sporting trophies that he and his dad and grandad had won playing football, cricket and athletics. I would sit with her on a chair at the kitchen table where she lit a candle since she rarely had enough money for the electric meter. She usually had a blanket over her shoulders; coal was rationed and too expensive to burn all the time. I did a few chores, bringing in coal, lighting the fire and checking to make sure the outside lavatory was in working order; then I would report back to Mum and Dad on the state of the house and Grandma's complaints about the neighbours, who seemed to be prostitutes.

Although Dad visited Gran regularly to carry out various plumbing repairs and once to put in a new fireplace, there always seemed to be quite a tension between Dad and his mother, although I could never work out why. Mum seemed to write Gran off as being simpleminded for letting herself be used and brought down in the world. Gran was, however, kind to my brother and me

Doting parents in the back garden of 174 Charlbury Road in June 1941. The railway embankment and Dad's bean poles in the background.

when she was asked to look after us if Mum went off to town or when Mum and Dad had a night out on holiday.

Dad was educated at Lenton Secondary School and when he left as head boy was awarded the 'Albert Ball Prize', in honour of the handsome flying ace born and raised in Lenton. For his first job Dad was apprenticed to a motor mechanic. He also joined the Denman Street Lads' Club where he started boxing, something he quickly mastered. On the strength of his boxing ability, Dad joined the Nottingham City Police Force even though he was half an inch below the required six feet in height. With encouragement from its famous chief constable Captain Athelstan Popkess, the Nottingham City Police boxing team became internationally famous. In 1938, after knocking out the German champion in Stuttgart, Dad became European police light-heavyweight boxing champion. 'We have nothing to fear from Hitler with men like George Scott in our midst,' was how one newspaper recorded it.

There are plenty of tales of Dad as a bobby on the beat armed only with his truncheon, whistle and boxing skills. The latter came in useful breaking up a fracas with his friend and fellow boxer, PC Jerry Beaves, at a notorious pub on Denman Street. Bottles and chairs were flying around the room, but a few well-directed straight-arm jabs laid some brawlers out while the rest rushed for the door. After that the pub became quite respectable – or so the story goes. Another time, a dray horse bolted down Friar Gate towards a busy road junction. Dad ran alongside and pulled the horse's head down by its reins.

3

He received a police commendation for his quick thinking and was later promoted to sergeant, but never could pass his inspector's exams. Mum had us all creeping round like mice while he studied for them.

So I was born the son of a boxing champion, on 29 May 1941, having been conceived during the Battle of Britain at the start of a war whose outcome was wholly uncertain. For my parents and the city of Nottingham it was a life-and-death struggle to preserve democracy and civilisation, yet my childhood seemed entirely normal. We lived on the edge of town in a semi-detached house on a cul-de-sac still lit with gas lamps at night, sandwiched between a railway embankment and a disused canal leading west out of the city.

At the end of the road were miles of green fields to roam in and woods in which to make dens and climb trees for hours after school and on fine weekends. Beyond the woods were ponds and scrublands and gangs of youths from other communities who either became instant friends or with whom we fought running battles. There was Wollaton Pit with its slag heaps and workings to explore. Five miles away was the Hemlock Stone, thirty feet high and said to have been thrown by a goblin inhabiting Helsby Crag in Cheshire at his enemy on Nottingham Castle Rock. The stone had fallen short but it provided us with a good objective for long hikes.

Dad had an allotment in farmer Frank Earp's field only a short walk from our house. It got a direct hit during a bombing raid on 16 November 1940 and became a bomb crater, another casualty of war. In the same raid a bomb landed in the canal pond and though it failed to explode, the impact still sent pike and other fish over houses and on to the road and field. My mother must have found all this quite harrowing, carrying me in her womb without her mother or mother-in-law to help, wondering if she would be a victim of the next air raid. We shared an Anderson shelter of galvanised corrugated steel with next door. The inside was painted white and clay heaped on the outside. It was soon covered with grass and a cascade of aubrietia.

The wailing of sirens had everyone along our road scurrying off, down into their shelters, except for the night of Good Friday 1941, at the bend in the road, when a woman called Maude Tomlinson was caught out and killed as a bomb destroyed her house just a few weeks before I was born. Altogether four houses were rebuilt and were always known as the 'bombed buildings'.

The worst raid was on the night of 8 to 9 May, when a hundred German aircraft attacked Nottingham, dropping 500 high-explosive bombs and thousands of incendiaries. Bastards! Our road escaped this time but there was terrible carnage in town where the Co-op bakery was hit and forty-nine people killed in the Co-op shelter. The situation at that time was dire. Although the Battle of Britain had been won and the British Empire still covered a quarter of the globe, Britain felt very much alone. The possibility of defeat was in most people's minds since every time British armed forces met the Germans they got pushed back on land and sea. After the loss of Crete to a smaller German force, it seemed the Germans were unbeatable.

A month after I was born the nation's situation improved. Hitler launched Operation Barbarossa against the Soviet Union, and in December the Japanese bombed Pearl Harbour, bringing America into the war. Later I asked my parents whether in those dark days of 1940 and 1941 they expected Britain would be defeated. They both said they had every confidence Mr Churchill would pull them through and were quite disgusted when, after the war, he was not re-elected.

Mum boasted I was a strong baby with powerful lungs, able to rock the crib across the bare boards of the bedroom floor from one wall to the other as I screamed for attention between feeds. She said the screaming was awful but Dr Loewenthal, an Austrian Jew who had escaped the Holocaust, warned Mum against spoiling me. Given that I have been screaming for attention ever since, it might be said the doctor had quite an influence on my future life, although not as much as that other Austrian, Adolf Hitler – and his war. Husbands were taken from wives and children into the armed forces, denying sons and daughters the firm hand of a father. I became something of a tearaway and Mum was only too pleased to have me out of house and into the woods and fields beyond.

My parents were immensely proud of their infant son. They entered me in a local baby show in August 1942 when I was fifteen months old. As reported in the *Nottingham Journal*, I won my category; the actor Tod Slaughter, famous for playing Sweeney Todd, presented me with a rosette and the actress Patricia Hastings gave me a kiss. There was also a cash prize in the form of a National Savings Gift Token sent by post from the secretary of the West Bridgford Urban District Council to 'Master Douglas Keith Scott as First Prize in the Holiday at Home Week, Bonniest Baby Competition, Class II.' While some are born famous and some seek fame, others have fame thrust upon them, thanks, in my case, to doting parents. Even though there was a war on and our situation dire, it was a case of keep calm and carry on.

In 1942 Dad was called up into the army, first in a Royal Artillery regiment but later, when his commanding officers recognised his natural sporting talents, transferred to the Army Physical Training Corps for the last three years of the war. Dad wasn't just a boxer. He played football for Nottingham Boys at Lenton School and made the annual town swim from Wilford Bridge to Trent Bridge. He was an athlete too and later became an official for the Nottingham Amateur Athletics Association. The ideals of amateur sport ran through his veins.

My earliest memories are of Dad returning on leave with his white canvas kitbag in a corner of the hallway and the shiny peak and regimental badge of

'Master Douglas Keith Scott, First Prize in the Holiday at Home Week, Bonniest Baby Competition, Class II.'

his army cap on the clothes peg. In 1943 he came home on leave from the army with several wooden toys, including a rocking horse he had made and a sheet of plywood with a quote from Grantland Rice carved into it:

> For when the one great scorer comes
> To mark against your name
> He writes – not that you won or lost –
> But how you played the game.

It was the only wall-hanging in my otherwise spartan bedroom and stayed above my bed until I left for college.

I can still picture Dad marching down the road at the end of the war wearing his khaki uniform with his kitbag on his shoulder and being scooped up. I can still feel the rough serge of his battledress top. He was given the usual demob suit. It was pinstripe and had sharp lapels, and came in useful later whenever I went to fancy dress parties as Al Capone.

Although our house was rented and there was no support from family money, I never thought of our family as poor. By careful management of their finances, along with recycling and buying second-hand, my parents were able to provide all the necessities. Their generation was used to frugal living, having vivid memories of the Great Depression of the early 1930s. Compared to the terraced houses my grandparents occupied, we seemed quite well off in our semi-detached.

I remember the blackout curtains and a Morrison shelter – a metal, box-like table – in the middle of the dining room. The walls were a dreary mix of old mustard and green paint but we could draw near to a fire of glowing coke, which was cheaper than coal. Just before bed a shovel of slag, or powdered coal, was heaped on which kept the fire alive until morning, taking the chill out of the air. There was no central heating. Dad fetched the coke from the Radford gasworks, two miles away, carrying the sack over the crossbar of his bike with me sitting on top.

During the war and the period of austerity that followed there was a good deal of mutual support among neighbours and friends who all seemed to take pride in coping, finding a certain dignity in belt-tightening and an egalitarian lifestyle that put everyone in the same boat. The constant worry of war and the rationing of essential items made everyone more equal and the gap between rich and poor seem less.

To celebrate VE Day, the end of hostilities in Europe on 8 May, everyone carried their tables and chairs into the centre of our road and filled them with sandwiches, cakes and jellies. Effigies of Hitler were burned, leaving small craters in the tarmac that got wider and deeper with each passing year.

The Charlbury Road VE Day party. Mum is standing second from right, and Brenda Jones is the fourth child back facing the camera on the left-hand side of the table.

Nottingham had escaped the worst of the bombing with 179 people killed and 350 injured – nothing like the carnage in London, where 50,000 died, and other major cities like Liverpool. There were many British servicemen killed in action and several grieving families on our road. Troops returning home went through a stressful period of readjustment. Mr Boothwright next door came back emaciated from intense fighting in North Africa.

My strongest memory of the war was Lord Haw-Haw being hanged for treason. His strange name stuck in my mind every time he came on the radio with the words, 'Germany calling, Germany calling,' denouncing Jews and urging us to surrender. I later discovered he wasn't English at all, despite the accent, but was in fact an American-born Irishman, William Joyce, who had a terrible scar from ear to mouth from being slashed across the face at a Conservative election rally in the 1920s. The scar split open when he was hanged.

Neighbours were always round to gossip over cups of tea and most evenings play cards on the green baize covering our steel table. All this stopped for the nine o'clock news as everyone listened to the latest progress of our troops in North Africa and Italy and after the Normandy landings in France. The wireless was always on and my parents were avid listeners. Dad's favourite was Tommy Handley and his *ITMA* team – *It's That Man Again!* I will always associate Sunday roast dinner with *Much-Binding-in-the-Marsh*, starring Kenneth Horne and Richard Murdoch as senior staff officers battling red tape on a fictional RAF station. When the BBC put on *Dick Barton, Special Agent* after the war, every child on the street stopped playing just before 6.45 p.m. and rushed indoors to hear ex-commando Captain Richard Barton MC and his friends Jock and Snowy saving the nation night after night. The only problem was the timing; being indoors when it finished at 7 p.m. meant there was little excuse for not being in on time for bath and bed.

Despite the privations of rationing everyone on our road ate well and seemed healthy. With so many children of a similar age, there was an endless series of parties and even with rationing there were always cakes and sandwiches left over and presents and prizes for the winners of musical chairs and pass-the-parcel. Children were given free bottles of cod liver oil and orange juice; once a day I was given a tablespoon full of glutinous Virol, said to be full of essential vitamins and other mysterious ingredients required by the body. Dad was adept at supplementing our meals with venison from Wollaton Park and rabbits and wood pigeon. Being a policeman probably helped with this.

By the end of the long summer holidays we were covered in scratches from gathering blackberries along the railway embankment. Families climbed over their fences, crossed a ditch of stagnant water and waded into the prickly bushes clutching bags and basins before returning with them brimming with fruit. Mum put ours in the sink to soak and drew my attention to the little grubs that had floated out of the berries. It was a sure way to prevent me eating more than I brought home.

Gardening and growing vegetables in allotments was a constant in Dad's life. He encouraged Mum and later his sons to save every scrap of waste vegetable and other organic matter for the bean trench and compost heap. He grew a huge amount, not only vegetables but also tomatoes and soft fruit, in a relatively small space. I was naturally happiest imitating everything Dad did and was therefore subliminally inducted into gardening at a very early age. My parents fenced off the bottom of the garden for chickens. One Christmas Dad took the cockerel on to his lap and, after stroking it, wrung its neck for dinner, only the bird's head came off and the cockerel escaped, running around the garden with blood spurting out of its neck.

Early every morning the milkman came up our road in his horse-drawn cart leaving horse muck on the road and bottles of milk on the step. I can still hear the ring of Dad's shovel on the tarmac, as he rushed out to scoop up precious manure for his vegetables and Mum's roses. Mum quickly brought the milk into the house since the sparrows and starlings would peck through the cardboard cap to get at the cream. It was the cream Mum was after, to make butter and also cottage cheese after the cream had hung from the clothesline in a muslin bag for a day or two. Another of Mum's seasonal jobs was blanching the runner beans, before salting them for the winter in large earthenware pots.

Mum was a supervisor at the John Player cigarette factory when she became pregnant with me. Forever after she remained a housewife, always hard at work gardening, cooking, washing and mending clothes on the Singer sewing machine, knitting jumpers or darning socks over a Bakelite mushroom. Apart from visiting Dad at Larkhill near Stonehenge in Wiltshire during the war, Mum had hardly been further away from Nottingham than the east coast. Her world view was constrained by what she read in newspapers, heard on the wireless or gleaned from conversations with friends and neighbours. She put family first and was a little suspicious of everyone beyond it. When I nibbled at the rind on the thick wedges of Cheddar Mum bought, she'd warn me not to do it since 'niggers had touched it.' I had no idea what 'niggers' were; nor had my mum ever met anyone from Africa.

Every so often gypsies would appear on the road, prompting an encounter between two very different worlds. The gypsies were usually youngish women with dark faces, long black hair and flashing eyes, wearing voluminous skirts, carrying a baby on one arm and a large wicker basket full of clothes pegs in the other. We all stopped play to gather round. Mum usually had a long chat with the gypsy woman who came to our door, before buying some pegs, but there was a sigh of relief when the nomadic gypsies moved on from our community, with its set values and codes of behaviour.

Mum also spoke fearfully of the Earp's farmhouse where, she said, they had 'galloping consumption'. She also said it was haunted. Her anxiety impressed me, because I never did go to that farmhouse – not even into their orchard scrumping apples. I listened as Dad passed the time of day with Frank Earp. Frank had led a colourful life travelling around North America before the Great War, where he did some panning for gold. He had also suffered, having lost two daughters to tuberculosis and was later crippled after a dray horse bolted and the cart ran over his legs. After that he turned his tenanted farm into a market garden, letting Dad and other keen gardeners have strips of land at the beginning of hostilities so they could all 'dig for victory'.

Meals were always eaten sitting around the dining table. There was beef on Sunday with Yorkshire pudding, lots of gravy and our own potatoes and greens, usually followed by bread and butter pudding. There was more beef on Monday, with all the vegetables mixed and fried up as bubble and squeak, a simple meal because Monday was washday. There was enough leftover beef fat and gravy to have bread and dripping sandwiches with lots of salt for a few days. We had liver on Tuesday, tripe and onions on Wednesday, stew or belly pork on Thursday, fish on Friday, sausage and chips on Saturday.

I never tasted cake better than Mum's flapjack made from treacle. I never had a better dinner than Mum's stew and dumplings made with parsley and so light and puffy, floating on the gravy; no bread made my mouth water more than

Mum's bread baked in the back oven with the aroma filling the house. I once asked Mum if she could make mashed potatoes like they did for school dinners. 'How could you like potatoes from processed, powdered potato and not from our own, home-grown potatoes?' she asked angrily, which made me think.

There was a sudden evacuation of the kitchen when all the hot, sweet rice and milk in Mum's new pressure cooker came spurting out of a failed valve and hit the ceiling, spraying the whole of the kitchen, including Mum, who then went back to using saucepans. There was always great consternation when the red gas meter, tucked away under the stairs, ran out of shilling pieces and the gas cooker went out, until more shillings were found after rummaging around handbags and coat pockets.

Until her first washing machine arrived, Mum was kept busy boiling clothes in the steaming-hot gas copper, rubbing clothes and sheets down the washboard and finally rinsing off the soap in the dolly tub and putting them through the mangle. Then they were hung out on the clothes line, if it wasn't raining, otherwise there would be clothes and sheets all over the house. Her workload only increased after my brother Brian arrived in April 1944.

I wasn't much help, quite the reverse, since I often caused her worry coming in late or going missing for hours at a time. Her constant lament was, 'You will drive me into Mapperley, Douglas,' when I finally reappeared, Mapperley being the local lunatic asylum, as such places were then called. The one advantage of Dad being away in the army was the chance for me to snuggle up in bed with Mum when it was freezing out, or after a bad dream, or when miserable with chicken pox. That came to an end when Dad was on leave. I would slip into their bed only for Dad to carry me back to mine, cold and alone in the empty room, cut off and miserable, especially when I had wet the bed. One night Dad gently led me back to bed from the landing where he had found me peeing down the stairs in my sleep.

During the day I went off with the older boys along the canal or to 'the land of ferns', as we called it, and beyond to Bilborough and Strelley. I was drawn to open country; looking over the horizon, having unexpected encounters with other children and then, exhausted, finding my way home again. It gave me huge satisfaction. I remember going off with the gang in a new green coat Mum had saved up to buy for my fifth birthday. The older lads had an altercation with a gang of youths on a building site and I got caught in the crossfire, returning home caked in clay and crying with earache. Mum put me to bed with warm olive oil pouring out of my ears on to the pillow and the pain subsided. Mum's usual remedies were Indian brandy and lemon in hot water for tummy troubles, Vicks and eucalyptus oil for chesty colds and, if that failed, I'd breathe in the steam from a basin of hot water and Friar's Balsam from under a towel draped over my head.

There were often hushed discussions about diphtheria, scarlet fever, polio and pneumonia, all of them a threat to life and limb – my first playmate, the neighbour's three-year-old son, Philip Jones, died of pneumonia. In 1941 a patient had been successfully treated with penicillin but it was a few years before it was in common use. However, the National Health Service came into being in 1948 and Mum was quick to take advantage of it, having me admitted to hospital to have my tonsils removed and a year later having my ears syringed. Both have been perforated ever since. I was again admitted into hospital to have my sinuses drained, leaving me with a poor sense of smell.

It was a half-hour walk to the shops and Mum would often persuade Brenda Jones, Philip's sister, who was quite grown up and lived next door, to take me with her. I would go along on my tricycle, coming back with a stick of liquorice in my teeth, sucking a Sherbet Fountain out of a cardboard tube. Brenda was nine or ten and would tease me on the return journey, threatening to leave me, which had me in floods of tears. Eventually Brenda's family left, never having got over the loss of Philip during the war. Our new neighbour was a Pole, Val Maciejewski, and his English wife Hazel. Val had fought for the Allies during the war and was now a hard-working electrician at Castle Donington power station.

I often walked with my father up to the Raleigh Bicycle Company's playing field where Dad was allowed to use the sporting facilities for training. In 1945 he had become British heavyweight amateur boxing champion and had set his sights on the 1948 Olympic Games. I would sit in the gym with its smell of leather punchbags as Dad and others slogged away at the big body-sized bags or rapidly pounded the smaller, rounder leather balls at head height, as they sprang back and forth. Skipping ropes swished through the air, flicking the boards, raising chalk dust as weightlifters hissed and groaned under their burden. I overhead the frightful tale of the groundsman rushed to hospital after a rat ran up one trouser leg, bit him between the legs and then ran down the other.

Eventually Dad had to come to terms with his age and the fact his wife wasn't happy about him continuing to box; for a short time, it was a source of heated arguments. Mum was genuinely worried that Dad would suffer permanent injury since he was now boxing at heavyweight despite trying to diet down to light-heavyweight. So Dad gave up his Olympic ambitions for Mum and his family. At the end of every week he would put all his wages on the kitchen table for Mum to distribute.

I was sometimes taken to see Dad box in 'exhibition bouts' with famous professionals of the time, Freddie Mills and Bruce Woodcock. This was usually in aid of local charities and to promote upcoming bouts. I became aware of the clear distinction between an amateur and a professional; there was

Dad in a boxing pose, with the Army Physical Training Corps badge on his vest.
He was British Army boxing champion in 1945.

always the underlying assumption that those who boxed for money were not quite kosher – not true sportsmen. I don't recall Dad making a big thing about it, beyond mentioning it in general conversation with friends. He was visibly disappointed if boxers, footballers or any other sporting personalities were featured in the newspapers for scandalous reasons. That was letting the sport down.

I would sometimes walk alongside Mum pushing Brian in the pram around Wollaton Park, a journey of about four miles. Wollaton Park was a wonderful asset to the city with a seven-mile boundary wall that, according to Dad, took one bricklayer and his two apprentices seven years, seven months and seven days to build. There had been 2,000 American paratroopers camped on the park ready for D-Day and towards the end of the war we would see Italian and German prisoners of war lined up for exercise or being marched off to work on community projects.

The centrepiece of the park was the Elizabethan Wollaton Hall, set on a man-made hill and sold to the city in 1925 by Lord Middleton to become a natural history museum. During good winters the grounds around the hall were a mecca for sledging, with parents and children trudging across the snow-covered fields from all the housing estates around about. There were also avenues of mature chestnut trees, and in the autumn, first with Dad and then with friends, we would scout around for perfectly weighted sticks to throw at the prickly fruit to knock it off. We'd take the chestnuts home and roast them on the fire, or in one of our dens.

In 1946 I started Harrow Road primary school. The reception class teacher was Mrs Perrins, whose husband went down with his ship after being torpedoed by a U-boat. I remember the polished desks, the green checked tablecloths for when we had morning milk and lunch, the wooden bricks and Bakelite tubes. There was Annette Burton who couldn't stop crying, a boy with greasy black hair who wouldn't stop bullying and the screeching of chalk on board that made me shudder. We chanted the times tables, the only useful thing I learned in class. Mum had me learning the alphabet, which I would recite to Dad when he came home on leave; that helped me to read before I went to school. But I was never among the clever pupils, who were asked to write the number of milk bottles required on a slate and put it outside the classroom door.

Nor was I the best-behaved pupil, certainly not in the eyes of the school dinner lady, Mrs Wall. Mum cycled to school one day to give me a message and asked Mrs Wall if she knew where I was. 'If you ever find that little bugger, keep him away from me,' she said. Mum questioned me later about this but I honestly had no idea what I'd done. Maybe I just had too much energy. I was forever running around the school playing fields, flowerbeds and outbuildings, one of a gang of kids in perpetual motion, chasing each other. The only time I sat still was when the teacher, for half an hour a day, read from Hans Christian Andersen. The whole class would sit rapt in the story; I have the clearest memory of those wonderful readings – like a familiar taste or smell.

In the terrible winter of 1947 the snow was so deep it blocked our road completely and so we couldn't get to school for three weeks. That was a magical time. I remember constant hot aches, building giant snowmen, igloos and a huge barricade, which survived long after the rest of the snow had gone. Dad persuaded the local blacksmith to make me a sledge with tubular steel runners that was incredibly fast. I had great fun whizzing past and flipping over other sleds, but then picked the wrong lad, as his brother, a huge, ginger-haired youth, boxed my ears. I often took things a little too far.

When the big thaw came, the River Trent poured over its banks, flooding most of the low-lying area of The Meadows. Turgid river water came up through the sewers, flooding Grandma's house at Queen's Grove without warning. The first Roy knew of it was waking to hear the kitchen table banging on the kitchen ceiling underneath his bed as it bobbed up and down. Gran started downstairs and on the first step put her foot into the cold water. Dad reached the back of the house in a rowing boat to retrieve the more valuable items of furniture but most of it was ruined. Roy came to stay with us at Wollaton and after a few days the water subsided. Everyone got stuck into shovelling and bucketing out the mud. There was no insurance; the only help came from family, friends and neighbours.

To keep me out of trouble, Mum persuaded Dad to take me with him to watch Notts County at Meadow Lane when he was on match duty. I settled into the crowd of men in their cloth caps and long gabardine macs. Tommy Lawton was playing for County, and every time he did something exciting the men beside me would leap off the benches. I soon lost interest and reached into my old gas mask case for the sandwiches that Mum had packed only to find that the top had come off the orange juice bottle and everything was soggy. The whole experience was miserable; I never watched league football from the terraces again.

I fared better at Nottingham Ice Rink. Dad was on duty again and had inveigled a ticket for me on the front row to watch the Harlem Globetrotters give a demonstration of basketball. To my amazement and embarrassment, the star of the show, known as 'Goose', loped across and pulled me on to the court to demonstrate the set shot at the basket. I remember his huge, long fingers. He told me to put my little ones down each side of the ball, bring it down between my legs and throw it up towards the basket. I watched the ball's trajectory as it flew through the hoop, earning me huge applause.

That summer I turned seven, but before transferring from Harrow Road school to Robert Shaw Primary, our year was lined up en masse for a half-mile running race. This was the first time the staff had us competing against each other. The emphasis in school so far had always been self-improvement; the better pupils were simply examples to be emulated. I was way out in front, galloping along, when Mick Palmer, a much smaller boy, came racing past like a little steam engine. How could a smaller boy beat me? Mick's speed and determination impressed me such that I always respected him and never underestimated other competitors thereafter. Mick and I were way out in front of the rest of the children and we were both lionised so, even though second, I was suddenly a bit of a star – there was no longer the need for me to seek attention by doing crazy things. I once ran through the open-air lavatory area and slipped on some wet concrete, bashing my head on a washbasin. Since I saw stars I made quite a meal of it, pretending to be unconscious until a group gathered, including my teachers. They pulled me back on my feet with instructions not to waste their time – again – so no ambulance then!

Our parents often bicycled the three miles to Trent Lock and Beeston where Mum's Aunt Edie lived in a big townhouse. To ease her parents' financial burden, Mum had spent most of her formative years being brought up by her Aunt Edie and her husband Walter. My little brother Brian sat on Mum's bike and up until that summer I travelled on Dad's crossbar. Now I was seven, I had my own small bicycle. Aunt Edie lived with Great-Grandma Sanson who was well into her nineties. There was a huge Victoria plum tree in the garden with fruit so big and juicy my mouth waters at the memory.

Great-Grandma had been born in the 1850s and dressed in the Edwardian style with lace-up boots, long black sateen skirts, a pinafore and a white, crimped collar. It occurred to me later that she must have known someone born in the middle of the eighteenth century, since her own great-grandmother had lived to a great age; the past is always close behind. She was a wonderful pastry cook, always dishing out slices of apple pie and she usually sent us home with half a crown.

In the kitchen, behind a heavy curtain hanging from a wooden pole, was the door to the cellar. Plucking up courage while everyone was talking, I went down the cellar steps with the help of a little light filtering through the wrought-iron coal grating. I felt like an explorer, pushing into the unknown, opening chests and cases to see what I could find. Then the cellar door opened and Great-Grandma called down the steps: 'Joe Lob lives down there, Douglas!' and then she slammed the door shut. I was back up those stone steps as fast as my little seven-year-old legs would carry me.

Mum and Scotty by Wollaton Canal, with 'Halfway House' in the background.

THE CANAL

From the changing of the teeth ... to puberty at 13,
14 or 15 the life forces are made available for thinking,
memory and imagination. Thought forces ... are not
of an intellectual nature.

The Number Seven, A.E. Abbot

The feeling appropriate to an infant in arms is his feeling
of rightness or essential goodness ... Without that conviction,
a human being of any age is crippled by a lack of confidence,
of a full sense of self, of spontaneity, of grace ... A person
without this sense often feels there is an empty space where
he ought to be. Many a life is spent in seeking nothing
much more than proof that one exists. Racing-car drivers,
mountain climbers, war heroes and other daredevils who
flirt with death by predilection are often only trying to feel,
by contrasting it as closely as they can with its opposite,
that they are, in fact, alive.

The Continuum Concept, Jean Liedloff

Now the war with Hitler was over, the fight for social justice began; it felt as though utopia was just around the corner. Whether such optimism was justified, there was no going back to pre-war polarities. In December 1942, when I was a toddler, the momentous Beveridge Report was published, the foundation stone of the welfare state. The report identified the five evils facing the British people – squalor, ignorance, want, idleness and disease – and would have far-reaching implications for all walks of life. The report was almost universally popular with the public who were promised an extension of National Insurance and creation of the National Health Service as a reward for the sacrifices everyone was making to win the war.

The terraced houses off Nottingham's Radford Bridge Road had been built for coal miners at Radford Colliery and factory workers at Raleigh and John Player. Radford was one of the more deprived districts of Nottingham. Only a generation before I was born, scores of inhabitants in these slum areas died of enteritis and typhoid; the back-to-back houses had no proper sanitation facilities, only the 'privy midden' system, which didn't get rid of the waste properly. Sanitation had improved but conditions were still pretty grim, as Alan Sillitoe described in his autobiographies and the 1958 novel *Saturday Night and Sunday Morning*. As late as 1937 a quarter of the city's households had an income of less than £1. 10s. a week, wages far below cities of similar size. Children were expected to leave school as soon as possible to help contribute. Many families managed on scraps, spoilt fruit and stale bread. Infant mortality was above the national average.

To get to the shops we had to go along Radford Bridge Road and close to these terraces. Their cobbled streets were full of life, especially on sunny days, with dozens of street urchins running about, young mothers pushing prams and old folks sitting outside on the front steps. I was fascinated but Mum was not impressed; she constantly reminded me to keep away or I would get nits in my hair, impetigo and, even worse, tuberculosis.

Charlbury Road was new, built through a field that stretched for a mile up from Radford Bridge Road all the way to Woodyard Lane. When war broke out, the road was only three-quarters complete and building stopped just four doors up from our house. Each semi-detached had a front and back garden with net curtains and an aspidistra. The community was determinedly lower-middle class. Mrs Griffiths at the fish and chip shop on Radford Bridge Road reminded me of this whenever I was boisterous or impatient waiting in the queue: 'I thought you people off Charlbury Road had better manners than that.' Sometimes she'd add: 'and isn't your dad a police sergeant as well?'

There was much on our road that helped form my view of the world. Mr Smith, in the house opposite, who cycled to and from the Raleigh bike factory every day, was made foreman of his department. From then on his health deteriorated and he looked increasingly worn out; within a year his hair had gone completely white. Gossip had it that, having been taken from the shop floor and put in charge, his former workmates had turned their backs on him, hardly speaking to him. It was like a scene from *I'm All Right, Jack*.

Three doors down, Mr Lake was made redundant from his job in an insurance office. He had been there all his working life but now, in his mid-fifties, found himself on the scrap heap – and depressed. Dad persuaded him to take an interest in helping out as an official at athletics events in an effort to draw him out. Sadly, a year or two later, he died of lung cancer. Dad was always taking on projects and helping friends and neighbours. He became editor of the *Police Bulletin*, which occupied a lot of his time since he found writing hard and spelling harder still, another of his characteristics I inherited.

Mum liked everything to be new, which was a nuisance being short of funds. She pestered Dad to put hardboard down the length of the doors and up the staircase to hide the ornamental mouldings. They only gathered dust, she said. Dad's workshop was where our weapons were made: swords, shields, catapults, bows, arrows, quivers, even a crossbow and an Indian headdress. We'd get feathers for arrow flights and headdresses from swans' nests along the canal, but the really big ones required our gang to lure a swan with bits of bread and then one of us, usually me, would yank a tail feather out while it was distracted. It would then rear up, flapping its wings and threatening us.

I am amazed more kids didn't lose an eye; so many of our playthings were projectiles of one sort or another, particularly bows and arrows, the head of the arrow weighted with electrician's tape holding a nail in place. There were pea-shooters, elastic bands with folded paper pellets, cork spring-loaded popguns, and airguns, which were usually kept under parental control. Dad had a small armoury of starting pistols for athletics events, which should have been kept well away from me. Galloping across the lawn one day, like a cowboy at the pictures, the gun went off. The bullet just missed my brother Brian's head and buried itself deep in the coalhouse door. I was so shocked at my stupidity I never fired a pistol again.

Our houses were built on Keuper marl, a clay that we rolled into balls the size of a marble and then baked on an open fire. These we used as catapult ammunition. Fireworks were available in the weeks before bonfire night and we'd lash bangers to arrows and fire them off in all directions. One irate neighbour screamed at us: 'It's like being back in the Blitz!' We also bundled them together like sticks of dynamite, and set them off under steel dustbin lids, which blew into the air higher than the street lamps.

With not much money about, we had to be imaginative and make our own playthings. An old treacle tin with holes punched through the sides and a long wire loop was all we needed to make a 'winter warmer'. We'd fill the tin with hot coals from the fire and swing it around faster and faster until it really glowed. Most summer evenings there would be kids playing cricket on the street, or games like 'stringy dobby' and 'hot rice', played with a ball that once caught me on the ear leaving me deaf for a week. There were skipping ropes stretched right across the cul-de-sac and kids chanting the rhythm as we waited to take our turn, games of hopscotch and marbles, spinning tops and flying kites.

Parents, busy in their homes or gardens, were only too pleased to see the back of us. Time passed so quickly; full of imagination and always active, we created our world, so much so that we ate well, slept well and could hardly wait to meet up the next day: John, Audrey, Lesley, Michael, Bill, Janice, Tony Squires and Jennifer Lowe – especially Jennifer, a kindred spirit, a bit of a tomboy, full of life and ready for any adventure across the fields or along the canal. The only distraction was Dick Barton.

At weekends I was up at the crack of dawn knocking on doors, getting the gang together, often too early for some mothers, who would lean out of upstairs windows with their hair in curlers, yelling that their son or daughter was still asleep. I came to understand that everyone was different. What interested one friend left another bored. I learnt to give and take and had less trouble as the rough edges were knocked off my character. I was made to see the folly of self-importance, of being jealous, of lying and being unreliable during the course of our play. Little by little it became apparent that if we wanted to build a den or go on a journey, it worked better if we cared for one another.

There were exciting play areas close to our road, like the railway embankment, where we'd dig tunnels, or clambering around the canal locks, building rafts and fishing the ponds. The canal ran parallel to our road and the gardens from the houses on the opposite side to ours stretched right up to the canal bank. Completed in 1796, it had once brought coal into Nottingham and also timber, iron, stone and corn as well as passengers. South of Nottingham the canal had taken away night soil from Nottingham privies to fertilise the Vale of Belvoir. Our part of the canal was known as Wollaton Flight since the topography required several lock gates to lift the barges uphill.

The canal was built to last: the monumental walls and massive timbers of the lock gates and the wrought-ironwork of the sluice gates blended into the landscape as if they had been shaped together. All the ashlar stonework slotted together with the minimum of mortar; today it is still perfectly set and may prove to be as long-lasting as the Inca masonry at Machu Picchu. Even as a boy, I was aware of the workmanship on the overflow culverts, the canal bridge and lock gates. Compared to our 1939 home and all the prefabricated houses springing up around Bilborough, it was like clambering over the pyramids.

The canal was for us as important as the sea is for those living on the coast. Dad would sometimes climb down to the base of the lock gate to collect watercress for the table or for Mum to make into soup. Someone was always falling in and getting stuck in the mud but no one actually drowned. Walking back from the shops one day, via the Radford Bridge Road locks, Dad and I were approached by a group of young children who told Dad one of their brothers was missing. They thought he had fallen into the canal by the lock gate on his tricycle. Dad stripped down to his underpants and slipped into the cold, murky water, swimming down to the muddy bed of the canal, feeling around the sluice gate then coming up for air before going back down but without finding the boy or his tricycle. It turned out to be a false alarm; the child had gone home unannounced.

The canal was where I found out a lot about myself; it was where my personal qualities were put on trial, my essential nature and everything I had become – and always beyond the eyes and ears of parents and neighbours. It was where I met children from other areas of Nottingham, since the towpath was a popular route in and out of the city, and where I learned about the strangeness of the world, and its injustices.

As summer wore on, the canal became shallow, with dragonflies skimming the water and kingfishers diving into holes in the canal banks, and the numbers of frogs and toads increased. One day, I watched the lad who delivered papers from our newsagent standing above some frogs, firing his catapult at them, one after the other, pulling the elastic right back and letting go the stone, splattering frogs all over the place. I asked him if he wasn't being cruel; he said it didn't matter since animals don't have feelings. He was from the estate on the other side of the canal and as he headed home with his friend Baz Ingle, he fired his catapult across the canal hitting me on the temple. I dropped to my knees, quite stunned, as Baz shouted: 'You'll live Scotty!' I did, but knew I was lucky not to be blinded in one eye. Baz went on to become a prominent rock climber in North Wales.

During the hot summer months, kids from Gate Street came to 'our' lock trying to set fire to the tar-coated timbers, which seemed quite wrong to me. I was foolish enough to say so and one of the gang, a lad much smaller than me, though he looked tough and was smoking a cigarette, asked me if I was from Charlbury Road. I told him I was, at which point he advised me it was none of my business and stubbed his cigarette out my bare chest. I was so staggered that I just looked down at my burnt flesh, speechless, unable to take in such a nonchalant act of aggression. I asked him why; he simply shrugged his shoulders, looked me straight in the eye and said he felt like it. I turned away, unable to take it in. His mates thought it hilarious.

During the summer, we'd migrate along the canal up to the spoil heaps at Wollaton pit. Some of the earliest coal mining in Britain took place here, and further west, especially from 'bell' pits around Cossall. The very first railway – the Wollaton Wagonway – was constructed here in the early seventeenth century with horse-drawn wagons on wooden rails to take coal down to the River Trent. The Willoughby family used the profits to pay for Wollaton Hall. In my day, coal trains regularly took a spur off the main line into Wollaton Colliery. The engine drivers allowed us up into their steam engines to admire the shiny brass dials and valves, to pull the whistle and shovel coal into the roaring firebox. Once in a while they would take us down the line and drop us off near our road. With the railways recently nationalised and in public ownership, maybe the drivers thought they might as well let us on board.

How wonderful it was to go out of the gate, up the road to the cut and beyond. A really big outing, on foot or bicycle, was to continue well past the colliery and Martin's Pond to Bramcote Hills. Situated on the roadside of Stapleford Hill was the spectacular Hemlock Stone. On the north side of the hill was an old quarry with a thirty-foot cave at its base. All in all it was a wonderful objective and place to explore. The Hemlock Stone makes a big impression on anyone seeing it for the first time, a thirty-foot monolith of red rock. Bare to the elements, weathering along its bedding planes enables easy climbing low down but up above the rock is capped with harder, black rock overhanging the base. Since the protecting cap contains barium sulphate, it is thought to have been the remnants of an ancient dried-up salt pan. It was only after several visits that I managed to stand on the top for the climbing was quite strenuous and getting back down was even more difficult since it was hard to place feet under the overhang. Along with the canal the Hemlock Stone was forever etched into my memory, as it must be for many Nottingham folk.

I was also drawn to a knobbly old oak that reached out over the canal and was taller than our house. It had clearly lured many a Nottingham youth into its branches. Steps had been chopped into the trunk but bark had grown back into the scars. It was possible to use them to reach a dead branch, five metres above the footpath. That branch, rubbed marble smooth by generations of young hands, was the key to the oak. I went there often, with boys older and bolder who dared to swing up and out on to the highest branches, seemingly oblivious to the drop below. This is my earliest recollection of consciously facing up to the fear of falling, urged on by what others were doing. Despite my apprehension, it was a good feeling to stretch growing muscles. I sat for hours high up that oak, shaded from the summer heat, the humid air scented with its leaves, watching couples walking underneath along the towpath. I came to understand why the oak was so sacred to the Celts who considered it the most powerful of trees with as much of it above ground as below. It was a miserable day when they filled in the canal and cut down the oak to make way for more suburbs. I felt quite upset, perplexed that someone might not want that tree in their back garden.

Nottingham changed utterly as I grew up. The Collin's Almshouses on Friar Lane were pulled down to create Maid Marian Way. It seemed grotesque to me to use such a legendary name for a dual carriageway. By the 1960s the results of the 1949 Housing Act could be seen in Nottingham; the slums were gone, but the new high-rise flats had become slums in the sky. In the late 1960s, people wept in the street as The Black Boy Hotel in the centre of town was pulled down. An iconic Gothic Revival gem designed by Watson Fothergill, the hotel was among the best in town, hosting stars like Laurence Olivier and Gregory Peck. Despite a vigorous campaign, it fell to the contractor's wrecking ball and

Mum and Dad by the Hemlock Stone in the mid 1930s.

was replaced by a utilitarian Littlewoods store. There was very little that was constructed during the 1950s and 1960s that anyone would want to preserve for posterity. The council squandered the chance to build a better city by conserving the best of its heritage and planning more thoughtfully for the future.

Slum clearance in Radford began in the late 1950s and included Arthur Terrace, where Grandma Scott lived. She was moved out to Balloon Woods on the outskirts of Wollaton, to a new estate of prefabricated high-rise flats and walkways that proved a complete failure. There were construction faults that were left to deteriorate; graffiti sprouted everywhere and with it crime and vandalism. After only twenty years they were demolished, by which time Gran had died, of old age, in her eighties.

Another casualty of the slum clearance was the demise of the intimate social life of areas like Radford, Sneinton and especially St Ann's; crime and vandalism were kept under control through close contact between one family and the next. For fifteen years, the social worker and broadcaster Ray Gosling campaigned on behalf of St Ann's residents, battling with city planners against the wholesale destruction of these areas of the city bustling with life and vitality. Without Gosling's intervention there would not have been any of the selective demolition and simple improvements that made this 'new urbanism' more tolerable.

The open country where we used to roam rapidly disappeared. Frank Earp's field was sold in 1949 so Charlbury Road could finally be extended right up to Woodyard Lane. Not long after, the Earps' ancient, three-storey farm, known as Halfway House, was demolished to make way for a sports ground with a six-foot fence around it. The hills stretching out towards Bilborough and Strelley – the 'land of ferns' – became warehouses and residential estates of prefabricated houses thrown up to replace bomb-damaged buildings for demobbed servicemen and evacuees from the slum clearances.

So the building site became our new playground. In the evening, after the workers left, we moved in. Early one Sunday, finding the compound open, we commandeered wooden scaffolding poles, boxes of nails and barrels to build a big raft. We worked all day and into the evening, but the craft was too big to get through the canal bank hedge. That is where the builders found it next morning, stuck wedged in the hedge, and I was swiftly identified as the chief architect.

I seemed to be in trouble a lot. We got a visit from the railway police after extending our den in the embankment right under the track, trying to link up with friends on the other side. Although the embankment was covered in brambles and bushes, the amount of soil piling up had attracted attention. For a time the embankment was out of bounds, so no more putting pennies on the line to retrieve them later, wafer thin, after the trains had squashed them; no more shortcuts over the tracks to visit friends.

There was also a visit from the local bobby. He spotted us scrumping apples and gave chase on his bicycle. We broke into a run, ten delinquents throwing apples and pears from inside our shirts all over the road to slow him down as he pedalled furiously after us. That afternoon he paid a visit to my parents, which was just as embarrassing for the young constable as it was for my father since he was the young man's sergeant. Luckily the owner didn't press charges and we all got off with a warning.

Sometimes Dad would take me into the shed to cane my backside. It was more symbolic than painful, done to appease Mum because I'd been cheeky or ignored her. If it was more serious, like the visit from the local policeman, then Dad warned me he could lose his job if his superiors knew he couldn't control his own family. I can see now, under the circumstances, he was very tolerant of my behaviour. He did well never to seriously lose his temper. He didn't have an easy time, especially when working nightshifts. He would cycle home at six in the morning, soaking wet and full of cold to sit in front of the fire, feet in a bowl of hot water and mustard with a towel over his head, breathing in steam and Friar's Balsam.

When I was seven, for the next four years Dad worked away during the week at Sutton-in-Ashfield Police Training Centre. Being a policeman, we had a telephone and could speak to Dad every day. He was now a sergeant instructor, popular with recruits and colleagues alike. Brian and I loved visiting because there were so many facilities – like professional archery equipment. Mum was introduced to the hierarchy, right up to the chief. She never seemed comfortable with the officers' wives, especially those with big, confident smiles; Mum's teeth were small and uneven, something I inherited from her. I know how inhibiting that can be.

Mum was intimidated by displays of wealth and those who talked in 'lah-di-dah' accents. Despite her discomfort, she persisted in making incursions into higher echelons of society, determined to make a better life for us. Perhaps because Dad was away so much, Mum was more fraught than usual and less forgiving of my anti-social behaviour. Then, in 1952, our younger brother Garry arrived and she was ever busier. Feeling superfluous to requirements I decided to leave home. I sewed extra-long straps on to my rucksack so I could put a kitbag on top for all the food and other items I would need to survive on my own. When I announced I was off, Mum and Dad said they would help me pack. I never got past the front gate.

From the age of eight, I had a phase of collecting things, starting with train numbers. With my copy of the Ian Allan locomotives guide, I'd take off with friends to Victoria Station in town, bustling with passengers under its cavernous roof of glass and iron – like a cathedral. The giant locomotives pulled in, hissing jets of steam and clouds of sulphurous smoke that tasted salty and gritty.

Garry's christening, 12 October 1952. I'm on the right, and Brian is on the left.

I remember the firemen, with their smoke-blackened faces, working on the engines, the shiny pistons and their oily housings painted red and green. We would talk to the driver, his white teeth gleaming from his grimy face. There was the rumble of porters' drays clanking along the uneven, platform flags and passengers coming and going with their leather suitcases. Then the stationmaster sent the leviathan on its way with a loud, shrill whistle and a wave of his red flag, south to London or north to Sheffield.

Stamp collecting followed, and then I got interested in cigarette cards. Dad had boxes of cigarette cards he collected in the 1920s when his father ran a public house at Newmarket. (He also collected coshes and knuckledusters from Nottingham criminals, poachers and other assorted miscreants. It was a fearsome collection rightly kept locked away from my inquisitive little hands.) Sadly, over the years, Dad's cards dwindled away, lost by me in flicking competitions or swopped for more exciting fare such as sweets or comics. By the 1940s the only cigarette company producing cards was Turf and the main source were the dustbins behind the Crown Hotel on Middleton Boulevard. I had to climb over a ten-foot wall on the way to school to rummage through them. I also collected comics, particularly *The Rover* and *Hotspur*, which required a lot of swopping and cajoling. I was riveted by characters like Dan Dare and The Mekon and could hardly wait for the next week's edition of the *Eagle*.

In July 1949, along with every other child my age along our road, I moved to Robert Shaw Primary, built to accommodate the recent surge in population.

Mrs Webb, the headmistress, asked me to stand up in school assembly to read out the chorus of a song from the blackboard. I had to walk right up to it before I could read what was written; to my embarrassment I was told to get my eyesight tested. I was found to be short-sighted and after a few weeks was fitted out with National Health spectacles. Needing glasses was as much a problem for Dad as it was for me. Mother, looking on the bright side, said at least I didn't need a big square of white cloth stuck over one eye. So many children in our school did seem to have a 'lazy' eye. A lot of them had purple-coloured ointment on their cheeks to cure ringworm, while some had callipers, having suffered rickets or polio. Mum put it to Dad that I might not have wanted to be a boxer or a policeman anyway.

Like most children I responded to teachers who were enthusiastic, but teaching a class of forty-eight children must have been hard; discipline was strict and the leather strap often used. For a short while we had an American exchange teacher who taught music, introducing us to traditional English and American folk songs like 'The Drunken Sailor' and 'Pick a Bale of Cotton'. I loved singing and became 'a valued member of the choir', according to my 1951 school report. That was down to the teacher. She was a breath of fresh air, far less stuffy and threatening than her British colleagues, one of whom would creep up from behind me and then clout the back of my head.

The deputy headmaster, Mr Crooks, was a tall man with a long face and dark greasy hair combed straight back over his pointed head. He hated anyone being even five minutes late and would lay into them, girls included, pulling up their gymslips to slap the back of their legs with his bare hands. It was quite frightening to watch, never mind being on the receiving end. Those children given tokens for free dinners were the ones 'Crooksie' punished most. Mum talked of those children in pitying tones. I couldn't understand it; I thought they were lucky to be given dinners free of charge.

Playing the huntsman in the school's production of Snow White, I fell head over heels for the star. Alas, she didn't reciprocate my feelings, so I forgot my disappointment by playing for the school football team. My ability wasn't great but my fitness was high. We had to be fit living on Charlbury Road; it was reputed to be the longest cul-de-sac in the country. School was about two miles away and although Mum gave me bus fare, each lunchtime I would be first out of school, racing down the roads, alternately sprinting and jogging between lamp posts, along Woodyard Lane over Tin Bridge and down through the new housing estate and into the house, breathlessly asking Mum the time to see if I was any faster than the day before. After lunch I would race the two miles back to school just for the sake of enjoying the feel of my body moving without effort, having saved a couple of pence each way. I seemed full of energy but was often getting into trouble, misbehaving to get attention.

Academic work was not so easy. In my last year at primary school it was made clear that if I didn't work harder I wouldn't pass the eleven-plus exam. The stakes couldn't be higher. Success meant grammar school. Failure meant Cottesmore Secondary Modern School for Boys, which had a grim reputation. On the first day new boys were thrown into bramble bushes. Consequently, my schoolwork improved although as the headmistress wrote in my final report: 'although still below average I am pleased with the wonderful progress Douglas has made these last nine months. He is a completely changed boy … He has become more sensible … now carry on the good work at your next school.' I had been given responsibilities, prefect duties and so on, and had responded to their confidence in me.

I still failed the eleven-plus, much to the disappointment of my parents. The day came, after the summer holidays, when we all walked down the road as usual but this time some turned left at Radford Bridge Road to High Pavement Grammar School, while the rest of us turned right to catch the trolleybus to Cottesmore Secondary Modern. I think Dad was particularly upset I was not considered grammar-school material, especially as most of the children on our road did pass. Now that Dad had given up competitive sport and almost everything else for the family, he naturally had high hopes for his eldest son.

I learned a lot from Dad and imitated much that he did. He would sit me on the crossbars of his bicycle and take me down our road giving a cheery greeting and a wave to everyone we met. Sure enough, when I got my own bike and cycled down the road to school or to the shops I too would shout a cheery 'Good morning!' My parents were complimented on having such a polite son.

If he wasn't working, Dad was on call to rescue wellington boots from the canal bed or recover my sheath knife from the building-site privy. Just before I started at Cottesmore, he had to rush me to the doctor's with a deep cut in my thumb that needed stitches. The only advantage of having a huge dressing on my hand was that the older children at Cottesmore agreed to let me off being thrown into the 'prickle bushes' since I was clearly already injured.

Dad taught Brian and me a brand of unarmed combat – what we should do if someone attacked us. He was a good teacher, unsurprisingly given that he taught young police cadets the same skills. At Cottesmore, a gangly, red-faced boy called Clem, who slavered when he spoke, grabbed me from behind, wrapping his arm tightly round my neck. Without thinking I put both hands on his arms, held tight, pulled down and leaned forward. Clem went right over my head in a spectacular arc to land on his back. There was loud cheering from previous victims and from then on I was left alone. I could live on my reputation from that one very satisfying move I learned from Dad.

He also taught me to swim so I wouldn't drown in the canal. I learned at the Victoria Baths where 'Torpedo' Tom Blower swam, a Nottingham lad who

In Wollaton Park, August 1953. Wollaton Hall is visible in the background.

worked at John Player and smashed the record for swimming the Channel. In 1947 he became the first person to swim between Ireland and Scotland. Dad introduced me to Tom and I got his autograph, but he died in 1955 from a heart attack aged just forty-one years old. I loved swimming and was school champion every year until I left. Dad faithfully cut out newspaper articles from the *Nottingham Evening Post* and *Nottingham Guardian* about my swimming successes, just as he did for everything else.

Dad was meticulous in recording family life, lining us up on holiday to have our picture taken, insisting that everyone was smiling before he pressed the shutter. For my first twelve years, our family holiday was always taken on the east coast between Ingoldmells and Skegness. Etched in my memory are images of dozens of children watching enthralled as Punch and Judy were horrible to each other; the long lines of bony, moth-eaten donkeys crossing the sands, bells jingling; playing cricket with Dad; and rounders with Mum while Grandma Scott sat on her blanket watching. There were bus trips along Sunset Boulevard to Butlin's Holiday Camp where we heard Vera Lynn singing 'Auf Wiederseh'n, Sweetheart', the bestselling record of 1952. There was the early morning ritual of collecting mushrooms from dewy fields, playing with Charlbury Road friends, John Bradley, Jennifer Lowe and Tony Squires, and meeting lads with strange accents from other towns. For the whole fortnight we went barefoot, the soles of our feet becoming as hard as nails. We'd return home as brown as berries – the hallmark of a good holiday, according to Mum.

Perhaps because the car was too full, or I was fed up with Mum and Dad wrangling, or just for the adventure, when I was twelve I announced I was going to cycle the eighty-four miles to Ingoldmells. My bike lacked gears but it was mostly flat, apart from the Lincolnshire Wolds, and I was able to cope, standing up on the pedals when necessary. I had a pump and a puncture outfit, a bottle of Tizer and sandwiches and cake that Mum had packed for me. I arrived by lunchtime at the bungalow feeling very superior, although it was reassuring to see Mum and Dad en route just after passing Lincoln.

That summer, my parents rented their first television set to watch the coronation, on 2 June 1953. That morning the news also broke that Edmund Hillary and Tenzing Norgay had climbed Mount Everest. It barely made an impression on me. We were too busy at home preparing to celebrate with another street party. (We were all given a flag to wave.) The following year, the whole school, like so many others, was taken to the Albert Hall to listen to Sir John Hunt tell us about the climb. Like the news itself, this wasn't, as it was for others, a life-changing moment for me. I was so restless that the teacher in charge of our class warned me that if I didn't sit still and behave myself I would be sent out.

The television arrived in time for a host of neighbours to crowd into our living

Me and Brian with Mum and Grandma Scott at Ingoldmells, August 1947.

room to watch the FA Cup Final between Blackpool and Bolton Wanderers. Thanks to the determination and skill of Stanley Matthews, Blackpool won four goals to three. Stanley Matthews was held as a role model for children, not least by my parents. He didn't smoke, never drank and was never even booked, let alone sent off, in his entire career. He trained hard, played hard and never lost his temper.

I, on the other hand, around the age of thirteen, was punished every week at school. The only question in our minds when sent to the headmaster's study was: would it be the strap or the cane? With the strap across your hand, nothing could be done to make it easier. With the cane across the bottom, there was the chance to lessen the pain by wearing extra PE shorts or by quickly pushing two jotters down my underpants. Most of my misdemeanours were me seeking attention, although a few teachers were decidedly eccentric and some had a sadistic streak. Our French teacher Mr Dixon, known as 'Dicko', would stick a pin down the end of his pencil and then sit at his desk while he cleaned wax out of his ears on to his newspaper, before blowing the wax all over Victor Dunn who sat opposite. He called Victor 'Victor Victorious' since he could remember more verbs than anyone else. After French we went next door to have English with Mr 'Jock' Gallagher who patrolled the lesson with a leather strap in his right hand. A brave George Bates once told Jock that another boy had peed his pants. A stream of urine was flowing across the dusty parquet between the desks. Jock asked him why he hadn't gone to

Charlbury Road street party to celebrate the coronation of Queen Elizabeth II. L–R: Janice Bryce, Audrey Lake, Brenda Jones, my younger brother Brian, me, Garry (in high chair), Jennifer Lowe, unknown, unknown, unknown, John Bradley, unknown.

the lavatory. The class replied 'Dicko' wouldn't let him so Jock went next door for a heated discussion with Dicko. George was particularly pleased; at every opportunity Dicko would address him, with a smirk, as Master Bates.

A gangly, six-foot-four ex-army man called Warsop took a particular dislike to me – and me to him. Despite changing the bulb in the light above the blackboard, it still wouldn't work. I suggested he test it by putting his finger up the socket. He had me in front of the class, hands out, for six lashes with a leather strap, first to the left hand then to the right, with all the force his long arms could muster. I asked him if he had enjoyed himself and he slapped me across the face. I told him that Dad was going to hear about that, but Dad was the last person I would tell. His disappointment would have crushed me.

The majority of my teachers were good men who did their best. Mr Everett, the metalwork teacher, had been in the RAF and drove around in an open-top sports car that he parked near the workshop. He demonstrated operating the machinery by making parts for his car. Mick Graham taught us English and was not only a good teacher but played rugby for Nottingham RFC's first XV. Rugby became a way for me to lose myself in the moment, but because Cottesmore was one of very few secondary moderns to play rugby, our fixture list was limited. The advantage was we got to know the opposition very well – and became good friends. While playing our near-neighbours at the John Player School I got to know one of their stars, Dez Hadlum. Soon we would be going climbing in the Peak District together.

Mick Graham also got me reading more widely, opening my eyes to a world of classic literature about which I knew little; there were very few books at home, a set of encyclopaedia from 1937 and Mum's Mills and Boon novels. I had read Enid Blyton's Famous Five books and C.S. Forester's Hornblower series. Now I was captivated by Henry Fielding, George Eliot, John Buchan, Edgar Allan Poe and the work of more modern authors: John Wyndham's *The Day of the Triffids*, Ernest Hemingway's *The Old Man and the Sea*, George Orwell's *Animal Farm* and *1984* and Aldous Huxley's *Brave New World*. I also loved the satire *Clochemerle* and Giovannino Guareschi's Don Camillo stories.

Yet it was the epic myths and sagas of antiquity that really caught my imagination: Romulus and Remus, Horatius at the bridge, and the Spartans holding the Persians at Thermopylae. My mother's admonishments were nothing compared to that of the Spartan mother who, according to Plutarch, handed her warrior son his shield and told him to come back 'With it – or on it!' I was captivated by the adventures of Odysseus, told in my Newnes *Pictorial Knowledge* encyclopaedia, defeating the Cyclops and outwitting Circe the Enchantress with the help of the gods. I read and reread Norse tales of Asgard and was enthralled by tales of King Arthur and his Knights of the Round Table. These heroes inhabited a world of huge risks, uncertainty and sacrifice.

Feats of athletic prowess didn't interest me much until the day I turned up at Orston Drive playing fields where our PE teacher was trying to organise heats for the school sports day, the biggest event on the school calendar. I couldn't be bothered so played my usual trick of attracting attention by being standoffish, attracting attention away from others, like a vampire. I sloped off to a stand of trees and climbed one of them to the top where I was spotted and told to get back down to the running track. I was given a good talking to about being loyal to my house and finally agreed to enter the heats for the 440 and 880 yards. I not only won, I also broke both school records. That led to me representing the school and breaking city records. The next time I was in the headmaster's office wearing several pairs of PE shorts under my grey flannels, the headmaster Mr Skillbeck, essentially a kind man, gave me another lecture, but this time struck a chord, telling me what a fine athlete I was and what a credit I could be, if only I would just settle down. We were both quite emotional by the time he gave me three of the best.

I was growing fast. At fourteen, I could no longer fit in my standard-issue grey flannel shorts, so Mum took me into town to C&A to buy long trousers. My parents, almost always my mother, chose my clothes for me. It never occurred to me that I might have a say in the matter. As I grew, I borrowed Dad's jacket along with one of his ties or a cravat to go with my white school shirt. Dad gave me his spare steel cycle clips since Mum insisted that I shouldn't tuck my trousers into my socks. That was common. Mum herself dressed elegantly and had an innate sense of style. She was determined that we were well turned out for school every day, with a clean, white shirt and shiny black shoes.

I was now old enough for a newspaper round, getting up at six in all weathers, and earned extra pocket money by recycling old clothing, especially woollens, and scrap, mostly lead from old car batteries found on local tips. Our woodwork teacher, Percy Fox, a devoted communist who thought Churchill was no better than a warmonger, was nevertheless on good terms with the Lord Lieutenant of the county, a considerable landowner, who needed seasonal help with potato picking. The farm was at Car Colston and the manager Mr Frost was impressed enough to invite me back to help with the harvest. It certainly kept me fit, working on the farm, stooking hay high up on to farm wagons and then cycling twenty miles back home to Wollaton, all for five shillings a day. At least it was more than the twelve shillings a week I got for the paper round.

Delivering papers one day, I noticed a removal van emptying furniture into a house on my round. I immediately persuaded the new occupants to become my customers. I recognised the daughter, Jill, as she was at Cottesmore Girls School, separated from us by a hedge. I discovered her father, who had been a general in the war, had recently died. Her mother was busy with a new relationship and tailoring women's underwear. I was invited in to polish off scones and cakes from her mother's afternoon tea parties and over the weeks Jill and I became evermore friendly.

Like every child I had a strong exploratory nature, and not having a sister had made me especially curious about girls. As an eight-year-old, a mother discovered me on her doorstep kneeling over her daughter, poking around with sticks, her nurse's costume half undone, and heatedly asked us what was going on. We both instantly replied: 'Playing doctors and nurses.' Later, whenever the subject of the opposite sex came up, most of us asked an older boy up the road, who seemed to know what it was all about. The only advice I got from my parents was from Dad, much later, when he took me aside in the bathroom, to warn me there were two types of women, good ones and bad ones and the bad ones were those who took money for sex and were to be avoided since they would give you bad diseases.

Going through the physical and emotional changes of adolescence was something of a rollercoaster that only came into perspective, by chance, during Mr Fletcher's technical drawing lesson. He was asked a question by one of the lads about some aspect of growing up and he launched into an explanation of adolescence. It was the first time I had heard the word and the first time I realised I was not unique in having mood swings alongside all the physical changes taking place. I thanked him for taking the trouble to help us understand the transition we were making from childhood into manhood, and all the confusion that went with it.

Hauling myself up the climbing ropes in the school gym during PE lessons, my penis was suddenly erect, a new but pleasant sensation. It certainly gave me a new enthusiasm for rope climbing. I could never talk to anyone about all this, although I did wonder if there was something wrong with me after an incident at the dentist. He was a grim-faced butcher, known for taking teeth out at any opportunity, but he did have a very attractive female assistant. He gave me some gas, and I fell back in the chair. When I regained consciousness, the dentist was slapping my face and shouting: 'Dirty boy! You dirty boy!' The buxom dental assistant seemed embarrassed and flustered. I had apparently pulled her on top of me and wouldn't let go.

I spent more and more time at Jill's house and fell for her, with all the excitement of a first love. Neither of us had much idea; she could so easily have ended up pregnant. One summer's evening we walked together up Woodyard Lane to the canal bridge and I left my bike and canvas paper bag propped up by a stile. We were standing under the arch of the bridge with Jill's ample bare breasts against my bare chest when Mum appeared out of nowhere, clearly upset at what she saw. She told me I was 'a disgusting boy' and that I should get the rest of my papers delivered. I was mortified.

Not long after, having finished my Saturday round, I raced as usual to the Savoy Cinema to meet Jill and the rest of the gang on the back row, only to discover – in the light of the usherette's torch – Jill in the arms of Georgie Cropper, a boy two years older than me. I was devastated and fled in tears. On the bus home one of Jill's friends must have seen how upset I was and reported back, because the next week a note arrived from Jill begging forgiveness and offering herself body and soul. She obviously had not realised how strong my attachment to her was. By then, however, I had discussed my distress with a friend I went climbing with who had experience of being jilted. He advised me to have nothing to do with women; they were only trouble. So that was that. From then on, all my time was taken up with schoolwork, sport and the Scouts.

The Scouting movement was a big part of my development as a climber. I'd started going to Cubs at All Saints' Church, where the Cub leader, known as 'Akela' after the character from Rudyard Kipling's *Just So Stories*, was Cecil Wall, the son of my old dinner lady. Cecil didn't like me much. I enjoyed summer camps, although my first night under canvas was less successful. Brian and I put up a white cotton tent on the back lawn at home, stocked with food, drink and bedding. Neither of us could sleep and I was chattering away to Brian when Mum called down from the bedroom to ask if we wanted to come in. The two of us were back in like a shot with me leading the charge. It was the rats. We had just learned at school about the Plague and there, at the bottom of next door's garden in a concrete pit where their Anderson shelter had been, was a stagnant pool of fetid water full of dead rats.

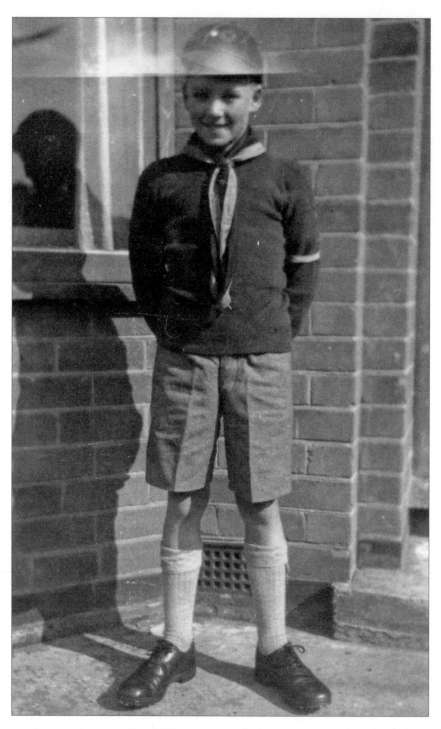

In my Cubs uniform on my ninth birthday, 29 May 1950.

When I joined, the Scouting movement had just initiated bob-a-job week and I entered into the spirit of fundraising with enthusiasm, doing jobs for family and friends. The Cubs had stimulated my interest by making it a competition to see who could bring in the most money, so after exhausting all the neighbours, I started cold-calling complete strangers, offering to clean cars, dig gardens, paint doors and wash windows. I found I could be quite persuasive and most households showed considerable patience.

On the final day, our Cub pack was sitting in a circle as Cecil strutted around. I wasn't feeling well disposed towards Cecil. At the last camp, I had watched his friends shampoo his black, curly hair and then put curlers in it, which I thought a bit odd. Now I found him very annoying; he was being sarcastic about me, even though I had earned more money than everyone else. So as he passed me sitting down in the circle I punched him between the legs. Cecil doubled up in pain and when he finally recovered he simply screamed 'Out!' and pointed to the church hall doors. At the age of eleven, my life in the Cubs was over. Soon afterwards I was invested into the 1st Nottingham YMCA Scout Group in the centre of town.

Getting into town in winter was sometimes a problem because of smog so dense that the buses and trains stopped running. One night I became completely lost, inching along as I pushed my bike, having to backtrack in conditions so dire it was impossible to see the pavement underfoot. Pollution was so bad in London during December 1952 that over 10,000 people died from smog-related incidents and illnesses. That was a particularly bad year with a high-pressure system over Britain that trapped sulphurous fumes from domestic fires, factory chimneys and power stations. Campaigners argued that 'industrial progress without pollution control is no progress at all.' The government was forced to take measures to reduce air pollution despite the poor economic situation. The result was the Clean Air Act 1956, making it compulsory for households in urban areas to switch to smokeless fuel and central heating. It was amazing how quickly the legislation brought change; by the 1960s 'peasoupers' were a thing of the past.

My first summer camp with the Scouts was on Exmoor in 1953, the year after the Lynmouth disaster. Floodwater pouring north off Exmoor had swept away rocks and shrubs, damming the upper reaches of the Lyn Valley until the pressure was so great it all gave way and a tremendous surge of water and debris flooded the town. A hundred buildings were destroyed in the middle of the night, killing thirty-four people and making over 400 homeless. It was sobering to see huge boulders washed down in the flood now embedded in the second-floor rooms of houses and hotels.

At our camp high on Exmoor, the weather was entirely different. The whole fortnight was hot and sunny, and we were soon red with sunburn. I tried my

L–R: me with Clive Smith and Wes Hayden, two Scout friends who at the time were keen climbers.

first cigarette while washing pots at the standpipe, and promptly turned green and threw up everywhere, retiring to my tent for the rest of the day. It put me off smoking for years. The attention-seeking behaviour that got me into trouble at school spilled over into the Scouts. I threw a bowl of dirty washing-up water over the Scoutmaster's son because he had been bugging me. Unfortunately he had just put on his best uniform to parade through town and I was mortified, consumed with guilt. I apologised sincerely and after that we became great friends.

There were so many interesting characters in our troop and a good energy that bound us together. We achieved far more as a group than we could alone. Wes Hayden, Ian White and I swotted up on first aid and became quite expert, winning a regional prize for our efforts. Scouts was also the starting point for all kinds of adventures and experiences. Our troop rented huts in woods eleven miles out of town, and we walked out there in the course of a night, ferrying all our gear on a cart. I remember particularly one winter walk, again through the night, down the frozen course of King's Brook to the River Soar. We kept to the river all the way, struggling to keep our balance where the ice was glassy and sloped steeply over rocks. Rods of ice, like candles, bobbed about like fishing floats, bumping against each other when we disturbed them so they tinkled like Chinese bells. Through gaps in the willow and hawthorn, frost on the snowy fields sparkled like silver in the moonlight. Winter, I discovered, could be more magical even than walking out on a clear summer's day.

In the woods I discovered the beech is a most satisfactory tree for climbing with its elephant-grey branches smooth to touch and tough to pull and stand upon. There were about a dozen in Rempstone Wood that I climbed one after the other just to feel the increasing sensation of power in my arms and shoulders, swinging and stepping from one hardy branch to the next. The beech I feel is a most elegant tree with a strong, feminine presence. The oak is the king and the beech is the queen, according to the ancients, to whom it symbolised knowledge and wisdom.

At Easter in 1955, I went on a Scout hike from our camp near Wirksworth in Derbyshire with a Rover Scout, a kind of young adult helper, called John Leonardi, known to us as Leo. During our walk, we came across Black Rocks jutting into space and its wonderful view of the Derwent Valley, Arkwright's Mill, the white cliffs of High Tor and Riber Castle high on the moors above. Having taken in the scenery for a few minutes, we realised there were others there, not just tourists enjoying the view, but men climbing the rocks themselves, cramming their fingers into cracks and grappling with the shapes, bracing their feet against the blank rock and hanging off their arms. Other men were concentrating all their attention on the white ropes hanging down from the climbers. Here was something completely new yet not so far removed from climbing trees and swinging around the scaffolding on building sites. I wanted to know more about these men in army anoraks and khaki trousers who were not soldiers, although they were shouting commands to each other. Leo was more a cyclist than a climber, and was soon alarmed to see his young charges swarming over the boulders below the main crag and shuffling up the gullies and chimneys either side of the prominent buttresses. He called us down but by then an indelible impression had formed in my mind.

I was more than curious; I was smitten.

A fortnight later, I decided with Clive Smith, who had also been on the Black Rocks visit, to return on our bicycles. Clive lived in a farmhouse on Aspley Lane now surrounded by a new estate. His mother always made me welcome and she became friends with Mum, despite their different backgrounds. His father was a chiropodist, also friendly but more distant and given to standing on his head every morning doing yoga. They both seemed genuinely interested in me. Clive had been at prep school and spoke with a posh accent like his parents. They must have hit on hard times since they were unable to afford to continue the cost of a private education for their children; Clive was now at Cottesmore School.

We persuaded Terence 'Stengun' Sturney, one of the lads in our class at school, to join us on our expedition and we set off on the twenty-five-mile journey to Cromford, pushing our bikes up the final steep hill to the rocks. I had Mum's washing line around my shoulders while Stengun had his dad's car tow rope.

Clive had a rucksack of food and drink on his back. We were still just thirteen years old. Our first climb was *Fat Man's Chimney*, a climb graded 'Difficult' and first climbed in 1890 by the Peak pioneer J.W. Puttrell. We followed this up with *Central Buttress* and *Lone Tree Gulley* and then harder routes for which we brought out the more substantial tow rope, pulling each other up, much to the amusement of regular climbers who told us the rope was only for safety and not direct help. We were supposed to be climbing the rock, not the rope.

These day-visits turned into weekend camping and climbing trips. The play-things I requested for my next birthday were a Primus stove, a nylon rope and a big pair of American Alpine boots from Flitterman's in Sneinton, heavy with clinkers and Tricouni nails. The best and cheapest footwear for gritstone were black PE plimsolls, the tighter the better. We taught ourselves to climb by trial and error and by emulating others who would sometimes offer advice. I was born curious but also cautious, with an inbuilt instinct for survival. We certainly didn't try to repeat everything we saw. I watched a youth climb right up the centre of Railway Slab in big boots without hesitation and in perfect balance. I found out his name was Steve Hunt and that Steve was one of the best in the area at the time. He was an early inspiration but not enough for me to climb Railway Slab direct. After a few more visits to Black Rocks we moved on to other crags like Birchen Edge and Gardom's near Baslow, climbing harder routes with ex-military karabiners and a couple of nylon slings to put around trees or thread behind chockstones for protection.

Then the school sent a group of us to White Hall near Buxton. White Hall was Britain's first outdoor pursuits centre for state-educated students, having opened in 1951. There were organisations like the Scouts and the Public Schools Exploring Society, founded in 1932 by George Murray Levick of the Royal Navy and a member of Scott's ill-fated Antarctic expedition, later renamed the British Schools Exploring Society. In 1941, the well-known German educationalist Kurt Hahn and Lawrence Holt opened the first Outward Bound school to help young seamen better survive harsh conditions at sea during the war. There was now a move to broaden access to the opportunities outdoor education offered.

Jack Longland was a well-known climber from pre-war days who extolled the ethos of outdoor education. Longland distinguished himself as a rock climber in North Wales with routes like *Javelin Blade* at Idwal in 1930, and then as a mountaineer on Everest in 1933 when he demonstrated a cool head during a whiteout at 27,000 feet to lead eight Sherpas from Camp VI down to safety. He became director of education for Derbyshire in 1949 and over the next two years persuaded his committee to fund White Hall Outdoor Pursuits Centre.

There was so much positive feedback from Derbyshire schools that students from other authorities were invited. Jack Longland's vision was key but engaging the services of volunteer, amateur climbers and cavers was important too; they would respect the young students' spontaneous curiosity and not stifle the joy of being out in open country with too much instruction. Volunteers were more likely than professional educators to keep the best traditions of British climbing alive. Longland was fortunate, also, to have excellent wardens, first Peter Mosedale and then, in 1955, Geoffrey Sutton and instructors like Joe Brown, Harold Drasdo, Gordon Mansell and Andrew Maxfield. With such men in charge and a great band of volunteers, many young people from the region were introduced to hillwalking, caving, skiing and, of course, rock climbing.

Wars usually bring about significant periods of social change. After the Second World War restrictions on access to open country were reduced, especially with the creation of the Peak District, Britain's first national park, designated the same year White Hall began its outdoor activities. The 1944 Education Act gave all children a free education and raised the school leaving age to fifteen, laying the foundation for a more meritocratic society and breaking down old polarities so more of us were able to take up previously esoteric pastimes like rock climbing. What had been the preserve of the middle class became far more egalitarian. Despite the concerns of regular climbers from senior clubs that newcomers would break with tradition, this did not happen. Even with the large number of people suddenly coming into climbing and a sharp rise in standards, the sport was able to evolve with, as Harold Drasdo put it, the 'margin of safety remaining satisfyingly narrow.'

The instructors at White Hall took us out to local crags such as Windgather and Castle Naze where they showed us how to belay properly. When they thought we could cope, they put us into the lead, helping us realise our full potential without any pressure. We also went on long hikes with map and compass. I remember one such walk with a temporary instructor called Johnny Russell who had once hitched all the way to New Zealand to go climbing. He had some fantastic tales to tell. Then we got lost in the mist and Johnny had us all walking on a compass bearing until, after a worrying couple of hours, we knew where we were. We got back to White Hall famished.

My friend Mick Garside had more experience of mountaineering than any of us. He was a year older and joined our school when his parents moved down from Yorkshire. Just as Mick was looking forward to starting his working life, the headmaster told his parents he should be doing O levels, so he stayed on at school but dropped down a year to join us. A group of us from Cottesmore, including Mick and Clive Smith, signed up for a Mountaineering Association course held one evening a week throughout the winter at Lenton Boulevard School. The instructor was Bob Pettigrew, late of Nottingham High School and Loughborough College. He co-opted Mick and myself to help demonstrate belaying techniques and mountain rescue. He was enormously encouraging and opened our eyes to the wider world of mountaineering with readings from books, tales of his own and film of expeditions to faraway places.

Mick had not only been to White Hall, he had also managed a week's course at the National Adventure Centre at Plas y Brenin in North Wales, where his instructor was Olympic runner and mountaineer John Disley. Such was Mick's enthusiasm for North Wales that he persuaded me to spend our Whitsun holiday there in 1956. We caught the Barton's bus from Nottingham to Llandudno and then walked south, hiking over the Carnedds to Ogwen Valley, where we camped disastrously.

Before leaving Nottingham, Mick had proofed the tent with a paraffin-based agent. In the night we woke up to check the time, first lighting a candle. Unfortunately, the match didn't go out and the tent was soon burning around us, despite the soaking mist outside. By the time we had the fire out, all that was left of the tent was the back triangle and two wooden poles held up by scorched seams. We huddled together until dawn and then found refuge with a local farmer who put us up for two shillings a night for the next four nights. I had to post him my share of the rent; my paper round didn't cover luxuries like farmhouse accommodation.

Not having a tent, we gave up on visiting Snowdon and stayed where we were, making the farmhouse our base of operations. Setting off to climb Tryfan via the Milestone Buttress we were intimidated by the scale of the crag. It did not help that the rock was polished and was also wet. After one pitch we lowered off and went round to Little Tryfan where we had more success and our first experience climbing routes of more than one rope-length, or 'pitch', when you have to belay halfway up the cliff. We then walked across Glyder Fawr and Glyder Fach before hiking back north to the Conwy Valley and through stands of oak forest carpeted with thousands of bluebells. We finally limped into Llandudno completely exhausted with blistered heels and toes to collapse on to the bus for the long journey home. At least we had been spared the weight of the tent.

THE 2ND AGE

In early childhood the boy or girl looks out on to the world with a certain amount of enchantment; but after puberty, when the soul is 'born' this world seems grey and so, during the early teens there may be shocks, or a veil of dreams may be drawn over what seems a cruel, hard world and a negative attitude to life can cause difficulties for both children and parents.

The Continuum Concept, Jean Liedloff

At about the age of fourteen ... The epoch of idealism, the head rather than the heart now becomes the bearer of thinking and all the characteristics of intellectual thought begin to occur. The critical faculty develops with all its good and bad characteristics. The adolescent no longer accepts authority, but wishes to form his own opinions. He is extremely clever and ruthless in argument, and the wise adult will avoid controversy with him. At the same time, in connection with the rapid growth of limb, new will-power manifests itself which he finds hard to control.

The Recovery of Man in Childhood, A.C. Harwood

Winter on the Kinder plateau.

EMPIRES

When I was fifteen, it occurred to me that, unless I took charge of my education, future options in life would be limited. Having been down Radford Colliery, right up to the coal face where men worked long hours unable to see more than ten yards ahead, I knew breathing coal dust wasn't for me. I also knew from an afternoon's work experience at the Raleigh factory that further education was a better option than becoming a grimy extension of an oily machine doing the same thing every day, starting and stopping to the sound of a hooter like one of Pavlov's dogs.

The headmaster told me that if I got O levels in history, geography, general science and English then I might make it to grammar school to do A levels and go on to higher education. So I badgered staff for the curricula in these subjects. The number of pupils in my class dropped from forty to a more manageable twenty-five, and staff no longer had to keep a strong rein on unruly elements now that most of us were thirsting for knowledge and outgrowing many of our teachers in size. My sudden interest in academic life must have been a relief to my teachers.

Maurice Davidson, a diminutive ex-miner, had left the pit to teach history, which he did with a passion. There was never any bother in his lessons, not after receiving a rat-a-tat-tat from the edge of his ruler across the knuckles. The only time I had been first in class was in Mick Graham's English class and now in history with Maurice Davidson. They had a calling for the job that shone through.

The main focus of O-level history was 'Empire', which was, as it happened, Mr Davidson's forte. He was a true patriot and his nationalism was infectious; we too revelled in the notion that over a quarter of the map of the world was coloured red for the British Empire. Even though the Empire was being transformed into the Commonwealth, our pride in being British was undiminished; we still appeared to be the most powerful nation in the world.

I knew of the great empire-builders from my set of 1930s encyclopaedia: General Wolfe storming the Heights of Abraham to defeat the French then dying from bullet wounds in the moment of victory; Robert Clive, 'the clerk who made an empire,' once again at the expense of the French, but this time in India; Horatio Nelson, 'Guardian of England', who also died from a French bullet; Captain Cook who perished on the end of a native's spear, just like General Gordon at Khartoum. It was a world of exotic locations, dogged determination, leadership and teamwork and enormous courage, all of which captured my imagination and no doubt inspired every other small boy who read about such heroes.

Mr Davidson put flesh on the bones of what I already knew, handing out reams of notes from the school's fading Gestetner machine that we'd go over with a pen. There was always an underlying assumption that the British were better at empire than the French and much better at it than the Germans and Belgians. The Belgian King Leopold, we discovered, was quite inhuman in his exploitation of the Congo, where those natives who failed to work hard enough had their hands and other extremities cut off. The British, by contrast, went to Africa in the footsteps of explorers and missionaries to trade and take on 'the white man's burden'.

That the romanticism of exploration led to commercial exploitation wasn't emphasised. Mr Davidson did balance the books a little; he told us about the hunting and extermination of the Aboriginal people of Flinders Island and Tasmania by British settlers, and the massacre of unarmed Indian demonstrators at Amritsar in 1919 by troops under the command of General Dyer. But these were merely 'setbacks' or anomalies; pride in the Empire remained undiluted.

Among this pantheon of heroes, one in particular caught my imagination. At the age of just twenty-three, Francis Younghusband travelled 3,000 miles from Beijing to India through the Gobi Desert, across Chinese Turkestan and over the Muztagh Pass, arriving after seven months of wild travel in November 1887. It was all part of the 'Great Game', the struggle between the British and Russian Empires for control of Central Asia. How could we not be impressed?

It was rumoured that a mysterious Russian Buddhist called Agvan Lobsan Dorzhiev was negotiating a deal with the thirteenth Dalai Lama on behalf of Russia. Lord Curzon, viceroy of India, pressed for a mission into Tibet to assert British dominance. In 1903, Colonel Younghusband was put in charge of Curzon's mission and the following year crossed the Jelep La from Sikkim into Tibet with a thousand troops, armed with mountain artillery and Maxim guns, their equipment carried on the backs of thousands of pack animals and porters. Blocking their path at Chumik Shenko was a Tibetan force of 3,000 men armed only with matchlocks and swords.

Fighting broke out as Sikh soldiers scuffled with Tibetans surrounding their general. One of the Sikhs was shot, the Maxim guns opened up, and in a few minutes seven hundred Tibetans were slaughtered. One British officer wrote: 'I hope I shall never again have to shoot down men walking away.' The British suffered half a dozen minor casualties. This last throw of the dice in the Great Game was hardly a glorious chapter in the history of the British Empire. When, after further skirmishes, Younghusband's mission finally entered Lhasa, they were unable to find any Russians or negotiate with the Dalai Lama who had fled to Mongolia. A punitive treaty was drawn up with the remaining Buddhist hierarchy but much of it was unenforceable and became redundant with the Anglo-Russian Convention of 1907.

Younghusband had been rather dismissive of the Tibetan people during his campaign, but on his last day in Lhasa he rode off towards a nearby mountain, under a clear blue sky, and suddenly found himself experiencing 'untellable joy. The whole world was ablaze with the same ineffable bliss that was burning within me ... I was beside myself with an intensity of joy, such as even the joy of first love can give only a faint foreshadowing of ... I was convinced ... that men were good at heart, that evil in them was superficial ... that men at heart are divine.' This revelation inspired him years later to help found the World Congress of Faiths, the conqueror, it seems, conquered by the spirit of place. The diplomatic ties he established also allowed him to pursue his other great passion – the ascent of Everest.

Mr Davidson fired my imagination and I read, under his direction, avidly around his lessons. I came to know how the British world view was underpinned by the theories of men like Halford Mackinder, who read his famous paper 'The Geographical Pivot of History' to the Royal Geographical Society in 1904, just as Younghusband was, in theory at least, stemming the onward march of the Russian Empire. This paper, as Mr Davidson explained, more or less invented geopolitics. Mackinder's 'Heartland Theory' suggested that whoever controlled the region between the Volga and the Yangtze, and between the Arctic and the Himalaya, controlled the world, thanks to its resources and its location. Should Russia become more technologically and socially developed, it would threaten everyone. His ideas influenced foreign policy deep into the twentieth century.

Not only were we being taught about global politics, we were being introduced to global economics and the arguments for and against protectionism and free trade. I wholeheartedly embraced geography, particularly for what it taught me about how underlying geology shaped landscapes, and the impact of erosion. Geography teaching was patchier though, until our sympathetic new headmaster Gordon Happer took over. I would pass both history and geography, my favourite subjects, and also general science – but not English.

My fascination with Mr Davidson's lessons on geopolitics was superbly timed, since our pride in the British Empire was about to receive a rude shock. This was the era of the Suez Crisis and the rise of the Egyptian nationalist leader Gamal Abdel Nasser, who nationalised the Suez Canal, prompting Israel, France and Britain to invade Egypt. At the time, I was on Kinder Scout, trudging across the groughs and peat hags in my nailed boots with Mick Garside, John Hudson and Pete Newbold. We'd caught the bus to Bakewell and then walked up to Ashford, where we'd tried to tickle a trout for our dinner. It did end up in our frying pan, but only after the unethical use of a lump of limestone.

After a wet night we set off towards Kinder, taking two days to reach the top of Grindsbrook Clough. We wandered around the centre of Kinder's drear plateau, hoping that one of the greasy mounds of peat was the highest point in the Peak District. Then we tramped east towards Madwoman's Stones, along the plateau's edge. We had never experienced landscape like this before. I found it compelling and it left an indelible impression that had me returning to Kinder, Bleaklow and all the moors around many times thereafter. Our map work was tested to the limit in the claggy weather as we wound our way through the streambeds, or groughs, cut deep into the peat. It was hard work with all our camping gear. Sometimes a red grouse would burst into the air, or a mountain hare sprint off into the mist, or we'd hear the looping call of a curlew in the sky above.

We came across a shooting cabin with a stream running under its flagged floor. It seemed a likely place to spend the night but there wasn't enough room for our gang of four and it had been partly vandalised so we put the tent up by the wind-blasted rocks of Madwoman's Stones, drawn to that place by the name and explanation from Bob Pettigrew who had told us that the stones were named for a jilted local woman. She was so bereft at being abandoned by her lover that she ran at the rocks headfirst until she dashed her brains out. This information was not conducive to a good night's sleep.

Next morning, John and I ran down to Edale for more supplies and to buy the newspapers, which were, almost exclusively, full of jingoistic support for our troops going in to regain control of the Suez Canal. They published maps detailing the numbers of ships, aircraft, paratroopers and tanks heading for Suez. To us it was stirring stuff; we never questioned the rights and wrongs of the conflict.

We left Madwoman's Stones and spent the last two days of our half-term walking down to Ladybower reservoir and along the eastern gritstone edges to Bakewell to catch the bus home in time for a Sunday roast dinner and to tell my folks all about our trip. By the time we were back at school the Israeli, French and British troops were well on their way to taking control of the Suez Canal, having already annihilated the Egyptian air force and army units at

Port Said and Port Fuad. The bold action of our paratroopers made us proud to be British.

Then, suddenly, as a column of tanks was heading down the canal towards Suez itself, all progress stopped and then went into reverse. We were disappointed and confused, until Mr Davidson explained. The allies' action had been widely condemned around the world; the Soviets threatened to send troops to Egypt and economic pressure swiftly followed. The Arabs cut off their oil and then America blocked the sale of their oil unless Britain ordered an immediate ceasefire and left Egypt completely. Sterling sank in value. It was a bitter lesson for the beleaguered prime minister Anthony Eden and for the country as a whole. It signalled the end of Britain's role as a world superpower. The duplicitous preparations for war had cost Britain much moral capital.

With the end of Empire, our world became framed by the Cold War. At the height of the Suez Crisis, the new Soviet leader Nikita Khrushchev, who had ordered the invasion of Hungary the previous April, told Western leaders that 'we will bury you'. There was the ever-present worry of a nuclear exchange and the vociferous campaign to 'ban the bomb'. Britain was testing the hydrogen bomb, and in 1957 suffered its worst atomic accident when a fire caused a dangerous leak of radioactive material at Windscale in Cumberland. The same year the Russians launched Sputnik. I remember being particularly affected by Nevil Shute's *On the Beach*, and a powerful play that later became a television drama called *The Offshore Island* by the author and journalist Marghanita Laski. It told the story of a handful of British survivors of a nuclear holocaust and after reading it I experienced recurring nightmares. In my dream, I'd be lathered in sweat, running this way and that across open fields, straddling hedges and jumping ditches to escape an advancing cloud of radioactive fallout only to run into another and then another, with the deadly clouds coalescing to trap me in the middle. It was a relief to wake up each time without my skin blistered and peeling off.

Despite the existential crisis of atomic war, and nightmares aside, by the time I was in my last year of compulsory education, I found school enjoyable on all fronts, stimulating in the classroom and challenging outdoors on the running track, rugger field and on the crags. I was a prefect and house captain – named after George Mallory, as it happened. Beyond school I looked forward to meeting up with good friends in the Scouts once a week, especially those with whom I went climbing each weekend and during the holiday. There was not a great deal of social life, no girlfriends, dancing, pop concerts or anything much musical, just the occasional visit to the cinema.

I had put aside Dick Barton in favour of *The Goon Show* and its surreal storylines and eccentric characters. After every episode, we'd come into school and imitate the antics of Harry Secombe's character Neddie Seagoon, Peter Sellers

Leading the way in the 880 yards at Cottesmore in 1957.

playing Bluebottle and Spike Milligan's Eccles. We'd sing the Ying Tong Song and pepper our conversation with catchphrases like 'You dirty, rotten swine, you!' The Goons paved the way to the boom in satire in the early 1960s, particularly *Beyond the Fringe* and *That Was the Week That Was*. I loved it all, but especially Millicent Martin in what became known as 'TW3', a programme that would empty the pubs on Friday night. The cultural revolution of the late 1950s and 1960s was astonishing: hugely popular music shows like *Juke Box Jury* and the *Six-Five Special*, the landmark Chatterley trial in 1960 and the introduction of the birth-control pill. It was an incredible moment in history to be young.

Ever since my revelatory performance in heats for the school athletics day, Dad encouraged me to train properly for the 440 and 880 yards. He had long been a tireless secretary for the Nottingham Police Athletic Club and organised the annual police sports day. He also became an Amateur Athletics Association coach. He must have thought there was a potential champ in the family, spurred on perhaps by Roger Bannister breaking the four-minute-mile barrier. He bought me my first pair of spikes, running shorts and jock strap and had me down Wollaton Park athletic track, timing my every circuit of its bumpy track with his stopwatch. In 1956 at the city sports meet, I broke records for both the 440 yards with a time of 57.3 and the 880 yards in 2.11.05. That 880 yards was a wonderful couple of minutes; running down the back straight on the final lap, running on air, accelerating around the final bend, in a state of

The record-breaking Cottesmore relay team: Robin Payne (seated), with (L–R) Clive Smith, me and Clause Duval.

relaxed concentration, I observed my body in perfect balance, heading down the home straight, all set to win. Then, in the corner of my eye, another, smaller athlete was suddenly there on my shoulder. I recognised him as Henry Simpson. With twenty yards to go the race was on. I pounded along the grass track with all the power I had left, drawing on reserves that had all but gone until there was only pain; my only thought was to push harder and I crossed the line first, every muscle spent. In the winter, at the city's cross-country championship around Wollaton Park, Henry crossed the line twenty yards ahead of me to win the race and even the score.

Dad persuaded me to continue training, either before my morning paper round or after the evening delivery, three or four times a week. He was tireless and so enthusiastic. I found it quite a trial, but not wanting to disappoint him I would relieve the monotony by having friends from school join in, including Clive Smith, Clause Duval and Robin Payne, who were all good rugby players as well as fast on the track. During the city school sports day of 1957 the four of us won the relay race in record-breaking time and I again broke the records for the 440 and 880-yard races.

A Cottesmore girl with long, curly black hair told me that it was quite something to break three records. She was sufficiently impressed to walk with me from the John Player Sports Ground all the way down Western Boulevard. Dad had been at the event and he cycled past at this moment without stopping. Just as I was wondering if he had spotted me, and without looking back,

Nottingham Moderns Rugby Football Club, 1957–1958. Back row, L–R: Mr Owen, Roy Webster, Pete Turner (climber), Tony Smith, Clive Smith (climber), me, Mick Garside (climber), Frank, Paddy Straughan. Front row, L–R: Neil Mann, Clause Duval (climber), Frank Hunt (climber), John Bee, Mike Towle, Rob Atkins, Roger Hunt, Dez Hadlum (climber).

his hand went up in a wave of acknowledgement. I was so embarrassed. She and I met up a couple of times but had little in common and nothing to talk about. I was so shy; I still didn't really know how to talk to girls and was still smarting from having my heart broken by Jill. It was probably best we moved on, anyway; I was too busy swotting for O levels and busy playing sport.

Dad had me training hard for the Nottinghamshire AAA Youth Championships where there was the chance I might be selected to represent Notts at the national school championships. He improved my diet, got me to bed early and had me lying out while he massaged my legs with liniment before the race. There was nothing to eat after breakfast apart from glucose tablets but it was all to no avail; I was well beaten into second place in the 880 yards by John Whetton from Brunts Grammar School who also broke the county record. John was built to run middle distance, his large chest set in a slight frame and consequently light on his feet. I knew I would never get past county standard and began to lose interest in competitive running, preferring cross-country and fell running alone. John Whetton went on to compete in the 1964 Olympics in the 1,500 metres and was British team captain.

Every lunchtime in good weather, we played touch-rugby on the sloping school playground; on Saturday mornings through the winter we played against other Nottingham secondary modern schools with staff keen enough to give up their spare time organising and refereeing matches. In November, thanks to

Gordon Happer and Nottingham's city youth organiser, a Welsh ex-navy man called Mr Owen, all secondary-modern pupils interested in playing rugby after leaving school were invited to a meeting to consider forming a new club. Mr Owen became the secretary, Mr Happer chairman and our climbing instructor friend Bob Pettigrew became trainer and coach of the new club, called Nottingham Moderns. I was selected as club captain, probably because Mr Owen knew me through athletics. I knew I wasn't the best player nor was I the best team player. The following year, an ex-Player School pupil, John Bee, was elected captain for two years running with our full support.

Hitherto, only public and grammar schools had been considered nurseries for senior sides. Now a serious attempt was being made to harness the potential of fifteen-year-old secondary modern boys by forming them into a team of their own to play other young sides from around the region. At the end of the first season we entered a team in the Nottingham RFC seven-a-side competition. The team included Dez Hadlum, Clive Smith and myself, all Scouts and climbing most weekends after rugby. In the game against Nottingham second team our old English teacher, Mick Graham, fumbled a tricky bounce of the ball as Clive and myself, two of the winning relay team, bore down upon him at top speed in a pincer movement to lift him bodily off his feet, taking the ball from him, allowing us to score the winning try. He feigned hurt that two of his former pupils could have been so ruthless.

The Moderns became more organised when Sam Lewis, a young teacher who had played rugby for Carmarthen, came to teach at Cottesmore and joined the club. Sam had a Rover car large enough to take one third of the team to away fixtures. This helped supplement public transport and parents' cars until some of the team were old enough to buy motorbikes. Mick Garside learned to drive quite early on as did Peter Turner, another John Player school-boy and rugby player who took to climbing.

Clubs were not grouped together into a league so there was no champion-ship, only the game. As frustrating as the bounce of a rugby ball can be it was after all the shape of the ball and the inherent uncertainty as to where the ball would bounce that ensured rugby would always be a more interesting game than soccer. I could have played from dawn to dusk, I so enjoyed the camara-derie and the contest, but most of all I played for those rare, transcendent moments. I gained a somewhat dubious reputation for deception and would hear the other team warning each other to watch out for me selling a dummy, which I found I could do with complete conviction. Ducking and weaving, with the opposition transfixed, I floated through in the experience of the moment, out of mind and out of reach of grasping hands. I should have looked for someone to receive a pass, but often I would find the ball glued to my hands. When in full flight all too often the red haze came upon me, not that

I could see very well without my spectacles. I had only one objective in mind and that was the try line, occasionally crossed but more often not. Then I would hear the accusation: 'Tacky hands!'

After the game there were pies and peas or sausage and mashed potatoes prepared by parents, and later girlfriends, and later still wives, as the Moderns grew into a community club, a virtual one for a long time, with no settled home ground or clubhouse of our own. Since the club had been set up by the Nottingham Education Committee we did have access to council grounds such as Peveril School and Harvey Hadden Stadium, where the national cycle champion Reg Harris trained. The pitches were on clay and often waterlogged. There were disappointments too, particularly when talented friends stopped playing rugby for work or a different lifestyle. My old classmate Peter Newbold, who was a brilliant forward, transformed himself into a Teddy boy.

The sudden emergence of youth culture during the mid-1950s was quite a revolution. Plenty of Nottingham youths became followers of fashion – and the new rock 'n' roll. Peter was one of the new tribe of Teddy boys with their draped coats, dark velvet collars and lapels, drainpipe trousers, crepe-soled shoes, and Brylcreemed hair swept back into a 'DA' with a quiff at the front. They tended to slouch as they walked around town, usually smoking, with their shirt collar up or buttoned down if wearing a typically narrow tie. In school we had classroom debates during English lessons, which included one on the Teddy boy phenomenon. The point was often made that having taken off one uniform after leaving school they had simply put on another.

There were occasionally knife fights in town between rival gangs. Friday nights in Nottingham were not for the faint-hearted. Occasionally aggression got out of hand, especially during the race riots of 1958 when over a thousand people were involved in violence in the St Ann's district. West Indians and Asians newly living in the city were blamed for job shortages, quite unfairly. There were so many people stabbed that the *Evening Post* described the scene as a 'slaughter house'. 'It's a rough old town,' the broadcaster Ray Gosling once said. 'I absolutely love it.'

I cycled up to Peter's home a few times, trying unsuccessfully to persuade him to play when we were short, but eventually gave up and lost contact. Sometimes one of the teams was short of players, so the reserves usually got to play. The weather could be savage. Someone suggested I apply liniment to my legs, a brand known as Fiery Jack, to warm me up before the game. I over-did it a bit, smothering it between my legs. It was a minute or two before the pain kicked in and then I spent the first half in the changing rooms, sitting in a bowl of hot water scrubbing away at my tender parts.

The fitness I developed running and playing rugby was of great benefit in the hills. During the Easter holiday in 1957 I was in Scotland around Ben Nevis with Wes Hayden and Geoff Stroud, walking all of the Mamores; starting off from Polldubh Barn we climbed up to Mullach nan Coirean and then continued along the connecting ridges and over all the summits to Sgùrr Eilde Mòr. There I parted company from my companions, who walked back down to Glen Nevis and the barn to put a stew on. I was still feeling fit and set off across the glen to traverse all the peaks and ridges of the Grey Corries on the opposite side of the Water of Nevis from Stob Choire Claurigh to Càrn Mòr Dearg.

Spring snow made the going interesting as I coasted from one summit to the next. Despite the warm sun, the air had a bite to it. There was no wind, only complete silence. I was surrounded by snow-covered mountains that lay one behind the other for miles in all directions and, towards the end of the ridge, I watched a huge stag stand for a few seconds on the superb snowy summit of Aonach Beag. He had come up from the other side so we were both as surprised as each other; but neither of us panicked, he just gently turned and ambled down towards Aonach Mòr.

So far the Grey Corries ridge had been gently undulating; now there was a steep loss of height down to the *bealach* between Aonach Beag and Càrn Mòr Dearg. By the time I dropped down and climbed back up the sun had set and my energy levels were finally wilting. All the distant mountains were now in outline, one silhouette after another stretching into the distance under a clear, evening sky. With not enough time or strength to scramble up Ben Nevis, I descended the rock and heather hillside to Polldubh. It had been the best day I had ever had in the hills and the feeling of contentment I experienced persisted for days. After this epiphany, I forgot my blisters, forgot tearing my sleeping bag on the iron bedstead in the barn and the feathers that covered everything for the rest of the holiday. No other activity bore comparison. Those fourteen hours climbing twelve Munros was a turning point in my life. Cross-country running and athletics had been superseded by an insatiable urge to visit more of the hills in Britain – and mountains everywhere.

I continued to enjoy Scouting and during May we went to Gilwell, the headquarters of the Scout movement in Epping Forest. There we met Scouts from all over the UK and swopped county badges to add to our collections that we sewed on to our campfire blankets. Every night we sat around a huge fire singing the traditional Scouting songs – 'We're riding along on the crest of a wave!' – and took a daytrip into London, with Wes Hayden leading the way since he had experience of the underground, and the Lyons Corner House down the Strand where you could eat as much as you wanted for 4s. 6d. At the closing ceremony I was given my Queen's Scout Certificate. I still have it.

Otherwise, I began an intense period of study, either up in my bedroom or, if it wasn't raining, sitting on the back lawn. During our last term at Cottesmore, Mick Garside and I walked up Derby Road at lunchtime to visit the local

Soloing *Sunset Slab* at Froggatt in 1961. I'm wearing Dad's old police trousers, which were useful for pegging as you could put the hammer in the truncheon pocket.

recruiting officer. With National Service looming we wanted to inveigle our way into the mountain rescue section of the Royal Air Force. Conscription had begun in 1941 and continued after the war ended. From the age of eighteen every young man had been obliged by law to complete two years of military service. Most were stationed in Germany, defending the free world from the USSR. A few saw active service in Korea, Malaya, Kenya and Cyprus. To our astonishment, we discovered our country might not need us after all. It seemed there was hardly any Empire left for my generation to defend. I would have relished being part of some heroic action, like the 'Glorious Glosters' defence of Hill 235 that kept communist China from Seoul. Whether I could have stood still as some corporal with a chip on his shoulder bawled obscenities into my face is another matter.

The one thing that took me away from my books was weekend camping and climbing trips to Derbyshire. We usually hitchhiked out to Black Rocks or the Robin Hood pub near Baslow. The Robin Hood was a one-off; there was straw on the stone flags and old Gladys the landlady would take a quart jug down to the cellar to pull beer from large oak barrels. We camped on Smedley's Farm behind the pub. In the morning old Ben Froggatt came round to collect the camping fee of two shillings. Ben Froggatt's campsite and barn was a great meeting place for Nottingham climbers hitchhiking up the newly extended M1 and within easy walking distance of what some would say is the finest crag climbing in the world on the millstone grit of Birchen Edge, Gardom's Edge, Chatsworth Edge and not so far from Curbar and Froggatt.

This whole business of climbing had become a large part of my life. There was a lot more to it than simply spending time on rock. With rugby, most of the time was spent actually playing rugby; the rugby grounds were near to home and it could all be fitted into one afternoon. Climbing involved far more travelling, meeting up in pubs and restaurants, sitting around shouting the odds on wet days and sleeping out in barns, cricket pavilions, under bridges and in caves. I think I've only read one book on rugby – Michael Green's *The Art of Coarse Rugby* – but climbing had produced a huge literature, although there weren't so many manuals then.

The recommended instructional book was John Barford's *Climbing in Britain*. Barford was secretary of the newly constituted British Mountaineering Council, and under the influence of the great Geoffrey Winthrop Young, the BMC decided to produce an elementary introduction to hillwalking and mountaineering. Barford wrote most of the text, taking advice from some of the great names of British climbing before the war: A.B. Hargreaves, J.H. Bell, A.S. Piggott and Young himself. In a very short time 125,000 copies were sold. Not much had changed in the twelve years since Barford's book was published in 1946; there was less emphasis on clinkers and Tricounis and more on Vibram-soled boots, developed in the war, and plimsolls were now recommended for 'advanced' rock climbing. The only running belay explained was a loop of nylon rope put on a spike of rock or threaded around a chockstone in a crack with the main climbing rope running through a snaplink clipped to the sling. Since the leader's protection was limited the emphasis in these manuals was on climbing within the limits of experience and never to fall off. The use of pitons for running belays and for direct aid was described and illustrated under the chapters for alpinism. I'm not sure I learned much more from instructional books that I hadn't already assimilated from other climbers and Bob Pettigrew's evening class.

I hadn't been climbing long before I realised there were other lads more naturally gifted than me. Compared to Dez Hadlum, for example, I always had more of a struggle, ending up more battered and bruised. There was definitely room for improvement. Yet I never became discouraged; more than anything I simply enjoyed being out in the Peak District discovering the different crags, working out moves with the rest of the crowd and all the banter that went with the climbing life. After two or three years, when I began to climb more than play rugby, I did become fitter for climbing, strong in limb and with skin hardened from hand-jamming the classic gritstone cracks. I began to trust myself to pad across open slabs – but not without a wobble or two and even a rescue now and again.

On our trip to the White Hall Outdoor Pursuits Centre, Mick and I had been offered the chance to help out as temporary instructors. I had so enjoyed my visit that I took up the offer several times. The practical advantage was that temporary instructors, although unpaid, had travel and other expenses covered. We were also made very welcome. White Hall was such a friendly place to be, like one big family. Its ethos was quite different from the strict, somewhat regimented Outward Bound centres. White Hall had been created to interest a much younger age group. The courses were designed to last for either a weekend or at most a week; there was less emphasis on character building and more on enjoyment.

The bus would drop us off quite late on Friday night. Invariably, the warden Geoff Sutton, tall, broad-shouldered and usually wearing thigh-length sealskin boots from a Greenland expedition, was there to greet us and invite us into the kitchen. His charming wife Anne would cook us delicious, garlic-flavoured omelettes for supper as we sat listening to stories told by permanent staff members Harold Drasdo and Andrew Maxfield.

Geoff became one of climbing's most influential writers, particularly as a translator of important books like Lionel Terray's *Conquistadors of the Useless*. He also wrote of the history and great traditions of British climbing in his very readable and compelling style, weaving all manner of anecdotes into his narrative.

He was a big influence on me. Here he is in his first major contribution in the book he co-authored with Wilf Noyce – *Snowdon Biography* – commenting on the surge of recruits into climbing after the war: 'The number of people coming to the Welsh hills with the intention of using a rope has seemed to double itself every two or three years since 1946. Age cannot wither nor custom stale their infinite variety: they are of every shape and age and ideal and sex and condition of life – greeting them on the hill it is fascinating but vain to speculate whether the reply will come in the most dulcet of Oxford modulations or a good outright adenoidal *scowse*. In only one thing are they uniform, and that is their appearance. During the war numbers of wind-proof camouflaged smocks and trousers, karabiners and ice-axes were produced to serve our men in bloodthirsty battles on mountain tops and icebergs which fortunately never took place. Since that time they have been made inexhaustibly available, at an ever-increasing profit, to the fortunate climbing public: and indeed it is true to say that, if drab, they are practical, strong, and were once cheap.' He also wrote a biography of the tortured climbing genius Menlove Edwards, again with Wilfrid Noyce. Increasingly Sutton made his career out of writing and in 1960 was succeeded at White Hall by his friend Eric Langmuir, moving to Geneva. In 1962 he wrote a small handbook on artificial climbing which was the only guide in the English language on the subject and would be significant to me when I came to write my own book on big walls.

His most popular book was *High Peak*, written with Eric Byne. In it he refers back to his time at White Hall when, between writing and translating and running the centre, he found time to go out with the permanent staff, climbing in the Peak and also in the Poisoned Glen of Donegal. They created minor classics on the grit and an important climb on limestone when Harold Drasdo and Gordon Mansell climbed *The Stalk* on Plum Buttress down Cheedale in 1955. It was the first time a significant and later popular VS route had been climbed free of pegs on limestone.

Geoff was also an important alpinist. After leaving Cambridge, he and Bob Downes, an assistant instructor at White Hall, were with Joe Brown and Don Whillans on their first attempt to climb the west face of the Blaitière in 1953. In 1955, after following Don Whillans up the first ascent of Skye's Old Man of Storr, he made the first British ascent of the north face of the Piz Badile with fellow Cambridge men Bob Downes and Eric Langmuir and also Alan Blackshaw, then at Oxford. Geoff also made the first British ascent of a fine new route on the Gugliermina in the Mont Blanc range. This new wave of alpinists inspired the formation of the Alpine Climbing Group, which produced translations of foreign guidebooks, a great spur to post-war British mountaineering.

Mick and I were lucky enough to travel to the Isle of Arran as volunteers on a White Hall trip. On a break from instructing, we set off with Harold and

Gordon to climb the *South Ridge Direct* on the Rosa Pinnacle of Cìr Mhòr, the splendid, symmetrical peak in the centre of the island. It was the longest route I'd yet done. I was pushed into the lead, spurred on by these luminaries watching from below, feeding my ego as I made short work of the layback crux. The rock was just wonderful, the setting superb and the company always inspiring.

Harold was one of the original Bradford lads and a contemporary of Arthur Dolphin; he later wrote several influential guidebooks and important essays on the ethics and philosophy of climbing. Intellectually, he leant towards the anarchism of Alex Comfort, but also had a strong interest in environmental campaigning. Gordon Mansell strummed his guitar and regaled us with songs, backed up by his beautiful wife Maureen, and climbing stories of Joe Brown the 'human fly', who completed the first ascent of *Cenotaph Corner* with his belayer knocked unconscious by Joe's dropped peg hammer. The same Joe Brown had just returned from climbing a steep jamming crack at more than 28,000 feet on the first ascent of Kangchenjunga. People like Geoff, Harold and Gordon were all larger than life characters, so full of infectious enthusiasm for the climbing life. They were all highly individual but had one thing in common – they made me, and everyone who came to White Hall, feel at home.

Good jamming at Black Rocks in 1964.

On Scafell, December 1957. **Photo:** Wesley Hayden.

HISTORY LESSONS

While I was up on Arran climbing the Rosa Pinnacle, my O-level results came through. I had failed English, but passed the others and my grades were good enough to earn me a place at the co-educational Mundella Grammar School. So, in September 1957, full of apprehension at what lay ahead, I cycled through the meadows to Mundella, still wearing my Cottesmore blazer. I needn't have worried. Both Wesley Hayden and Geoff Stroud were in the upper sixth and they gave me a tour of the grand halls. Masters in flowing black gowns glided down long corridors as pupils, in uniforms of maroon and gold, stood respectfully to let them pass.

The headmaster took me to my first lesson to meet Tom Robinson, who taught history. Under Tom Robinson's tutelage, I learned how to learn for myself. The other pupils helped me settle in and could not have been better company. We were encouraged to find evidence for ourselves, delving in the school library. I remember reading Parson Woodforde's diaries; it was like opening a window on the eighteenth century. What amazed me was the non-stop entertaining and the huge amount of food the parson shared with his guests: 'We had for dinner some fresh Water Fish, Perch and Trout, a Saddle of Mutton roasted, Beans and Bacon, a Couple of Fowls boiled, Patties and some white soup – second course – pigeons roasted, a Duck roasted, Piggs Pettytoes – Sweet breads, Raspberry Cream, Tarts and Pudding and Pippins.' This wasn't standard fare on Charlbury Road.

I also read Pastor Moritz's *Journeys of a German in England*, about his impressions of England in 1782. He was amazed at the quantity of beer drunk but also the high standard of education across all strata of society. Moritz visited the High Peak. He walked over Mam Tor, the 'Shivering Mountain', and went down the Devil's Cavern, near Castleton, before walking south and coming upon the fair vista of Nottingham as it was in the eighteenth century. 'Of all the towns I have seen outside London, Nottingham is the loveliest and neatest. Everything had a modern look, and a large space in the centre was hardly less handsome than a London Square. How Nottingham stands on a hill, and, with its high houses, red roofs and church steeples looks excellent from a distance. At no town in England have I enjoyed so beautiful a prospect.' I was proud to read that, but knew how Nottingham had changed.

Tom Robinson gave me a love of learning for its own sake and while I couldn't know everything, after two years with Tom, I knew where to find it. 'Curiosity is, in great and generous minds, the first passion and the last,' observed Dr Johnson, another author Tom had us reading. 'What is written without effort is in general read without pleasure,' was another of Johnson's maxims he favoured, along with: 'the greatest part of a writer's time is spent in reading, in order to write; a man will turn over half a library to make half a book.' Consequently, there would be a group of us at the Mechanics' Institute library long after school – all the lads in the history class, Mick Poppleston, David Summers, John Stenson and myself. At 6 p.m. hunger drove us over the road to the local YMCA to buy a bowl of soup – with a free refill or two and access to a stack of white sliced bread and butter – before another couple of hours back at the library.

During my first term at Mundella, Wesley and I took two fifth-form girls to the Goose Fair, Nottingham's four-day festival that has been an annual event for 700 years. Wesley walked with an attractive blond called Carol Pullen from Wollaton; I walked with the equally attractive but raven-headed Susan Webster, the daughter of an Anglo-Indian doctor and a mother originally from the West Indies but now living in Carlton. As Wesley slid his arm around Carol's waist I moved to hold Susan's hand. She asked me if I always copied Wesley.

I went to my first dance with Susan, the school's Christmas ball up in the grand main hall. Susan was looking breathtakingly beautiful: black hair, olive complexion, flashing eyes and a warm smile. She was dressed in layers of chiffon skirts. I inevitably tripped, falling on to my back with Susan on top of me, her skirts revealed to all, including Tom Robinson who looked down at us and smiled: 'Better at climbing than dancing, hey Scott?'

One misty day in January, I set off with Susan on the bus to Bakewell and then walked up to Baslow and beyond. There was snow on the ground, fast disappearing in the rain. I clumped along the lanes and footpaths in my climbing boots, which Susan thought ridiculous for such a walk. She was quite right; it was me trying to impress her and everyone else we met that I was a real climber – just like the novice climbers I had noticed coming into pubs and restaurants with a belay length of nylon around their necks, weighed down with a snap-link.

It must have been Susan's idea to go to the Theatre Royal. I had often been to the theatre but to sit up in the gods with my mother and brothers to watch a

Christmas panto. We met under the Corinthian pillars of the theatre entrance; I was wearing Dad's green jacket and red silk cravat. We took our seats and settled in to watch Julian Slade's musical *Salad Days*, an appropriate choice since it's all about the light-hearted innocence of youth. I found myself entranced by the lyrics and the performances of the actors and the whole theatre was laughing, me louder than most. Susan said it wasn't that funny. Alas, we didn't have that much in common. Susan was far brighter than I and had little interest in sport and none in mountaineering. I lost out to an older and much more suitable chap. But we remained friends and stayed in touch; our parents were friends and her brother Michael took up climbing.

The headmaster at Mundella, knowing of my interest in climbing, put my name forward for interview to assess my suitability to take up a place offered to the Nottingham Education Committee at the Eskdale Outward Bound Mountain School. In February the director of education wrote to congratulate me on my selection for a month's course over Easter 1958. I couldn't wait to go on my first trip to the Lake District but was also apprehensive at going away for a month with complete strangers. That side of things, putting young people into challenging and unfamiliar situations on land and water, was part of Kurt Hahn's philosophy. It seemed to help them gain confidence and become more self-reliant. Lawrence Holt, a senior partner in a shipping company and a Gordonstoun parent, was the co-founder of Outward Bound, choosing a name that was the signal used to alert sailors their ship was departing and to leave the comforts of home for the vagaries of the open sea. Bracing myself for all the uncertainties of Eskdale Green in the Lakes, I knew how they felt.

I arrived by train wearing a pair of Arvons, the latest climbing footwear that I bought from Arvon Jones himself on Bethesda's High Street in North Wales. They had Vibram rubber soles, which had now made the nailed boot redundant. One of the young instructors greeted me rather acidly: 'Oh, you've got a pair of Arvon's 'Tigers' have you? What do you think you will be doing in those? Does it make you feel like a real climber?' I thought it best to keep my powder dry and told him I would see what I could do. Happily he turned out to be a supercilious oddball out of so many first-rate instructors.

Every morning we were up at dawn running around the lake in PE shorts, usually with frost on the track. Then we had to dive in. There was a crag in the grounds, about thirty feet high, which I couldn't resist. I was reprimanded for climbing without ropes or permission. Apart from that I seemed to get along fine and in particular with a captain from the army seconded to Outward Bound. He had been at Eskdale long enough to know quite a bit about the area. He told us of a local character who had gathered wool from the hawthorn hedgerows and first spun, then woven and finally sewed himself a suit. After the

Me, front centre, with my patrol of Ford Dagenham apprentices at the Outward Bound Mountain School in Eskdale, 1958.

first week the captain decided I would be leader of one of the twelve patrols for the next three weeks. I knew this was going to be tough since most of the lads in our group were two or three years older, mainly from London and several of them young apprentices from Ford.

The course was non-stop activity: first aid, mountain rescue, athletics, rock climbing, fell walking, bivouacking, map reading and natural history. It made quite an impression on me to hear, read and then see how the natural landscape had evolved over the centuries, the deep forest cut down to make pit props for the mining industry and fuel for furnaces, and then sheep farming ensuring there would be no regeneration of trees or anything else apart from grass – certainly not much wildlife.

Towards the end of the course, the excellent warden, John Lagoe, who had taken over from Eric Shipton, led group discussions about our futures. I was taken aback by the attitudes of some of the London lads; they seemed despondent about their prospects and life in general. They sounded old before their time. For me it had been such a wonderful four weeks rock climbing up on Yewbarrow, ranging right across the Lake District during the final expedition and climbing Scafell and Scafell Pike, Skiddaw and almost Helvellyn, all in three days from Eskdale Green and back. I was glowing with contentment. Maybe it was the thought of going back to Dagenham that was bothering them. One of the co-leaders was an Eton schoolboy with whom I got into regular conversation. We shared stories and seemed to complement our contrasting backgrounds. He was the first public schoolboy I had known and I was impressed with his quiet confidence and affable nature.

That course whetted my appetite for the Lake District. What lovely country it is. I found it more beautiful and inviting than Wales. Geoff, Wes and I decided to go back for Christmas and New Year. We changed buses at Manchester and arrived in Windermere long after dark. Looking for somewhere to camp, we hopped over a wall and found a wonderfully flat field. Next morning we discovered we were camped on the lawn of a very grand mansion. A butler appeared and, not unreasonably, ordered us to pack up and go. So we walked up into Langdale and across to Wasdale, camping in driving rain at Angle Tarn. Our borrowed mountain tent leaked like a sieve. Next morning, with the rain turning to snow, we wrung out the tent, rolled up our sodden sleeping bags and salvaged our food from the puddles.

We waded through the deep snow from cairn to cairn, eventually reaching England's highest point on top of Scafell Pike before dropping down through the mist and heavy rain to rest and to dry out at the Wasdale Head Hotel. The proprietor in those days was a burly ex-wrestler called Wilson Pharaoh, who said we could dry out in the barn. It was chock-a-block with climbers, mostly from the Rock and Ice Club, but we managed to find a space to cook the last of our food on the Primus. That night, after everyone returned from the bar, a large plastic bottle was placed in the middle of the barn. The climbers split into two groups and moved to either end of the barn before charging forwards to grab the bottle and then touch it against the opposite wall. This was barn rugby, also called 'murder ball', and I couldn't resist joining in. Right in the thick of the action was Don Whillans.

Don was twenty-four and, along with Joe Brown, already a legend among British climbers. He was born in Salford in 1933 and, although only five-foot four, he was broad shouldered and obviously fit. He also had a strong accent, peculiar to that part of Lancashire, and spoke it in a measured monotone that began deep down at the base of his neck before emerging with a slight vibrato through his sinuses. Not that he had much to say to us apart from to ask how we had managed to get all our gear soaked – and rugby. Everyone seemed to defer to him on account of his reputation for hard climbing and hard living.

I would play barn rugby again with Don, including one rather supernatural bout that resulted in some natural justice. Bas, a friend from Nottingham, was distraught when his girlfriend disappeared with a big lad called George Potts for the New Year weekend in Wasdale. So Bas made an effigy of George out of fruit and olives and then stuck cocktail sticks into the effigy's eye and also its ribs. Up in Wasdale, a furious game of bottle rugby was underway, and during the ebb and flow, Don Whillans landed a fist in George Potts' eye and then I landed on top of him, cracking his ribs so severely that he had to retire, much to the satisfaction of Bas when the story was put together back in Nottingham.

Back at school the tempo of work increased. I needed to have five O levels altogether, including English, if I was to move on to further education. My first lesson in A-level geography was with Miss Winter and just two other students, Elizabeth and Pearl. Miss Winter, a rather homely lady in her retirement year, gave us a chapter in F.J. Monkhouse's *Principles of Physical Geography* to read while she brought out her copy of *The Times*. She was soon asleep and only woken by the school bell at the end of the lesson. Once again, by making certain I knew the curricular requirements by checking out previous exam papers and by reading widely, I made good progress, according to Miss Winter, who would at least mark our answers to previous exam papers.

The deputy headmistress, a rather grand lady of some bearing, gave me one-to-one tutorials in O-level English whenever we were both free. I read *Macbeth* and *Morte d'Arthur*, and learned about onomatopoeia, alliteration and metaphors. Despite my newfound grammatical knowledge, I failed English for the second time. Then I had some good luck. I became fascinated by the contrasts in character and leadership style of the great Antarctic explorers, my namesake Scott and Shackleton. In my next attempt to pass O-level English one of the topics for the long essay was on leadership and I wrote reams on the subject. This time I passed.

Geoff, Wesley and I combed the school library for maps of the Alps for our next expedition. With the Mamores and the Snowdon Horseshoe under our belts, it seemed obvious our next objective should be walking along the crest of the mountains between Mont Blanc and the Matterhorn. Non-climbers listening in sensibly told us that would be impossible and got quite worked up saying we should be stopped from risking our lives and maybe the lives of others. Eventually we settled on spending five weeks on the Continent, three in the Alps and two behind the Iron Curtain in Yugoslavia, just to see what it was like. It seemed sensible to travel out as Scouts with the support of our 1st Nottingham YMCA Rover Crew. We left Nottingham by bus in late July, spending the night in the East End of London at Roland House, the Scouting hostel. Then we caught the boat train for Dover and my first trip abroad.

We stretched out in an otherwise empty carriage and slept all the way to Basle, where we changed trains for Kandersteg. Our faces were glued to the window, staggered by the scale and grandeur of the Alps rising up from behind vast forests of pine. Peak after snow-capped peak revealed itself as the train made its tortuous way through steep-sided valleys and through the longest tunnels we'd yet experienced. At Kandersteg's International Scout Centre we put up our Bukta Wanderlust tent and settled in.

The heat seemed incredible, especially crossing the snowfields and glaciers above the beautiful Oeschinensee. We hoped to climb the Blüemlisalphorn but were defeated by the heat, its height and our inexperience. After a week spent plodding across soft snow and reaching various passes we left the Bernese Alps for Chamonix as wiser men. At least our introduction to the Alps had made us accustomed to the scale of the landscape, which was utterly magnificent, the blue of the lakes, the huge rock walls rising up to ice and snow. From the passes, we saw snow peaks panning out around us in all directions, as far as we could see.

In early August, having sent most of our kit and supplies by rail to Leuk, we walked twenty-four miles up and over the Gemmi Pass with its fine views of the Matterhorn. At Leuk, we decided to try our luck hitchhiking for the first time abroad. In Derbyshire in the late 1950s there were so many people on the roadside hitching that if we missed the bus back to Nottingham we always tried thumbing a lift and often got back before the bus. I soon graduated to thumbing lifts to Wales and Scotland. So it wasn't such a big deal to try our luck in Europe.

With so much competition, especially outside some of the big towns and cities and in particular Calais, the only way to move on quickly was to have an identity. I once joined a group of twenty hitchhikers on the outskirts of Calais and then watched in amusement as two of the crowd put on kilts and another went behind a building and came back dressed as a priest, wearing a cassock and a wide-brimmed hat and counting off his rosary beads. They were picked up in no time. I was impressed. Motorists would want some idea of the person they were taking into their car, so I pulled the rope out of my rucksack and attached it so that it was obviously visible. The youth in breeches and climbing boots was indeed an alpinist and the youth was consequently soon on his way, trying to convince a complete stranger that climbing wasn't dangerous.

There were good times and bad. Sometimes for no apparent reason there would be one car stopping after another and then other times, as on the outskirts of Metz one day heading for Paris, I waited for hour after hour as I sat all day on my rucksack, despondent and homesick, until a lorry stopped and took me 250 miles through the night into Paris. He was a Swiss from Basle with green eyes and slits for pupils, like a cat's eyes. They gave him something to talk about, he said.

There were times when I would take up the offer of a lift just for the company and to get out of the cold and wet. Hitching up on January to Garve Station outside Inverness to meet Ray Gillies I stayed in the warm cab of a lorry all the way to Aberdeen and then started walking as snow fell on the empty roads. By 11 p.m., now in Bucksburn on the outskirts of Aberdeen, I was beginning to wonder where I could stay the night. Through a gap in a tall privet hedge, I saw a house – 'Hope Croft' – and knocked on the door. A window opened and an old man in a nightshirt and pointed nightcap holding a candle asked me what my problem was. I told him I had nowhere to sleep and asked if I could sleep in his shed. Sleep in the kitchen, he answered, and blew the candle out before coming downstairs to let me in. His wife, covered neck to toe in a thick cotton nightie, fed me oatcakes and cheese. I slept on a couch and in the morning, after a bowl of porridge, went on my way. We kept up a correspondence for years. Next day, Ray and I waded up Ben Wyvis in the snow.

Given the amount of time I spent on the roads of Britain and Europe, hitch-hiking must have shaped my character, encouraging me to be patient and to develop a philosophical attitude to adversity. I learned not to be upset or lose energy when, for example, a car full of young people stopped fifty yards up the road and then, just as I ran up to it with my heavy load, so looking forward to sitting down, drew away and then stopped again, playing cat and mouse before leaving for good without me. Hitchhiking was always interesting even if it did involve long periods of inactivity and frustration. For good or ill, it was something to look forward to because the result was greater awareness of myself and particularly the places and people I visited.

Our first experience went well, and we were pleased to arrive in Chamonix within a few hours of each other. The town seemed full of English climbers, including friends from White Hall. Food was more expensive than Switzerland but the bread was wonderful, far better, as I wrote home, than Nottingham Co-op's white sliced. 'We had our first bottle of wine today,' I wrote to my parents. 'It cost about 2/- and I don't think I want any more, though it was not so bad after sugar had been added.' We managed to keep to our budget of £1 a day between the three of us. What we bought was supplemented with huge quantities of wild strawberries and fruit and a few tomatoes and spring onions we managed to scrump travelling down the Rhône Valley.

As for climbing, I wrote in my diary I was 'feeling more confident. We began our last week in the Alps by going along the length of the Mer de Glace crossing many crevasses and séracs which we agreed should be avoided next time.' That was an understatement. Geoff recalled later being terrified as we inched our way above deep crevasses holding on to rotten ice with no protection at all. Then we walked up towards the Géant Icefall where we got into conversation with a gangly Englishman who gave us the daft advice that we should buy a 200-foot lightweight rope for abseiling. Unfortunately, we were daft enough to listen. We returned to Montenvers and walked down through the forest to Chamonix proud we weren't wasting money on trains.

Next day we were walking back up through the forest, sticks of French bread poking out of our huge rucksacks, heading towards the Aiguille du Midi with the vague plan of continuing from there to the summit of Mont Blanc. It was well after noon by the time we started rock climbing up several pitches, including two of Severe standard. Suddenly it seemed prudent to return; it was late, snow melt was pouring down the rock and I fell off, tumbling about sixty feet until Geoff stopped me, suffering rope burns across his hands as he did so. Later we discovered that in our attempt to climb the Midi we had in fact gone some way up the Boeuf Couloir – rather like a bull at a gate – on a completely different mountain, the Aiguille du Peigne.

Prudently, we gave up on Mont Blanc, packed our gear and began hitchhiking across northern Italy. It was a wonderful experience from the start. I went into a shop below the Saint Bernard Pass and asked for some cheese. The large lady behind the counter was so warm and full of good cheer and answered my question in a singsong voice I would never forget: '*Ah, formaggio! Gorgonzola? Quanto costa? Cinquecento lire!*' We stopped for two nights at Peschiera just so we could enjoy being in Italy. There was music at night and dancing in the streets, the night air full of the smell of tasty fish grilling on fires. In Venice we toured the canals on a gondola and visited the Lido where we got on a bus with some American tourists who said with great glee, waving their feet in the air, that this was the first time that they had been on a public bus. That night we slept outside on the sand bar of the Lido below an amazingly starry sky.

Early next morning a sea mist hung over the town. The gondolas bobbed up and down like ghostly galleons as we walked out of town to start hitching to Trieste where we treated ourselves to a lunch of chips and a salad covered in olive oil, something I had only ever had put in my ears. That evening we reached Yugoslavia, the one communist country opening up to tourism. Everything was ridiculously cheap. We took a ferry down the Adriatic as far as the island of Rab. That night there was a violent storm and a huge tree blew down in the grounds of the Franciscan monastery of St Euphemia. In return for reducing the fallen giant to bundles of firewood, the monks fed and housed us for a few days. One hot afternoon, we walked down to the sea and saw a yacht mooring in the bay. By the time we reached the beach, the passengers were ashore lying on the sand, and all of them naked, men, women and children. They were German, and we three teenage lads picked our way through them, like pink seals in the hot sun, mumbling *Grosser Gott* and trying not to look.

Returning to school, I had decisions to make. I thought about journalism as a career, and even of becoming a doctor but realised I didn't have the ability to do either easily. Nor did my parents have sufficient income to support me at university without a huge struggle. If I had been really keen they could have somehow managed. My brother Brian did become a doctor, studying at Barts at the University of London before becoming a consultant. My youngest brother Garry also went to university, studying civil engineering at Nottingham. I applied instead to Loughborough College for a teaching certificate in PE and geography. There must have been some other reason for taking the comparatively soft option of trying for a teacher training college. It was the holidays. If I became a teacher, I would have more free time to climb.

Having made the decision, Dad went into overdrive, encouraging me to get 'another string to your bow' by studying for certificates in first aid from the St John Ambulance Association, Dad being a serving Brother of St John of Jerusalem. He was also an examiner for the Royal Life Saving Society so I got a certificate in that as well. Out of the blue came an invitation to take part in a pilot project for something called the Duke of Edinburgh Award Scheme. Dad was involved as an examiner for the section on athletics. I passed the bronze and got my silver certificate in December 1958. At school I kept up with running, mainly to keep fit for rugby, and shared the *victor ludorum* with a fine athlete called Alan Warsop. At my last school speech day, I collected the prize for geography: a newly published history of the Eiger's north face by Heinrich Harrer, called *The White Spider*.

Wes had now left school to work at Rolls-Royce in Derby; Geoff was working as a technician at the Sutton Bonington Agricultural College. We kept in touch through Scouts and weekend climbing trips although now I mostly climbed with Dez Hadlum. Dez, like me, had started climbing through the Scouts and he too juggled climbing in the Peak District with playing rugby. He also helped his family run one of the best fish and chip shops in Nottingham, mostly by peeling huge amounts of potatoes, and was an apprenticed toolmaker.

During the summer of 1959, before college, Dez, Wes and myself decided to go to the Alps together. Most of my climbing friends were now working and so although short on holidays they were in the money. I was in the reverse position. Dad had to take care of three sons and put some aside for the family holiday as well as pay the weekly bills. My parents wouldn't buy anything on the 'never never' and criticised those who did. Somehow there was spare cash for a new coat or a wheel for my bike. I managed to cover the cost of weekend climbing and equipment by delivering mail for two weeks during the Christmas holidays.

Dad was friendly with the owner of a pork pie factory and got me a part-time night shift that I worked after my job delivering the post. My task was squirting gelatine through the pastry into the pie. I had my first insight into British labour relations, when the foreman, a lecherous, red-faced man who was forever telling us he had a 'promise' from one of the secretaries, upended the night's production all over the factory yard in front of the boss's Jaguar. I also worked weekends on the farm at Car Colston and had just enough funds for six weeks in the Alps with a bit over to buy an ice axe and crampons.

Mum bought me lots of 'Pom' potato powder and 'Swell' dehydrated vegetables and let me fill my rucksack with tins from the pantry. She warned me to boil the water in France before drinking it. Two hours after leaving school,

I shouldered my sack of climbing gear and tins of baked beans and was hitching out of Nottingham.

After four days, I reached Chamonix and pitched my tent among the trees at the Biolay campsite, close to the cemetery on the shady, damp side of town. An hour or two later Dez arrived and next day we bought ourselves new ice axes and crampons from Snell Sports. Derek Burgess, a climber from the Oread Club, and a friend of Bob Pettigrew, gave us advice and let us copy descriptions from the Vallot guidebook. We were ready to go.

Our first objective was a magnificent pyramid of granite, the Dent du Requin – the shark's tooth. We carried a heavy tent, food and fuel for about a week up to the Requin hut, putting most of the gear on the train to Montenvers and walking up to save money. Scrambling down to the Mer de Glace, we hugged the bank of the glacier to avoid crevasses but didn't understand that the true left bank of the glacier meant the right bank as we hiked up it, and we ended up having to cut steps in the ice to get back on track when we saw the hut sitting high above us on its rocky outcrop. It was a long slog up and then it took us a while to find somewhere flat enough for the tent that wasn't covered in garbage tossed out from the hut.

By late afternoon the Bukta tent was up and the Primus stove roaring away. I wrote in my diary that I finished reading *The Third Eye* by Lobsang Rampa, the incredible story of a monk with extraordinary powers who helps the young Dalai Lama. I'd picked up a book on yoga from a second-hand bookshop, partly to help with athletics and climbing, but the book also switched me on to Eastern religions. *The Third Eye* was a bestseller and really caught my imagination. The author described how, while in his lamasery in Tibet, he had an operation that opened his 'third eye' in the middle of his forehead. His lama told him: 'you are now one of us, Lobsang. For the rest of your life you will see people as they are, not as they intend to be.'

The book had been published in 1956, but Heinrich Harrer was sceptical. He hired a private detective who discovered Lobsang Rampa was in fact Cyril Hoskin, the son of a plumber from Devon who had never been to Tibet. I knew this when reading the book, as did most other people, but it was still a thought-provoking read; it certainly had me reaching out for more information on Tibetan Buddhism. It's surprising how many academic Tibetologists had their interest sparked by Hoskin's yarn.

It rained during the night, moisture permeating the tent fabric in a fine drizzle. We wouldn't have the flysheet until Wesley arrived. At 7 a.m. the rain stopped and the clouds lifted to reveal a sparkling view of the many iconic mountains we had read about: the Dru, Grandes Jorasses, Dent du Géant. I had never felt so much a part of the mountains before, an experience heightened by the Requin's position at the heart of the range.

With the sun shining on the Requin's south face, we set off, both of us wearing crampons for the first time. We had the novel experience of roping up for a crevassed section before climbing up to a snowfield that led to the base of the rocks and the start of our route – the relatively straightforward *Voie des Plaques*. I felt quite confident, smearing on suntan lotion against the fierce glare of the sun on snow, although people watching us from the hut made us a little self-conscious. We loved the rock, coarse-grained granite that was a pleasure to climb, and we led through easily past some prominent pinnacles. Then, in late morning, cloud developed, billowing up into a full-blown storm of hail, snow, thunder and lightning. We took shelter against the blizzard on a ledge under an overhang of crystals, watching as the granite became soaked with melting snow. Dez wisely counselled for retreat, which was hard to take; we seemed only a pitch or two from the shoulder, and not more than an hour or so from the top.

I now realised how stupid I had been to buy the 200 feet of lightweight line to abseil off. The thin, brand new cord quickly tangled and jammed before one of the two strands frayed right through. We reached the snow in the dark and only reached the rock near the hut at 11 p.m. I reflected in my diary next morning: 'One thing we soon realised – we had the technical ability to do much harder climbs but we did not have the experience of long climbs to estimate times – to be still on the Requin at 11 p.m.?!'

We left the tent where it was and headed down to Chamonix to meet Wesley and spent the next day resting at the Biolay, periodically hiding in the surrounding woods to avoid the 'taxman' who came round demanding camping fees for the non-existent facilities; the smelly forest was a minefield of human waste. Then we walked back up to the Requin with Wesley, phlegmatic as ever, uncomplaining at being so high so soon. At 6 a.m. we were once more walking up to the *Voie des Plaques*. Reaching our previous highpoint, we discovered it was three pitches to the shoulder, not the one I had previously estimated. I led a thirty-foot hand traverse, which turned out to be straightforward. The last few pitches were more interesting as we lead through, climbing up chimneys and an overhang to reach the top.

Storm clouds were massing again as we reached the summit, but in our haste to leave, we abseiled down the wrong side and had to climb back up. Then we made good progress until the storm hit, first drenching us with rain before a blizzard of wet snow drove us off course. We found ourselves on a solid rock that overhung the Envers du Plan, and below it a hundred feet of fresh air to the bergschrund below. We had one wafer-thin leaf peg, which we bashed into a hairline crack. Dez bravely put his weight on it and then, hanging free, abseiled down until he was able to swing across the bergschrund on to the glacier.

Wes came down last, by which time the bridge of snow spanning the berg-schrund had collapsed so Dez and I hung all our weight on the ropes to pull Wesley across. Fortunately the peg held and we were able to descend the glacier, albeit in the dark. The snow became thinner until we were walking on water ice, slippery from the deluge. Lightning flashes lit the route and when we leapt across crevasses we weren't always sure we would reach the other side. We discussed a bivouac, even though there was nowhere suitable, but then got a second wind. The epic retreat continued. By midnight we were stumbling around the hut, shattered and a bit out of it, trying to find our tent as the storm continued. Our crashing around woke the *gardien*, who grumpily muttered something about the Requin being '*le dortoir des anglais*' and pointed to our tent. By the skin of our teeth we had avoided a night out and dived into our dry, warm sleeping bags. We had survived our first Alpine climb.

Back in Chamonix we ran into Bob Pettigrew, who at the time, was leading a Mountaineering Association course. Bob introduced us to a friend of his from Derby, known only as Wilks, and he joined our trio for a route on the Aiguille de l'M. The route was on excellent rock but local guides held us up while they dragged their clients up jamming cracks they didn't know how to climb, confirming our British prejudices about French guides and Continental jamming techniques.

Next day we set off for Mont Blanc. Dez had a bad stomach so we put him on the cable car while the three of us walked up through the forest. We met him at Bellevue at the bottom of the Tramway du Mont Blanc and then walked up beside the rails. We camped by a wooden hut, cooking dinner on an open fire and then rising before dawn to cook porridge, aware that we had to cross the rock ribs near the Tête Rousse hut before the sun, or other climbers, sent down rocks.

We made good time up to the Goûter hut and cooked a second breakfast on the veranda before continuing up and over the Dôme du Goûter to the Vallot bivouac hut beyond it. Wilks wasn't acclimatising well and struggling without crampons; since I was annoyingly fit from athletics and rugby, I gave him mine. After lunch in the Vallot we went up the steep ridge of Les Bosses to the summit of Mont Blanc. It was now 4 p.m., the very best time to reach the summit of Western Europe, with so much of the Alps in sharp relief all day under a clear blue sky and the only cloud deep down in the valleys below. The climb had been a slog but worth it for the sense of accomplishment and the incredible views.

Within an hour we were back in the icy aluminium box of the squalid Vallot hut, listening to a party of Austrians puking up from the altitude, adding to a frozen cascade of vomit that had formed like a stalactite down one corner of the table. They were up all night, retching and then melting snow to rehydrate.

Only Wes was able to sleep through it, and we were pleased to hurry down at dawn after a bowl of porridge, the long shadow of Mont Blanc stretching west towards the Dauphiné. There was a sea of cloud below us with only the highest peaks and ridges catching the early morning sun. I thought of Wordsworth's *Prelude*:

> I found myself of a huge sea of mist, which, meek and silent
> rested at my feet
> … the vapours shot themselves
> In headlands, tongues and promontory shapes.

We clumped back to the Col du Dome and then turned down the north side of Mont Blanc on good snow, stopping outside the Grands Mulets hut for our second breakfast before descending again to the Plan de l'Aiguille and the forest below, where we somehow lost the track. Just as we were looking forward to flopping down in our tent at the Biolay, we spent an extra hour pushing through the pine trees. Despite the delay we were still back at a little after noon, and bought pints of cold milk and lazed around, luxuriating in that wonderful period of rest after satisfying activity. It was a good end to the season and I was happy to have started my mountaineering apprenticeship. Already I was looking forward to extending my climbing to other ranges.

I also discovered I had passed my A levels and been accepted at Loughborough College. I would be starting in mid-September. So with time on my hands, when Dez and Wes left to go back to work, I hitched over to the Julian Alps, to walk and scramble with schoolmates Mick Poppleston and Geoff Stroud. On this second visit to Yugoslavia I decided to revisit a family that had taken me in at the Villa Giorgio in the small town of Dolo just before Venice. They had been so spontaneously generous refusing to allow me to camp and insisting I stayed in their house where they not only accommodated me but had me sitting around the family table for dinner and breakfast before sending me off with as much fruit as I could carry. Oreste Novello, the husband with whom we had exchanged Christmas cards, was not in and as none of the family spoke English, another family member and myself went off on bicycles to visit relations and friends who did speak English, one of whom knew Mansfield well since he had been there as a PoW for three years. The family the previous year, on hearing I was from Nottingham, became quite excited since they were all into lacemaking, samples of which they had given me for my mother. Satiated with good Italian food, drink and such a warm hospitality, I left for Venice and Yugoslavia after giving them samples of Nottingham lace.

After a week in the rugged Triglav Mountains, we split up to hitch to Vienna. At Klagenfurt I was offered a lift by two young men wearing what I thought

Wes Hayden (left) and me in St Mark's Square, Venice, 1958. Photo: Geoff Stroud.

were Scout uniforms. They turned out to be part of a movement campaigning for the unification of Europe as a bulwark against Soviet communism and the American way of life, particularly the 'military-industrial complex' that thrived on war. After a few miles they drove into their camp by a lake where we went for a swim and then sat around their kitchen organised very much on Scout lines. (I did notice, with the contemptuous pride of the true Scout, they had used nails to put their homemade furniture together.) The driver of the car, called Gerhard, gave me dinner and then made cocoa, and we sat around the fire talking long into the evening.

I wrote in my diary: 'they believe in a strong Germanic race preserving their own characteristics and institutions and had a similar wish for other European countries wanting a unified Europe to stand apart from the dominance of both Russia and America ... European civilisation, culture and political creeds had in many ways been accepted around the world so Europe should be preserved and not lapse into [a] mere colonial status ... They were to fight the menace of communism, not with guns but with enlightened moral ideals ... it called for a change in the home, the factory – a better and more harmonious relationship between the workers and the boss and also with the political leaders of the country.'

They asked my views and so I talked about the Commonwealth providing a third force for freedom against the dominance of Russia and America. They listened politely but I soon realised they thought I was living in the past.

They knew about the Nottingham riots and said that sort of thing could best be avoided only when Britain was strong economically and that could only happen in a strong Europe. I was impressed by their sincerity and willingness to communicate their ideas in a friendly, gentle fashion with a complete stranger. Their ideas reminded me of the philosophy of the American missionary Frank Buchman. I had read Buchman's book of speeches *Remaking the World* twice over and had written to his organisation Moral Re-Armament.

The MRA came into being in the late 1930s as Europe was re-arming for war. Buchman gave a speech to 3,000 people on 29 May 1938 at East Ham Town Hall in London, suggesting the looming crisis 'fundamentally is a moral one. The nations must re-arm morally. Moral recovery is essentially the forerunner of economic recovery. Moral recovery creates not crisis but confidence and unity in every phase of life.'

Buchman was a Christian but MRA included people of all strata of society, faith and nationality based on the four absolutes: absolute honesty, absolute purity, absolute unselfishness, and absolute love. Change starts, Buchman said, 'by changing oneself.' After the war, MRA helped the economic recovery of Eastern Europe by bringing groups of workers, management and owners of industry together and uniting disparate groups in colonial territories as they made the transition to independence. The core idea was always to change the world by changing oneself.

After a visit to the Opera House, Geoff and Mick left Vienna by train while I carried on hitching around Austria before heading home via Innsbruck and Paris. In early September, I was on the home straight, hitchhiking up the Great North Road, normally the best road for lifts with so many roundabouts to slow traffic. Unfortunately I was dropped on a fast section of dual carriageway and had to walk for miles, becoming quite tired and hungry. Then I noticed an open gate leading into a large garden with an apple tree. As I was picking up a few windfalls, the irate owner came out and began haranguing me. He asked me where I was from and where I was going. I told him I had been all around the Continent and received nothing but kindness. He exploded with anger.

'I've met your sort before,' he bellowed. 'Scrounge your way around the world and now here you are stealing my apples. Do you think the world owes you a living?'

THE 3RD AGE

And then the lover,
Sighing like furnace, with a woeful ballad
Made to his mistress' eyebrow.

As You Like It, William Shakespeare

The idealism of youth which brooks no
compromise can lead to over-confidence, the
human ego can be exalted to experience godlike
attributes but only at the cost of over-reaching
itself and falling to disaster. This is the meaning
of the story of Icarus, the youth who is carried
up to heaven on his fragile, humanly contrived
wings, but who flies too close to the sun and
plunges to his doom. All the same, the youthful
ego must always run this risk, for if a young man
does not strive for a higher goal than he can
safely reach, he cannot surmount the obstacles
between adolescence and maturity.

Carl Jung

The Nottingham contingent of the Oread Mountaineering Club at Darley Dale in 1959. On the wall, L–R: Wes Hayden, me, Geoff Hayes, Ken Beech. Standing, L–R: Mary Shaw, Beryl and Roger Turner, Annette Rabbits, Mike and Celia Berry.

JAN

Wearing my new duffle coat, I took a bus down to Loughborough in September 1959 to begin two years of teacher training. My first lecture, on how to conduct a PE lesson, was called 'Maximum Activity in Minimum Time' and was given by an ex-professional footballer called Archer, who peppered his talk with phrases like 'man in terms of himself' and other such jargon. It was obvious to me and probably everyone else in our group that those who had completed two years of National Service were more mature and worldly wise than those of us who were eighteen and had not had a break from education. I would have gained far more from the course if I'd had the courage to take time out to work or travel for a year or so.

During my first term the anatomy lecturer, with the help of third-year students, had our group lined up in the sports hall, stark naked, to be somatotyped. In turn, full-length photographs were taken of our bodies – front, back and side. Our percentage of fat was measured by a third-year using callipers to grip our folds of flesh, and many other measurements taken to determine our position on a three point graph devised by Dr William Sheldon of Columbia University. He had devoted his life to showing there was a correlation between body type and personality. To this end he had produced a book, *Atlas of Men*, containing 1,175 naked examples of somatotypes at various Ivy League universities. An 'atlas of females' was in the pipeline but never appeared as Sheldon's methods and underlying philosophy were increasingly being questioned. The idea was linked with eugenics, a controversial subject with Josef Mengele still on the run.

My physique was expressed in relation to three main types: endomorphs, who have a tendency towards plumpness with wide hips and narrow shoulders and who, according to Sheldon, are generally tolerant, good-humoured, fun-loving, enjoy comfort and are quite extrovert; mesomorphs, who have a strong, muscular body, are broad shouldered, narrow at the waist and tend to be temperamentally dynamic, gregarious and assertive risk-takers; and ectomorphs, who are slight with narrow shoulders, thin limbs and little fat and are often artistic, sensitive, introverted, thoughtful, socially anxious and keep themselves to themselves. The anatomy lecturer told us the majority of suicides at universities were from this group. I remember being a little anxious not to be from this group, but as it turned out I was a mesomorph.

I got hold of a book circulating at the time with all the associated characteristics outlined. On the physical side, it said people like me were prone to abdominal hernias, something I was suffering from at the time, and that got me reading more, especially about a mesomorph's tendency towards aggression. I wanted to know why, as a boy, I enjoyed smashing my broken Hornby train on the concrete yard and then pounding it with the coal hammer. Mrs Boothwright next door had been watching from her bedroom window and called down: 'you are a destructive little boy, aren't you Douglas?'

I had regiments of lead soldiers, all immaculately painted in bright colours, until I discovered they could be melted down in a saucepan over the gas stove. I watched them, fascinated, as they became silvery blobs and then the whole regiment coalesced into a single pool of metal. There were moments of madness, like the time, going home from school, I leapt on to a parked car and ran along a whole line of them. The hernia I got fixed in Nottingham General Hospital, waking up to hear *Hancock's Half Hour* on the ward's black and white TV, and trying not to laugh. The character flaw would be harder to fix.

In general, my somatotype suggested characteristics that I recognised. I was indeed energetic, always on the go, often taking risks in everything I did. I could be gregarious and didn't always consider the needs of others. I could be competitive when I got the bit between my teeth, although by the time I was eighteen I must have reached saturation point when it came to collecting awards. I had enough 'strings to my bow', as Dad called them. In a doctrinaire fashion, I decided what mattered most was taking part, not receiving certificates. With this sudden realisation I refused to go to Buckingham Palace to collect my Duke of Edinburgh Gold Award, much to the consternation of Nottingham Council, which hosted the pilot scheme. It was also a concern for Everest leader John Hunt, who headed the award.

A meeting was arranged at Nottingham Council House, the grand city hall, for me to explain myself to John Hunt himself. He proved sympathetic and I did eventually receive my certificate from my brother Brian, who collected mine at the same time as being presented with his at Buckingham Palace. My sudden reluctance for conventional channels continued at college where I was surrounded with top athletes, county rugby players and swimmers representing their country, all of them hungry for gold and glory. This may have had something to do with my ethical stance. I remember the great delight I felt when one of these heroes came up to me in the refectory and pointed to the college newsletter where I was praised for climbing Joe Brown's classic climb, *Cenotaph Corner*.

I didn't spend that much time at college, preferring to go climbing over the long weekends, working on the farm on Wednesdays and so reducing college to two days a week. My first year passed in a haze of lectures, teaching practice, sitting up late to write assignments, and practical lessons on how to teach swimming, athletics and major games. I coped and even found some of it interesting. At the end of my first year, I put a lot of thought and research into an essay on Bertrand Russell's theme of authority and the individual, but my English tutor, the brother of the politician and journalist Woodrow Wyatt, lost the fifty-odd pages I had so carefully hand written for the third time. He wasn't that apologetic although he did say he liked it.

My first stint of teaching practice took place at the William Crane School, Nottingham. I was fortunate to have assigned to me a dedicated teacher with a calling for the job. He gently enthused me for the profession and for teaching underprivileged children. He let me into the background of each child, so many of them living in difficult circumstances; most were simply crying out for someone to care for them. Under his guidance I connected well with the class and ended up with a good report; most of all I was touched by the boys' genuine sadness when I came to leave at the end of my practice. I am sure that a couple of days walking in Derbyshire with them had helped to bond us together.

At the end of the summer term, I hitchhiked to Chamonix where the weather was terrible. I mostly sat around the Chalet Austria, a scruffy hut near Montenvers where we could stay for free. The rising rock-climbing star Martin Boysen was there, and also Wes Hayden and other frustrated Nottingham lads. Early in August I gave up and hitched to the Écrins to meet two new college friends, Lyn Noble and Mark Hewlett. We based ourselves at La Bérarde, a summer settlement in the lovely unspoilt Vénéon valley, so different from Chamonix. Over the next four days, we completed a marvellous circular tour over Pic Coolidge, the Dôme de Neige and the Barre des Écrins, dropping down to the village of Ailefroide and returning via the Col de la Selle.

Towards the end of August I left the Alps, hitchhiking south to Morocco with the aim of climbing Toubkal, the highest mountain in North Africa. I walked five miles in humid heat from one side of the splendid city of Arles to the other and then meandered through the amazing *étangs* of the Camargue, incongruous in big mountaineering boots and carrying a rucksack with rope and ice axe on display. I plundered an orchard of the sweetest, most succulent pears I've ever tasted, but had to share them with my next benefactor as we sped through the countryside in his sports car. A year ago I had been close to the source of the Rhône, now it was a mighty river, loaded with Alpine sediment, pushing on into the Mediterranean.

I had arranged to meet Brian and a friend at Le Grau-du-Roi post office but it was shut for a festival, so I left my sack outside and went off to scour the beaches and narrow streets of this pretty fishing village for any sign of him. Brian came into view, fit and tanned, wearing my old sweater with his school friend Boris walking alongside clutching a bottle of rum. It was so good to see them and catch up, ranting on for hours at their campsite, sharing travellers' tales. We set off for Barcelona, but I got marooned for five hours until a Cadillac pulled up offering me a lift all the way. The driver was a generous Venezuelan who picked up the other two further down the road and took us all into the city.

Brian and Boris set off for home, while I headed south, finding a single ride to Valencia, 350 kilometres away. The couple in the car had picked me up to help their thirteen-year-old son improve his English, which was fine, except the grilling went on mercilessly for hours as the day got hotter and my eyes grew heavier. Two days later, making slow progress down the coast of southern Spain, I was dropped in a village just as a fast car careered past and smashed the hindquarters of a collie dog. It pulled itself across the road towards me, leaving behind a trail of blood. I remember the agony in its eyes. I gently hugged it, then found a huge rock and smashed it down on the dog's head. Then I walked on, out of the village and up a hill, feeling miserable. The road was straight as a die, and at the top of the hill was silhouetted a solitary tree. As the afternoon wore on and the temperature dropped, I gritted my teeth and stumbled on to reach that tree and made it just as the sun was setting. It was an almond, heavy with ripe nuts that I gathered by spreading my sleeping bag and clothes under the branches and then climbing up to shake the branches. I ate them all the way to Gibraltar.

Walking over the border and seeing British road signs and telephone boxes, I had to gulp back a feeling of homesickness. I'd spent almost nothing since leaving the Écrins but was still down to my last £8. I would have to get a job. After asking at the labour exchange and in shops and restaurants in town if they needed help, I tried my luck down at the waterfront. Captain John Carey of the *MV Saint Ernest*, an old pre-war ferry boat that had once plied the west coast of Scotland but had been languishing in Gibraltar for a few years, said I could help out on the boat's refit and in return he would take me to the Channel Islands. From there I could get a ticket to Southampton for £3. Did I have any skills? I told him I could map read and take a motorbike to bits. On the strength of my knowledge of motorbikes, which was meagre, he said I could sign on as second engineer.

I told him my story, that I had been planning all year to climb in the Atlas, and asked if I could have a few days before starting to cross the straits and visit Morocco. He wasn't keen, but his wife Katherine persuaded him to let me have three days as I had come so far. I left all my climbing gear and most of my belongings on board and caught the ferry to the Spanish enclave of Ceuta. After carrying my climbing gear all that way, through all those towns and villages, in the searing hot sun, I had no time to climb Toubkal. I'd overestimated how fast I could hitchhike and underestimated how much money I needed.

After three nights in North Africa I returned to start work on the *Saint Ernest*, chipping thick paint off the wheelhouse and taking the two lifeboat engines to pieces. During the day we ate at Smoky Joe's, just like any transport caff on the A1 with a greasy full English breakfast and a cup of sweet tea, lovely after such a frugal time on the road. John and the other crew decided that at nineteen I was ready for a nightclub. The main entertainment was a woman my mother's age, although somewhat more voluptuous, who sang and performed a belly dance. The highlight of her performance as far as the crew were concerned was seeing how embarrassed I got when she sat on my knee.

We spent the next few days chugging across the bay, once getting as far away from Gibraltar as Cádiz, only to see the oil pressure plummet, forcing us to return. On one return trip I spotted a body floating in the water. I climbed down the side of the ship and pulled a nine-year-old boy out of the water. I had to make a statement to the police, who told us the lad was last seen by his parents on the beach near Algeciras eating a bunch of grapes. His death was something of a mystery.

By early September I had to leave the ship. Even if the engine was repaired successfully, there was no time now for me to cross the Bay of Biscay and reach college before the start of term. Captain Carey gave me £12 for my twelve days of labour and wished me well. I took a train part way across Spain that went so slowly up steep gradients that I actually got out and walked alongside it. Then I hitched day and night to Calais but still arrived home at Loughborough a week late. The vice principal asked if I thought I was cut out for teaching. I told him, on the strength of my teaching practice, that I was – but without much conviction.

Eighteen months later, the *Daily Mail* reported that the 137-ton coaster *Saint Ernest* had vanished in a gale crossing the Channel. Lifeboats and life buoys were washed up along the Sussex shoreline along with a mass of daffodils, the ship's last cargo from the Channel Islands to Southampton. The crew of six and Captain Carey were presumed drowned. Katherine Carey was quoted in the article saying the ship had been fitted out with new engines and that there were good seamen and bad – and John was of the best.

During my second year I did a further stint of teaching practice, this time at a huge new comprehensive school in Leicester. The staff found me a nuisance and gave me very little support but I did know one of the teachers, the climber Peter Biven, who had pioneered new routes on gritstone and spectacular artificial climbs with Trevor Peck on High Tor. He told me that there was still much to do and also, more to the point, where it might be done.

During my first year I had lived at home, riding my motorbike into college. In my second year I was offered accommodation in college and got a grant of £50 each term. That was enough to purchase a second-hand Excelsior 250cc Talisman Twin. Dad found me a worn-out police helmet and a long water-proof coat from the traffic department. Although the insignia were gone, it was noticeable, especially at night, how cars ahead of me on the road would slow down thinking I was a traffic cop. The Excelsior's top speed was only about seventy miles per hour and a lot less going uphill. The bike wasn't that reliable either, especially when it was raining. Water kept seeping into the magneto. I was not then into the art of motorcycle maintenance and the bike often came to a halt in the most inconvenient places.

Driving home in the rain for a long weekend's climbing, the bike coughed to a halt on the outskirts of Loughborough. Water in the magneto, I thought sagely. There was nothing else to do except push it in the direction of Nottingham, fifteen miles away. Perhaps the rain would abate and the electrics dry out. It had stopped raining by the time I had reached Rempstone but even freewheeling down Bunny Hill and slamming it into third gear, the bike wouldn't start. I decided to push it all the way home as a challenge. Just after midnight, approaching the new Clifton Bridge over the Trent, a small truck stopped. The driver had seen me a few hours earlier and, now on his return trip, took pity on me. He suggested I get on to the bike and hold the back tailgate hinge of his truck. He would continue on slowly to Radford. Going down a slight hill on Middleton Boulevard I put the bike into gear and the engine spluttered into life. I was able to pass my Samaritan, waving thanks, before riding the last mile into my parents' front yard.

The bike paid for itself getting me out to Car Colston to work on Manor Farm every Wednesday with a bit left over for a weekend ride into the Peak District. My problem was being temperamentally unsuited to riding motorcycles. I so easily lost concentration and misjudged conditions, which was surprising given how acrobatic I was on my push bike, weaving in and out of traffic at breakneck speed.

One Friday evening, late meeting the team at Stanage Edge, I took the bend of a newly surfaced road covered in loose chippings so fast that the bike slid across the road in front of an oncoming car and hit the kerb. I was catapulted up and over a drystone wall into a field. I checked my limbs, particularly my elbow and ribs that seemed sore but weren't broken. Then I heard shouts and shrieking. I climbed on to the wall and saw my bike at full throttle, jammed under the front bumper of the car. A hysterical woman was screaming: 'He's in the engine, he's in the engine!'

'No I'm not,' I shouted, 'I'm here,' and hopped over the wall. I managed to twist the throttle shut, forced open on its slide across the road, but the woman now collapsed in shock so I joined her husband in trying to revive her. She came to and recovered and we put her back into the car, which was undamaged. The driver went on his way and I got out my peg hammer to bash the rear mudguard into shape before continuing on mine.

I was less lucky the following winter. I drove home one damp, foggy Friday to pick up my climbing gear and then roared off into the night towards Matlock. It had been a tiring week and I was miles away in my thoughts overtaking a car when I realised there was a sharp bend ahead and a pair of bright headlights coming towards me. I came to in the gutter, having gone right over the car. A woman leant over me, obviously fresh out of the pub, urging me to have a smoke of her cigarette. 'I don't smoke,' I said. My knee was in agony, full of glass from the car's headlamp. Someone must have called an ambulance, and I was soon on my way to hospital to have my broken kneecap put in plaster.

Once a month, our old history class gathered for a reunion in the Golden Fleece pub on Goldsmith Street and it gradually developed into quite a crowd. One night I was walking home, pushing my punctured cycle along the pavement, when on the other side of the street I saw a woman sobbing. I walked over, recognising her as one of the Golden Fleece crowd; she had been a Mundella School pupil in the fifth form when I left. Her name was Janice Brook. Being shy and not that articulate I had hardly spoken to Jan before. Now my feelings of compassion for her compelled me to enquire after her situation.

As I walked her to the bus station, she told me her dad was a captain in the army, and her family had been moved so often that she had been to thirteen different schools. She was now a student nurse in Nottingham and fed up travelling to her father's latest posting in Sheffield every day. She told me about her frustrations and the loneliness she'd felt moving so much. It was the first time a woman had really opened up to me in that way; it felt as though I was speaking to the core of someone, rather than playing some kind of game. In the dark, we could talk freely, but I had already seen enough to know she was pretty, with long hair that in those days was auburn. She was quite tall, and with a strong sense of style too. She always looked attractive. We agreed to meet up the following week and began to look out for each other.

Jan came out at weekends and she gamely tried her hand at rock climbing, she was not a natural at sport, least of all climbing; she never liked exposure.

Jan, back right, as a student nurse at Nottingham General Hospital.

I worked on the principle that just as it was better for someone else to teach your wife to drive, someone else should take your girlfriend climbing, so Dez Hadlum and Clive Davies would often take her out, climbing the quite exposed *Spiral Stairs* on Dinas Cromlech. Jan's first route was at Birchen Edge where Dez and I tried to encourage her up a steep chimney. 'Come on, Sue!' I shouted, confusing her with a previous girlfriend. That was one way to get her moving. Dez thought it was hilarious.

From those early visits to Black Rocks I got to meet and climb with an ever-widening circle of friends. It started with Scouts like Wes Hayden and Geoff Stroud and then schoolmates like Clive Smith, Mick Garside, Graham Spooner and Clive Davies, and Bob Pettigrew at the Mountaineering Association. Playing rugby I got to know Dez Hadlum and Peter Turner and from Loughborough College Lyn Noble. All these friends brought along their friends and soon there was a loose band of likeminded souls meeting at the crag or in the pub, singing and shouting the odds on the bus back to Nottingham after another day on the moors. After each encounter with the wind and rain we came home like men and women reborn since, as John Muir observed, 'Cares drop off like autumn leaves.'

I took Dad up a route at Black Rocks one Sunday when it was packed out with other climbers. On the way back to Nottingham I explained that I was off to the Alps again soon. He seemed genuinely pleased I had these opportunities even if in his day he could not possibly have gone off for long weekends or taken long holidays. Was it just that his horizons were my starting point and the next generation reaches out to new frontiers? Perhaps so, but climbing until this point had primarily been a sport pursued by university graduates and professionals. Factory workers had reached out in the 1930s for the freedom of the hills, often in opposition to landowners protecting their grouse moors. Now the lingering restrictions were being swept away.

Even though there was a sudden influx of working-class climbers on to the crags after the war, and later out in the Alps, the basic traditions were passed on and preserved. By the late 1950s and 1960s climbing abroad was open to everyone who had the initiative to take up the challenge. The cost of travel came down and affluence increased. It was not unusual for young, committed climbers to leave well-paid, secure jobs to hitchhike out to the Alps and Dolomites for four months, living off their tax rebate or casual work on building sites. Social security had improved and there was now the National Health Service.

By 1961 there were enough of us to form the Nottingham Climbers' Club so that we could organise bus trips to Wales and the Lake District. There were lots of new climbing clubs springing up after the war in the Midlands and the North, like the Oread, founded in Burton-on-Trent in 1949. It soon moved to Derby, where most of its early recruits were based. In Leicester another group formed the Bowline Club and in Beeston, on the west side of Nottingham, the Rock and Heather Club formed in 1953.

Our Nottingham crowd were drawn to the Oread because of our links with club members like Bob Pettigrew, Geoff Hayes, and Beryl and Roger Turner. But the Oread had become rather formal and respectable and we could never quite reach their standards of acceptable behaviour. The weekend I turned eighteen, the elder Oreads awoke to discover the Nottingham contingent were sleeping alongside the young women who had been put in their charge for a weekend's induction into camping at North Lees campsite and climbing on Stanage Edge. The Oreads came from the professional middle class whereas the majority of the Nottingham climbers tended to be working class.

We started meeting once a week to discuss that weekend's climbing trips, first in coffee bars, then in pubs like The Spread Eagle and the Salutation Inn, so forming a club seemed a natural thing to do. After we started the Nottingham Climbers' Club, we continued to climb with everyone in the area, Oreads included. Dez Hadlum had left the Oread for the Rock and Ice, introduced by Dennis Gray, who had left Yorkshire to work at the well-known printing firm Bemrose in Derby.

Dennis was from Leeds and, like me, had been out with the Scouts when he first came across rock climbing. It captured his imagination and he started climbing with an informal group called the Bradford Lads. With the tragic death of Arthur Dolphin, the leading light amongst the Bradford Lads,

The look typical of the NCC and many other climbing clubs in the 1960s. L–R: Clive 'Claude' Davies, David 'Dan' Meadows, Terry 'Sherpa' Small, George 'Yoff' Jones, Rod Hewing and me. **Photo**: Rod Hewing Collection.

the group dispersed. Dennis became a member of the Rock and Ice and a mainstay of the club after it reorganised in 1959. He was a great storyteller, especially when it came to the legends of the Rock and Ice. It all helped to pass the time sitting in his van, heading off to Wales for another weekend down the Llanberis Pass.

I climbed quite a few routes with Dez and Dennis, mostly middle-grade climbs at a time when Dennis was moving into alpinism and expeditions to the Andes and Himalaya. He was a clever lad with a sharp edge to his wit. He often came across the NCC camping out in Derbyshire or Wales. He would call us 'the cricket club', barely concealing his disdain, and on spotting me would say: 'Ah, Dougie Scott, tough as teak, but twice as thick.' He didn't always go down well with the lads who saw him as 'a sarky little bugger' but he helped the club generously, giving lectures or after-dinner speeches to help us raise funds for our expeditions. It was encouraging to have Dennis on the rope, as he knew where to go and could usually talk Dez or me up the crux.

On our way to the annual Dovedale Dash fell race in November 1960, Dez and I arranged to meet Dennis at the house of Nat Allen and his wife, Tinsel, on Macklin Street in Derby. Soon after we arrived, there was a knock on the door and in walked Don Whillans in his motorbike leathers. He pushed his goggles up on his flat cap, revealing white eyes in a face otherwise plastered with oil. He was on the last lap home to Lancashire after riding 7,000 miles from Pakistan on his Triumph. It was lucky for us that his first port of call in

Britain was to see his great friend and climbing companion Nat Allen, them both members of the Rock and Ice. Don sketched out his recent epic climb on Trivor in Pakistan's Karakoram mountains and all the trials of his remarkable six-week solo journey across lawless tribal lands in central Asia and his altercations with corrupt policemen in Yugoslavia. He'd navigated all that way using the world map in the back of his diary.

The following Easter, the Nottingham Climbers' Club had its first meet, climbing on Dow Crag in the Lake District. I can still remember who came: Harry Cluro, Clive Davies, Mick Garside, Ray Gillies, Bas O'Connor, Bas Shakespeare, Peter Turner and several of our girlfriends. Soon more lads from Nottingham signed up and the club grew rapidly. Within a couple of years we'd started hiring a fifty-two-seater bus rather than the usual forty-seater. The more that came the cheaper the seats.

Later that year, in December, we went up to Glen Coe for the Christmas holidays. Mick Garside and I set off from our camp by the Queen Victoria Cairn at midday on Christmas Eve to climb Bidean nam Bian. Paying the price for our late start, we reached the top in swirling snow and mist after dark, unable to find a way off. We seemed to be on top of a castle with steep walls all around below us and decided to bivouac. Dressed in light anoraks, a jumper, old breeches and not much else, we were horribly exposed. Desperately, we made a pile of snow and pressed it down with our bare hands until eventually there was enough of the stuff to burrow into.

In this way we managed to construct a dome of snow over our heads and keep the freezing wind from killing us. We spent twelve hours in this makeshift igloo; I shivered through the night, sometimes shaking uncontrollably, rubbing life into my fingers and toes to keep the blood flowing so we didn't suffer frostbite. Mick hardly said a word; he just put his head inside his anorak and slept, lying there on the frozen rope and hard ground.

On Christmas morning we found a way off between the huge crags and eventually reached the Glen Etive road. Knocking on the door of a large house, we peered through the window at presents wrapped and stacked against an oak-panelled wall, almost to the ceiling. After a few grumbles, the lady of the house, who had obviously just woken, allowed us to use her phone and alert the mountain rescue that we weren't dead. Hamish MacInnes and his team were, it turned out, just getting ready to search for us. Later I heard of four mountaineers who had perished on the summit of Ben Nevis in a similar storm a few years earlier, in December 1956. They had spent the night huddled together in a hollow but without any protection from the wind. It was lucky for us we knew how essential it was.

During the early 1960s our main activity was doing new climbs on the limestone crags of the Derwent Valley: High Tor, Wildcat and Willersley Castle.

Weekend after weekend a whole crowd of us came to climb, drink in the local pubs and live out under the caves and overhung rock with girlfriends and wives all enjoying the change from Nottingham. Jan came too, regardless of weather, just to be there in the open after being cooped up in the city. The routes we did were both free and with aid, placing pegs to hang off them. The first new route I did was with Ray Gillies, the 450-foot traverse of Raven's Tor one October day in 1961. This was an exciting route, both free and artificial, particularly crossing a shield of black, loose rock halfway across. Next, Clive Davies and I climbed a route of aid and free climbing to the left of the main gully of High Tor. We called it *M1* and followed it with the more serious *Flaky Wall*, right up the centre of High Tor. This involved intricate, time-consuming artificial climbing up blind cracks and loose flakes, which took me ages, not helped by the falling snow. After fiddling around for about half an hour with one placement, I looked down at Clive, stoically sat in his etriers in the middle of the wall, covered in snow. Between us, where there was a dip in the rope, about two inches had settled on it. We finished in the orange glow of street lights along the A6, illuminating the large fluffy flakes that fell all night.

Dez and I had first tried pegging at Lawrencefield quarry above Grindleford Station. This was to prepare ourselves for climbing in the Alps and Dolomites. We had heard that pegs should not be banged in too hard and so Dez used his hammer gently. When he was near the top of his route, the peg he was standing on came out and he fell backwards, ripping out all the others. He landed awkwardly and sprained his wrist but was otherwise unhurt. We gradually became more proficient and realised that once the techniques were mastered, artificial climbing became a simple mechanical exercise with limited appeal. It lacked the commitment and intrinsic interest of free climbing.

By 1962 I was really enjoying my rock climbing. I had led all the routes on Dinas Cromlech at the time, except *The Girdle* and *The Thing* and discovered Cloggy, leading some of the modern classics like Joe Brown's routes *The Corner*, and *The Boulder* with its committing traverse. What I found most satisfying was to know the crag inside out, to develop a close, personal relationship with it so I knew all its hidden places. I loved that feeling of making moves with confidence, oblivious to the drop below, pulling up on strong fingers, my body trained from so many other climbs. It is never boring, this climbing, but always intriguing. I loved snooping about on warm, dry rock, revealing for myself an unknown country, reaching up for each tiny imperfection, twisting my fingers into a crack so I can hang from them, my mind detached but delighting in the feel of each solid hold, until, exhilarated, I reach the top – and am able to share the mystery with others who have been that way before me.

In July 1961, newly qualified as a teacher, I left Nottingham with Dez to climb among the granite peaks of the Bregaglia in southern Switzerland and

Me on the first ascent of *Limelight* (A3) at High Tor, with Terry Bolger belaying. **Photo**: Bob Holmes.

in particular Riccardo Cassin's route on the Piz Badile. In 1956 Gaston Rébuffat's book *Starlight and Storm*, detailing his ascents of six great north faces in the Alps, was published in English. My parents bought me a copy for Christmas; Rébuffat's account of his descent from the Badile with Bernard Pierre was compulsive reading. By 1961 several English parties had already succeeded and the route didn't have quite the same reputation it once did. Geoff Sutton told us we were good enough and should get on with it.

Like a tramp with a purpose I hitched south again, sleeping in a potato field outside Paris and waking in a park by the Rhine in Basle, lit by glow-worms. On the fifth day I arrived in Promontogno in the Bregaglia and holed up in a builder's hut, challenging a prowler, who turned out to be a sympathetic policeman. The workman who woke me in the morning took me to his house for breakfast.

It was a hard four-hour slog up the Val Bondasca to reach the Sciora hut but good to be among the most spectacular chain of pale granite spires. Lyn Noble, David 'Ben' Sykes and other friends from Loughborough were already there but not Dez, so next morning Lyn, Ben and I climbed the north ridge of the sensational Ago di Sciora, a granite wedge tapering to a needle with exposed climbing at the summit. Descending the snow slope at the base, I slipped, slid a hundred feet sideways into a boulder, and disappeared down a gap between the snow and the rock. Lyn and Ben found this quite amusing since I was there one second and gone the next, swallowed by the snow. It was some time before the bruising on my hip disappeared – a warning but not one heeded.

Dez arrived that evening and after a period of bad weather we set off to climb the *Ferro da Stiro* – the Flat Iron – on the Pizzi Gemelli; it took delicate footwork in our big boots on magnificent open slabs and strenuous lay-backing up clean-cut corners. Climbing such a sustained route early in the season, especially one so varied and in under guidebook time, filled us with confidence. We followed it up with the north ridge of Piz Badile itself, a classic route in a wonderful position without being too difficult except for snow on some of the slabs. We traversed over the summit and frontier ridge and descended into Italy to visit Riccardo Cassin's equipment store in Lecco.

When we returned, we set off for main objective, the *Cassin Route* on the north-east face of the Badile. Despite the fact other British parties had repeated this route, we knew the first few ascents had required two bivouacs because of bad weather and the hard climbing. Once we began all our fears evaporated. One superb pitch followed another, one perfect granite crag, corner or chimney after another. The only problem was passing several slow teams of Italians. With so many weekends climbing on gritstone cracks we were in our element, especially Dez who powered up every pitch without hesitation as we lead through. We arrived on the summit at 1.30 p.m., eight hours after starting, although with all the hold-ups our climbing time was around five hours. It was the finest rock climb I had so far experienced but I knew we had been lucky with the weather.

As testimony for this, in the upper regions of the climb we found a large number of shiny new Cassin pitons, presumably left by climbers fighting their way off in a storm. As we hammered out some of these pitons there was a cry from the Italians far below: 'Engleesh, you take out all ze pitons?'

'No, there are plenty left!' we shouted back. We reached the summit with about twenty of those pegs that seemed superfluous and also a gold wristwatch I discovered when reaching deep into a crack to get a good jam. After a long rest we abseiled down the north ridge with two Swiss climbers using our rope. The whole excursion had taken twelve hours.

Picking our way slowly down in the dark across moraine and scrub, I found myself on a bald granite slab running with water. I was too tired to climb up so decided to traverse directly. In the middle of the slab my feet slipped on the greasy rock and my legs went from under me. I hurtled down on my back, sliding totally out of control in a stream of water, slithering ever faster down the lichenous slabs. Time seemed to stretch. I managed to flip over on to my belly and tried to stop myself with the pick of my north wall hammer, without success. I slammed down on to a notch in the slab right at the edge of an abyss with the water pouring over my shoulders and on in a huge cascade down to rocks hidden in the darkness below. Dez rushed down the grass at the side of the slabs and threw me a rope, helping me to safety.

I had lost my spectacles and was sore in my rear end, but at least I was still alive. It had been a near thing. Once I reached safety I relaxed and had a good laugh as Dez described the stream of sparks firing out from under my pick as I frantically tried to dig into the granite. We climbed up a few feet and decided to sleep out under boulders to avoid further incident. We were both exhausted and I was soaking wet so Dez gallantly gave up half his clothing and we shivered until dawn. When we got to our feet we discovered we were only a few yards from a well-made path and half an hour from the hut and our tent.

For a few days we lazed around the hut. Lyn's girlfriend June had arrived, bringing up welcome letters from Jan and home. Lyn and Colin Mortlock went off to climb a new route on the Ago di Sciora. Colin had a lot more experience than any of us. He'd climbed with Wilf Noyce, making three significant first British ascents of classic Alpine routes including the *Furggen Direct* on the Matterhorn. He had also been to the Karakoram the year before with Noyce and Don Whillans, helping make the first ascent of Trivor.

While they climbed, we sat around sewing clothes, chatting over cups of tea and watching a farmer way down the valley putting salt out on prominent boulders. Then he began shouting and pounding his metal bucket on the rocks.

Slowly the hillsides around us seemed to move towards him; there were hundreds of sheep on the move, coalescing around the salty boulders below.

As we watched, Colin arrived in a state of collapse, telling us Lyn had fallen fifty foot above his last peg runner. His foot had slipped on wet rock while lay-backing up a shallow corner. As he fell more than a hundred feet, the rope had wrapped around his leg and snapped his femur. Colin's hands were burnt through to the bone as he held the fall. Somehow, after making Lyn safe, he managed to climb down a knotted rope, despite his injuries. Colin's wife Annette attended to his wounds. We were lucky that two experienced Piedmontese members of a mountain rescue unit were staying in the hut. With their help we managed to get Lyn down to the snow and into the hut. He was very stoical, never once complaining as we took turns to carry him on a stretcher to where a helicopter could land. Within minutes of arrival Lyn was airborne, flying to Samedan hospital. The holiday was over.

On the walk out to Promontogno, Colin and Annette introduced Dez and myself to Johnny Lees and Gwen Moffatt, Britain's first female mountain guide, who had just published her autobiography *Space Below My Feet*. We were both a bit 'cap in hand' and more than willing to give her and Johnny a description of our climb up the Badile. At the Promontogno post office there was a large bundle of letters for me from family and Jan, which I read many times over consuming me with reveries of delight. She wrote good letters in a bold hand with every thought clearly put. Frustration was mounting as I became ever more eager to be with her. There was also a letter from Geoff Sutton offering me work as a guide for the Mountaineering Association, starting in ten days' time, so I wrote immediately accepting his offer and after visiting Lyn in hospital hitched back to Chamonix.

While I was camped at the Biolay waiting to start work I met a Cambridge undergraduate called Mick, my second Old Etonian. I once again had a favourable impression. Mick had been climbing for only a year or two so was a little slow, but he was full of enthusiasm and unflappable. We walked up to the Chalet Austria and then walked up early to the Couvercle hut to try a route on the east face of the Aiguille du Moine. We climbed the hard section, but it was plastered in ice higher up and we retreated, climbing the south ridge as a consolation. Then I dashed down to Chamonix to meet my six clients who had just arrived.

They seemed tired from the journey and wanted a day off, so while my clients sampled the delights of Chamonix, I turned around and went back up to Montenvers and the Chalet Austria with a Bristol University student called Jerry Lovatt. We were up at 5.30 a.m. and on the steep granite of the east face of the Pointe Albert. There was supposed to be an awkward aid section across an overhang, but the Commando climber Mike Banks had fallen off it a few days before and ripped out the pegs, turning the climb into a hard free route. We reached the summit in five hours and then raced down to Chamonix, where I said goodbye to Jerry and caught a bus to Le Tour and the cable car to the Col de Balme to spend the night at the Albert Premier hut with my clients.

Not surprisingly, I struggled to rouse myself at 2 a.m., but had everyone moving across the glacier towards the *Forbes Arête* on the Aiguille du Chardonnet an hour later. A wonderful moonlit night turned into an equally fine sunrise as we crunched across the frosty snow and up steps expertly cut by a guided party ahead of us. Thanks to this trail, we were soon on the summit and back at the hut by mid-morning to sunbathe and read for the rest of the day. Guiding didn't seem so hard.

After the Chardonnet I took my charges up to the Couvercle hut. Only one had any experience of rock climbing and that was Shirley Angell, the only woman in the group. Shirley, a member of the Pinnacle Club, had led Very Severe rock climbs in Britain and had already climbed in the Alps with her husband, Ian, who had gone off to climb the Matterhorn. She was great fun, very game and easily persuaded to lead a second rope of three while I went ahead leading a rope of four. We climbed the granite peaks above the Couvercle – La Nonne, L'Évêque and the Moine – all by moderate routes but on consecutive days so that the others were more than ready for a day off.

Shirley and I went off to climb something more technical and found some wonderful climbing on the Aiguilles Ravanel and Mummery involving V+ crack climbing, quite sustained and always on superb rock. There was a French couple about to abseil down the Mummery when I insisted on testing the peg they had threaded their abseil rope through. The peg came out of the rock in my hand. The woman was thankful and looked across towards her partner who simply shrugged his shoulders as only the French do and found a better placement for the peg.

The rest of the group were keen to climb Mont Blanc, which we did over a couple of days. As we arrived we were a little surprised when a helicopter flew in, disgorging a journalist clutching a bottle of wine and letting off purple flares. It wasn't for us, as we discovered when first Don Whillans and then Chris Bonington arrived from the Italian side of Mont Blanc having made the first ascent of the very difficult Central Pillar of Frêney, a route which had caught the imagination of some of the finest climbers in Europe over the last decade.

It was good to see Don again. I hadn't seen him since the previous Christmas at Wasdale Head playing barn rugby. We shared what little food we had and then descended to the Vallot hut where we put on a meal for them. Don told us it was his first ascent of Mont Blanc despite having come to the Alps for the last ten years. Chris was ravenously hungry and so busy eating he didn't have much to say. Don was curious as to what else I had been up to that season and seemed quite impressed with our ascent of Piz Badile.

Later it struck me how unfocused I was for the big routes. My natural inclination was to visit and climb as widely as possible. I didn't mind what I did as long as I was climbing. Now I had regrets that I'd spent the last two weeks of perfect weather guiding when I might have climbed more interesting routes with friends. Did I really want the bother? The money was useful. On the proceeds of this course I was able to kit myself out with twelve-point crampons – and my first duvet jacket. But I also noticed a lingering satisfaction from helping clients cope and enjoy all that has to be done to climb high.

I hitchhiked back to Nottingham where I found Jan at an NCC party underway at Judy Darnell's mother's house. After the excitement of seeing Jan again I proudly displayed my brand new Lionel Terray duvet. Jan and her girlfriends had obviously been discussing the possibility that we might sleep together for the first time and were giving out covert warnings about Jan becoming pregnant and what would Judy's mother have to say about that? After three days hitchhiking with very little sleep, our relationship remained unconsummated as I fell fast asleep, waking up to find the party over.

A few days later we lay together in the darkness of night under a spreading beech tree near Willersley Castle Rocks. On the Monday I started my first job as a schoolteacher. My old headmaster Gordon Happer had invited me back to Cottesmore Secondary Modern, much to the amazement of some of my former teachers. I'm not sure I did enough to reassure them, especially when I applied for, and received, a leave of absence to go to the Atlas Mountains in the autumn of 1962.

Steve Read new routing Wildcat in the mid 1960s.

Schoolboys aiding on the bridge at the disused Tissington railway station (courtesy of Mr Beeching's cuts in the mid 1960s), during a geography lesson at Cottesmore School's outdoor and field study centre.

ATLAS

Early in 1962, I told Dad I intended to marry Jan at Easter.

'Douglas,' Dad said, 'you're far too young to marry at Easter next year.'

'No Dad, I meant Easter this year, in three months' time. Good try, but we've made our minds up.'

The truth was Jan thought she was pregnant. Mum guessed because when she heard of our intention to marry her only comment was: 'Been playing with fire, then, Douglas?' The first time either Jan or I had made love was with each other and after we had been together for about a year. We were very much in love and that night together, camping out in the open under that beech tree in Derbyshire, seemed the natural way to seal our commitment. For some reason we couldn't tell our parents Jan was pregnant out of wedlock. We suffered huge pangs of guilt until Jan announced it was a false alarm but, despite the fact I was only twenty and Jan was just eighteen, we decided to continue with our plans to marry and came to terms with Jan's irregular periods and my obsession with climbing. I had told Jan that it was unlikely I would ever give up climbing even if we were to start a family. Jan said that she could see there was no doubt about that and said she was prepared to support me.

Among the guests at our wedding were Dez Hadlum and Dennis Gray, whose wedding present was a pair of PAs, the first rock boots I ever owned. Jan was a bit miffed but then Dennis drove Dez, Jan and me in the back of his van to North Wales for our honeymoon. Sitting in the back of Dennis's van we had our first marital disagreement when we discovered neither of us had brought any money. Thankfully Dennis loaned me £5, which paid for one night in the Pen-y-Pass hotel. The next few nights we spent under the famous Cromlech boulders in the Llanberis Pass where Harry and Shirley Smith were camping, luckily for me, because Jan and Shirley got on well, allowing Harry and me to go off climbing on Dinas Cromlech, Harry leading

With Jan on our wedding day, April 1962.

Climbing and school friends at our wedding. L–R: Dennis Gray, Clive Davies, John Stenson, Ray Gillies, my brother Brian (the best man), me, Mick Garside, Dez Hadlum, Geoff Stroud and Mick Poppleston.

1 Grandad George Scott (seated, first left) with the Newmarket Town FC team and their trophies in the 1920s.
2 Dad (sitting, front left) played with the St Mary's School boys' football team, also in Newmarket.

3 Dad in his police uniform.
4 Dad in his army uniform during the war.

5

6

5 With Mum and Dad at Stonehenge in August 1943.
6 Robert Shaw Primary first eleven school photo, 1951–52. Derek Smith, our teacher, and me standing next
  to the goalkeeper, Christopher Spears.

7

7 Tissington railway station bridge.
8 Nottingham Climbers' Club on Scafell at Christmas, 1961. L–R: Rod Hewing,
   George Jones, me and Steve Bowes. **Photo**: Clive Davies.
9 Camping at Nant Gwynant in Snowdonia in in the 1960s.

11

10 Leading Don Whillans' fine route *The Sloth* at the gritstone edge of The Roaches in Staffordshire. I first led it
     in 1961, and am pictured here in 1968 with George Jones belaying below the roof. **Photo:** Clive Davies.
11 *Peapod* at Curbar Edge is one of Joe Brown's most famous gritstone routes.

12

12 The Vallée Blanche leading down to the Refuge du Requin above the Mer de Glace. The mountains above, from left to right, are: Aiguille du Dru, Aiguille Verte and Les Droites, with the twin rock spires of the Aiguilles Ravanel and Mummery in-between the Verte and the Droites. **Photo**: John Tasker.

13

14

13 The huge Aiguilles de Sisse in Chad tower over one of our lorries. **Photo**: Peter Warrington.
14 When the rear differential on one of our lorries collapsed, Ray Gillies and Pete Warrington
worked for eight hours in oppressive heat to fix it. **Photo**: Peter Warrington.

15 A Tibbu woman in Modra in 1965. **Photo**: Mick Garside.
16 A Tibbu tribesman of the central Sahara.
17 There is little shade in the Sahara. **Photo**: Tony Watts.

19

20

18 Layers of loose conglomerate near the summit of Tarso Tieroko. We established three new routes during our expedition.
19 Friendly Kurdish nomads who visited our camp in the Cilo Dağı.
20 The 1967 Hindu Kush team. L–R: (standing) me, Ken Vickers, Bill Cheverst, Brian Palmer, Mick Terry, Guy Lee. (sitting) Bob Holmes, Ray Gillies, George Jones, Tony Watts, Dick Stroud, and two hitch-hikers.

21 The east face of Koh-i-Sisgeikh.
22 The view from Koh-i-Sisgeikh over to the twin peaks of Koh-i-Morusq.
23 Ray Gillies descending Koh-i-Bandaka following our ascent.
24 Mick Terry on belay just before my sixty-foot fall on the Cima Ovest north face.

25 Climbing around the big roof on the Bauer-Rudolph route on the north face of the Cima Ovest.
Ted is below; Jeff is belaying me as I go around the first roof. **Photo**: Mick Terry.

26 The north face of the Cima Ovest. **Photo**: Leo Dickinson.

Cemetery Gates in his big boots and me leading *Cenotaph Corner* so much easier in my new PAs. I really enjoyed climbing with Harry, who was a member of the Rock and Ice; he was incredibly safe and full of banter. We hitchhiked back to Nottingham and began married life at our flat on Lenton Boulevard, just around the corner from school.

With the end of petrol rationing and increasing car ownership, branch lines on the rail network began closing, including the Tissington line in Derbyshire. So Gordon Happer rented the now unused Tissington Station as an outdoor activity and field study centre for the school. It was a great place to take our city-centre children. On wet days the road bridge near the station was a good place to practise artificial climbing. The dales provided wonderful country for walking and the study of limestone geomorphology. Not far away there was gritstone for rock climbing. It was remarkable how a week at Tissington, sharing experiences and walking and climbing in all weathers, improved relationships between pupils and staff.

At the end of the summer term I hitched down to Chamonix and met Jan, who had travelled with the Nottingham Climbers' Club. A group of us went up to the Nantillons Glacier, where I encouraged Jan to step out on to the ice for the first time. Bad idea. One of the lads dislodged a rock that hit Jan on the arm, chipping the bone. She completely lost it with me, demanding that we both went home. I pointed out that the holiday had hardly started, and what about our contract? Back off the glacier, I began smashing my ice axe against a rock, shouting at Jan: 'I won't be needing this again.' By the evening it had all blown over and we resumed normal behaviour and I packed my rucksack in readiness for my first climb of the season.

Lyn Noble had recovered from his broken leg and we went up together to the Grand Capucin, a granite skyscraper on the shoulder of Mont Blanc du Tacul, to attempt Walter Bonatti's route. Luck wasn't with us, and we were caught in a storm just below the summit. Abseiling off, the rope became stuck and we had to climb back up in a blizzard, eventually cutting the rope. That meant many short abseils down the face and we only reached the safety of the Torino hut at midnight. The weather was better next day, so we traversed over to the Dent du Géant, a fang of granite set above a dramatic snowy ridge called the Rochefort Arête, to climb its south face. There were several parties already climbing, so we made a return trip along the Rochefort to let them get ahead.

By the time we returned the sky was overcast and as we pegged our way up the granite cracks the thunderclouds were gathering. Just as we reached the Géant's twin summits, the storm broke. Lightning flashed around us, and the pitons hanging from my neck began to spark. I threw them to one side, urging Lyn to hurry, becoming anxious and impatient when the lightning arced between the summits, causing my crew cut to stick up, dragging my hair first one way and then the other. Lyn was just as anxious to leave the summit and he carried on over and down the fixed ropes of the ordinary route with me following behind as bolts of lightning slammed into the granite slabs. With every strike, water streaming down the slabs sizzled and steamed and the air stank of sulphur. I went beyond fear. There was nothing I could do other than put my trust in fate. It was the first time I had written myself off. I reached a point where I thought: 'If it's going to happen, then it's going to happen.' With that I calmed down sufficiently to focus on a safe descent.

The season continued in similar vein. A few days later I climbed the Aiguille du Plan with Brian Chase, a friend from Derby, and then the Aiguille du Fou. Climbing from one ledge to another up a chimney, I did a mantelshelf move on a giant chockstone but just as I was stepping off it the whole thing gave way. Slowly at first, but then gathering speed, it bounced down towards Brian who was belaying at the bottom of the chimney. I yelled to him as I dug my fingers into the gravelly bed of the chimney and Brian leapt instinctively to one side. The boulder brushed past him, missing the rope as well otherwise we'd both have been killed, tumbling one after the other down the broken rocks to the glacier hundreds of feet beneath our feet.

For the next route I teamed up with old friend Ray Gillies, now a motor mechanic. We both climbed at the same standard although Ray, as with most tradesmen, usually made a better job of it than me, being neater and faster. We settled on the Mer de Glace face of the Grépon but in rushing to get on the climb I misread the guidebook and we set off in the wrong direction. We ended up doing a hard new route on the neighbouring Cornes du Chamois but only realised our error when we reached the top. We now faced the embarrassment of going back to the Biolay and telling our friends we'd not only been off route but had been on the wrong mountain.

The first abseil was from a horn of rock with a bunch of slings around it. Ray put the abseil rope through the slings and was just about to lean back and slide past the overhang below when, on impulse, I suggested we tested the slings. He took his weight off the rope and I took the whole bunch of slings in my hand and gave them a sharp jolt down. They disintegrated in a puff of powder; the polymer structure of the nylon had crumbled with time, the weather and UV light. Ray sat down to get over the shock of what might have happened and we threaded a sling of our own, abseiled down and walked back through the woods to Chamonix.

Jan and I hitched to the Oetztal Alps in Austria to meet another Mountaineering Association group. With my expedition to the Atlas coming up I needed the money. We met them off the train at Innsbruck and took them up some easy climbs. I remember one Pakistani client known as Stan who found it impossible to acclimatise. When he didn't arrive at the hut one day,

I set off down the trail to find him crawling up on all fours. He looked up at me in some distress and said: 'Oh dear, I have the high-altitude lassitude and must go slowly.' Stan never did climb any significant routes but we all appreciated his humour – and the fact he was just happy to be in the mountains. The other member of the group I remember was Brian Manton who would strip naked and dive into glacier pools and lakes at every opportunity. He became a good friend. When the course ended, I put Jan on the train with the clients including Brian, and hitchhiked south to the Sierra Nevada in southern Spain, first stop on my journey to Morocco.

By now I was twenty-one and getting a lot of satisfaction from rock climbing in Britain and visiting the Alps each summer. I had a good job, a flat and a wife. So it may seem strange that after one year's teaching, nine months of marriage and a good season's climbing in the Alps I was so desperate to go to the Atlas. I had to convince Jan to accept my absence for two months and persuade my employer to do the same. In my first letter of application, I explained to the director of education that I feared I was slipping into middle-class complacency. To remain an effective human being, I would have to step away from domesticity and the daily routine every so often. Gordon Happer suggested I didn't send that version. I wrote another suggesting a trip to Morocco would make me a better geography teacher and enrich the children's lives.

But why North Africa? I suppose it was somewhere I could climb after the season in the Alps was over. I knew that climbing in Morocco would be relatively inexpensive. But the real reason was pure curiosity, to see the mountains and how the people who lived there coped. It wasn't a conscious decision at the time although I had seen quite a few European countries by then and while I enjoyed the peculiarities of each, they seemed culturally similar. Visiting Africa, the Dark Continent of my Empire history books, was tantalising.

In my immediate circle of climbing friends I soon found kindred spirits. Ray Gillies, Clive Davies and Steve Bowes were all struck with the same romantic curiosity. I plucked up courage to approach Wilf Noyce, famous for his contribution to the ascent of Everest and author of the bestseller *South Col*. Wilf was just back from the Atlas when I spotted him in the bar of the Pen-y-Gwryd hotel below Snowdon and was happy to offer advice.

One wet day in Chamonix, I pulled out my maps of the Atlas and managed to enthuse Steve Read to join us, so now we were five. Steve and I had put up a number of routes together in Derbyshire, especially in the Derwent Valley. He was an impressive figure of a man – tall, broad-shouldered and with a loping stride and long, strong arms. Steve had won the approval of Don Whillans after climbing with him in the Dolomites, and had been to Kullu in the Indian Himalaya with Bob Pettigrew and other members of the Oread. Perhaps by nature, perhaps by nurture in the mountains, Steve was self-contained, very much his own man, confident but a bit taciturn unless there was something worth discussing.

The five of us split up in Chamonix, me for Austria, Ray hitchhiked back to Britain to claim his tax rebate, via Paris to pick up a French climbing guidebook to the Atlas. Clive was recovering from injuries sustained abseiling off the Aiguille du Peigne and Steve Bowes was keeping him company. Steve Read continued climbing in the Alps and would see us later in Gibraltar. None of the others had any particular time limit, being between jobs. We were free spirits; with no ties or commitments for a few months, we could direct our energies wherever we fancied. Any compunction I felt at leaving my colleagues to cope with my class and my wife to cope on her own was overridden by the rat in my gut, the need to go off down the road again. Carving out a career, accumulating wealth and status as hard climbers: these for me would come later.

We found each other in Granada and boarded a tram that took us up the Rió Genil into the northern hills of the Sierra Nevada, reaching the village of Güéjar Sierra at nightfall. The stationmaster invited us to stay with his family. His daughter-in-law spoke fluent French and, being a keen skier, was able to fill in the gaps of our inadequate map. We talked late into the night. The next morning was sunny and fresh, a welcome change from the heat and dust of the plains. We washed our travel-stained clothes and then set off to explore the surrounding country.

The village, a collection of whitewashed houses surrounding a fine church, made a pleasant contrast with the green fields and olive trees. Maize, tomatoes, melons and millet grew abundantly on the small terraced fields with their intricate irrigation channels. The villagers, protected from the sun by huge straw hats, were harvesting crops, stacking produce in baskets strapped to the backs of mules. Above the terraces where the soil was too thin or the slope too steep, the barren granite rose up to a serrated skyline of gendarmes and strangely eroded pinnacles.

Early next morning, having reassured the stationmaster's wife we'd be careful, we stashed our spare gear and climbed steeply out of the valley, zigzagging up the rough path. At first we were sheltered from the sun by apricot and olive trees, but soon the fields ended and we were exposed on the bare, rocky hillside. Eventually, we joined the metalled road that runs from Granada to the very top of Veleta, at 3,398 metres one of the highest mountains in Spain. The peak came into view and we judged that its steep, northern face might offer some rock climbing possibilities. That night we dossed in an abandoned military installation, watching the sun dropping behind the plains of Granada, the lower hills in silhouette, each one separated by a faint haze.

By sunrise next day we were standing on the summit of Veleta. There was a small diesel engine on top that powered a ski lift. Somewhat disappointed

In the Sierra Nevada, Spain, September 1962. L–R: Clive Davies, Ray Gillies, me and Steve Bowes.

at arriving so easily on the summit of such a high peak, we scrambled down its eastern shoulder. The north side turned out to be made of unstable shale; we didn't want to go near it. There was snow at its base, in a cwm that showed the last vestiges of the glaciation that had carved out the deep U-shaped valleys of the Sierra Nevada and the sharp ridges in-between.

On the col between Veleta and Tajos de la Virgen we found an empty shepherd's hut. After renovating the roof it provided us with a fine Base Camp for the next few days. We toasted maize cobs over a fire and ate flapjacks with honey, watching another fine sunset. With two easy days behind us we wanted a more ambitious programme and so at dawn we headed along the ridge towards the Pic del Tajo de los Machos. The landscape was wild and bleak, despite its proximity to the city. Keeping to the crest entailed difficult rock climbing over gendarmes, one of them two pitches long and up to Very Severe in standard. Although the ridge was only a couple of miles, these difficulties slowed us down and it was mid-morning before we reached the top.

The ridge carried sharply on beyond the summit, tempting us forward even though we'd reached the end of our map. We continued for another five miles, dropping down to the clear waters of the Río Lanjarón, where a herd of ibex were grazing. They were soon off, bounding up the opposite hillside. From the last summit we had a fine view of the Mediterranean and the Rock of Gibraltar, still a hundred miles or so to the south-west. We ate a frugal meal of almonds and apricots, and then followed the river upstream to the little lake at its source, surrounded by springy verdant moss. Climbing out of the cwm beyond to reach the ridge we'd been on that morning, we finally reached our hut.

We sat outside around a juniper wood fire drinking coffee and lying snugly in our sleeping bags. The lights of Granada were visible but up on our ridge, far away from the bustle of the city, not a sound disturbed the starry night except for the crackling fire as we slowly drifted off to sleep. Heavy dew froze overnight on our sleeping bags and we were reluctant to move in the morning. But after a quick breakfast we set off to climb Pico del Caballo, the westernmost of the Sierra Nevada's 3,000-metre mountains. There were more gendarmes to climb, although we could have avoided them, and then the ridge dipped down for a thousand feet to the beautiful turquoise lake of Laguna del Caballo, a jewel against the bleak grey rocks.

Scrambling up the other side we gained the summit of Caballo and got another view to the south-west. The air was so clear that we could see the coast of North Africa from our elevated position. From the top we dropped down to the south and found some solid cliffs 200 feet high where we spent the afternoon. Towards evening we hurried back, absolutely ravenous as mists rolled in on a strong wind. We made our fire in the doorway so we could shelter in the hut and feasted on pancakes and a huge stew.

We left the hut for good next day, crossing Veleta again and then taking an awkward, twisting line down to Lagunillo del Veleta. From the lake we could gain the ridge between Veleta and the highest peak in the Sierra Nevada, Mulhacén, following this ridge with difficulty to Cerro de los Machos and then descending to a beautiful corrie lake, Laguna de la Caldera. Here we met the only other climber we saw in the Sierra Nevada, a young lad from Barcelona, who seemed just as pleased to see us. His rucksack was bulging with food whereas we had run out of everything apart from a handful of porridge. The salami, cheese and bread our new friend offered us were very welcome. Together we contoured around the back of the cwm to regain the ridge at a col and half an hour later we were on top of Mulhacén, at 3,478 metres the highest point on the Iberian peninsula.

It was fifteen miles back to Güéjar Sierra and, glancing anxiously at oncoming storm clouds, we jogged back down the scree to the col, sending up clouds of gaily-coloured butterflies. Our route down the northern slopes crossed awkward rock steps covered in debris and there was no trail. Then we reached the Río Valdecasillas and the gradient eased. We began to see herds of sheep and goats and then a shepherd appeared, wearing the largest sombrero we'd yet seen. He gave a long yodel that echoed around the hills and from all directions sheep and goats streamed towards him. He was throwing out salt just as we had seen the year before in the Bregaglia and was soon completely surrounded.

Smoky Joe's, where one could get wonderful greasy English food – a plate of fat with a slice of fried bread floating in it.

At the junction with the Río Genil, we came across what must have been the highest farm in Spain, a few terraced fields, irrigated from the two rivers with a dwelling under a bricked-up boulder. The work must have been tremendous. They were obviously subsistence farmers growing just enough to exist on. The farmer waved us towards the path we had lost among the stony fields. Luscious blackberries growing all the way down to Güéjar Sierra were very welcome. We had a short rest by an almond tree, cracking shells. The stream to our right was now a raging torrent, thundering hollowly in a deep gorge.

There were no other dwellings for three miles and then those we saw were no less primitive than the farm we'd left, being little more than caves with four or five stony fields with scraggy goats or sheep on the rocky slopes above. We met mule parties taking their small surplus down to Güéjar Sierra. Weary after jogging down the rough track for so long, we spent half an hour at the small hamlet of Casas de las Hortichuelas. A Coca-Cola sign heralded our return to the modern world. By nightfall we were back in Güéjar Sierra, much to the relief of our kind hosts who once again gave us shelter. We were invited back for the night and stayed another day for a village fiesta, before saying goodbye to the generous stationmaster and resuming our journey to Morocco.

In Gibraltar I took the lads to Smoky Joe's for a full English breakfast and strong, sweet tea and then we caught the ferry to Algeciras to meet up with Steve Read. In two days we hitchhiked from the Spanish enclave of Ceuta, down through Casablanca to Marrakesh. Stormy weather had passed through, leaving the air clear and the snow-covered Atlas thirty miles to the south in sharp relief above the palm trees and minarets. It was good to be in this town so steeped in history and so different from any town in Europe with its souks and twelfth-century kasbah. From now on we were conscious of a different tempo to life and soon learnt to expect the unexpected.

The bus to Asni was all set to leave Marrakesh when the driver decided the brake linings needed to be changed and we ended up spending the night at the bus station while Ray, our newly qualified motor mechanic, lent a hand. He had us making washers from an old tin can while the bus driver disappeared on a wobbly bicycle to fetch various spare parts and tools from rival bus companies. Next morning, some eighteen hours behind schedule, the bus left, filled to capacity with women clutching children and chickens, while their husbands sat aloof from all the hubbub and confusion.

The overladen bus chugged its way up the steep mountain road to the high Atlas village of Asni. It was the end of the road for us, since the road beyond had been washed away. We were a lightweight trip, because of hitchhiking, but to survive in the mountains for the next few weeks we needed a mule to carry our food: a sack of potatoes and another of onions, flour, large tins of jam, rice, sardines, sugar, tea and coffee and also a stack of chapattis that neatly fitted one on top of the other in a kit bag. We declined the service of a local guide, Lahoussie, despite his impressive letters of recommendation from Wilf Noyce and Mike Westmacott, and at midday set off following a valley into the heart of the Atlas and the village of Imlil.

Wherever the valley allowed, terraced fields and mud-brick houses clung to the hillsides, yellow maize cobs ripening on the flat roofs. Small boys slashed away at the walnut trees, showering us with nuts, much to their amusement. Occasionally we would catch sight of a red headscarf amid the maize and millet. Sometimes a woman would appear bent almost double under a huge load of fodder. The Berber women here had more freedom than their Arab counterparts but they went about unsmiling and silent for they had little to be joyous about. From morning until dusk they fetched and carried heavy earthenware water containers, brought firewood off the mountainsides, gathered crops and fed the animals, as well as the usual domestic chores; what a life for the men with two or three wives.

That night, in a swirling mist, we settled down in a shepherd's hut at the small hamlet of Sidi Chamharouch. After flapjack and a stew, we sat around burning gorse bushes while our two muleteers, with subtle flicks of the hands, went through the ritual of making mint tea. In the morning we reached the Neltner hut and bargained hard with the muleteers, but still had to pay them £1 each. After their departure I found a way into the locked hut where we spent the night. It was a sturdy structure and spotlessly clean, named for one

A view of Mount Toubkal, with the Tizi n'Ouanoums pass in the centre of the shot.
We scrambled up the 1926 Bentley Beetham route on Toubkal.

of several French climbers who explored these mountains between the wars. In 1922 a local CAF section was established and several huts were constructed. In 1938 a comprehensive guidebook, edited by Jean Dresch and Jacques de Lépiney was published. Lépiney died three years later climbing near Rabat.

We moved further up the valley to a good bivouac under a huge boulder and while Clive and Steve Bowes started work improving it, the rest us walked up to the Tizi n'Ouagane, a pass offering an easy scramble up a ridge to the twin summits of Ouanoukrim, Timzguida and Ras Ouanoukrim, the second and third highest peaks in North Africa. Then we dropped down to the Tizi n'bou Imrhaz, reaching our new five-star bivouac at dusk.

In the morning, we all walked up the steep zigzag path to the dramatic pass of the Tizi n'Ouanoums and the start of the west-south-west ridge of Toubkal, a route first pioneered by the redoubtable Lakeland mountaineer Bentley Beetham in 1926. It was a fine route, although never harder than Very Difficult. The first challenge was a monolithic pillar and then a series of rock towers we had to climb over or around. Above all this, we reached the west shoulder and a scramble through increasingly deep snow up to the main summit and wonderful views of the rolling arid country to the south and the town of Marrakesh to the north. Taking the ordinary route off the summit, we scrambled down scree for a thousand feet to reach our bivouac. That evening we were full of contentment, having climbed the highest peak in the Atlas.

Illness then laid three of us low, me included, and I spent the day with Steve Bowes and Clive wandering around in our shirt tails and boots – and nothing below – ready for a fast trip to the loo. While we discussed the dangers of eating unwashed fruit and not bringing the necessary pills from home, Steve Read and Ray went climbing. Camped by a clear gurgling stream in the fresh air of the mountains, we soon recovered; the following day Steve Read and I set off to climb the south-east face of Tadaft n'bou Imrhaz. The route had not been tried before, and it was interesting work, exploring the couloir and chimneys splitting the face. Two abseils from the summit brought us to the Col de l'Amguird and back into the grassy cwm of the Irhzer n'Bou Imrhaz.

It was early October and cold winds now swept across the mountains promising snow. We elected to head eighty miles south to our next objective – the Volcan d'Siroua, remnant of a Miocene strato-volcano that links the Atlas with the Anti-Atlas. We set off down a rocky gorge on a seemingly endless stony path, the river below the merest thread, carving its way through hard volcanic rock full of quartzes and amethyst. Climbing steadily towards us was an old man carrying a staff and wearing home-made sandals on his feet. To keep out the cold he had a cloak spun from goat's hair wrapped around him. We stopped and chatted. His features were gnarled and rugged like the bark of an ancient olive tree. He must have started out before dawn and

Starting the Beetham route on Toubkal.

Brewing up with a friendly Berber. L–R: Ray Gillies, Berber, Steve Read, me and Steve Bowes. **Photo:** Clive Davies.

he wouldn't reach his destination, the distant village of Asni, before dark. These old Berbers are capable of great feats of endurance.

At last we reached Lac d'Ifni, a green jewel against the brown rock, which, so the old man had told us, contained huge trout, though the only fish we ate that night came in tins. After a brew we left the pretty lake in a violent storm for Tizgui, a small village some way down valley. At Ligrane, we were invited into the headman's home for mint tea and boiled eggs. We sat on cushions and a beautifully designed, homespun carpet. The mint tea was delicious though the price demanded came as a shock. We settled for five dirhams, about eight shillings, a small fortune, and continued on our way, passing through villages with the terraced fields between them fed by ancient irrigation channels.

At Tizgui we passed a good night near a clear spring and awoke surrounded by a crowd of giggling youngsters. The women were already going about their many tasks and gave us sly glances as they worked. We became quite friendly with the villagers after giving first aid to an old man with a badly lacerated leg and a youth with a swollen infected finger. We treated them with impressively coloured ointments and white bandages in the headman's house, who invited us to stay in his home until the stormy weather passed.

The village was built on steep ground that was often just bare rock. The shallower side of the valley was needed for cultivation. It was a contrast to Nottingham, where I'd see the best farmland eaten up by urban sprawl.

Our first aid box made many friends in Morocco. **Photo:** Clive Davies.

This was the first time any of us had stayed with villagers living a life so vastly different from our own. From this brief visit it soon became apparent there was at least one other solution to the problem of finding food, shelter, bringing up children and organising community activities. Here all the basic amenities that I had always taken for granted were lacking; no electricity or water on tap, no mechanical transport or shops to spend the cash they didn't have, yet the people seemed content. Living on a steep mountainside in an area prone to drought made life in this isolated area very difficult and one of unremitting toil – at least for the women.

During our first evening the stream became a raging torrent, the hillside awash with running water, breaking down walls, eroding soil and washing crops into the river. The side of a mud and stone house collapsed, allowing goats and cows to escape, grunting and steaming in the rain. Small boys ran about barefoot in ragged, rain-soaked smocks rounding the animals up. The side of another house collapsed as we sat watching from our veranda, but our host and his friends looked on phlegmatically and continued drinking their mint tea as the storm passed. Next day the women were out first, down to the river, shovelling soil into wicker baskets with the help of their children. They carried their heavy loads, bent double under the weight, back up the hillside in an effort to re-establish their meagre fields, some of which were too small to take an ox and plough. The men were busy repairing stone walls. Such is life living on the side of a mountain, always fighting gravity.

After four days with the villagers, helping where we could and using our first aid to good effect, we carried on to the Anti-Atlas and the fringes of the Sahara. Two days later we reached Askouan, fifty miles south. From now on the hospitality of local people seemed boundless. In every village the headman would invite us to join him and his family for mint tea and chapattis. At Askouan we stayed a couple of days with the khedive, a sort of regional administrator. We ate large meals, sitting around a low table on cushions, dipping into a large bowl with our fingers. Only the dancing girls were missing.

We left the track and headed east toward Siroua, through a strange land-scape of bizarrely eroded rocks. Streams had etched out deep gorges and left standing pillars of rock with protecting boulders capping them. We passed grottos, curious arches and towering pinnacles. Then we found a little valley of green amid the barren rocks. It was covered in mushrooms. By the time darkness fell, as we reached a fine bivouac beneath a shoulder of Siroua, we were carrying fifteen pounds of perfectly formed white field mushrooms. Before turning in for the night they went into a stew of maize meal with our last Oxo cube. We now had only a kilo of flour and a tin of gravy powder left.

After a good night's sleep, we climbed up to the shoulder and contoured round the head of the northern salient and on to a ridge leading to the top of Siroua, 3,305 metres above sea level. We scrambled up for 200 feet and were finally on the summit. Two huge bosses of rock sprouting out of the earth like teeth nearby immediately caught our attention; we christened them molar and pre-molar. They offered some great rock climbing, as would the crags a thousand feet high that we found just behind them.

It took two days of walking to reach the road back north. All the way we experienced the sort of hospitality one usually only reads about. It came spontaneously and the villagers seemed offended when any attempt was made to pay them. By the end of our walk we were full of mint tea, eggs, honey and chapattis, made fresh on our arrival over charcoal fires. At Ouarzazate we found ourselves back in the modern world. Everything was so expensive. A few months before the town had been full of Hollywood stars and film-people working on David Lean's movie *Lawrence of Arabia*. We left for Tangiers and the ferry to Gibraltar. Money was always a problem. It was a source of great pride that our six weeks from the Alps, our hillwalking in Spain and our trip to Morocco had only cost us £22 each.

Steve Bowes had been getting progressively weaker and was now really suffering so I took him to hospital on a wet, stormy night, thinking he had dysentery. The duty nurse asked me where I was staying. I told her I was planning to sleep on the beach. She said that as the weather was so bad, why didn't I stay in the hospital? She found me a bed on a ward but next morning

I awoke horrified to discover that the patients all around me were bright yellow. I was sleeping on what turned out to be the isolation ward.

Steve recovered and we all hitched home, but I managed only one day's teaching before I too turned yellow. I was diagnosed with hepatitis B and sent to hospital immediately where I remained for ten days and was put on a strict diet – no greasy fish and chips and definitely no alcohol for the next three months. Fortunately I qualified for full sick pay, having completed that single day back at school.

Apart from a large collection of slides and a superficial geographical study, which would be very useful in schoolwork, material gains were few. But we felt enriched by overcoming the adverse weather, the tiredness, ill health and hunger, losing the route and sometimes our tempers, and all the other obstacles. It was deeply satisfying to move about a relatively unknown country as a self-contained unit; everything we needed we carried or found near to hand. We had no sponsors back home to tie us down to a pre-arranged route, from port to base, to summit and back. For six weeks we went our own way, unfettered, wherever we felt we could practise our mountaineering skills, see a new country, and taste some of the delights of mountain exploration. We had reached that feeling of 'never-ending-ness', deciding our next move and then seeing where it took us, always wanting to look over the next horizon.

On the Comici route on the north face of the Cima Grande with Bill Cheverst in 1963. A continental team can be seen on the Brandler-Hasse in the background (this was impressively soloed by Alex Huber in 2002).
Photo: Bill Cheverst.

DOLOMITES

By the start of 1963 I had more or less recovered from infectious hepatitis, put on weight, gained strength, resumed playing rugby and rock climbing and had settled back into teaching and married life. My absence had been a trial for Jan. Years later she wrote about being separated for that first expedition: 'During his first trip to the Atlas in the year we were married I seemed to spend the whole time feeling desperately unhappy and in fact I literally just about took to my bed with missing him so much. It took quite a few trips for us to realise what had happened – this adjustment of mine. It's the weeks immediately after his return that are always the most traumatic for us. It's very hard for me to accept him as part of my life again. He comes back panting to be a husband, father, etc again and I sort of look at him and say, "Who is this guy?"'

During the winter of my convalescence and Jan's readjustment, I wrote a comprehensive report of our visit to the Sierra Nevada and the Atlas Mountains for the director of education. I also wrote an article for *Mountain Craft*, then the only climbing periodical that wasn't a club journal. It was published in the summer and I got paid £7. 10s.

When Dez saw it, he told me he wasn't surprised. He had long ago detected that I wanted to be famous. Other friends, half in jest, half seriously, asked if I was turning professional, while some said they enjoyed reading about our wander through southern Spain and Morocco on a shoestring. So there it was in embryo, a way to continue climbing, motivated partly by fame and fortune but also for the sake of doing it and then sharing the experience with others. Tony Howard, one of the leading exploratory climbers of my generation, saw the article and went off to roam around neighbouring areas of the Atlas, just as we had been encouraged to do by the information Wilf Noyce gave us.

Having seen the edge of the Sahara I became excited at the idea of crossing it, partly for the experience, partly to visit the Tibesti Mountains of northern

Chad that reach almost 3,500 metres. Examining the dotted lines on my Michelin road map, I realised that the road south from the coast to the mountains was a camel route. Crossing the Sahara by camel train would have been interesting, but I had no experience of camels and no time to make the necessary contacts. Clive, Ray and Steve Bowes said they were also curious, having been brought up on stories of Beau Geste, the French Foreign Legion, the Bedouin and Wilfred Thesiger. Mick Garside, now studying to be a geography teacher, was also taken by the idea. The plan gathered impetus only slowly though. Having been away and then sick for six months, I needed to catch up.

Cottesmore was now fifty per cent immigrant children, mostly Asians and West Indians living in the substantial Edwardian villas of the school catchment. They were far less of a problem when it came to discipline than the indigenous children. Old hands advised that on the first day of each school year I should identify the main troublemaker and deal firmly with him. The theory was it would save a lot of nonsense in the future and allow actual teaching to take place. With a year's probation completed, I was given a more difficult class and told who to watch.

On the first morning I gave a lad a long window pole and asked him to pull the windows open. He smirked and set to work as I went through the register until another pupil yelped in pain. He'd been jabbed in the face by the window pole. I leapt out of my chair, shouted at the youth to come to the front, bent him over and slapped him hard on the bottom with a school-issue plimsoll. The youth, not much smaller than me, shuffled back to his desk and for the rest of the year I had no more trouble with him or any other members of the class. I now lived on my reputation.

The school had offered me a leather strap but I preferred a plimsoll; it was only at the start of PE lessons that I needed to punish anyone, usually those miscreants who always failed to bring their PE kit. One newly arrived Indian boy who looked fit and athletic failed to bring his kit several weeks in a row, with the excuse that he didn't understand English. Eventually, having asked other Indian boys to impress upon him that it was the law of the land that every boy did PE, he continued to stand on the sidelines of the PE hall distracting the class. I finally lost patience and produced the slipper. He put his hands together and bowed his head. 'Oh please, *sahib*, no physical violence.' The game was up. He had been duping me and several other members of staff. At least he actually started doing physical education. An overweight Indian boy tried my patience by agreeing to bring his kit each week, but never doing so, despite his family being informed that it was a statutory requirement. He seemed to think it was a joke until I gave him the slipper and then he became sullen and resentful. A teaching friend later met the boy's sister, after I climbed Everest, with the news the boy had become a doctor and thought I was a psychopath.

There was, as you would expect in a large school, a wide cross section of teachers, from the young and idealistic, full of enthusiasm with a genuine calling for the job, to the old lags, disillusioned and hanging on for their pensions. Mr Dickens, an older teacher, overweight and lacking in energy for teaching and life in general, was having a hard time at Cottesmore during his final year. One morning, as I was trying to teach geography, I heard such a noise coming from his class next door that I decided to see what was happening. As I passed the window of his classroom I saw Mr Dickens with his head bowed, his back against the radiator, staring down at the floor. The class was in uproar. Some of the boys were wrestling with each other, others flicking ink-soaked blotting paper missiles across the room. It was like a scene from the Bash Street Kids. I made an excuse to enter and as I did every boy immediately jumped back into his chair and sat bolt upright, an expression of innocence on every face. I had the same effect on dinner duty; the dinner ladies loved me and so did those of the kids who preferred to eat in peace.

During most breaks and lunchtimes there were fights in the playground. I'd hear a chorus of 'Scrap, scrap, scrap!' and find a crowd of boys in the yard gathered round two more wrestling on the ground. Usually they stopped fighting when they heard 'Scotty' was coming. Sometimes I got carried away. I once found two boys rolling around fighting in the school corridor. When they carried on despite having seen me standing above them, I gave one of them a kick up his backside. As soon as I did it, I knew I shouldn't have, especially as I was wearing shoes.

Next day I was called into the headmaster's study, where I was introduced to the grandma of the boy I'd kicked. Both parents had abandoned the boy and grandma had taken him under her wing. She said she realised he had problems but underneath his rebelliousness he was a good lad at heart. I agreed with that and with genuine remorse apologised to the grandma and later to the boy for my totally inappropriate behaviour, something I never forgot. As she was leaving the headmaster's study she sympathised with us having to handle difficult children in overcrowded classrooms. Mr Happer left it at that, knowing one of his young teachers had, in turn, been taught a valuable lesson in humility.

For the first time I questioned the use of corporal punishment in school. I realised I tended to use it out of impatience when routines were upset by unruly behaviour. I now understood you could only have an environment for effective teaching through mutual respect and not through the fear of being beaten. I saw that my methods, however justified out of expediency, could lead me to an arrogant disregard for the children as individuals whose personal histories and needs had to be considered sympathetically.

One of the unexpected results of taking the children on long hikes and rock climbs in Derbyshire was the complete change in our relationship. As a result of those experiences out of the classroom there was far more understanding and empathy on both sides. Discipline ceased to be a problem, especially as the regular rock climbers sorted out troublemakers for me, allowing me to get down to actual teaching. They became a valuable asset in a school with, as in many tough inner-city schools at the time, class sizes of up to forty-five pupils.

I helped run the school rugby teams with Sam Lewis and later Neil Highfield, training at lunchtimes and travelling to various grounds around the city on Saturday mornings in an old Humber ambulance that we also used for field trips, although not having passed my driving test, I needed to find a driver. I started running basketball teams and eventually had four on the go, training in the school hall after school until 6 p.m. I then went home for tea before returning at 7 p.m. to take evening classes, for which I was paid an extra £1 an hour. Bob Pettigrew had left Nottingham to teach in India and I took over his Mountaineering Association course and also took a keep fit group, mostly made up of the Moderns Rugby Club and the Nottingham Climbers' Club. More difficult was teaching adult immigrants English. It all helped me afford weekends and holidays in the hills.

I certainly surprised myself by slotting so many activities into the day. My Loughborough tutor, Mr Archer, would surely have approved: maximum of activity in the minimum of time. I'm not sure he would have approved of my attempt to teach yoga to a particularly boisterous class. The headmaster had told me to get rid of their energy but when he came to see how I was getting on, he found forty or so boys lying flat out on their backs, some of them asleep. I had told them to focus their attention on all the points of their limbs and bodies that touched the ground. The headmaster had to agree there was an improvement in the boys' attitudes as they walked out of the hall to the changing rooms.

Jan's suspicion that she might be pregnant was confirmed this time. The baby was due in mid-July. She decided reluctantly to leave nursing and took a job in the local tax office. We also moved from our rather grim flat to a better flat on Derby Road, still close to school. Luckily there was a telephone box just outside, where I spent increasing amounts of time trying to organise our expedition to the Sahara. I was the one most driven to go and therefore worked hardest at making it happen. I tracked down people who had been to the Tibesti, including the Cambridge academic Roger Akester who graciously invited the whole team down to his home for a briefing.

Had Roger not been so enthusiastic we might well have given up when he told us his last trip to the Tibesti in 1961 had cost £6,000. The most depressing news was of the bureaucratic restrictions imposed on climbing by departing French colonial officials. Our team, being used to travelling on a shoestring budget, reckoned on reducing the cost to a fifth and hoped that with the departure of the French the local regime in Tibesti would have a more open mind. We also now had a definite objective, the unclimbed Tarso Tieroko, which, from a distance, Wilfred Thesiger had pronounced 'probably the most beautiful mountain in Tibesti'. This information, more than any other, gave impetus to preparations. Roddy Tuck and Peter Steele had attempted the peak on Roger's first Cambridge expedition in 1957. Crumbling rock had defeated them 200 feet from the summit.

After school, the telephone box was in almost constant use with embarrassingly long queues of impatient neighbours waiting outside to make calls. On more than one occasion the phone would ring as other users were about to make their call. They would lean out of the phone box, asking if there was a Mr Scott outside because a secretary at the French Embassy wished to talk to him.

I handwrote a large batch of letters requesting food, but all I got back was one pound of dehydrated onions through the post. I sent off more letters and this time got an invitation to visit a local health store. I arrived with other members of the team, only to find a photographer from the *Nottingham Post* ready to take photographs of the manager handing over sixty pounds of dried dates – the proverbial coals to Newcastle.

On a more positive note, we were invited for an interview with the Mount Everest Foundation at the Royal Geographical Society about a possible grant. That prospect stimulated fundraising lectures and dances for the autumn. I went to see *Lawrence of Arabia* to relive the splendid film sets we had crossed in southern Morocco and whet my appetite for the future expedition. The Lawrence portrayed was not of the same cut as pre-war Empire heroes. There was a strong suggestion of his homosexual leanings and his superiors were nothing like the fair-minded colonial administrators dispensing justice in the back of beyond throughout the Empire. Allenby and the British were portrayed as duplicitous, double-crossing the noble Arab after their courageous defeat of the Turks with no compunction whatsoever.

Britain was changing fast. This was the era of the Profumo scandal and Mandy Rice-Davies appearing in the Old Bailey, young, beautiful, working-class and self-assured, contradicting Lord Astor's denial with her line: 'Well, he would, wouldn't he?' The country felt a more democratic place and the Empire was being dismantled, our colonies given independence. America was changing too. I remember being electrified by Martin Luther King's 'I have a dream' speech on 28 August 1963 from the steps of the Lincoln Memorial in Washington to a crowd of 200,000. It was incredibly powerful seeing so many black and white people standing together.

The integration of immigrant children at Cottesmore never seemed a problem; as with most newcomers, they were more enthusiastic. The immigrant students contributed positively to school, the Asian kids often doing well academically and the Afro-Caribbean kids well at basketball, athletics and rugby. Very few carried on rock climbing after their introduction. It seemed at the time that they were more concerned with integrating socially and financially within society and could see no sense in taking up such an esoteric pastime. Not all the staff found the change easy to accept. One old buffer came into the staff room staggered to have been asked at his bus stop by a black man with a suitcase: 'where is the place they give you the free money?' All the younger staff members just laughed; we had mostly accepted that the new arrivals had made an almost exclusively positive contribution, most obviously in the National Health Service and on the buses and trains.

I recall in particular one young man of Jamaican parents who took part in every aspect of school life. Neville Ballin was a breath of fresh air, always so positive, always with a huge smile. He had the ability to jolly along his peers out of bad behaviour and into something more constructive: sport, mountaineering and school trips. One of his schoolmates had spina bifida and in the days before disabled access was obligatory, Nev, who was big for his age, took it upon himself to carry this lad on his back from one lesson to the next. Nev decided he wanted to be a doctor and worked hard to gain the necessary O levels to transfer to grammar school. A few years ago, out of the blue, Nev called me. He had returned to Jamaica and was now the island's chief anaesthetist. He said that since I was getting on in years, he wanted to take the opportunity to thank me before I died for helping widen his horizons while at Cottesmore School.

In between bus trips to Wales, we spent weekends in the Peak District, particularly on the crags of the Derwent Valley, unearthing virgin crags from under the ivy. Steve Read had climbed on the rocks between High Tor and Willersley Castle in the 1950s and had come across an old map of the area with the name Wildcat written across it. He showed us his earlier routes and in 1963 he and I pioneered two particularly good climbs, *Cataclysm* and *Catastrophe Grooves*. Our club, including old friends Steve Bowes, Clive Davies, Ray Gillies and newcomers to the NCC Mick Terry, George Jones, Dan Meadows and Terry Small, climbed all the obvious lines. They weren't the hardest routes in the Peak District but we had good fun and always climbed from the ground up, without practising them first. Although many of these routes seemed piddling little climbs they were new and therefore intrinsically more significant than climbing something old; pioneering is naturally at the essence of rock climbing and mountaineering.

Limestone in the late 1950s and early 1960s was a realm of its own, still to be fully integrated into mainstream climbing; limestone was considered handy for pegging practice in winter but was too dangerous for free climbing in summer.

Ray Gillies at Wildcat in the 1960s.

Although pegs were placed on many climbs, very few were used for direct aid, as had been the case up *Flaky Wall* on High Tor. Pegs were used mainly for protection on rock that was featureless and sometimes loose; nylon slings, chockstones and machine nuts – at the time all we had to protect climbs – weren't so useful. It was nothing like *Cenotaph Corner* where you could easily place a dozen pieces of protection, all of them bombproof.

We returned to the familiar caves and overhung rocks to sleep after a lively night in the local pub. The Nottingham Climbers' Club were keen folk singers, encouraged by the strong voice of Terry Small who hailed from Northern Ireland and introduced us to songs from across the water. Judy Darnell had a lovely voice and a fine repertoire of traditional ballads. Terry Bolger would have us in fits of laughter with his variety songs. Mick Terry's voice was indistinguishable from that of Tom Jones. Instruments started to appear: Bob Wilson from Newcastle arrived in Nottingham to sing raucous songs accompanied on his own guitar. Then others joined the club who were accomplished on the banjo, double bass and accordion. Non-climbers began asking us where we would be meeting the following weekend – for the music. The NCC developed quite a following.

Not every night ended well. One evening in the Prince of Wales pub at Baslow, we crossed swords with a rowdy element from Chesterfield. One youth grabbed someone's hat and wouldn't give it back without a fight, a challenge I foolishly took upon myself. We ended up rolling around on the grass of the churchyard next door. When the crowd shouted the cops were coming, I took off, hiding in a nearby bunkhouse where a young constable found me. I ended up in court for disturbing the peace, with Jan by my side, highly pregnant, to discover, fortunately for me, that my adversary had given a false name and address. I was given an 'Absolute Order of Discharge', to my great relief – and that of my father, who was still a serving policeman.

The winter of 1963 was one of the coldest and therefore one of the best in years; for months the hills and mountains were covered in snow and ice under a blue sky. Even in Derbyshire we found good sport, climbing the frozen Kinder Downfall and all along the Eastern Edges where we had to dig our way through huge snow drifts into Robin Hood's Cave on Stanage to spend the night. The best winter climb we found was on Back Tor near Edale where loose shale and sand, covered in ice, was frozen solid. In Wales, Snowdonia was quite alpine and all the gullies on Snowdon were full of snow and ice. I got to use my ice axe and crampons for the first time in Britain.

Jan felt she needed to be with her mother Helen to have our baby so a few weeks before the due date she went up to Carlisle where her father Tom was now based, overseeing the local Territorial Army unit. Each weekend after school I hitched up the A6 to be with her. Things did not start well with my

Climbing on Wildcat above the River Derwent, with Arkwright's Mill and the A6 behind.

in-laws, who were plain-speaking Yorkshire folk. On the first weekend I came through the front door, swung my rucksack off my back and knocked a full can of gloss white paint all over the hall carpet. Tom got the blame for leaving the lid off.

The following weekend he managed to get hold of a racing cycle for me to use. I spent the Saturday cycling into the Lake District but, rushing back for dinner, I hit a rock in the middle of the road coming down the Kirkstone Pass. I went over the handlebars, put out a hand to break my fall and the road sliced deeply into my outstretched palm. I had to stop at the hospital in Penrith to have it stitched and arrived home late, covered in blood with a buckled front wheel. They must have wondered what their daughter had got herself into, although my mother-in-law did once pay me a compliment: 'say what you like about our Douglas, we've never had an argument.' I would never cross her.

On the third weekend there was still no sign of the baby. This time Tom had managed to borrow a homemade plywood two-seater sea kayak. He'd also recruited a young TA lad to go out with me on to the Solway. We decided to paddle from Silloth across the estuary to Dumfries and back. My companion was of similar age and in civilian life was a salesman – and not that fit. By the time we were halfway across he was beginning to wilt and only kept going so he could take a rest on the far shoreline. As it was now well into the afternoon, we gave up on Dumfries and settled for Southerness Point. Having rested we set off at a fine pace, paddles whirring like matching windmills, for the ten miles back to Silloth. Slowly it dawned on us that not only were we not closing on Silloth, we were drifting away from our destination on a strong tide towards the Isle of Man and the now-setting sun.

We desperately tried to paddle back up the estuary but as the lights of Silloth started appearing in the dusk, we could see we were even further away. My companion had been quiet for some time, in a state of complete exhaustion, as was I. He stopped paddling and quietly placed his paddle alongside the kayak, pressed down with both hands on the hull, stood up and stepped out of the boat right in the middle of the Solway Firth. He stood there, like a divine being, his feet just below the water's surface. He had, he said, brushed a sandbank with his paddle and realised we could walk home. We walked up the estuary, the kayak pulling against the tide rushing over our feet and right up to our thighs, for more than an hour until we were level with Silloth. Then we paddled to shore to be met by the only person awake at 1 a.m. on a Sunday morning, Jan's father, Tom, who, it turned out, had quite a bad temper. He managed to cancel the coastguard call-out before driving us back to Carlisle.

On the fourth weekend, sitting on the lawn at Tom's house, sewing leather patches on to my-worn out rock boots, Helen shouted down from the back bedroom window that our child was born. I rushed upstairs to share tears of relief and joy with Jan and to hold our baby boy – Michael. After ten days, being superfluous to requirements for all practical purposes, I left Jan and Michael with Tom and Helen and hitchhiked down to Dover and Calais and in one long day reached Innsbruck. The Nottingham Climbers' Club had given up on me and moved on and I had no idea where. Luckily I ran into a youth called Steve Smith, known as 'Sid', who had been on one of our bus trips. We decided to hitchhike to the Dolomites, try to find the NCC and, if not, climb together. Sid was very fit, as he was just as keen on cycling as rock climbing.

The Dolomites were a staggering prospect, their scale almost too much to comprehend. We climbed a route on the Cima Piccolissima and the north face of the Punta di Frida. The exposure was incredible but we kept our heads and slipped down our ropes from the abseil stations, and when the scary bits had faded, headed up to the Cima Piccola to try the famous grade-VI route the *Spigolo Giallo* – the Yellow Edge. Before setting off, I'd calculated this route was eight times longer than the longest climb on High Tor – and it felt it. Neither of us had been on anything quite so steep and exposed before. Yet by taking it one pitch at a time and making each belay rock solid, we made progress. Before long we had one of the classic rock climbs of the Alps under our belts.

After Yellow Edge, Sid and I managed to track down the NCC. I had agreed to climb with Bill Cheverst, a college lecturer originally from Birmingham who had joined the club following his move to Nottinghamshire. He was short but wiry and strong and smiled like Alfred E. Neuman, mascot of the American satirical magazine, *Mad*. He was quite eccentric himself and seemed always underfunded; he mostly slept in the back of his minivan in the college car park with his toothbrush next to his pens in the top pocket of his corduroy jacket.

As you'd expect of an academic, he had a philosophical bent. It was Bill who explained to me that *Alice in Wonderland* wasn't just a fairy story and that Lewis Carroll was playing around with logic and the principles of mathematics. As a climber Bill could push the boat out, as he did on the aptly named *Jericho Wall* on the Cromlech. He started to lose control but continued racing across loose rock until finally he was airborne, still clutching a flake of rock as he went flying past me. One strand of our Viking nylon rope was completely severed in the fall. Although we were poles apart intellectually and two quite different characters I always had a strong connection with Bill. Whenever I was about to phone him, he phoned me and vice versa. He was such lively company and a very caring sympathetic chap. It was a great sadness to me and the rest of our club when he died climbing unroped on the Matterhorn's Hörnli Ridge in 1972. His partner was waiting for him at the Solvay bivouac hut but Bill never arrived. He left a widow, Margaret, and their daughter Abigail.

That summer of 1963 we climbed the Emilio Comici route on the Cima Grande's north face where again the exposure had me worried. In fact both

Bill Cheverst.

of us fumbled about until we were beyond the point of easy retreat and only then did we settle down to enjoy the climbing and the exposure, climbing the route in a day from the Lavaredo hut.

Resting after our climb, we heard there was help needed for a rescue on the south face of the Cima Ovest. Bill and I rushed off with a huge chap from the local mountain rescue team and as we neared the face, someone pointed the way to the casualty from the path. Bill and I scrambled over the scree and were first to reach the body. The man had fallen all the way down the ordinary route, bouncing from ledge to ledge. His head was a mess of skull, hair and brains crushed together. Our companion arrived and promptly vomited while the rest of the team put their handkerchiefs around their mouths and started to pray. Bill and I took the body bag they were carrying and manoeuvred the poor fellow in it. Out of sight seemed to be out of mind for the Italians; the rescue team was soon disappearing down the path with the body. I wondered why Bill and I had not reacted as they had. Were we unnaturally cold and heartless? Or were the Italians more excitable?

I came home with renewed enthusiasm for our expedition to the Tibesti and arranged lectures featuring well-known climbers to raise funds. The famous French alpinist Lionel Terray was first in this series and proved very popular, especially with Jan. Lionel met us in the pub and looked around at our expectant faces.

'Ah,' he said sadly, 'you are all so young.' Then he took Jan's hand and kissed it. 'And you, mademoiselle, you are so beautiful.' I thought it best to mention Jan was my wife.

If I had an early climbing hero it was Lionel; he had my total respect. He had made the second ascent of the Eigerwand in 1947 and was a major player in climbing Annapurna in 1950. Later he made the first ascent of Makalu. I found his approach inspiring, particularly his energy, going twice a year to the Himalaya and somewhere else in-between, something I wanted to do. The year before his lecture, he'd climb the stunning peak Jannu in Nepal, gone to the Andes to climb the east peak of Chakrarahu and then gone back to the Himalaya to climb Niligiri.

There was a full house of over 450 people to hear Lionel but just as he began a jazz band struck up in the basement, the music filtering out from the air-conditioning system. 'So,' Lionel said to the audience, apparently uncon-cerned, 'we 'ave ze lecture to ze music.' The audience burst into applause. He got a much warmer reception than Gaston Rébuffat, whose projector kept breaking down, sending Gaston into fits of rage. 'What is wrong with Nottingham? Everywhere else is perfect but here in Nottingham only prob-lems.' Several people got up and walked out and the applause was lukewarm at the end.

A month later Dennis Gray gave a lecture, which drew in the crowds and was well received, and in November we had Don Whillans. He walked on stage and greeted the packed hall: ''ow do, I'm Don Whillans. They say I'm working-class but you should know I've not worked for ten years.' The audience spent the whole lecture laughing. He put a slide of the Rock and Ice Club all lined up at the Roaches and identified each one individually. 'And you see the woman stood at the end? Well, she became my wife. You never know where danger's lurking.' Chris Bonington was supposed to round off the series but sent Ian Clough instead to talk about their climbs on the Frêney Pillar and the Eigerwand. To supplement income from the lectures, Mick Garside organised dances, usually at the Trent Bridge Inn. One night we went there to listen to Monty Sunshine on the clarinet and the wonderful blues singer and entertainer, George Melly. He told the audience he had a girlfriend called Pat who was, he said, a bit grotty so he called her Cow Pat. He kissed Jan's hand too.

The weekend after Dennis gave his lecture we drove to Wales for one of the Nottingham Climbers' Club's regular bus trips. As usual, we stopped at a pub just before Capel Curig, but the bar was silent when we walked in. John F. Kennedy had been assassinated in Dallas. The world seemed to be changing fast: mods and rockers fighting in Brighton, The Beatles on top of the charts and the end of capital punishment. Having bought his driving licence before the war, Dad bought his first car, like so many others did in the 1960s, which, thanks to Mr Beeching, did for the railways. Charlbury Road changed when everyone started buying cars; it wasn't so safe for kids to play out like we had. Brian was now at medical school and a champion hurdler. Garry was at secondary school.

Jan, Michael and I moved from our flat on Derby Road to The Park, a leafy, less polluted area of Nottingham but unfortunately without a telephone box outside. Mrs Robinson, the kindly school secretary, would take messages for me, selling tickets for NCC lectures and booking places on the bus service. There were calls from firms offering equipment and food for our desert journey, which was now scheduled for February 1965. As the departure date drew nearer, so the number of calls increased.

After asking others who had been across the Sahara, we decided the best option was to buy three ex-army Morris Commercial MRA1 trucks, by auction, at the Ordnance Disposal Depot outside Nottingham. We would drive two and cannibalise the third for parts. Mick, Ray and I bought one as a trial and parked it up alongside the Lenton Abbey Scout Hut, where Clive Davies' father Skip was the Scout leader. He generously gave us parking space and a place for Ray to work on the vehicle. The truck seemed a good buy for £65 since it had very low mileage and had been serviced every six months. It was cheap to license and insure so we used it to take club members and schoolchildren out to the hills.

The north ridge of the Aiguille du Peigne.

As a way to raise funds, we decided to drive the truck to Chamonix for the summer of 1964 and sell seats to climbers and walkers. Somehow I over-recruited. When I calculated the number of passengers, each paying £10 a head, I realised we had twenty-one for a twelve-seat vehicle. The only solution was to put in an extra level in the back of the truck. We made a platform from old British Rail fencing and fitted it into the tubular frame on the back of the wagon. When the passengers arrived on the last day of the school term, I explained nervously there would only be seats for the drivers, and they would all have to manage as best they could in the back. Everyone accepted the situation. The more ascetic passengers squirrelled themselves away among the luggage and only emerged to relieve themselves. The rest hung on the back like it was an overcrowded bus chugging across the Punjab.

The weather in the Mont Blanc range was far better than in previous Alpine seasons. I climbed the north ridge of the Aiguille du Peigne with Will McLoughlin and on the strength of that consulted those Brahmins Joe Brown and Don Whillans, also camping on the Biolay, about their route on the west face of the Aiguille de Blatière. With their encouragement we climbed it in under guidebook time, mainly because the famous crux pitch, the Fissure Brown, which Mac led, had huge wooden wedges hammered into it. Mac and I then did the Frendo Spur on the north face of the Aiguille du Midi, which I thought was a wonderful, varied and for once safe route on good rock and reasonably angled ice. Mac was an excellent companion but we never again climbed together. He discovered a strong religious conviction, married his girlfriend and moved to Norfolk where they began a very different kind of life as Jehovah's Witnesses.

Having come out on the truck, I planned to go to the Dolomites with Sid Smith, on the back of his BSA 650cc Super Rocket, while Mick Garside drove our passengers home. The truck's gearbox chose this moment to seize up while driving down Chamonix's high street. Local mechanics took out the engine and gearbox only to realise the parts needed were not available in France. So Mick hitchhiked to Folkestone where he bought a copy of *Exchange and Mart*, called various scrapyards and then hitched north to Northamptonshire, sleeping under a hedge just short of Burton Latimer.

Next day he walked into the scrapyard run by an extended family of gypsies. The patriarch of the clan, a huge, bearded character was obviously moved: 'I couldn't sleep thinking about you hitching all that way,' he told Mick. They found a gearbox, smashed the aluminium casing, packed all the cogs and bearings into Mick's rucksack and, after numerous mugs of tea, Mick was charged £5. Two days later he was back in Chamonix. The French mechanics emerged from the garage and when Mick pulled out the parts, they cheered: '*Les pieces!*' The passengers were amazed to arrive back home only three days late.

The famous Fissure Brown pitch on the west face of the Blatière.

In the Dolomites I ran another Mountaineering Association course, with Sid's help. We climbed every day mostly in the Sassolungo and everyone survived – but I struggled to cope with the wide range of ability and fitness among the clients. I made a resolution not to take on any more guiding work; not only could I not relax, it was taking time away from the climbing I really wanted to do. I found the job emotionally wearing and thought it best left to those more temperamentally suited, who had actually been trained for the job.

Sid and I did some good routes around the Sella Pass but as I was fixing the last abseil off a climb, the large rock Sid was squatting on began to slide. He shouted a warning and then jumped off on to a ledge. Luckily for me I had started wearing a newly acquired construction worker's helmet, made of very thick fibreglass. The rock still smashed it into my skull. I managed to stay conscious, urged on by Sid who was shouting at me to stay awake, and the rock thudded into the grass 150 feet below. I managed to clip on to the rope, much to Sid's relief, and abseil down. Sid took me to the local cottage hospital for stitches and I came away with a dramatic white head bandage. We managed one more climb before heading home. The journey back to Nottingham was tedious; we suffered several high-speed punctures on Germany's autobahns. Now the climbing was over, I was desperate to be home with Jan and Michael; five weeks was my limit before homesickness kicked in – and I felt conscience-stricken for leaving Jan to cope with our young son for so long.

Our Tibesti expedition was proving difficult to organise; progress was intermittent. At the time it was frustrating, but in retrospect we had no previous experience of taking on such an expensive and difficult project. Northern Chad was incredibly remote, certainly in those days, and reaching it involved a great deal of bureaucracy, which sapped our enthusiasm. We needed visas for all the North African countries and *carnets de passages* and insurance all the way from Calais, through Spain to the Sahara.

We got a second wind with our application for a grant from the Mount Everest Foundation. I remember sitting nervously outside the council room at the Royal Geographical Society waiting for my interview, but it was worth it, because the committee gave us a grant of £400. It was a tremendous boost. We bought two more Morris Commercials and Ray set to work, putting an extra leaf in each spring to boost the suspension and fitting seventy-gallon petrol tanks behind both cabs. That meant we could carry a total of 200 gallons across the Sahara and back, essential given that petrol in Chad cost ten times what it did in Tripoli. Clive Davies, a sign writer by trade, expertly painted the lorries white and put the expedition's name on the doors. Mick, now a fellow geography teacher, began to assemble all the equipment necessary for the geographical survey we intended to make of the remote Modra valley.

Before we left, I had a book to finish. Climbing in the Dolomites had inspired me to take a deeper interest in limestone climbing at home and I'd taken on the task of producing a guidebook to the Derwent Valley. In 1961, Graham West and friends from the Manchester Gritstone Climbing Club had published *Rock Climbs on the Mountain Limestone of Derbyshire*. That gave a tremendous boost to exploration on the limestone crags of the Peak District and we planned to update their work. As our book neared completion, there was a great impetus to do as many of the unclimbed routes as we could, before everyone else found out about them. Most weekends, after playing rugby on Saturday, I would hitch to Cromford or Matlock Bath to meet the lads and record all the routes climbed. Steve Read and I climbed a couple of classic routes on Willersley Castle Rocks, *Lone Tree Groove* and *Gangue Grooves*, which were both excellent. Willersley, I always thought, is one of the finest limestone crags in Derbyshire.

I was still doing artificial climbing on crags in Yorkshire like Malham Cove and Gordale Scar. I did a route there with Pat Harris we called *Grot*, since it was very loose, up a fractured overhang of limestone and quite the most difficult pegging I experienced. It made everything I climbed in the Dolomites seem quite easy. I also climbed an aid route on High Tor in Derbyshire we called *Twilight* with thirty-five pegs and a bolt. It was the first time I had drilled a hole in the rock for protection and I didn't feel too guilty about it; lots of other people had bolted High Tor.

Early in the New Year, with the expedition looming, Ray and I went up to Yorkshire for a last climb, putting up a direct route under the big overhang at Gordale. We also looked at putting up a new route around Kilnsey Main Overhang. After drilling half a dozen holes for bolts with a rawl drill we gave up. Nat Allen, Dennis Gray and Dez Hadlum were also on the crag that day enjoying a free route and asked us why we were bothering, drilling holes to produce just another risk-free artificial route parallel to the first one. It was food for thought.

Dennis had recently organised the Rock and Ice Club dinner in Grassington, just down the road from Kilnsey. That year Tom Patey was a guest, singing his comic songs lampooning the great and the good of the climbing world, like Chris Bonington and Joe Brown. Dennis introduced me to a fit-looking youth he called Dan Boon, who proceeded to get up on the stage and sing Bob Dylan's song 'The Times They Are A-Changin'', all five verses and pitch perfect. I was staggered at this bravura performance but also at the embarrassed silence that followed. I suddenly realised how basically conservative working-class climbers could be. They didn't want to hear, from a nineteen-year-old, that their old road was rapidly ageing. Dan, whose real name was James Fullalove, was even then a hugely talented climber; he climbed the route

Great Western at Almscliff in Yorkshire in a pair of sawn-off Wellington boots. Coming from a poor background in Bradford, he was always short of funds, but climbing opened the world to him, just as climbing became part of 1960s counter-culture.

A month after the Rock and Ice dinner the Nottingham Climbers' Club met at the Dog and Partridge near Ashbourne in Derbyshire. It had been a typically raucous evening, and as instruments were being tuned, ready for the singing, the publican announced the bar was closing earlier than arranged. Things quickly got out of hand. The landlord grabbed a banjo and started whacking Steve Read with it when his back was turned. The rest of us waded in with the landlord's two sons, both wrestlers. The landlady called the police and soon the blue lights of a panda car were flashing through the pub window.

As we took off in the expedition truck and the police gave chase, we shouted at Ray to drive faster. Just as they were gaining on us, Ray reached the ford just south of the town at Clifton and went through it at full throttle. The river was in spate, and the wagon sent a sheet of water over the top of the cab. The engine spluttered but we had enough momentum to make it through and Ray powered up the other side. The police slammed on the brakes short of the water's edge and we all gave a cheer. We spent the night sleeping under the arches of Baslow Bridge, with our precious truck hidden from sight behind the cricket pavilion.

A few days before we left for the Sahara, our guidebook – *Climbs on Derwent Valley Limestone* – was typed up and Dick Stroud had it duplicated and bound, selling it at five shillings a copy, with all proceeds going to the Nottingham Climbers' Club. On 10 February I took my driving test for the second time, with a miserable examiner who looked like failing me again. I told him: 'Look, before you make your decision please consider that tomorrow I'm driving south to the Sahara where I can improve on any deficiencies in my driving without fear of harming other road users.' He told me it was quite wrong to try to influence his decision but as it happens he was going to pass me anyway. And so on 11 February, after a resounding send off from friends and family crowding the Salutation Inn, we left Nottingham for the desert.

The striking line of the grade-VI route *Spigolo Giallo* – the Yellow Edge – on the Cima Piccola, which I climbed with Steve 'Sid' Smith in 1963.

The team and trucks, ready to depart for Tibesti. L–R: Mick Garside, Steve Bowes, Pete Warrington, Dan Meadows, Ray Gillies, Clive Davies and Tony Watts. I'm crouching at the front.

TIBESTI

I was now twenty-three, married with a young son, holding down a steady job I found interesting, and was fit enough to play rugby every weekend and climb at a reasonable standard on rock and ice. So why was I again leaving all that behind to spend this time two months crossing the Sahara to climb in the Tibesti Mountains of Chad? I'd made the decision on the spur of the moment, on the edge of the Sahara just as we turned for home in 1962 after three weeks wandering in the Atlas. I felt a strong urge to continue exploring through that ever-changing landscape, where there was something new at every turn. For every mountain pass we struggled up, our reward was to see beyond the limits of our near horizon to a mysterious, empty land stretching far to the south, to an endless solitude.

My Michelin road map for North Africa indicated likely venues: the Jebel Marra, a volcanic plateau which rises to 3,000 metres in South Sudan and further east, Ras Dashen, at 4,550 metres the tenth-highest peak in Africa, in the Simien Mountains of Ethiopia. These were interesting areas, but they were not that far from main roads. There were no roads at all for hundreds of miles around the Tibesti of northern Chad. To reach the Tibesti from the north would take us right through the Sahara Desert, along gorges, over rocky plateaux, past the Aiguilles de Sisse and around the flanks of vast calderas to the unclimbed peaks of Tibesti. With its remote settlements in scattered oases this wilderness seemed the perfect place for our group to immerse itself.

There is a paradox in our blissful state of isolation, standing on the summit, that we wish others could share the experience and yet it never is quite the same experience when others actually do share the summit, like the summit of Snowdon on a bank holiday. The Tibesti had all the lure of simplicity of form without the distraction of crowds. As Wilfred Thesiger put it: 'I was exhilarated by the sense of space, the silence and the crisp clearness of the sand.

I felt in harmony with the past, travelling as men had travelled for untold generations across the deserts, dependent for their survival on the endurance of their camels and their own inherited skills.'

My fascination with this dry, eroded landscape also went back to my childhood visits to the Hemlock Stone. Its rocks had been formed in a similar desert 200 million years ago. On my first visit to Black Rocks ten years earlier, one of my fellow Scouts had spotted fossils in a spoil heap dumped next to one of the climbing routes. He had me searching through the rocks and, switched on to their significance, I became more and more interested in geology, finally taking an A level in the subject during the summer of 1964. It was mainly the outer geomorphological structure of rocks that grabbed my attention walking in the hills. Seeing the bare bones of the earth exposed on a mountainside, and especially in the bed of a youthful mountain stream. There, where the swirl of the rushing water armed with grit and pebbles had worn away at the bedrock to reveal faults and folding and intrusions, the subtle coloration made more vivid after rain, gave me so much pleasure. I have an equal fascination with rocks worn smooth from centuries of use, like the paving stones of the old road that crosses Stanage or the steps of temples in Kathmandu.

Beyond this simple calling, I did wonder if there was more to my ambition than a fascination for wild spaces. Before we left, there were reports in the local papers about our plans, quoting Doug Scott, 'the expedition leader'. The justification for publicity was attracting sponsorship for food, clothing, spare parts and batteries for the lorries. Yet what if this rationale were spurious? What if, as the climbing historian Roger Frison-Roche put it, 'the most powerful driving force was usually the desire for fame?' Even when I jumped into a project feet first, could I have been driven subconsciously by a need to impress others? In retrospect, I believe I wanted to be in the desert for the sake of it. When I made my decision, it was spontaneous, unclouded by any other consideration.

Just as I found rocks like the Hemlock Stone compelling, I have always been captivated by tales of those who went out from the comfort of hearth and home to face unpredictable hardships crossing oceans or exploring the unknown – like the legends of Odysseus in my encyclopaedia that I read by the light of Dad's police torch, under the sheets after lights out. I wonder often if there is something of the explorer in some of us if not everyone from ancient times, when our ancestors were first on the move out of Africa, looking over the distant horizon, facing up to uncertainty and risk on a daily basis. The one that went first was the one rewarded by the rest. That is how it is now and there is no reason to suppose it was any different in the beginning.

Could that be the driving force? Knowing he would be fêted on his return, admired and rewarded with the choicest food and most admired woman, achieving renown according to the magnitude of his journey. So it was for Gilgamesh, in the epic poem of his search for immortality written more than four thousand years ago: 'He was wise, he saw mysteries and knew secret things, he brought us a tale of the days before the flood. He went on a long journey, was weary, worn out with labour, and returning engraved on a stone the whole story.' For some that impulse to explore is so strong that it transcends reward. They go for the journey's sake.

These glorious quests into the unknown that set everyone's imagination soaring did not always end well. Alexander the Great was dead at thirty-two, Columbus was put in chains and died a broken man, the last voyage of Henry Hudson trying to find the North-West Passage ended up with a mutinous crew setting him and his small son adrift in an open boat, then there was Franklin and so many others who perished in the Arctic. In warmer climes, after three incredible journeys of discovery, James Cook was clubbed to death on Hawaii. But for every disaster there were those who made it home again, for every Scott of the Antarctic there was a Shackleton and a Wally Herbert, the hugely successful Charles Darwin on the Beagle Expedition, the courageous Thor Heyerdahl and his Kon-Tiki expedition across the Pacific and so many others. It seems to me that deep down in the soul of all these men, and women too like Freya Stark, Isabella Bird and Fanny Bullock Workman, if not in all of us, there is an impulse to look over that distant horizon, fascinated by the unknown. For some that impulse is so strong that it takes men away from kith and kin to explore the unknown country, not because the one who goes first is rewarded by the rest but they go without fear or favour for its own sake. I sometimes wonder if I don't look into things too deeply, for instance, the decision Jan and I made to get married was because at the time we were fed up of saying goodbye at the bus stop. The reason I hitched down through Spain to Morocco in 1959 was because I had already been the other way to Yugoslavia and now the next obvious destination was south, just to see.

Going to the Tibesti was the opposite of a cutting-edge, technically difficult climbing expedition; it was the kind of enterprise Harold Drasdo, in a polemical essay called 'Margins of Safety', described as the preserve of a 'tame tiger'. There are, he wrote, 'climbers who direct their energies into the opening-up of remote but minor mountain areas where the difficulties of access join with the mountain objectives to give a sense of commitment.' Although we didn't think about it at the time, for much of the journey across the Sahara to and from the Tibesti there would have been no chance of rescue if anyone had been injured or fallen ill. There was no radio contact and we didn't have much idea about technical difficulties we would face on our main objective, Tieroko.

By 28 February 1965, our two old army trucks with eight of us on board were on the edge of the Murzuq Sand Sea in southern Libya, 100 miles from the nearest oasis. I can't tell you how much time and effort I, and the rest of the team, had put into making this moment possible, how we had pressed family, friends and colleagues to help. It had been a giant jigsaw whose many pieces – leave of absence from school and family, climbing permits, raising funds, sorting out visas and carnets, keeping the team together – only fell into place after doggedly tackling each problem one at a time. The challenge was to keep up the momentum in the face of relentless bureaucracy. At Calais the French customs officials held us up for a day and then sealed the wagons for the entire drive across France to the Spanish border. Then it all began again: listing, twelve times over, every single item we carried.

Less than twenty years after the Allies had beaten Rommel, I found myself sitting on the stone benches of the Roman theatre at Sabratha on the coast of Libya, speculating on whether it was climate change or the goats I could see nibbling at bushes sprouting from the ruins that had caused the Sahara to advance. A British Army officer approached briskly and introduced himself as the commander of the Medenine barracks, Britain's last outpost in Libya, inviting us to stay. We were royally entertained, eating well and visiting Leptis Magna. The army even serviced our trucks.

The largest area of sand any of us had seen before was Skegness beach with the tide out. With our complete lack of desert travel experience setbacks were not unexpected. Now, on the edge of Murzuq, putting the trucks into four-wheel drive and selecting first gear, the drivers edged forward, cross-country tyres biting into the sand. Soon we were chugging along at a stately five miles per hour. Then we heard the dreadful sound of shearing metal. The bearing in the rear differential of the lead vehicle had broken into little pieces as the gears sheared off. The worst had happened in the worst possible place.

Ray Gillies, with help from Peter Warrington, got to work stripping down the differential and replacing the broken parts from the spares. Temperatures reached 46° Celsius and the hissing wind blew a fine layer of sand over the oily machinery. At first we congratulated ourselves on having reached the middle of the Sahara and that now we had something interesting to write about in our diaries but as the hours ticked by, the sense of isolation grew. Finally, after eight hours, we were ready to move again. Someone recalled Roger Akester advising us to deflate the tyres, spreading the load like a camel's foot, to ease the stress of driving on sand. From now on, whenever the trucks started to dig into the sand, we also used tracks, eight-foot lengths of heavy punched metal, to keep moving forward. Working in pairs, sweat dripping off our half-naked bodies, we picked up the heavy tracks from the rear of the wagons and jogged them to the front. We kept this up for a couple of hours until we were deep into the sand sea. Gradually the drivers were able to move up the gears until we were away, gathering speed, over the sand all the way to the last oasis of Al Qatrun.

Meeting the Bedouin at Al Qatrun while en route to Tibesti.

There was a customs post here, which took time, but that gave us the oppor-tunity to meet the Bedouin who were there en masse after travelling hundreds of miles with their camels from Sudan. They stood apart from the coastal Arab officials scrutinising our passports. The Bedouin were fair skinned with strong, hooked noses – proud, self-contained men of the desert. The Libyan authorities had promised them work, a home and £50 besides if they would settle in towns. With the sale of their camels the Bedouin would be relatively wealthy. Yet how could they possibly settle down after a life wandering the desert? Inspired by Wilfred Thesiger, most of us wished we had been able to join such a camel train.

We retrieved our passports after parting with a couple of bottles of whisky, topped up our water tanks, purchased a large pile of dates that had been buried in the sand to preserve them, and set off for Chad with no more officials or anyone else for 400 miles. About fifty miles south of Al Qatrun we came across clumps of fossilised trees and drove across the fine silt of an ancient lakebed. In parts the wind had scoured through the deposits, creating parallel humps, known as 'yardangs', up to ten feet high, streamlined by the prevailing wind. Here and there we found snail fossils and nodules of a metallic substance rather like the haematite or 'kidney ore' of Cumbria, most likely formed from volcanic dust from the Tibesti falling into water and coalescing to form in these strange concretions. As we left the lakebed, we found on the ancient shoreline more clumps of fossilised trees, this time clearly showing growth rings.

En route to Chad. Ray driving one of the trucks, with Clive, Dan and Tony on the roof and Pete in the back.
Photo: Mick Garside.

A few miles further on we reached an area marked on the old French maps as *Terrain Roches Chaotiques*. They weren't joking. The vehicles lurched and creaked over bare rock carved into blocks rather like the clints and grykes at Malham in Yorkshire. Fortunately, there was only a three-mile stretch and our overladen lorries performed magnificently, inching forward with the sand tracks clanking on the sides. We had crossed the Tropic of Cancer, the first time any of us had done so. Navigation in the desert wasn't easy in the 1960s, long before satellite positioning systems. We didn't have a sextant either, just a Silva compass. Thanks to our unofficial navigator Dan Meadows having the uncanny knack of always knowing precisely where he was, we drove directly to the Korizo Pass, about fifty miles inside the border of Chad. We were anxious about crossing this, since deep sand dunes periodically blocked the route, but they were insignificant obstacles when we passed through, and with the use of sand tracks, easily negotiated. The pass, gateway to Chad and the Tibesti, had been partly blasted out by General Leclerc in 1941 when he came up with the Free French from French Equatorial Africa in a convoy of over fifty vehicles. They joined the Eighth Army and played a useful role in the North African campaign against Rommel. Several abandoned vehicles and oil drums bore testimony to their passing.

We camped near to the Aiguilles de Sisse, huge, cathedral-like sandstone towers rising sheer from the desert floor for a thousand feet. We could drive right to the foot of these towers since there was no debris or scree. Marked on the rock were petroglyphs depicting ostrich, giraffe and other animals long extinct in Tibesti – driven south by the expanding desert. We did see small herds of gazelle and one lorry gave chase, its passengers armed with red and white survey poles like lances poised for the kill. With a short burst of speed the gazelle were soon out of range. We debated whether or not we could have shot such graceful and harmless creatures had we been carrying a gun. On the return journey, with depleted food reserves, I doubt if the question would have arisen.

At last, we had our first view of the mountains we'd come to climb, a serrated skyline hovering above the desert haze as we followed a track rising eastwards towards Pic Toussidé at 3,315 metres, the westernmost volcano in Chad. Just as the sun was setting behind the Aiguilles we arrived on the rim of Trou au Natron, a vast, volcanic caldera. Suddenly we were looking down some 2,000 feet into a crater approximately five miles in diameter with an extinct central sulphur cone and a volcanic plug sprouting out of the white sodium salts of the crater floor. It was among the most incredible things we'd ever seen. Roger Akester told us that in 1961 a DC3 airliner was chartered to fly around the inside of the crater, below the rim.

The route on to Tieroko took us first to Bardai where a Berlin University field study group welcomed us to their well-equipped research building and a fridge full of beer that quickly disappeared. The Germans had a longstanding interest since the first European to explore Tibesti was the German Gustav Nachtigal in 1869. He was the first European to penetrate the massif but during a particularly dry period. After 'discovering' Trou au Natron, which was very well known to the Bedouin, Gustav made his way to Bardai where the hard-pressed Tibbu took most of his food and possessions. He managed to salvage his maps and notes, which were later used by the next European expedition to Tibesti, that of the French commandant Jean Tilho. Tilho subsequently spent five years mapping the whole area, including the surrounding deserts. We later met the black African administrators who now governed the Tibesti and the Tibbu. Before the French arrived in the 1920s the Tibbu had kept them as slaves; now this once proud warrior race sat about their villages sharpening swords and spears, dreaming perhaps of the time when they rode a thousand miles across the desert to the Hoggar, raiding the Tuaregs and bringing back their women and camels to Tibesti.

Having completed formalities without any fuss, we left one truck at the research centre and drove the other on rough tracks through a lifeless landscape, save the occasional acacia tree, to Yebbi-Bou, 120 miles further east. We put up in an old French fort now guarded by one local soldier and his friends from the village. Tony Watts, Steve Bowes and Dan headed off, after a five-day wait, with a heavily laden camel to the volcano Tarso Toon to climb all the high peaks in the area. The rest of us, after failing to hire camels at a rate we could afford, drove forty miles south and then north-west up a wadi that led us to within five miles of the village of Modra. After four weeks' driving, we had arrived at our base.

In 1938 Wilfred Thesiger had been the first European into this valley and there had most likely not been any visits since. Clive Davies and I were the first into Modra and were immediately invited into a hut by two tribesmen, once they had got over their surprise at seeing two young Englishmen wandering around their village. They did not speak French but we were shown by sign language to sit and rest on a mat in front of a crackling fire. Cool water from the wadi was passed round, which was a luxury to be savoured after weeks of drinking water stored in jerry cans that tasted faintly of turpentine. A bowl of dates was handed round and slowly consumed, while an old woman, dressed in a tattered black dress, tended the fire.

It grew dark soon after our arrival, but in the firelight I watched the long fingers of our host as he carefully prepared tea. Then a long, sinewy arm reached out across the charcoal embers, handing us both a small glass of a very strong and refreshing brew infused from local herbs and spices. The moonlight filtering through the door allowed us to take in our strange surroundings. Closely woven reed baskets hung from the palm-wood frame of this guest room. By the low entrance hall stood a tall, wooden bowl with a long, wooden pounder, used to crush corn for the evening meal of couscous. The floor was sifted gravel, spotlessly clean and with no odours at all until we arrived covered in grime and sweat.

Our two male hosts had daggers hanging below their armpits. They sat cross-legged, in the lotus position, both wearing turbans and long, striped smocks; their feet were partly covered by open sandals and bore the scars from a lifetime stepping on sharp rocks and prickly thorn bushes. With conversation reduced to the occasional sign from our hands, we had time to consider the enormous difference between this simple hut and our own complicated homes in Nottingham 5,000 miles away. We also contemplated our good fortune in finding the inhabitants so friendly and hospitable, although we turned down their offers to stay the night and walked the five miles back to our lorry for a stew and a regular cup of tea.

In the morning we all moved to the village with our baggage where the villagers, realising we were not just passing through, offered us a hut which we gladly rented for the next three weeks. Our daily routine was to wake early in the cool of morning, when we would fetch water and dead wood from around the wadi and have porridge and coffee. Then Mick Garside and I, armed with theodolite and plane table, worked on the map we were triangulating. We also aimed to indicate on our plan of the settlement how the land was used and the system of irrigation. Two local lads, dubbed Coke and Freddy,

Tarso Tieroko, from the south-west.

were useful assistants, holding poles and stretching out the chain measurer. Coke agreed to organise donkey transport to take water and food up towards Tieroko. Fred became our faithful Tibbu servant around the hut, fetching wood and water and putting on brews for bed tea for as long as our barley sugars held out. This gave us an extra hour in bed, which was well worth foregoing sweets.

With the sun at its zenith we walked back to the hut and slept in its cool interior until late afternoon, when villagers began arriving to demand pills for headaches or stomach cramp and treatment for cuts and festering sores. We treated septic wounds quite effectively with antibiotics but for ailments we couldn't handle we worked on the principal of psychological healing and gave aspirin from our first-aid boxes, donated by Boots – the Nottingham chemist. As in the Atlas, our first-aid provision gained us many friends among the Tibbu.

There was one illness we couldn't do anything about. Clinging high above the wadi was a spring-line settlement, over a thousand feet higher than ours, where an old woman lay in her hut, grossly swollen around her stomach and ankles. We offered her some food, aspirin and vitamin pills and just to comfort her we walked up twice a day. We were given cool goats' milk and dates by her daughters. Below the old woman's hut was a waterfall that sparkled as it cascaded over a black, basalt dyke into a deep green pool. The water was led along a large channel cleverly contouring above the fields. From this main channel the water passed through an intricate maze of subsidiary channels to each of the small fields below. After watering the terraced fields at four or five levels, only a small trickle arrived back at the wadi floor.

It never ceased to amaze us how self-sufficient the villagers were. Material for huts came from within a few yards of where they were built; dates and millet grew abundantly, as did tea and various root crops. Goats provided fresh meat and daily milk. Goat hair was used for spinning into yarn and woven into rough clothing. Goatskins made a variety of domestic utensils, dagger-sheaths and gourds but were most useful in making sandals and saddles for the camels. Date palms provided food, fuel and shelter; the stones were ground down to a powder for animal fodder. Fibres from palm trunks were matted together to form pads for saddles and also twisted into stout rope and woven into baskets with reeds from the wadi. We watched as the women wove rush mats and wound rushes into coils and then into bowls that were so closely fitted as to be watertight. Only fabric for clothes and a few metal goods came from beyond Modra Wadi, paid for from the sale of dates, goats and, on rare occasions, camels. Anything else seemed superfluous to their needs.

We soon adapted to our new environment, sitting for hours bartering for a woven reed bowl with an old woman wearing crude, leather sandals, a black smock, a ring in her nose and a colourful scarf, gypsy fashion, around her plaited hair that glistened with goat fat. Pete played his mouth organ while Clive began sketching the Tibbu by the white light of the pressure lamp. The young men had brought their wives along and they collapsed in hysterics at the drawings. The men broke into excited chatter when we showed them photographs of Thesiger's Arabs from Arabia, pointing out the differences in apparel and their camels – and the rolling dunes that were absent from Tibesti.

Time passed all too quickly in Modra, and we needed to focus on Tieroko. On the drive round we had seen it from every side but at a distance it was little more than a silhouette. Our French maps did not explain the complicated gorges that carved up the region. A sketch from the first Cambridge expedition in 1957 helped fill in the picture. They narrowly failed on Tieroko but climbed other peaks in the vicinity. Tieroko, at 2,910 metres, is actually the highest point on the south side of another eroded crater rim. The area is particularly isolated, barren and difficult to traverse. Torrential downpours that occasionally drench the mountains cause the temporary streams to eat deep into the soft volcanic rocks. They have cut the mountains into serrated ridges and crazy pinnacles that make route finding a formidable problem. Yet the main problem was maintaining adequate water supplies. In the whole of our journey in North Africa we only saw running water at Modra and the only water in the mountains comes from rock pools known as *guelta*.

We left Modra with two heavily laden donkeys and Coke whom we hoped would point out the waterholes. Walking over ten miles of boulder-strewn country, we then crossed dry valleys draining the south side of Tieroko's crater, eventually coming to the wadi that drained Tieroko itself. We slept the night by some stone circles and Coke returned home after indicating that water could be found at the bottom of the wadi. We climbed down and then back up towards the west ridge of Tieroko, carrying the maximum amount of water we could manage, two gallons each, which weighed in itself twenty pounds. With all our climbing gear and food, our sacks weighed fifty pounds. To reach the ridge, we crossed rough slabs to a dyke of softer rock that provided a line of weakness. It was five very tired, red-faced ramblers who settled down for the night. According to my diary, we cooked our thirtieth stew of the expedition and watched the fabulous sunset.

Perhaps because of the altitude, we did not sleep well and were up early, shivering in the cold of morning. I had read that snow falls in the Tibesti at this time of year on the rare occasions there is precipitation. Now I believed it. After coffee and porridge, we explored the western side of the peak to find a route on to the final summit cone but our search was in vain and we were forced to climb back up 4,000 feet to our bivouac. Running short of water, we turned down the west ridge to Paradise Wadi – so named for the trees around some murky, stagnant pools. Very tired, we slung off our packs and soon had a roaring fire, feasting on corned beef hash and settling in for a better night's sleep by the glowing embers.

Food was now the issue, so we rose early for another attempt to find a way on to the upper section of Tieroko, following the gorge, sometimes on the left bank, sometimes on the right, around deep pools on the wadi floor. We saw wild Barbary sheep, powerful beasts with magnificent horns and capable of gigantic leaps but still able to maintain their balance on the most crumbly rock. Finally, having turned up a right branch of the wadi's gorge, we came to a pool that proved to be one of the highest in all the Tibesti, from which we based our final attempt.

A peak overlooking the pool gave us a good view of Tieroko and then we settled in by a fire of acacia wood, singing songs late into the night in honour of St Patrick's Day. With the last of the porridge gone, we left our gear behind and, taking only water, headed back to Modra in six hours to begin a marathon pancake session. We spent the next few days in the village to rest, and then returned to our camp by the high pool, leaving Mick behind to continue our geographical work. The next day we reached a shoulder on the north-west side where, to our delight, there seemed a reasonable route to the steep summit cone of Tieroko. Ray and I went up to have a look at the route while Pete and Clive went down for more gear and water, as we thought the steep rock above might involve considerable pegging.

A montage of the huge north face of Tarso Tieroko.

When we got to the west ridge and traversed 400 feet towards the south-west ridge, we found a shallow gully of smooth, weathered rock that we felt could be the key to the summit. The couloir gave us 150 feet of interesting, delicate climbing at about Very Severe standard that we protected with two pegs we had with us. From its top we gained access to a *brèche* from where we could look down the north side of the mountain.

From below we heard our two 'coolies' shouting up at us; we spotted them sitting among the rocks surrounded by a pile of equipment and cans of water they had just lugged up from below. They told us we were nearly at the top. After 250 feet of more Very Severe climbing and then some easy scrambling we were, much to our amazement, both sitting on the summit of Tieroko. We hadn't even brought a camera and there was now enough gear at the bottom to climb the north face of the Cima Grande. I have to admit that although ours was the first human ascent, we found wild-sheep droppings on the summit. We built a cairn and then abseiled down to the *brèche* and to the shoulder below it. Soon I was back at camp reading James Bond and drinking a brew. Both Ray and I felt quite guilty that the whole team had not been up there together. Clive and Pete were far too polite to complain and simply offered their congratulations and looked forward to joining us on further ascents next day.

Pete, now climbing with Ray, went round to try the south ridge and after some complicated route finding and abseils, reached the ridge and climbed pleasantly to the top. Clive and I tried the top part of the peak's north side; after 400 feet zigzagging about the face on difficult ground, we came to the *brèche* of the previous day. On the way we found an abseil piton from a previous attempt, either the British in 1957 or a Belgian team, Michel Demeulemeester and Jean Lecomte, who visited the area in 1961. We all met up on the top, having now climbed Tieroko by three different routes. We took bearings on other peaks and drew a rough sketch map. From our vantage point we could see, fanning out in all directions, fossilised water courses that may well flow inter-mittently on those rare occasions when Tibesti is drenched in rain. We thought of the lads over in Tarso Toon and wondered how they were getting on.

We also looked across at the peak to the north called Imposter by the 1957 expedition and thought of their disappointment at having found that Tieroko was indeed higher than the peak they were on. Thanks to their information we went to the right mountain first time. Then we returned to the high pool and the following day reached two cols to the north and climbed minor peaks in-between, to take bearings for our sketch map. We had thought of descending to the crater floor and leaving by its north exit but the abseils and long walk might have delayed us beyond our water reserves so we abandoned the idea and returned to Modra. I suppose, as is usual when the main objective is realised, some of our enthusiasm for further climbing evaporated. We did

Ray leading on Tieroko.

register the fact that it would be worth returning here to tackle the whole of the north face rearing up from the crater floor, involving some 3,000 feet to the summit of Tieroko.

Back at Modra, Mick was pleased to hear of our ascents. In our absence he had been able to press on with our field study of the valley. We began to pack our gear for the return drive to Bardai while Ray, Pete and Clive prepared to walk back – a distance of eighty-five miles. It took them two and a half days and it soon became an ordeal; they spent the final day without any water with their tongues swollen and lips cracked walking under the white sun blistering their faces. At one point they spotted a lone goat which they attempted to catch and milk. Their feeble efforts to trap it against a rock cliff were observed by a very surprised herdsman who emerged from behind some rocks to show them a damp patch on the wadi floor. They hastily dug for water and drank their fill of the chocolate-coloured nectar that filtered into the hollow they had made. While this epic unfolded, Mick and I finished off the geographical field work, settled up with the villagers at Modra and, after a bone-shaking ride, arrived back in Bardai just after Tony, Dan and Steve. They were very impressed with the Tarso Toon region where they managed to climb several pinnacles of excellent, solid rock. They also found several caves and numerous artefacts and pottery of considerable age.

Luckily for us, we were there when the German ambassador's wife came to visit the field study centre. We were treated to rotwurst, herring in mayonnaise, tinned camembert and more, all washed down with heavenly cold beer hoarded for the occasion. We took the opportunity to have a long chat with the centre's professor who answered many of the questions we had about the Tibbu and their customs. The men, we discovered, have several wives scattered among the mountains and spend their lives wandering from one to the other, living off plots of land and date trees they own in each wife's village. The local administrators had a difficult time when a wife wanted a divorce because several different families may own different parts of a date palm. One may lay claim to the leaves, another to the dates and yet another to the trunk. The same applied to the goats and to the land. It all added to our determination to return to the Tibesti in the future.

Ray and Pete were able to repay the Germans' generosity in a small way by servicing their vehicles. Then we left Bardai to visit several sites of Neolithic rock carvings and to walk down to the crater floor of Trou au Natron. We collected rocks from each horizon on the way back up including the green, glass-like rock from a lens of obsidian. From the rim of the crater we photographed the Pic Botoun in case we needed another excuse to return to this incredible region. In so many ways it had been an unforgettable journey, partly because of the landscape but most of all because of the Tibbu and their communities, outwardly so vastly different from our own and yet having the same aspirations and fears all of us share.

We halved the return journey to the coast but not without incident. As we left Bardai smoke billowed from under the canvas of the leading lorry, which carried all 120 gallons of petrol we needed to reach Sebha. Our first reaction was to leap out of the lorry, run across the sand and take cover behind rocks. It didn't take us long to return, having realised if it did blow up we would be stuck in Tibesti for a very long time. We pulled off the oily tarpaulin, now actually on fire, to find a crowbar had fallen across the nine terminals of our very powerful chrome-nickel batteries. We levered the crowbar off with a Tibbu spear and squirted the neighbouring forty-gallon petrol drum with the fire extinguisher since its paint was now bubbling from the heat. We then continued north.

After crossing the *Roches Chaotiques* we sadly abandoned one of the lorries. The major difficulties had passed and the ferry fare to Sicily would have cost more than the lorry, not to mention petrol and other costs. Leaving a lorry invited trouble and it came in the form of four punctures and an oil leak in the transfer box of the remaining vehicle. Eventually we re-crossed the Murzuq Sand Sea and reached the North African coast and Europe via the ferry from Tunis to Palermo. After an interesting visit to Pompeii we drove over the Saint Bernard Pass to Martigny, Geneva, Calais and home for Easter.

Perhaps this expedition made such a powerful impression because it was our first, but the truth is that travelling to the Tibesti was one of the most incredible journeys anyone could make, crossing the Sahara and staying with the Tibbu, locked away in those isolated mountain valleys. Perhaps also the impressions of our journey registered so strongly because the contrasts were so marked. During the day temperatures were so high in the desert, reaching an unbearable climax just before noon, with heat striking up from the rock and the air itself hot and heavy. There was no greenery among the harsh, shimmering red rocks, no peace from the revving engines and the clanking sand tracks hooked on the sides of the lorries and all the time the sickly smell of spilt oil and evaporating petrol. Everything – clothes, hair, skin – became coated in dust, even the food.

The sun would go down, the noise stopped, and we would wash away the dust and there was time to enjoy the peace of the evening, especially when stepping out from our little world, illuminated by the headlights. Only then did the desert impress itself upon us with the sun setting in a fierce array of colours, as we reflected humbly on the enormity of the Sahara. On walking back into the light of our camp, sitting around the simmering stew on the Primus stove, I thought how much this adventure had brought us all together, up in the mountains, toiling in the sun and resting in the evening in the clean mountain air, of being away from our ordinary lives among new kinds of people, from the disappointment of retreat and the elation of finally reaching our objective. Although not a mountaineer, the desert traveller Wilfred Thesiger put it best: 'No, it is not the goal but the way there that matters, and the harder the way the more worthwhile the journey.'

We made plans for our return and Wilfred Thesiger himself agreed to act as our patron. Within a few years, while King Idris was in Turkey for medical treatment, he was deposed in an army *coup d'état* lead by Colonel Gaddafi who went on to play war games in the desert, laying land mines all around the approaches to Tibesti from the north. A few years ago a Swedish expedition was approaching the Aiguilles de Sisse when their vehicle hit a landmine and all four occupants were blown to pieces.

Jan and Michael at Black Rocks in 1964.

HINDU KUSH

At Sebha, capital of the Libyan district of Fezzan, Steve got a letter from his mother. On the envelope she'd written: Steve Bowes, Sebha Post Office, North Africa. How it got there I don't know. I also had a letter, from Jan, who vented her frustration at being left with two-year-old Michael for two months and the tension that had developed between Jan and my parents. Mum was sympathetic, up to a point, but she naturally compared Jan's situation to her own. At Jan's age she was bringing up two children with Dad away in the army for three years. That was no help to Jan. We weren't at war and she wasn't part of a community like Charlbury Road, brought together by a common enemy to help each other cope.

A letter from Dad made no mention of Jan's unhappiness but he told me my brother Garry had been seriously ill from meningitis. Fortunately he recovered without side effects. Dad had been laid low with a slipped disc but was now busy doing up the house, which he'd recently bought as a sitting tenant – for £700. After thirty years in the police service, Dad had taken compulsory retirement, though he was still only forty-nine years old. It might have been psychologically devastating, but he never seemed bored or depressed at having to leave the police and he was soon offered another job, this time in social services. While still in the police he had helped establish the successor to the borstal system of punishing young offenders, the Nottingham Attendance Centre for Juveniles. Now he joined social services' children's department, where he introduced many young people to walking and camping in the Peak District.

Jan was a lot happier after being accepted on a three-year course at Nottingham Teacher Training College. I agreed to help support her, both financially and with looking after Michael, as best I could, allowing for the extra overtime I would have to do in the evenings. Our flat in The Park was, on the face of it, ideal, being a quiet residential area not far from the centre of Nottingham.

I even had a tree opposite to practise pegging and prussiking. There was an Irish family on the floor above who were willing to babysit, but on more than one occasion Jan came home early to find the husband shouting and swearing at his own children and terrorising Michael. He was not the kind of man to change by us having it out with him so we decided to move.

Now I had a driving licence, I bought a minivan, our first car, which made our daily lives even more hectic. Each morning I took Michael to playschool two miles across town, dropped Jan off in the middle of town and then drove like a madman through rush hour to take the register at 8.55 a.m. In the evening, after basketball club, I did the journey in reverse, collecting Jan and poor little Michael who had been at playschool for ten hours, before eating tea and then driving back to school for two hours of evening classes.

Michael developed a rash on his face and under his arms that got worse with constant scratching. Our GP, Doctor Sprackling, confirmed eczema, something one in ten of us suffer. He didn't think it was to do with our lifestyle or with drinking cow's milk necessarily. In any case, he said, we weren't to worry; there was now a wonder cure – cortisone cream. His daughter, similarly afflicted, had used it. Michael's eczema miraculously disappeared for a while but soon returned and using the cream made his skin hypersensitive. We took matters into our own hands and gradually overcame the problem. He wore gloves at night, and we kept him away from wool, bathed him in warm water and used a moisturiser on his skin rather than soap. We also reduced his intake of cow's milk and watched out for other foodstuffs he was allergic to, particularly gelatine. While driving to Cornwall, with Michael sitting happily on the back seat eating jelly babies, Jan turned round to discover that his head had ballooned to almost twice its normal size. In a panic we rushed off to the local cottage hospital where they reduced the swelling with injections of antihistamine. No more gelatine after that.

We bought a house in Chilwell on the west side of town, a little box on a hill but with really friendly neighbours, most of them with young children. Janet opposite was more than willing to babysit Michael along with her own children. She knew my mother and Grandma Gregory; they had once been neighbours in The Meadows until re-housed under the slum clearance scheme. There was a police sergeant living next door, which worried Dad. The officer had a reputation as a stickler, issuing tickets to 500 cars during the Nottingham Goose Fair, and catching a hundred drivers still over the limit on New Year's Day from parties the night before. I tried to maintain good relations with the neighbours, possibly because of my childhood embarrassment at Mum's steaming rows with Mrs Boothwright next door. I even managed to stay calm with the copper next door, even when he claimed that our expedition lorries, parked in our drive alongside the wall of his house, were interfering with the reception on his radio. I moved them back to Skip Davies' Scout hut.

The expedition approaches the castle of Hoshab in Turkey.

Sitting in the Salutation Inn discussing the next Nottingham Climbers' Club project with Steve Read, I suggested an idea we'd had at Loughborough College to climb in the Cilo Dağı, a range of mountains in the predominantly Kurdish region of south-east Turkey, south-east of Lake Van and not far from the Iraqi border. Steve was in his probation year as a teacher and shared my interest in taking children into the hills. We decided to look into taking Cottesmore students with a keen interest in the outdoors to the Cilo Dağı as well as lads from the Meadows Boys' Club; the leader there, Dick Bell, had asked me to take some of his lads climbing in the Alps.

I put the idea of taking twenty boys to Kurdistan to my headmaster, Mr Happer. He said he would have to think about it. I saw him next morning in the school corridor: 'Scott,' he said, 'I have been considering your proposal to take the boys down to south-east Turkey. In the end I thought to myself, would I want Scott to take my own two sons down there? I decided I would. So off you go.' And that was it. There were no risk assessment forms to fill in and the only insurance we took out was for the vehicles. It might seem, on the face of it, that Mr Happer was being irresponsible, but I knew that when he said he had considered his own children, he meant it. Mr Happer, being old-school, was not the type to absolve himself of responsibility by putting his trust in certificates. He knew anyone could be coached to get a certificate without having much common sense at all. There was no substitute for experience.

As a result of Mr Happer's confidence, a few months later I found myself walking behind a big brown bull lumbering up a stony, twisting path in the Diz Valley towards the Cilo Dağı. Behind us stretched a column of thirty aspiring mountaineers from Nottingham schools and youth clubs and climbers from the Nottingham Climbers' Club. Our two lorries and a Land Rover were parked five miles away and 4,000 feet lower down, by the Great Zab river, which drains most of Kurdistan before it joins the Tigris south of Mosul in Iraq. After twelve days of almost continuous travel from Britain, it was pure joy to leave the hot and humid Zab for the clear, cool air of the mountains.

The bull and its amiable Kurdish drover were both a pleasant surprise, because until we met them we had no idea whether or not the Diz Valley was inhabited. Hans Bobek's German map of 1937 indicated only abandoned settlements and the writings of more recent travellers to the area had offered no clue. The ancient Christian sect known as the Nestorians had inhabited these highlands in recent centuries. On the outbreak of war in 1916 the Turks attempted to enlist their support. They failed and the Nestorians mobilised for the Allied cause after a Russian promise of help that never materialised. The Turks sacked their villages, massacring thousands and sending the survivors fleeing to all parts of the Middle East. They did make a comeback when 8,000 of the original 40,000 tried to resettle the old villages after the

The high peaks of the Cilo Dağı.

Ottoman Empire collapsed. In 1924 a Turkish column, harried by British aircraft, reasserted its authority in Hakkâri Province and drove the Nestorians from the mountains forever.

At midday our caravan halted at the village of Suva. A village elder dressed in a white smock and sporting a cloth cap made in Bradford and a pair of rubber shoes from Hong Kong bade us sit on the flat roof of his home, which was pleasantly shaded from the now glaring sun by giant walnut trees. Gradually the party gathered and rested aching backs and sore heels while chapattis and tea in small glasses were passed round. We feasted on goat cheese flavoured with onions in copper bowls, and sweet melons to round off a pleasant meal. Our efforts to repay this spontaneous hospitality with tins of coffee were met with embarrassed refusal. As we left, we waved to the villagers working in the fields of maize and tobacco and higher up the hillside setting up sheaves of straw for winter bedding and fodder.

Our route wound round jutting spurs and through deep gorges until the gradient eased somewhat and we could take in the sparkling snows and towering buttresses of the glaciers and mountains of the northern Cilo Dağı. This breathtaking view gave us new impetus and as the evening shadows lengthened so did our stride. We reached a perfect campsite at the junction of glacial streams draining the two major corries of the northern mountains to form the Mia Hvara river. The lush grass was covered with bright red, blue and yellow alpine flowers. On the opposite bank were pitched twelve black tents belonging to nomadic Kurds who herded their goats and sheep throughout these mountains. Groups of them came across the river with offerings of goats' milk, yoghurt and bread. In return they were pleased to get our empty coffee tins. They invited us over to their camp where women were agitating a goatskin gourd, full of milk, across a trestle. In five hours they would have butter. Older women stood spinning goats' hair on to a bobbin while younger women set up looms to weave fabric for their tents. The children overcame their shyness to join in games of football with some of the lads. In the evening herds of goats and sheep were brought down from the slopes above; there were bears in the mountains and most of the Kurds had an old Lee-Enfield with them as they walked along.

At first light the lads would leave in small groups with one or more experienced NCC members who acted as guides and climbing companions. Each group would try to climb routes on the rock faces and towering pinnacles above the surrounding glaciers. Some of these attempts were successful, some were not, but either way the experience was rewarding. A descent from a rock face and an unplanned bivouac at 12,000 feet often proved a more critical test of character and resourcefulness than if the climb had been straightforward. Of course the exhilaration of standing on top of a previously unclimbed summit is something to be savoured, however hard the route has been.

We hadn't planned the trip as a character-building exercise but every youngster had the chance to discover more about themselves. The lads were often hungry, thirsty and burdened with heavy sacks and found themselves living among strange people whose language they did not know and whose customs they were only beginning to understand when it was time to leave Kurdistan. Problems seem sharper when stripped of the comfort and security of a familiar city life. The boys displayed much good humour, and showed stoic indifference to the rigours of travelling, persistence and courage in the mountains and genuine concern for one another in times of difficulty and uncertainty. They had many shared experiences to look back on.

I loved being in the Cilo Daği. I hadn't expected the mountains to be quite so alpine. Nor had I expected the Kurds to be so friendly and hospitable. With Brian Palmer, I made the first ascent of a slender 700-foot pinnacle called Cafer Kule. The rock was quite solid and from the summit we had a wonderful vantage point to survey the whole of the Cilo Daği with its small glaciers nestling in corries below dramatic rock faces and the serrated skyline all around. The little climbing I did made up for the huge amount of time and energy I put into organising the venture – and the frustration of having to cope with Dick Bell, the youth leader whose boys we had hosted.

The expedition got a good deal of local publicity and because I was the one with the previous experience, I was the one journalists quoted. With every

Kurds at our base camp in Cilo Dağı.

radio interview or article that was published, Dick became more negative and resentful. He caused me more trouble and took up more time than all the twenty lads put together. As we drove across the mountains of northern Turkey, braking for a corner, the lorry lurched across the road unexpectedly, overturning the trailer we were pulling. Three lads had been sitting on it and were thrown clear along with sacks of flour that burst open, covering them from head to foot. They were grazed and shaken up, but luckily no bones were broken. This became a stick for Dick to use against me and he raged about my dangerous driving until the expedition's mechanic John Simmons emerged from under the lorry with a broken shackle pin that had destabilised the suspension. I was still in shock, imagining what might have happened, but the climbers and boys gave me their support and Dick was relegated to the second vehicle.

Unbeknown to us, just as we were preparing to leave Hakkâri, Turkey suffered a massive earthquake, to the north of where we were, close to the Iranian border. On newspaper billboards in Nottingham, parents were reading, 'City Boys Lost in Turkey Quake'. One hysterical mother burst in on Mr Happer, tearfully telling him that it had cost her £25 to send her son to his death. One tabloid reported that we were helping to rescue survivors. The first we heard about any of it was when we got our mail in Ankara, on the way home. It struck me then I would do well in future to treat the press with caution, given that they seemed to print anything to sell more papers.

I spent that next winter dreaming of new adventures. By the middle of winter, the frustration and hardships of the previous summer's climbing are forgotten. All you remember are precious moments above the snowline, out on some snowy ridge awakening from a bivouac, looking down on a sea of cloud and across to other peaks and distant mountain ranges. Those memories are enough to trigger months of planning. Following our visit to Kurdistan, I developed an urge to travel further east and climb higher peaks. After eight years and hundreds of routes in Britain and the Alps, I wanted to know if I could do similar things on higher peaks. The logical objective had to be the Hindu Kush mountains of Afghanistan, since at the time the Himalaya was largely restricted thanks to political tension across the region.

I had hoped Mick Garside would come with us and produce another geographical study, this time of the Panjshir Valley but Mick chose instead to marry his girlfriend Liz that Easter in Dublin. He gave me the honour of being best man. Jan had been offered a lift from Carlisle, where she was staying with her parents, but there was a mix-up and her lift disappeared without her. I was helping the bridesmaids to their seats in Dublin's main Catholic church when the door opened and Jan appeared, silhouetted against the bright sunshine, having hitched on her own from Carlisle. She promptly burst into tears.

After a lovely wedding, a team of us went off to Donegal to check out the coastal crags. We pulled up for the night by a barn near Enniskillen and early in the morning I went into the village to find water for a brew. Sitting on the stone surrounds of the village well was a little man dressed entirely in green who asked me: 'Would you be needing water?' I put the billycan on the side of the well and he pulled up a bucket full of sparkling fresh water and tipped it in. I thanked him. 'Not at all, not at all,' he replied and I walked back a little dazed. Not believing my own eyes, I went back with Jan and some of the lads, but he had gone. I wasn't totally surprised nobody believed me as I could hardly believe it myself. It's not as if we had been drinking heavily the night before.

During the mid-1960s I became increasingly fond of Ireland, particularly Donegal. Many of our visits were during the Easter holidays and were accompanied by April showers and rainbows galore, the landscape vibrant in the clear fresh air blowing off the Atlantic, driving the waves up the cliffs. There was fishing off Teelin pier and nights in Hughie Gallagher's bar in Bunbeg. The pubs would be open until 11.30 p.m. and then we'd move to an adjoining room and local musicians would start playing until the small hours. Sometimes there'd be a dance with all the ladies down one side of the room and all the men along the other.

I sympathised with the Irish people's determination to regain their freedom from English rule. As a separate people they had different aspirations. The main one, it seemed to me, was to remain as far as possible rooted in the land,

The impressive face of Sail Rock.

Ray Gillies on *Roaring Forty*.

growing spiritually without being entirely consumed by material things. That view was articulated on St Patrick's Day in 1943 by the first Taoiseach, Éamon de Valera, how the 'Ireland which we dreamed of would be the home of a people who valued material wealth only as the basis of right living, of a people who were satisfied with frugal comfort and devoted their leisure to the things of the spirit.' De Valera saw how important it was to cultivate those things 'which mark us out as a distinct nation,' and the first of those things was the Gaelic language. 'It is for us what no other language can be ... It has been moulded by the thought of a hundred generations of our forebears. In it is stored the accumulated experience of a people, our people, who even before Christianity was brought to them were already cultured and living in a well-ordered society ... To part with it would be to abandon a great part of ourselves ... '

With Sam Lewis and other members of staff we ran youth-hostelling trips to Donegal with boys from school and began exploring with friends from the NCC, climbing on Mount Errigal and exploring in the Poisoned Glen. We looked also at Slieve League, since, at 2,000 feet high, it was routinely described as the highest sea cliff in Europe. It may well have been the biggest but it was far too broken to climb, with little continuously solid rock. Then, on a school outing from Teelin pier to Slieve League we came across a Martello Tower, which was interesting enough, but just below I spotted a huge unbroken slab that looked much more solid, named by local fishermen as Sail Rock, since that was how it appeared from the ocean.

After Mick's wedding, Ray Gillies and I explored all the sea cliffs between Teelin and Slieve League and agreed there was little of interest except Sail Rock. Finding a way down to its base, we climbed up its left edge for 230 feet to the top. The crag was solid and weathered with plenty of protection; it was quite a find. We called our route *Roaring Forty* and came back the following year to do more. We also spent a day fishing off Teelin pier but caught nothing. We were thinking of giving up when a tall man approached us carrying a long, bendy wooden pole with a line on it. He introduced himself as Jim and said he had been watching us from his cottage. Then he cast his lure and immediately pulled out a pollock, and then two more in quick succession. That was enough for his supper, he said, and he stopped fishing. Jim told us he had been waiting for the tide to change. His technique was to fix half a red rubber seal from under the lid of a marmalade jar on to the hook and then throw it out and wriggle it back in. He passed us his pole and hook and within half an hour we had yanked out over thirty fish, including, just before dark, a five-foot conger eel.

A month after Mick's wedding, in late May, a dozen of us from the Nottingham Climbers' Club set off in two ex-war department Austin K9 one-ton lorries, crossing Turkey and Iran into Afghanistan, in those days a

The south face of Koh-i-Bandaka in the Hindu Kush.

more open society more oriented to the West under its last king Zahir Shah. The target of our ambitions was the Hindu Kush, the range of mountains that radiate south-west from the Pamir Knot into Afghanistan. The highest mountain, at 7,690 metres, is Tirich Mir close to Pakistan's north-west frontier with Afghanistan. The highest point in the central Hindu Kush is Koh-i-Bandaka, 6,850 metres high, which had been climbed half a dozen times via the west ridge, mostly by German and Austrian groups who had been very active in the area.

Having so many in the team and travelling overland reduced the costs substantially; the organisational challenges of such a large group were solved in Kabul by dividing the team in two. One group headed off to the Panjshir Valley to climb Mir Samir, with Eric Newby's *A Short Walk in the Hindu Kush* as guidebook. The other six, including myself, went north through the Salang Tunnel towards Fayzabad, to concentrate on the central Hindu Kush and Koh-i-Bandaka.

The rest of this northern group included Guy Lee, then a fitter, with a list of good Alpine peaks under his belt, and Mick Terry, who worked at the Royal Ordnance factory in Nottingham and was also curious to test his Alpine climbing experience at altitude. Ken Vickers, an architect from Leicester, was the only member not from Nottinghamshire. We had met Ken in the Alps and during weekends in Wales and Derbyshire. Ray Gillies, Tony Watts and myself completed the team.

It took three days of negotiation to come up with a reasonable deal for sixteen mules and muleteers at Hazrat-i-Sayet, south of Fayzabad in the province of Badakhshan, but once we got going, things went well. We followed a wide track alongside the Kokcha river past the mines at Sar-i Sang, where the lapis lazuli used in the mask of Tutankhamun originated. Then, on the third day, we met a group of porters recently employed by a Japanese expedition. These porters had been given new training shoes and wristwatches and even a duvet jacket or two. As if it were the signal for battle to commence a Japanese alarm clock went off. Our porters immediately took the loads off the mules and asked for their shoes and watches. They also demanded double wages. We were definitely not going any further that day.

The following afternoon we were busy trying to jolly our lads along with arm and leg wrestling when Ray, a brown belt, began a judo demonstration with Mick. At this moment a tall, straight-backed Nuristani came walking into camp. He took the rifle from his shoulder, placed it on the grass and stood there taking in the scene. One of the porters, meanwhile, could not resist trying his hand at judo. To the delight of the crowd, Ray threw him over his back, all in the wink of an eye, the porter flying in an arc of swirling clothes to land in a cloud of dust where he was pinned to the ground by Ray. The Nuristani, who had been speaking quietly to the head porter, now addressed all of them. They all stood up and walked over to their loads and loaded them on to the mules. The strike was over. After a brew we shook hands with this diplomat of such noble bearing and set off up the valley puzzled but pleased at the turn of events, wondering if he could possibly be a descendant of Alexander's Greeks. On the fourth day of actual walking we arrived at Skazar from where our Hazrat men turned with their donkeys for home, leaving us to engage local transport. Three days later, having crossed several swollen streams, we arrived at Base Camp with half our baggage. The rest we left at the Alakadoree police post by the Munjan River. We would need these supplies later in the Sharan Valley.

At Base Camp we found the Japanese, an expedition of students from the Chuo University Alpine Club in Tokyo. Their leader, Professor Itakura, received us very hospitably. They were already hard at work siege-climbing the west ridge of Koh-i-Bandaka, fixing ropes and establishing camps. We hoped to climb the south face, but with the same tactics we used in the Alps – packing a rucksack and going in one continuous push. By the time we had reconnoitred the route Mick and Ken decided they would rather climb the attractive peaks further north above the beautiful Sakhi Glacier basin. The rest of us established an igloo camp under the face at about 5,700 metres. It was near here, in 1965, that the British climber John Wilson, deviating from a known path across the glacier, perished falling 120 feet down a crevasse and breaking his neck.

Me (left) and Guy in the igloo camp below the south face of Bandaka.

We all had headaches but that wasn't surprising; we had hardly stopped to acclimatise other than making one trip down to Base Camp for more food. Our chosen route up the south face of Koh-i-Bandaka looked quite easy compared to the climbs we had been doing in the Alps and Dolomites, so we were tempted to rush. Then we could move on to the relatively unexplored region of the Sharan Valley as soon as possible. We failed to bear in mind all that we had read and learned about altitude sickness. Guy and Tony were feeling the effects a little more than Ray and I so after crossing into the main couloir of the south face they sensibly decided to descend. It all happened quite suddenly, one minute we were four then we were only two.

It was a sad parting and I felt my own resolve dwindling as soon as they left. Ray and I talked ourselves into continuing by agreeing to go a little further – just to see. Carrying forty-pound packs, we got our heads down, looking neither to the left nor the right but concentrating only on the steep patch ahead. There was not much to see anyway. Cloud clung to the mountain and the higher we climbed the thicker it became. Finding the route was now a problem as the couloir steepened and narrowed, terminating at a rock step. It was 4 p.m. and having climbed from 5,500 metres to 6,500 metres with loads that severely aggravated our poor acclimatisation we felt shattered.

Lacking the strength to negotiate the rocks ahead safely, we dropped our heavy sacks on the snow, pegged them down and began to dig a snow hole for the night. Breaking through the crust, we dug out softer snow with the shovel until we hit hard black ice after four feet, chipping away at this like coal miners in the confined space we'd excavated, lying on our backs and jabbing away. It was better than being outside stamping about with frozen boots. Our heads were spinning with altitude and we were in some danger of tumbling backwards down to the glacier below. The sky darkened but our cave took shape and finally we both had room to lie flat out. We pushed the sacks and a length of sponge under our hips, kicked loose ice chips into the entrance and snuggled into our sleeping bags. After a brew of tea and a tin of ravioli, we were asleep and remained so for eight hours until woken by spindrift inching its way into our sleeping bags and chilling our necks.

It was good to lie up there with Ray, stocky and built to last, doggedly determined and with the ability to climb steep rock and ice fast and safely. His familiar company helped me fight off the temptation of Base Camp. We didn't speak much; we had been together so often during the previous ten years there wasn't a lot that had not already been said. We just got on with what we had to do, saving our energy for what was essential. As Ray had prepared the evening meal I organised breakfast. I felt shattered just trying to sit up and my befuddled brain required some prompting to unearth the gas stove and make some hot sweet tea. That was all we could manage without vomiting.

By 8.30 a.m. we had put on frozen boots, fixed crampons and left the little snow hole, leaving chunks of sponge stuck to the floor. We wanted to get up and off quickly, not relishing another night on the face, so we gave each other a pep talk before making a long traverse to the right. Then we collapsed over our axes, gasping for air. We just about managed to keep going, encouraged by our sighting of a way through a difficult step above. After several abortive attempts we traversed around a buttress and on the far side found a steep gully filled with almost vertical snow. This led for a hundred feet to a cornice. Ray belayed and I knocked in a piton at the base of the buttress, conscious of the extreme effort required at nearly 6,700 metres.

I breathed deeply for several minutes, fighting for oxygen, and then started up the buttress, jamming my hands in a crack and doing a bridging move with one foot on the rock and another stuck in the vertical snow. I fumbled in another runner and took off my gloves to clip the rope. For some unaccountable reason I left my gloves inside my anorak pocket and took to the snow, digging in with my bare hands and banging my frozen boots, now like wooden clogs, into large bucket steps. Ray patiently payed out the rope not knowing what I was doing, being out of sight and beyond hearing. I found the hard climbing reinvigorated my weary muscles and I was surprised to find my head banging against the lip of the overhanging cornice. I could look down at a neat set of steps dropping away and round the corner to Ray.

Large lumps of snow dropped away as my axe cut through the overhang. I sank the shaft over the top, well back from the edge, wriggled and mantelshelved over the axe's head and found myself above the rock step. Looking up, sprawled out on the snow, I saw a long, easy-angled ice field leading to another rock step. Then I braced myself against a rock frozen into the ice and took in the rope through now unfeeling fingers. The pain was awful as my extremities recovered, and I lay back groaning.

It had taken nearly two hours of hard labour to climb the gully, but Ray made short work of it. The slope ahead was easy-angled but deceptively dangerous; crossing the wind-scoured ice took three hours. With each buffet from the wind we were knocked off balance. We had to catch ourselves and pause before resuming our plodding gait ten paces at a time before flopping down pathetically for a few minutes while the other took over the lead.

It was during one such rest, crouched over crampon points and ice axe, that we realised there was no going back the way we had come. We'd ditched our snow stakes lower down to save weight and we now no longer had the strength to climb down safely. There was no other choice except to reach the summit and traverse down the easy-angled west ridge. Thoughts of going down ended there; all our energies were now channelled upwards. With this new commitment we gained our second wind and moved up more readily, if still very slowly. The ice tilted more steeply as we approached the second rock step, and the weather worsened, so that it now loomed up out of cloud, snowflakes and spindrift.

At only 3 p.m. we had no more strength to continue so we dug another cave to guarantee a night safe from the predatory wind. Our decision to take a shovel rather than a tent had been a wise one. Yet while snow holes don't blow away, they do fill with spindrift as we discovered next morning. I grabbed the stove, which promptly stuck to my bare right hand. In trying to pull it off, I ended up with it stuck to both my hands. Eventually, holding it against my crotch, the stove warmed sufficiently to handle and I made some tea. We'd only managed two pints of fluid in the last two days, so we drank three cups each of sickly sweet Ovaltine and then broke our way out of our tiny cave into the swirling spindrift outside.

It took us ages to fix Ray's crampons on his boots. The straps had disintegrated on the ascent and were now held on by bits of cord and nylon tape. Eventually we fastened them with spare bootlaces and began wading through mounds of fresh wind-driven snow to gain the rocks. We now faced a vertical rock pitch that would have been pleasant at sea level but here, covered in ice, with hands frozen and toes without much feeling either, proved extremely difficult and drained the few reserves we had built up during the long night. By the time we reached the top we were shattered. The rock step was finally passed in five short, strenuous pitches and we trudged on through soft snow, passing rocks standing like ghostly sentinels in the seething mist until we noticed that one of the rocks had a red and white Japanese flag attached to it. We were on the summit.

What a relief it was, knowing that the Japanese lads had come up our descent route a few days before. Food was low and there was only sufficient gas for one more hot drink; so with nothing to see but cloud we left the rocky cairn below the snow summit and headed into the teeth of the west wind biting and stinging our nose and cheeks, down the west ridge with a drop of 5,000 feet on the left side and 6,000 feet down to the Sakhi River on the right. Soon we were climbing down bluish ice as the new snow slid away to the void on both sides. Without warning, Ray's crampon slipped off his boot and his legs shot out from under him. Down he went, sliding on his back at a frantic rate, desperately trying to turn over on to his ice axe. I stood horrified, waiting for the rope to tighten and pluck me off the fifty-degree slope. But the pull never came, as Ray was caught on a pile of boulders protruding from the ice some forty feet below. I climbed down to find Ray cursing his straps. We were both white with fear at what might have happened and to add emphasis the clouds now parted revealing the glacier and the ugly moraine piled up at its snout thousands of feet below. We continued with greater caution in case either of us made another false move.

Sitting and walking ten paces, and then sitting again was all we could manage along the undulating ridge. We stuck to the right side, keeping an eye open for cornices, and by 4 p.m. were below the cloud ceiling. Now we could see that the ridge was obvious and safe and we felt some of the elation normally felt on the summit. We were actually enjoying ourselves; breathing became noticeably easier and we descended more rapidly. The remaining difficulties were *penitentes* – snowy excrescences sometimes three feet high, which are a feature of the Hindu Kush due to the intense heat of the sun. In their shadow the snow was often soft and we'd plunge in and lose our balance.

At last, in total darkness, we reached the moraine we had left five days before. We decided to sleep among the boulders. Nothing could keep us from sleep, not our sore hands and painfully frost-nipped toes or the light snowfall that coated our sleeping bags. In the morning, in that chaos of broken rock, Ray helped me tie my bootlace and pack my sack. I was paying the penalty of climbing the steep snow gully in my bare hands; the tips of my fingers had open sores and would take a week to heal. We hobbled along valleys in the moraine, where little clumps of flowers clung to the rocks, and trudged across the muddy lake bed to the tents of Base Camp. The others were stirring from their slumbers.

Our kitchen boy, Sher, was pumping life into the Primus stove in an effort to give us tea. We drank a gallon of liquid each over the next few hours trying to assuage our raging thirst. A goat was slaughtered and we gobbled that down too while we made plans and talked over the past week. Ken and Mick had made an ascent of Koh-e-Safed and described the wild, remote Sakhi Glacier and the beautiful peaks at the head of it. Guy and Tony had fully recovered from altitude sickness and had fetched most of the gear down off the mountain, leaving a tent as a safety precaution for Ray and me as the weather deteriorated. They had now brought it down, leaving the mountain clear apart from a few scraps of sponge, squashed ravioli tins, a few pegs and the snow stakes.

Eating Tony's home-baked bread and Mick's chocolate cake, we contemplated our ascent. A longer period of acclimatisation would have made the climb more enjoyable and allowed more of us to reach the summit. The personal reward for Ray and myself was, on the face of it, small. There was no fabulous view from the top. We had lacerated fingers and aching toes and Ray's injured backside kept him awake. Yet we felt immensely satisfied that we had survived three bivouacs on the mountain in comfort and had managed to overcome the altitude – and pioneered a new route. It was not as steep as the walls of the Alps yet our horizons had widened considerably. I felt we understood the challenges of high altitude much better. I also knew that as far as I was concerned the harder the way, the more worthwhile the journey. I therefore looked forward to visiting the really high mountains of Nepal and the Karakoram.

On 15 July Guy and myself climbed a peak at the head of the Sakhi Glacier and then left Base Camp for pastures new in the Sharan Valley, some forty-five miles to the south-east. On our first night we camped at a small hamlet where our muleteer Bojan baked bread and we cooked the last of our food: rice and tomato soup. Next morning the villagers caught trout on Ken's line and gave us warm goats' milk with hairs floating on top. Our poverty must have made an impression because as we carried on a lad rushed out of a small shepherd's hut with six round cakes of *kurut*, a palatable dried yoghurt.

As the Sakhi Valley dropped down towards the Munjan, the temperature began to build. Rounding a final spur we had a view directly on to the Munjan plain and the river itself, now a placid turquoise thread among the shimmering brown hills. Ken became quite excited about the prospect of fishing the river, which only two weeks before had been brown and turbulent with snow melt. Presumably most of the winter snows had now gone. At the junction of the two valleys stood the village of Keran and its green terraces and sparkling irrigation channels overhung with willow trees. Stately poplars rose from the fields of corn and meadow grass.

We wound our way through the mud walls of the village to the police post at Alakadoree where we again dropped our rucksacks. Our equipment and food had been well looked after and we chatted with the newly appointed assistant police chief, whose command of English allowed us to ask all our queries about family structure and local customs. We stayed at the post for a couple of days, washing clothes and feasting on chickens, goat and chapattis. On the second day the chief and his constable appeared from the mud-walled station wearing pressed suits and shiny black shoes. They wanted to have their Polaroid taken and were delighted with the results, tucking them away in their wallets.

Packing two weeks' food and loading the donkeys, we set off for the Sharan Valley. We would return to Alakadoree, and then Ray and Mick would walk back down the Kokcha Valley to Hazrat and bring the truck back to Kabul. The rest of us would cross the Anjuman Pass and meet the rest of the expedition in the Panjshir Valley on their return from Mir Samir. Heading for the Sharan Valley we crossed the Pajuka Pass and as we were ambling down the other side, an old man with wicked, slanting eyes dressed in ragged hessian came up to us, demanding a doctor, or so we thought. The herdsmen with us pointed to me since I had been handling the medical box.

Guy and I followed the old man up a side valley for about an hour carrying the Boots first aid box and we eventually came to a warren of rough cave dwellings surrounded by sheep and goats. We had got the impression his wife was ill and needed treatment but, with our limited Farsi, we had got it all wrong. The old man was in fact a pimp, touting for clients on behalf of the more attractive women in his extended family, who emerged in fits of giggles to size up the customers. We settled for a cup of tea, explaining that while the women were beautiful, despite the goat fat and charcoal, we were in fact married and English wives could be very annoyed if we were not faithful to them. The herdsmen were not so saintly, and we were forced to drink several more cups of tea, to an accompaniment of giggles and soft grunts from within, before we could rejoin our caravan.

Towards evening we reached Sharan after a hard five-hour walk. The entrance to the village was along an avenue of willows. There were so many trees in Sharan that you were always protected from the hot sun. White stone walls marked the field boundaries; glancing briefly you might think you were in Derbyshire, except these walls were made of granite and not limestone. The river, the Darrah-i-Sharan, had been diverted into a complex system of irrigation that watered around a hundred fields, the water splashing and gurgling past the houses closely packed around narrow alleys and built from rough stone cemented with mud. The flat roofs, covered in reeds and branches, had a hole to allow the smoke out. As in mountain villages from Tibet to Morocco, the roofs were used for drying fruit or crops and storing fuel and utensils.

Towards evening we watched the women milking cows and goats, grinding corn and preparing meals on charcoal fires. We watched them hand over grain to the miller who emptied it into a wicker basket which funnelled it through a hole in the granite millstone, turned with the power of a water channel on

Tony Watts on the lower slopes of Koh-i-Sisgeikh, above the Suigal Glacier.

a solid block below. The women scooped up the flour and paid either in kind or cash. We had seen exactly the same method used in Kurdistan and further still in the Atlas at the western end of the vast Muslim world. There were similarities in the way these mountain people dressed and in their custom of treating strangers hospitably.

Our early morning start next day became a noon start in the face of prolonged negotiations for transport animals and we started up the Darrah-i-Sharan at the hottest part of the day. Reluctantly, we left the shade of the trees and the last fields of beans and tobacco to enter the valley. The Darrah-i-Sharan tumbled noisily over white granite boulders speckled with tourmaline on their journey down the slope to the Munjan and beyond. As the sun dropped, our pace quickened until quite suddenly the roar of the river stopped and we arrived at Maria Lake, a streak of turquoise mirroring the mountains in its calm surface. We walked along by the lapping waters and arrived at a flat, grassy meadow covered in edelweiss at the inlet to the lake. The violet sky grew a shade darker and we yelled at the donkey men to hurry. Distant ranges stood in silhouette, one behind the other, as the donkey men huddled round their bracken fire cooking chai, as we put up our tents and settled into our new Base Camp.

Over the next ten days of perfect weather we went on an orgy of peak bagging, with ascents of eight previously unclimbed summits between 5,500 metres and 6,110 metres. We were all very fit now that we had climbed Bandaka, except Ken who suffered a persistent chest infection. It felt marvellous to be roaming around the upper Sharan Valley without headaches as though we were back in the Alps. It was also very beautiful, with carpets of wild flowers reaching up to the snow line.

One porter, named Sultan, decided to stay on at Base Camp after the other Sharan men returned to the village. He carried huge loads up to the base of various peaks wearing only the clothes he wore around the village and supporting himself with a staff as he nimbly jumped across wobbly moraine. He even returned to the Munjan River to bring us fresh trout as well as eggs and chapattis from Sharan. He knew we had very little money and brushed the subject aside, indicating that a pair of old boots Tony had given him was payment enough. He seemed curious to know more about these young Western strangers and their baffling impulse to risk their necks climbing mountains in his back garden. I think, too, that he delighted in exploring the rocky cwms above the grassy pastures. Such a man had all the attributes of a guide for future expeditions.

The last peak I climbed in the Hindu Kush was Bechap Sharan Kuh. Tony and I were keen to see if we could make it in one long day from the Sharan Valley and curious to take a look down the far side. The pioneers in this region were Scots from the Corriemulzie; no one had approached these mountains before. They went on to climb ten peaks including Koh-i-Sisgeikh, close to our peak. (An account of their adventure is told in *No Tigers in the Hindu Kush*, drawn from the diaries of Philip Tranter, who died in a car crash ten months after his return, and edited by his father, the author Nigel Tranter.)

Just as the morning sun was catching the highest peaks, we crossed the divide between the Sharan and Suigal glaciers, crunching across frozen ripples of snow in our crampons. An immense feeling of solitude and wellbeing swept over me as we sat on a boulder watching the sun sparkling on the surface of the snow, bringing life to the mountains. Eight hours later we had climbed 3,000 feet of snow, steep ice and warm red granite to the summit and were rewarded with a wonderful panorama of peaks and glaciers stretching away in all directions. We spotted Mick and Guy nearing the summit of a 19,000-foot peak two miles away. As the sun wheeled above us, loosening rocks from the softening snow, we abseiled down and then hurried on over the col and out of danger. Then we marched down the valley to join the others. We had climbed three peaks between the six of us that day, marking the end of the expedition as far as the climbing was concerned. Just as we finished packing up Sultan arrived with his friends to help us down to the village. We were sorry to leave him and the other villagers. Of course, we said we would come back but I never did. Afghanistan has spent much of the decades since in a state of war and unrest.

Back at the police post we heard a rumour that a European had met with an accident further south. We hoped he wasn't one of our six friends in the

Tony Watts climbing, with Koh-i-Morusq in the background.

Panjshir Valley. At Skazar, Ray and Mick walked back north along the Kokcha Valley. The rest of us prepared to walk south along the Karan River to the Anjuman Pass. Villagers at Skazar also told us a foreigner had met with an accident. They thought he had died. To find out as soon as we could that no harm had come to the rest of the expedition on Mir Samir, we hired horses and set off up valley.

We arrived at a point where the steep, rocky hillside descended right to the river. The herdsmen indicated we had to cross over to the other side. The river was fifty yards wide, fast flowing and seemingly deep. We needed to get someone over with a rope to belay the horses across so on an impulse I stripped off to my underpants, handed my spectacles to Guy, tied on one of our climbing ropes, ran down the bank, took a deep breath and dived in, immediately thrashing against the water with my arms. Then I realised I was tight on the rope thirty yards downstream and being bashed around by the strong current. I had overestimated my powers as a Nottingham City swimming champion and completely underestimated the power of a youthful mountain river.

We weren't sure when, but at some point we left the province of Badakhshan and entered Nuristan, the land of light. This area at one time was known as Kafiristan, a region of non-Muslim people suffused with Vedic religious beliefs and also practising animism. Then, in the 1890s, Abdur Rahman, the 'Iron Amir', conquered the area and converted the population to Islam. The Greeks knew the people of Nuristan as being different from the surrounding tribes and to be fierce fighters. The mujahideen under Ahmad Shah Massoud, the Lion of Panjshir, was never defeated by the Soviet troops in nine campaigns in the early 1980s. Nuristanis are also physically distinct. We met families travelling to and from Nuristan many of whom had fair skin, light-coloured hair and blue eyes.

The Panjshir is a wonderful valley, dry rocky hillsides vibrant against the blue sky with lammergeiers circling high overhead, emerald green pastures and clear mountain streams and lakes teeming with trout. Further south, we came across ancient, twisted mulberry trees heavy with ripe, juicy berries. At the first village over the pass we heard from the headman that the dead climber was an Englishman; he had fallen into the river and his body had not been found. We galloped on downstream to Kaujan, the appointed meeting place with the rest of the team. After the long ride we were saddle sore weary and anxious that one of our friends was dead. One of the villagers put us up. He knew more, that it was one of the climbers on Mir Samir who had disappeared in the river. He told us the climber's name was John and we knew that could only be John Fleming.

Two days later, Bill Cheverst, Brian Palmer, Dick Stroud and George Jones walked into the village and confirmed John's tragic death. Early one morning he had gone out walking; he crossed the river high up near the Anjuman Pass, either first thing or later that day when the river was swollen. His rucksack

The village of Kaujan.

was found by the riverbank with its contents intact. Despite a thorough search by the lads and the villagers no trace was ever found of his body.

The group returned to Kabul to alert John's parents and deal with the embassy. Knowing we were not due back for several weeks they decided to return to Mir Samir – except for Bob Holmes who was so upset at John's death he lost all interest in climbing that season and carried out a useful study of various Afghan tribes to the south with the help of contacts made through the British Embassy. The other four lads grew closer after sharing the grief of John's death and pioneering a fine new climb on the steep granite flanks of Mir Samir – a fitting tribute to their friend. We all walked down the valley together and met Ray, Mick and Bob in Kabul. Short of funds, we offered space for twelve independent travellers from the Kabul Hotel and left for Europe. The last I saw of the Panjshir Valley was clandestine footage on television in the early 1980s showing Russian helicopter gunships strafing the village of Kaujan.

Strone Ulladale.

STRONE

Ten days later our two lorries pulled into the Biolay campsite in Chamonix with eleven expedition members and the dozen assorted travellers who had contributed to the cost of fuel. The trucks' old ammunition lockers were full of ancient flintlock rifles dating back to the Afghan wars of the nineteenth century, antique swords, beautifully embroidered ladies' Afghan waistcoats and full-length coats, leather bags, lapis lazuli jewellery and much else. Like merchant adventurers of old, we traded our wares in the smart shops of Chamonix, making a good profit on our sales. It all helped keep our heads above water financially.

The campsite was mostly full of English climbers keen to travel back home on our lorries now that the Alpine season was drawing to a close. Bill Cheverst and I had time for a route before the lorries left, so we walked up through the forest to the Plan de l'Aiguille to try the *North Face Direct* on the Aiguille du Plan. It took us three hours to climb 1,500 feet up the lower rock spur and then we settled in at a well-used bivouac site among some gendarmes a safe distance below the final section of the route: a hanging glacier. Early next morning we cut steps up the left side of this steep ice, swinging leads as we slowly made progress.

The route's bad reputation was confirmed when some 300 feet across the glacier we caught sight of a climber whose legs were entombed in ice and whose torso hung down the slope with one arm outstretched, clutching a length of rope. Mine was the next pitch, a steep wall of ice, which took me a long time to negotiate as I cut steps for both hands and feet. We had three Stubai 'corkscrew' ice pegs with us. Bill was belayed to one and since I needed to belay with another there was just one left for protection up the eighty-foot wall. At last I was able to traverse out rightwards to a sloping shelf of ice to belay.

Bill Cheverst going up rocks to the start of the *North Face Direct* on the Aiguille du Plan.

Bill was soon up and crossing the shelf to join me when we both heard the familiar but ominous rumble of falling ice. It was soon pouring over the ice cliffs above and then roared down our route. When the dust settled there was no sign of the steps I had so laboriously cut, every single one had been scraped off by the avalanche. If we'd started just a few minutes later that day, we would both have perished. We climbed on up to the summit and down the glaciers on the other side to Montenvers and back to Chamonix without further incident. So much for the 'Playground of Europe' as Leslie Stephen called it. At no time was either of us so threatened in the mountains of the Hindu Kush.

Somehow word reached a reporter at *Le Dauphiné*, the local newspaper, that we had spotted a body frozen into the ice. He made contact saying that the body was probably that of a Czech climber from an accident a few days before. He asked for any photographs we might have so I gave him a roll of black and white negatives to develop, suggesting the paper should pay me well. When the rest of the team heard about this, they came down hard on me, particularly George Jones, and not just for making money off the back of a dead climber. They wanted to know how I would feel if it was my dead relative suddenly being sensationalised in the press. Fortunately the photo never appeared but this was not the last rap on the knuckles I was to get for being greedy.

In this case, it wasn't just the money. I was also blinded by my ambition to be in print. I had returned like some kind of hero, coming out alive while others lay dead on the mountain. It was no excuse, but Continental climbers often sold photographs of dead climbers to the press, most notably on the Eiger. I began to realise it was in the aftermath of expeditions that I discovered most about myself, not during the climb itself. Club members and the wider community of climbers soon knocked the rough edges off those of us who stepped out of line.

A few days remained before our scheduled departure so I thought about another climb but decided to telephone Jan first. She seemed indifferent about when I returned, worryingly so. I didn't know how to interpret her lack of interest for our imminent reunion. I simply knew that now I wanted to get home as soon as possible. So I engineered a more rapid return by suggesting one lorry set off four days early. The best laid plans: we were barely north of Geneva when the lorry refused to go any further. I put it into the local garage but after two days the fault remained a mystery. There were about a dozen expedition members and passengers all camped on the village green by a water trough and we soon ran out of food. The farm opposite had a yard full of caged rabbit, and the farmer's wife took pity on us, bringing over rabbit stew each night until Ray arrived on the fourth day in the second lorry.

He soon worked out there was a hairline crack in the rotor arm of the distributor. Lacking a replacement, he asked for a condom, put the rotor arm into it and then jammed it back in place. The current was restored and the lorry fired into life but it was some time before we could move. There was a heated discussion about the garage owner's huge bill, sorted out with the help of a local gendarme who, it has to be said, was very much on the side of the local man. We drove out of the village but after two miles the lorry spluttered to a halt. Some half dozen condoms later we gave up and the second lorry towed the first all day to the Austin agents in Paris. We reached Nottingham without further incident.

Life at home with Jan was frosty; ordinarily she wanted to hear all about my adventures, but not this time. I sensed something had changed, but wanted to pick up the threads of my life at home. Michael began his school life at the local infants' and Jan went off to college. I joined the team teaching group at Cottesmore, which had now become co-educational.

Our expedition's afterlife now began, the process of sharing our story and putting it into the history books. Peter Watkinson, secretary of the Nottingham Pegasus Caving Club, produced our Hindu Kush report at his printing works. Pete had just led a successful caving expedition down the Gouffre Berger cave system in the Vercors. After thirteen days underground they emerged having reached a depth of 3,717 feet – at the time a world record. We agreed to put on a joint lecture – 'Deepest Down, Highest Up!' – at the Albert Hall in Nottingham to help pay off some of the cost of our respective expeditions. Pete and the cavers would do the promotion while the NCC would organise the event. We'd soon sold 1,200 tickets. The hall lacked a screen so our carpenter, Tony Watts, made a huge frame of solid timber and we bought a piece of canvas more than 500 feet square and painted it with white gloss paint. This made the screen so heavy it collapsed a couple of hours before we were due to start. Tony quickly fashioned a much smaller screen, twelve feet by twelve feet, but now most of the image was projected on to the organ pipes behind the stage. Members dispersed round town on motorbikes to find a smaller lens and finally, half an hour after the appointed hour, one arrived on loan from the YMCA.

Luckily most people seem to attend climbing lectures for the socialising, so the Albert Hall was buzzing apart from the Lord Mayor and Lady Mayoress and various council bigwigs who sat grimly silent on the front row. Just as the new lens was successfully fitted, to my immense embarrassment, I knocked the slide trays over and all my images cascaded over the dusty floor of the stage. I broke into a cold sweat and then told myself to calm down and sort it out. We finally started an hour late but the lectures went well and we congratulated ourselves on an entertaining and profitable evening. Then a member of the audience asked where they should pay. In the chaos of sorting out the screen and projector, the doors had been left unattended and the entry fees uncollected. After all bills had been paid there was only £36 left in the kitty, £18 for the cavers and £18 for the climbers.

After climbing the Piz Badile, Colin Mortlock had persuaded me to join the Alpine Climbing Group, a ginger group of younger active alpinists affiliated to the Alpine Club. After I got back from the Hindu Kush, Tom Blakeney, the assistant editor at the *Alpine Journal*, requested an article on our expedition, which I sent him, adding in a note that I would accept the journal's usual rates of remuneration. Tom Blakeney told me in no uncertain terms that in the more than a hundred years of the *Alpine Journal*'s existence no contributor had ever been paid for an article and he didn't think they would make me the exception.

Since I had now climbed in four mountain ranges within the lands of Islam I was invited to lecture on my experiences at the Alpine Club's premises on South Audley Street in London. I had the same discussion about a fee – and another rap on the knuckles. Now I was standing in front of the venerable members of the Alpine Club, with the most venerable on the first few rows so they were better able to hear. Even before the secretary had read out the club's business, announced the deaths and invited remembrance, a few were asleep, one with his head back, snoring loudly. I was well into the section of my talk on the Atlas, with all the members in the front rows nodding off or sound asleep, when I mentioned that the route we had taken up Mount Toubkal had been pioneered by, as I explained to the members, 'the redoubtable Bentley Beetham who some of you may have known.'

Professor Itakura with us in the Hindu Kush. **Photo**: Guy Lee.

At this point Howard Somervell, veteran of the 1920s Everest expeditions, stirring from his slumbers, became quite animated and got to his feet: 'Bentley Beetham, I knew him well!' Then he regaled the rest of the audience and myself about Bentley's character and climbing activities, mainly in the Lake District. Howard then retook his seat and was soon nodding off again as I droned on about the Tibesti, Kurdistan and the Hindu Kush.

We managed to sell the Hindu Kush lorries to Durham University Climbing Club at twice the purchase price, which gave Mick, Ray and myself the idea of buying and selling lorries bought at auction from what was now called the Ministry of Defence. Business went well until after buying eight more lorries and selling them on to various climbing clubs, Skip Davies closed down our 'maintenance depot'; his Scout hut was beginning to resemble a scrapyard. Satisfied customers sent us postcards from all over the world, including one from the Sahara where a truck had broken down near the Murzuq Sand Sea. They had spent a day or so trying to fix a problem that appeared insurmountable. Then one of the team, out for a walk to pass the time, came across the lorry we had abandoned in 1965. They were able to cannibalise our truck for parts and continue on their way.

There was an interesting coda to our Hindu Kush expedition. Professor Itakura had been so helpful and generous at our Base Camp at Koh-i-Bandaka that I invited him to stay at our home should he ever find himself in Nottingham. Within a few months, the professor took time out from meetings at Nottingham University to stay with us. Both Jan and I enjoyed his company so we were a little put out to be stopped in the street by a neighbour.

'Is that a Jap you have in your house?' I told him it was and how kind he had been to us in Afghanistan. It made no difference. 'I couldn't ever have a Jap in my house, in fact I can't bring myself to talk to them, not after what they did to our chaps.' Our neighbour had been in the Royal Army Medical Corps at the end of the war, helping rehabilitate the British and Commonwealth prisoners being released from Changi prison in Singapore. 'I can never clear my head of the memory of human beings so sick and emaciated. I know I should forgive the Japanese, even if I cannot forget the results of their inhumanity, but I can't.'

It seemed such a different world from the one I had grown up in, yet in 1967 I was still only twenty-six. Change was coming thick and fast; it must have been bewildering for the generation that had won the war. The Wolfenden Report had been published in 1957, but it was now in 1967 that homosexuality was decriminalised. There was legislation too liberalising the law on abortion. The Beatles' *Sgt Pepper's Lonely Hearts Club Band* was the year's best-selling album. Youth culture had exploded, turning its back on the certainties of the post-war consensus. A more relaxed attitude to sex and the use of mind-expanding drugs was changing society. Around the world, the Vietnam War was at its height, Che Guevara was caught and executed in Bolivia, and Chairman Mao was inflicting the Cultural Revolution on his own people. The lands of Islam I had visited were also starting to change. In 1967, Israelis crushed their Arab opposition in the Six-Day War, occupying the Sinai Peninsula, the Golan Heights, Gaza and the West Bank, setting the stage for the next few decades of tension and conflict. The British government was in the process of giving up Aden, its last toehold in the Middle East, when its new British-trained police force turned on the army, killing eight soldiers in one night. Lieutenant Colonel Colin Mitchell of the Argyll and Sutherland Highlanders restored order, without much reference to the Labour defence minister Denis Healey, and became a national hero for a while. Fleet Street dubbed him 'Mad Mitch'; the BBC described him as a fearless soldier 'born a hundred years too late.' It felt like the last battle of the British Empire.

I was still playing rugby and climbing in Derbyshire at the weekends, and if there was no rugby then I went off to the Lake District or North Wales. Ray and I hitchhiked up to the Lakes one weekend to stay at Elterwater Youth Hostel. One of our club members had got a job as deputy warden and said we could come and stay for free as his guest. But when we got there late on Friday night, we found him in a vitriolic confrontation with the warden, who had caught our friend in bed with his wife. Not only were we refused a bed for the night, our host was kicked out of the hostel and told never to return.

Ray and myself found a concrete shelter in the village not unlike a wartime bunker. It was damp but clean and we slept well until woken by a river of ash landing on our heads. We both stood up in our sleeping bags and looked out through a slot in the concrete wall at an old lady about to throw another bucket of rubbish on top of us. She nearly fainted with shock at the sight of two protesting heads poking out of the village rubbish dump.

More often I was in North Wales. In 1966 I'd gone there thirteen weekends in a row, usually hitchhiking. The drive to Snowdonia was often an epic adventure in its own right. One Friday evening in June, Geoff Stroud gave me a lift on his Matchless motorbike. Possibly because of the rucksack sitting on the petrol tank between his arms, he miscalculated one of the terrifying bends near Betws-y-coed and hit a telegraph pole. I was thrown clear but Geoff smashed his kneecap on the post and disappeared off to hospital in Llandudno for a fortnight. I hitched on to the Llanberis Pass to meet up with the rest of the Nottingham Climbers' Club.

The drive home on Sunday evening down the A5 back to Nottingham was either relaxed or manic, depending on how late climbing ended or the pressure to be home from wife and family. One bank holiday weekend I had to be home in record time. All went well until near Corwen in Denbighshire when a large family saloon car slowed us down. Looking to overtake, I dropped a gear and drew alongside but the saloon promptly accelerated. My van was full of passengers and gear, and we only just tucked in before colliding with an oncoming car emerging from the bend ahead.

A week or two later I got a summons to appear at Corwen Magistrates' Court charged with dangerous driving, which I aimed to refute, but at the last minute I had to postpone the court date, and then did so for a second time. The prosecution witnesses, the driver of the saloon and his wife, had been forced to travel down from Stirling three times. By the time I did make it to court with my passengers in tow, I had run up court costs equivalent to three months' salary.

We sat through the prosecution's arguments; the driver's wife told the court that after I'd pulled in 'there was a round-faced man grinning out of the back window of the van, making rude gestures with two fingers.' Then my defence solicitor stood up and asked whether or not the prosecution had finished. There was some shuffling of paper, and then the prosecution said that it had. 'But, your honour,' my solicitor told the magistrate, 'the prosecution hasn't established that my client was driving the minivan.' In no time at all I was walking out of the court, smiling at the saloon car driver, who looked most dejected. It turned out he was a parking warden.

During those thirteen visits to Wales, I climbed a couple of new routes at Gogarth, the famous sea cliff on Anglesey, and came in for some criticism from Ken Wilson, who had just begun a long and distinguished career in mountaineering journalism. In May 1966, leading through with Bill Cheverst, I climbed a wet and loose route we called *Crowbar* using seven pegs for direct aid or tension on the rope. In June, Ray Gillies and myself climbed a much more interesting line although the second pitch was very loose. I was pleased with the first pitch, which was on excellent weathered rock above the waves and I used just one point of aid to negotiate an overhang. I fixed a hanging belay from several pegs hammered into the loose, flaky rock.

As we were changing the belay, Ray and I watched as Peter Crew and Dave Alcock arrived to climb a new route a few yards to the right, which they called *Jaborandi*. Pete was in the lead when we saw him take a bunch of wires, clipped to a karabiner, and start fiddling around in a crack until he had one of the wires wedged within; it was like, as Ray described it, a man trying to open a door with a bunch of keys. That was the first time we had seen such a variety of wire chocks being used. They also hammered in four pegs for direct aid. Ray and myself used seven pegs for aid on our route, now called *Syringe*, which proved to be much harder. A week later Pete and Joe Brown put up the very demanding and very loose overhanging *Dinosaur* with ten points of aid.

Yet it was Ray and myself that Ken Wilson took to task in *Mountain Craft* magazine for using too many pegs, while absolving the others. Ray and I were a little huffy when we saw him in the pub a short while later. We had in fact called our route *Crewcut*, as a poke at Pete Crew who was formidably competitive. One of our club, Peter Thompson, had been at Gogarth that day and saw Pete's reaction when he realised we'd beaten him to a route he wanted for himself: 'That bastard Scott has got there before us.' Between them, Ken and Pete renamed our route *Syringe*, a witty reference to the competitive needle in Wales at that time. They didn't bother to ask me.

Despite being disgruntled with Ken, his editorial stance helped to keep in mind the best free climbing traditions. Ken was from Birmingham and had studied architectural photography at Birmingham College of Art. He'd also started climbing, first with the Scouts and then in the Alps on a Mountaineering Association course. He was a passionate and sometimes vociferous supporter of the traditions of British climbing and an inspired mountaineering magazine editor. Ken loved to categorise things – and people – but he could never quite make up his mind on how to categorise me. Was I in his 'A' team or 'B' team? I was not that driven to reach the limit of my rock climbing potential. Even if I did, I would never have equalled the likes of Joe, Don or Pete Crew. There's no doubt that Martin Boysen and Baz Ingle, who had first discovered the potential of Gogarth in 1964, would have made a better job of *Crowbar* and *Syringe* than I did. Such arguments would soon become moot, as chocks on wires became ubiquitous.

I was capable of being fairly unpleasant myself. Terry Bolger, who had only just joined the Nottingham Climbers' Club, watched aghast as I tore the page with our intended route out of his brand new guidebook because, I told him, we didn't want the extra weight. I always felt bad about that. And on a visit to the Cromlech, Ray Gillies and I discovered someone had left runners in the whole height of *Cemetery Gates*. We climbed various routes, including the *Corner* and *Ivy Sepulchre* but by evening the runners were still there so Ray and I climbed it and returned to the valley, ten pieces of gear better off. On the way back to my car I was asked to hand them over to someone who knew their owner. I told him they were now in Ray's car on the A5 heading for Nottingham. I never felt good about that either. It cut both ways though. The first time I met that master of the revels Mo Anthoine was on *Cenotaph Corner*. Mo and his friend were doing the traverse of the Cromlech and asked if we would leave four runners in the mid-section of our route since they were running out of gear. A week or so later I called in to see Mo and reclaim my karabiners and slings. He told me they were with his mate who was now on his way to New Zealand.

Mostly I climbed the classic routes in North Wales, usually with Dez Hadlum or Ray Gillies, sometimes linking them together. One dry summer's day I started off at dawn on Clogwyn y Grochan in the Pass, then its neighbours Carreg Wastad and Dinas Cromlech, then crossed the valley to Dinas Mot and climbed *Direct Route*. From there we walked up to Cyrn Las and did *Main Wall* before finishing in the Pass with the five-pitch *Gambit Climb* on Clogwyn y Ddysgl. It was dark by the time we walked down the Snowdon railway tracks, having finished the day with a route on Cloggy – *The Corner*, I think.

Sometimes we might just go for a walk. The most memorable was walking all fourteen of the 3,000ers with Beryl Turner, Dez and Ray, in fourteen hours. The Nottingham Climbers' Club was full of such enthusiasm at the time; busloads arrived in North Wales at the weekend climbing on every crag along the Llanberis Pass, frequently yelling 'Milko' to each other, a call that was taken up and echoed the length of the valley. There were very few really dangerous incidents but one close call involved Harry Cluro who was following someone on the climb *Phantom Rib* at Clogwyn y Grochan. Harry had swung out on to the rib itself, which was very exposed and undercut but was finding the climbing difficult and so asked for a tight rope. His belayer took in the slack but the rope kept coming – without Harry on it. His knot had come undone and he was now stranded in the middle of the cliff. Harry was reduced to a quivering wreck but luckily the rope was thrown back down with a loop in it, which Harry grabbed. He was then lowered safely to the ground.

During our visits to Gogarth, I noticed an enormous 100-foot overhang beneath the fog warning station at North Stack. Brian 'Henry' Palmer, with

Brian (Henry) Palmer having a stint out front on the first ascent of *The Big Overhang*.

Henry, thirty feet out on the first ascent of *The Big Overhang*.

whom I had climbed in Turkey and had led the key rock pitch on Mir Samir that summer, was keen to give it a go, especially as Derbyshire was out of bounds because of a foot-and-mouth outbreak. By the time we were both free to go it was the winter of 1968 and there was snow on the roads, so we drove from Nottingham to North Wales in one of the expedition lorries for three weekends running, starting in late November. John Carey, superintendent of the warning station, kindly invited us to stay with him and became fascinated by our project. He was one of the few North Welsh I got to know. During two rugby tours of South Wales I found the Valleys to be exceptionally hospitable – staying in Treherbert with a man known as Howard the Coal – and full of good humour. People in Snowdonia, by contrast, seemed more naturally reserved, remote in their own language.

The first weekend we checked the line of the route and removed a mass of loose, slimy rock from the back wall to reach the start of the roof. Over the next two weekends we took turns out front, eventually reaching the top after twenty-two hours of climbing and some forty pegs. The roof in profile is in the form of a saw blade with several protruding teeth of rock that we had to climb down and then back up. It was all very strenuous, especially as we did not have harnesses, only an arrangement of loops of tape. With the back wall at right angles to the roof, keeping the ropes moving required great care. Hanging from the roof, we watched a litter of seal pups being born in the zawn below. At the top, John walked across with cups of hot sweet tea as I belayed Henry on the final pitch. The route, which we called *The Big Overhang*, became quite popular, especially as more pegs were left in. I later did it again with Bob Wark in just four hours, the two of us moving together about twenty feet apart; it was an indication of the difference between making the first and subsequent ascents of an aid route. One of our NCC friends, Paul Denney, even climbed it solo.

The manic way I was living my life had inevitably put a strain on my relation-ship with Jan. She was enjoying student life and looking forward to becoming a teacher. College was for her a liberating experience: an exit from the confines of marriage, a place where she was appreciated, even made to feel attractive from the attention of male students and tutors. I was full on, buzzing around town like a madman until I got home, at 9.30 p.m. most evenings. On Friday nights I was off climbing unless there was a game of rugby on Saturday afternoon in which case I went off climbing on Saturday night instead. I was contributing materially to the marriage but very little emotionally. Our marriage was on the rocks.

After our siege of *Big Overhang*, I'd been at home over Christmas with the family and then left to spend New Year climbing in Scotland, leaving Jan and Michael behind – again. During the festivities, I followed up on advances made in my direction by a young lass and suffered paroxysms of guilt thereafter, until a conversation we had on the back lawn in early summer. Jan said she was thinking of divorcing me; a doctor had asked her to marry him. I persuaded her to think again; there was Michael to consider. She agreed, but only if I could deal with the fact that in the last few years she had slept with a number of students at college, and one of my climbing friends. I noticed I felt no anger towards Jan, only to the 'friend', although I kept that to myself. But I did understand that Jan needed to spread her wings, having married at eighteen. A husband obsessed with going off with the boys again climbing, playing rugby and working all hours wasn't much help. The situation we found ourselves in was a result of my selfish behaviour.

After our expedition to the Hindu Kush, I was eager to return to the high mountains of Asia, although the political situation made it difficult. The state of my marriage made this impossible. Shorter trips seemed to be the solution, a decision that coincided with my growing interest in big-wall climbing. Jan had recently qualified as a probationary primary school teacher and was offered a place at a city centre school starting in September. So we made plans for all three of us to drive out together for my next season in the Alps. I spent the week before we left searching the scrapyards of Nottingham for a replacement engine for the minivan and two days installing it, with the help of friends. Miraculously it got us to the Alps to meet up with the rest of the Nottingham Climbers' Club.

We started in the Bernina in south-east Switzerland, largely because some of us had seen Arnold Fanck's 1929 silent film *The White Hell of Pitz Palu*, starring a young Leni Riefenstahl. It was hard to resist a dramatic title like that. The Bernina, although adjacent to the Bregaglia and Piz Badile, is very different in character to the granite spires and faces Dez and I had explored seven years before. The Bernina is predominantly snow and ice, being substantially higher; the Piz Bernina is the most easterly peak over 4,000 metres. Only remnants of glaciers remain in the Bregaglia but in the Bernina there are wide glaciers spreading out below couloirs of tumbling ice and elegant snow arêtes linking peaks together.

There is also a contrast in the development of the two ranges. The villages of the Bregaglia have changed little over the last century. The Bernina, on the other hand, has become a Mecca for skiers with the infrastructure to support them constructed on the hillside: the cable cars and ski lifts. Some of the most expensive hotels in Switzerland dominate the once bucolic villages of Pontresina and St Moritz. The high cost of living didn't much affect the Nottingham Climbers' Club; we lived out of our vans and avoided the expensive campsites. That brought the attention of the law. Parked up in a layby outside Pontresina, our convoy of ageing vans was disturbed by a policeman who arrived on a moped demanding we all paid a fine for parking overnight illegally. Communication was difficult, and we resorted to holding our arms together and inviting him to handcuff us. Four more rather aggressive officers arrived in a car, and so we had a quick whip-round.

That night, the non-climbers pitched camp at a legal site and the rest of us left town in poor weather for a bivouac in a cable-car station on the approach to the Piz Palü. Happily, the sky cleared and we set off, several teams roped together as we crossed the Pers Glacier under a starry sky. By dawn we were climbing the east ridge to the first of Piz Palü's three summits, continuing west along the narrow frontier ridge, walking a tightrope between Switzerland and Italy, in perfect weather. It felt as though we were on a summit all day and the views to the north and south were fabulous. It was a hundred years to the day – 22 July 1868 – since the mountain's first traverse ascent and, unlike in Fanck's film, all of us survived unscathed, apart from a little sunburn. Then we left for the more challenging mountains of the Mont Blanc range.

Arriving in Chamonix, we were amazed to find the Biolay campsite was now teeming with Czechoslovakian climbers. They arrived by all means of transport, mostly hitchhiking but also on scooters, two-up with all their gear, or in beat-up Ladas and Skodas. If 1967 had been the Summer of Love, with the Mamas and the Papas reaching number one with their hippy song 'San Francisco', then 1968 was a year of revolution. John Lennon and The Beatles even recorded a song about it. It started in Czechoslovakia on 5 January 1968 with the election of Alexander Dubček as the country's new leader. Dubček wanted to liberalise Czechoslovakia in the face of stultifying intransigence from his masters in Moscow; he wanted, in his famous phrase, 'socialism with a human face'. In April he began his programme of liberalising reforms and as a consequence Czechoslovakian climbers suddenly found they had access to the Western Alps.

The mood of revolution extended right around the globe. In May, France was convulsed by mass civil disobedience. There were general strikes and students occupied universities in Paris. For a while the French government of President Charles de Gaulle ceased to function. 'Les Évenements', as the unrest became known in France, was as much social as political, with art and literature to the fore. There was widespread civil unrest in the United States too. Martin Luther King had been assassinated in April, prompting riots in a hundred American cities; following the Tet Offensive in January 1968, demonstrations against the Vietnam War intensified, protests which spread to London in March, where police in full riot gear broke up anti-war demonstrations outside the American embassy. It seemed the whole world was shifting on its axis.

While we were climbing in Chamonix, large-scale riots began in Chicago, as Vietnam protestors gathered for that year's Democratic Convention, filling the city centre with tear gas. Later that year, watching the Olympic Games in Mexico City, I saw the African-American athlete Tommie Smith, who won the 200 metres in record time, and John Carlos, who came third, walk to the podium wearing back socks and no shoes, bow their heads and raise a fist in the black-power salute as the 'Star-Spangled Banner' was being played. It was an overt protest at the oppressive treatment of African-Americans. They were booed off the track and suspended from competition under pressure from the IOC president, Avery Brundage, who, in 1936, had approved the use of the Nazi salute at the Berlin Olympics.

In 1966, Chairman Mao had declared war on the 'Four Olds': old customs, old culture, old habits, and old ideas. In China, Mao's campaign heralded the latest and most extreme form of repression in his cruel regime. Yet it seemed in 1968 as though his ideas had been adopted around the world, most notably in Paris where Maoism had reinvigorated the French Left. Class boundaries had weakened after the war, but now the new generation felt confident to attack 'the system' and 'the establishment'. There was growing disillusionment with the consumerist fantasy of the 1950s and corporate manipulation, expressed in books like Vance Packard's *The Hidden Persuaders*. The catastrophic consequences of the post-war agrarian revolution had already been exposed in Rachel Carson's *Silent Spring*.

These themes in wider youth culture were enthusiastically taken up in the outdoor world, especially over in America. Edward Abbey, the Thoreau of the American West, in his passionate and uproarious book from 1968, *Desert Solitaire*, gave an excoriating account of where the world was heading while paddling down Glen Canyon in a rubber dinghy: 'My *God*! I'm thinking, what incredible *shit* we put up with most of our lives – the *domestic* routine (the same old wife *every* night), the stupid and useless and degrading *jobs*, the *insufferable* arrogance of elected officials, the crafty *cheating* and the *slimy* advertising of the businessmen, the tedious wars in which we kill our buddies instead of our *real* enemies back in the capital, the foul, diseased and *hideous* cities and towns we live in, the constant *petty* tyranny of automatic washers and automobiles and TV machines and telephones!' (In his preface for the 1987 'new and revised and absolutely terminal edition' he changes the rather cruel 'Same old wife *every* night' to 'Same dreams *every* night.' Maybe he grew more compassionate with age – or maybe he had a better relationship with his later wives.)

Desert Solitaire and his later work *The Monkey Wrench Gang* are not only seminal environmental works but hugely entertaining.

In Chamonix, I teamed up with Dave Nicol to climb the *Bonatti Pillar* on the Aiguille du Petit Dru. Dave had been with us on Piz Palü so we were both reasonably fit; Martin and Bill Hepplewhite made up a second rope, and Chris Radcliffe and Peter Scott a third. Walter Bonatti had first climbed the south-west

Dave Nicol on the *Bonatti Pillar*.

pillar of the Dru solo, over six days in August 1955. Bonatti felt bitter at the cynical treatment he received at the hands of the two lead climbers close to the summit of K2. The Dru climb was his response.

For us the whole outing proved exciting: dodging the showers of whirring rocks in the approach couloir below the Flammes des Pierres; overtaking the well-known French alpinist Yannick Seigneur and his fifty-five-year-old, mother-of-five client on the exposed Red Walls; a night spent roped to a sloping ledge just below the Shoulder while Martin and Bill enjoyed a better bivouac on the Shoulder itself. Thanks to our regular weekend climbing on gritstone, we really enjoyed the Dru's granite cracks, which were never that hard, especially with all the gear *in situ*. We were able to climb the *Pillar* with just one bivouac and returned to the valley pleased to have worked well together and to have climbed one of the great classics of the Western Alps.

By the time we reached Chamonix, Russian tanks were rumbling through the Czechoslovak countryside and down the streets of Prague where they were met with passive resistance from the Czechs. Swastikas were painted on the sides of the tanks and all street signs were painted over with the word 'Moscow'. By the end of the year, Charles de Gaulle had been voted back into office in France and Richard Nixon had been elected president in the United States. The Chicago police, despite their brutality, received widespread support from Americans for their actions. The silent majority, terrified by the year's events, had swung to the forces of reaction.

I wrote up our Dru climb for Ken Wilson's new *Mountain* magazine, and after it was published Stanley Pickard, an editor at publisher's Kaye and Ward, suggested I wrote a book updating Geoff Sutton's short work on artificial climbing. I gave it some thought and agreed, provided there was no rush. That autumn I began to teach social studies, part of a team of six dedicated staff led by Mike Adams. It was enormously satisfying to be part of such a tolerant and supportive group. We introduced a huge range of topics to our fifteen-and sixteen-year-olds, who weren't academically inclined: advertising, drug addiction, old age, mental health, minority groups, war, cruelty to animals and so forth. We drew on a whole range of what were then unusual teaching methods: visual aids, films, visits and guest speakers from all walks of life. It was something of an experiment and one considered a success; our team was able to engage pupils who wanted to be anywhere but in school.

Jeff Upton and I had decided to visit the Dolomites in the summer of 1969; we wanted to try the newest route on the hardest part of the north face of the Cima Ovest, climbed in the summer of 1968 by Gerhard Bauer and the Rudolph brothers, Erich and Walter. To prepare, we travelled to the Isle of Harris in the Outer Hebrides that spring, for the 600-foot overhanging north-west face of

27

27 Climbing the crux pitch on *The Nose* of Strone Ulladale. **Photo:** Leo Dickinson.

28 L–R: me, Guy Lee and Dennis Hennek before our first ascent of *The Nose* on Strone.
Graded A5, and climbed without bolts, it was our hardest new route on the Big Stone.

29 Jeff Upton on the final bivi on *The Scoop* in 1969. I slept on the ledge immediately below Jeff.

30 Strone Ulladale, with the major routes marked.

Moskill Grooves
1989 – Moon, Dawes,
Pritchard.

Knucklehead
1977 – Lloyd, King.

Scoop Variation (free)
1987 – Dawes,
Pritchard.

The Scoop
1969 – Scott,
Upton, Lee,
Terry.

Knuckle Sandwich
1987 – Dawes, Pritchard.

The Nose
1971 – Scott, Lee,
Hennek.

The Chisel
1989 – Waddy, Drury,
Biddle.

Sidewinder
1971 – Scott, Lee.

Stone
1969 – Porteous,
Spence, Mitchell.

Moskill Grooves

The Scoop

The Nose

Sidewinder

Stone

30

32

33

34

31 El Capitan, Yosemite. *The Nose* follows a line at the junction of sunlight and shade,
the *Salathé Wall* takes a rising diagonal line on the shaded wall to the left.

32 Me at the first bivi on the *Salathé Wall*. **Photo**: Peter Habeler.

33 My partner Peter Habeler, as we topped out on the *Salathé*.

34 Low on the *Salathé*, with the headwall leaning out above.

35 Peter leading on *Salathé*.
36 Peter belaying on *Salathé*.
37 Peter on the headwall of the *Salathé*.

38 Guy Lee climbing the Narrow Slab on the Troll Wall.
39 Jeff Upton high on the Troll Wall.

40

40 The west face of Mount Asgard, Baffin Island. Dennis Hennek and I attempted the left (north) summit via
the crack system splitting the sunlit pillar in 1971 and again in 1972 with Paul Braithwaite and Paul Nunn.
It was eventually climbed by Charlie Porter solo in 1975.

41 Our approach up Pangnirtung Fjord in 1971 using skidoos pulling boats on sledges.
42 Me wading a stream. **Photo:** Dennis Hennek.
43 Climbing paradise: Breidablik is up on the left, with Mount Thor centre.
44 The east side of Mount Asgard's north peak. Our 1972 route goes up the centre of the south-east buttress (right of the couloir). The route involved climbing up overlapping slabs to the shoulder, and the steep cracks and chimney of the headwall.

45 Rob Wood climbing on the superb granite on the north-east face of Pt. Killabuk.
46 Dennis Hennek on the lower slabs of the east face pillar of Asgard.
47 Dennis Hennek climbing the lower corner cracks on the west face pillar of Asgard's north peak.

48 Devil's Tower, Wyoming.
49 Dennis Hennek signs the book on the summit of the tower.

50

51

50 The 'King Swing' pendulum on *The Nose* of El Cap.
51 Rick White climbing on day two on *The Nose* of El Cap.

52 Changabang in the Garhwal Himalaya. The team contemplating crossing the Shipton Col in the foreground.
53 Breathtaking panoramic views of the Nanda Devi Sanctuary from Changabang.

54 Pik Lenin seen from the camp, with the Krylenko Pass on the left and the north-east face on the right.
55 The line of our route on the north-east ridge of Pik Lenin.

Strone Ulladale, Scotland's very own big wall and the highest overhanging cliff in Britain. The face, a concave scoop of fine-grained Lewisian gneiss towering above Glen Ulladale, was suddenly becoming a sought-after objective. Guy Lee had been there in 1968 with Pete Thompson, and had come back with dramatic tales. With insufficient gear they had given up on the face and left for the Isle of Skye to climb a new route on the Old Man of Storr.

The line Jeff and myself tried on the left of the face felt all wrong; it lead away from the real challenge, which went straight up the centre of the scoop. This, we could see, was a much more pleasing line. So we stripped our pegs from our false start, called this visit a reconnaissance and planned to return during the Whitsun holiday with reinforcements. We were determined to be first up the north-west face but competition was gathering. We returned on the boat to Skye with a group of Scottish lads, including John Grieve who had climbed new routes either side of the north-west face.

'Just what Big H has been waiting to get his teeth into,' Grieve whispered darkly.

'Who the hell's "Big H"?'

'Hamish MacInnes,' Grieve said. 'And he's coming up again in a few weeks with Ian Clough.'

'Would that be "Little I"?' we asked. 'What pegging has Big H done?'

'Well, there's the *Bonatti Pillar*,' Grieve said.

'Oh, but you don't have to put any pegs in,' we told him. 'In fact, it's a good place to take some out.'

'Anyway, they have the *right* attitude to big problems; they'll do it,' he concluded.

Stung by this, we went into a huddle, more determined than ever to get the first ascent. We studied the summer timetable and laid plans to arrive just before Whitsun. That way we'd beat the teachers and the students. Famous Glen Coe guides we could do nothing about. Week by week we heard of the growing number of parties interested in the Strone. We visited Denny Moorhouse at his workshop near Llanberis and bought huge numbers of pegs but learned also that a team from Sheffield had ordered a similar number to be sent direct to Harris. We speculated this was Paul Nunn, who could go some on pegs, or Jack Street. It turned out to be no one we knew. But we did learn that another consignment of pegs had gone to Glen Coe. Our morale dropped further when we learned that a team from the Edinburgh Squirrels were already on the island.

So back we went, Jeff and me with Ken Wilson in his car with all our gear. Mick Terry and Guy Lee would arrive as reinforcements, hitching up separately. Crossing the Minch, we drove the last dozen miles to Amhuinnsuidhe Castle. (This Scottish stately pile was built – from imported sandstone – in

John Porteous and Kenny Spence.

1865 for the Earl of Dunmore, Charles Murray, who spent a year exploring the Pamirs, another actor in the Great Game.) We could only find one person in residence, a cleaning lady who told us the current owner, Sir Hereward Wake, was absent but that it would be fine for us to walk through the estate to Glen Ulladale and the Strone. So we followed the winding path up the glen, staggering under the weight of our pegging gear, chuntering about Sir Hereward's putative forebear, Hereward the Wake, who roamed the Lincolnshire fens killing Normans.

The Strone slowly took shape, growing larger and more impressive as we approached our old Base Camp, increasingly confident that we had the place to ourselves. This misconception was rudely shattered by sudden shrieks and whoops from high up on the hill. Three wild Scots were descending, obviously happy and triumphant.

'Christ, we're too late,' I thought. But we had been so fixated on the scoop that we'd forgotten about the lines to the right of the Strone's nose. Fergus Mitchell, the first of the three to arrive, explained that he had been helping Kenny Spence and John Porteous put up an excellent new route to the right of our line over three days, one for the reconnaissance and two for the climbing. They filled us in on our competition, pointing out where MacInnes had reached and what the Sheffield lads had been doing. They also warned us that Brian Robertson, fresh from Yosemite in California, was bringing Rick Sylvester to take a look. We decided to make a start next day.

There were so many unknown factors to be considered, but it is this not knowing that makes first ascents so much harder. We had, for example, no idea whether there were ledges from which to belay. If there weren't it would be a far harder climb: arranging a hanging belay in slings at the end of every pitch and then sitting there for hour after hour would be no fun at all. The crag went out over our heads until the final overhangs, which were 150 feet out from where we stood at the base of the cliff. The other unknown factor was whether or not there would be suitable cracks to peg; the contorted gneiss in the lower reaches looked decidedly anti-peg. What if we got to the final overhangs and there was no way through?

In the event we did find ledges: one to stand on at the end of the first pitch, then another six feet long and three wide where I could bivouac while Jeff slept in a hammock strung out above. Despite such a good ledge we descended to regroup and meet Guy and Mick, who had managed to find sufficient lifts to make it up from Nottingham. Jeff and I then moved up to another ledge, also absolutely flat and slightly bigger at seven feet long and three wide, the ideal place for Jeff to while away the hours as I dealt with the most overhanging part of the climb and, as it turned out, where cracks were thin and far between. Meanwhile Guy and Mick began de-pegging the first two pitches.

I reached an impasse and for three hours tried every way possible to insert one of a huge variety of pegs from tiny RURPs – Realised Ultimate Reality Pitons – the size of a large postage stamp, to three-inch bongs, not unlike a Swiss cowbell cut in two. Guy and Mick had completed their work; now there would be no easy way off the cliff other than up and the only way to move up seemed to be drilling a hole and placing a bolt. So I called down for the hand drill and began hammering away at full stretch. After half an hour's hard work I had made a hole an inch deep. I then took a bolt, which I'd taken off my motorbike and tapered on the school lathe, and managed to insert it a quarter of an inch into the hole, Then I started pounding it into the hole, tied a sling to it and transferred my weight. At full stretch again, I was able to place a bong between two blocks of rock that somehow also took my weight and from there I could reach out to place small angle pitons in a deepening crack, one after the other, each more solid and secure than the last, until I'd crossed the lip of the scoop and on to the headwall. Soon I was at the top of the most demanding rock climb I had ever been on.

For the four of us, it was the culmination of a week spent in one of the most beautiful places on the planet. Yet I was disappointed we had been forced to resort to sieging the climb and drilling the rock. Our excuse was that with the lower part de-pegged placing a bolt was our only means of escape. The reality was that if we had not had a drill I am sure we would have still got off and probably found an alternative way to finish the route, perhaps less direct

On the first pitch of *The Scoop* in 1969. The wind is blowing my free rope out into the void. **Photo**: Ken Wilson.

but still preferable to putting in that one bolt. Our route was subsequently repeated and more bolts were inserted as they were on other routes pioneered on *The Scoop*. I soon realised that I had created a precedent; had I worked harder and avoided drilling, a remarkable rock formation in a country not over-endowed with big cliffs might well have remained a bolt-free zone. To my eternal shame I started a trend that cannot now be reversed, at least not easily. I decided after that I would never again use a drill – never again 'murder the impossible' as Reinhold Messner put it. It had been a rather hollow victory. The reason I did it was probably the same reason that I screamed in my cot – attention. The advice from Grantland Rice hung above my bed had clearly been forgotten; I'd been more focused on climbing the Strone than 'how I played the game.'

On the journey home Ken arranged to call in on the *Scottish Daily Express* in Glasgow hoping to sell our story to subsidise his travel costs. Ken, both a perfectionist and anti-smoking, handed over his rolls of film to a paunchy Glaswegian who was hard to understand partly because he only removed the cigarette between his lips to light another. Ken was following the chain-smoker round the dark room, pleading with him to make sure dust didn't get on to his precious film, when about half an inch of ash dropped off the end of the Glaswegian's cigarette. As if in slow motion, Ken reached out to catch it before it landed in the developing fluid and in the process knocked over several plastic bottles.

'Nae bother,' said the smoker.

Ken was now red in the face, flecks of spittle in the corners of his mouth. He demanded to see the picture editor.

'Ah *am* the picture editor,' the smoker replied.

The article that appeared with Ken's photographs was baffling but it made us laugh. 'This particular achievement involved the first principles of parachute jumping and bronco busting,' the article explained under the sub-heading 'Jargon'. The journalist responsible was called James Gibbins, who later worked for the *Daily Mail*'s Washington bureau where he was exposed for inventing his stories. True, he managed to report that *The Scoop* was overhanging, but then he lost touch with reality: 'One of the overhangs was a dangerous twenty-five feet, like all the others it was tackled by throwing out a hook to get purchase on the rock, then like a parachutist the climber would haul himself up. The Strone is ugly not only in appearance but in its habits, it is notorious for its rock falls. A shout of jubilation; even – some say – a cough or an extra loud tummy rumble could bring the rocks tumbling. Naturally no-one snored, if they had they might have been wakened up – by an avalanche.' A photograph of Jeff jumaring up a rope, hanging free, was captioned: 'Jeff parachutes in reverse up the unclimbable rock.'

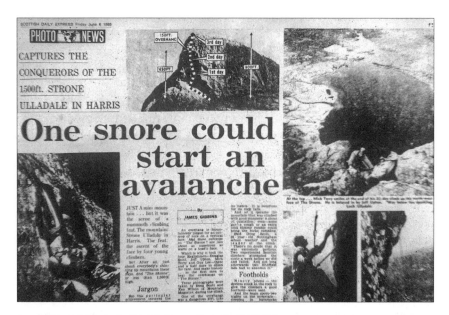

James Gibbins' article in the *Scottish Daily Express*. **Photo**: Scottish Daily Express.

Our main objective was realised with a cheque from the *Express* for £25, which covered the transport costs to the Outer Hebrides. The following week Peter Gilman wrote a more measured account of our climb for *The Sunday Times* under the headline: 'It's Done – Britain's Toughest Climb.' I tried to explain to the staff at school, who were starting to lionise me, that 'toughest' should not be confused with 'hardest' since a pegged route could never be as hard as the latest free climbs. That took some explaining and I soon gave up; it wasn't a bad thing to be thought the progenitor of the hardest climb in Britain when it came to justifying to staff that I should have another few months' leave of absence.

Ted Wells joined Jeff, Mick and myself on the big roof on the Cima Ovest's north face. I was keen not only to make the first British ascent but also to see if I could feel at home under those giant roofs. Surely, I thought, after *The Big Overhang* at Anglesey and now having succeeded in climbing *The Scoop*, I should be able to rationalise the exposure when hanging from the pegs and numerous bolts on the *Bauer-Rudolph* route. Although I wasn't placing the bolts myself, I wasn't averse to making use of them if they were already in place.

While we were reconnoitring the north face and the descent route, we ran into Tom Proctor, a well-known and highly respected Derbyshire rock climber who was on his first trip abroad. He told us he had just climbed Emilio Comici's classic route on the north face of the Cima Grande, a neighbour of the Cima Ovest and one of the Tre Cime di Lavaredo.

'How did you find that, Tom?' I asked.

Jeff Upton at the belay below the roof on the north face of the Cima Ovest.

'Eh, it were like being up in aeroplane all day, never known drops like it.' We left Tom to bask in his success and set off up the lower section of our route, climbing mostly free as there were so few pegs. It must be a new trend, we thought, with the Continentals reducing aid. After a strenuous long run-out, I rested on a loose fixed peg, only for it to come out with me hanging on it. I flew out into space for sixty feet before Mick held me tight. His hands were burned from the rope and so we went down to regroup. Mick decided to stay down and take photographs.

The next day I passed my previous high point and eventually came to a crack bristling with pegs and with a note scratched on the rock: 'Fuck off Scott, it's too loose for you – Leo.' Unknown to us, the photographer, Leo Dickinson, with Jeff Morgan and Brian Molyneux, both good rock climbers, had decided to beat us to the first British ascent. They had lost heart where they left the message and proceeded to strip out nearly all the pegs as they descended; it was all good fun, the sort of friendly competition you get on a first ascent, even on just a first British ascent. Brian and Leo went off to climb the *Brandler-Hasse* route on the Cima Grande.

We now reached the roof where I left Jeff belaying me in slings and Ted some 100 feet lower down at the previous belay. I had two cameras, one colour and the other black-and-white, which I passed from the roof to Jeff, who lowered them down to Ted. Ted had never used a camera before and so there was a long discussion on f-stops, shutter speeds and depth of field which all helped

Me on the north face of the Cima Ovest, swinging out under the 150-foot roof,
800 feet above the scree, with Jeff Upton belaying. **Photo**: Ted Wells.

to take my mind off the yawning space below me. I always preferred to go first rather than sit for hours with doubt turning into fear; to avoid panic attacks I felt better grappling with the problem at hand.

Some 120 feet out from Jeff my hands were knotting up with cramp. I could feel it creeping down my back as well. I wondered if I could get back to Jeff, but realised I couldn't; I had better concentrate all my efforts on completing the overhang and getting on to the headwall. Once I realised it was all or nothing, I calmed down and gained strength from the commitment. Finally, I reached the Kasparek Bivouac on the headwall, a well-known feature on the easier Cassin route. I was absolutely parched and used my helmet to collect water dripping down a crack from melting snow above and drank all the water in the sack I hauled round from Jeff. By the time Jeff and Ted were on the ledge it was dark and with nightfall it became colder and the source of the dripping water turned to ice. Ted was left with a parched throat, gasping for water all night, something he has never let me forget.

THE 4TH AGE

Then a soldier,
Full of strange oaths, and bearded like the pard,
Jealous in honour, sudden and quick in quarrel,
Seeking the bubble reputation
Even in the cannon's mouth.

As You Like It, William Shakespeare

From 28 to 35 is the time of the development
of the intellectual or rational soul, the human
being begins to think differently, develops more
consciousness in the sphere of judgements
and feelings, and a tendency towards a more
serious life. Before 35, activity is directed
to the development of the physical body.

The Number Seven, A.E. Abbot

Ken Wilson at Camp 1 on Everest in 1972.

A CHANGING WORLD

I arrived back in Nottingham from the Dolomites broke. To make ends meet before the start of the new school term, I took a job as bouncer in a nightclub in the old part of the city. It's not something I would repeat or recommend to anyone else. Listening to incredibly loud music from 8 p.m. to 4 a.m. every night left my ears ringing when I tried to catch up on sleep next day. The only interesting thing about the job was exploring the cellar; the club was expanding and the builders had unearthed part of the sandstone wall from the twelfth century that separated the Saxons from the Normans.

This was the time of Woodstock, 'three days of peace and music' held on Max Yasgur's dairy farm in upstate New York that was a pivotal moment in the counterculture just as the 1960s came to an end. Despite the crowds and the mud, the incessant rain and the endless traffic jams, the idealism of that era shone through. Yasgur himself, who said himself he was no hippy, saw the event as a victory for peace and love: 'If we join them we can turn those adversities that are the problems of America today into a hope for a bright and more peaceful future.'

Aspects of the counterculture appealed to me greatly. The remorseless pace of development after the war and the intensification of farming with its ever-increasing use of toxic chemicals put nature into decline and diminished the wild places I loved so much. The counterculture offered a more balanced approach to living on Planet Earth. The *Whole Earth Catalog*, for example, was launched in 1968, a bible of self-sufficiency and sustainable living. The Soil Association came into being with the ambition of reining in the use of chemicals on the land.

Climbers and mountain lovers played an important role in this awakening. David Brower, for instance, made many first ascents in Yosemite and climbed Shiprock in New Mexico in 1939, a seminal moment in American climbing.

Brower helped steer the Wilderness Act into law for the Sierra Club, but left in 1969 to found Friends of the Earth to protest against the nuclear power industry. The organisation's first employee was Amory Lovins, who served his time as a mountain guide in the White Mountains and also spent time in Britain, climbing in North Wales. Brower commissioned a book from Lovins about Snowdonia; Lovins remains one of the world's leading advocates and engineers of energy efficiency.

This link between climbing in the mountains and a respect for nature and the people who live there has been significant to me. There was something about Joe Brown and George Band, on the first ascent of the world's third-highest mountain Kangchenjunga, stopping short of the summit that struck a chord with me and everyone else who cares about such things. It was done out of respect for the local people and their reverence for the guardian deities that inhabit the mountain's five summits. Along many of the footpaths in the high Himalaya you can find banks of *mani* stones near monasteries or propitious features in the landscape, like caves. On each stone are carved the six Sanskrit syllables *Om Mani Padme Hum*, often translated as: 'Hail to the jewel in the lotus!' There are many interpretations, but the mantra is a tool, a way to transform your impure body, speech, and mind into those of a Buddha, to find the Buddha within. Most of us now look outwards for explanations, through our senses, and spend less time looking inward for strength and conviction. But we are not immune to the idea that there is something hidden away that would be important to us if we only had the inclination to find it.

If many saw Woodstock as the end of the 1960s, I have a more personal memory. That November, one of the great characters of British climbing, Eric Beard, was killed in a car crash on the M6. I never knew 'Beardie' as well as his friends in the Rock and Ice, like Nat Allen and Dennis Gray, who introduced me to him at the Dovedale Dash in the late 1950s. But over those ten years Beardie had become for me, as he was for so many others, a pillar of our community of climbers. He was absorbed in all aspects of outdoor life, on and off the crag: fell runner, star of Ilam Hall pantomimes, folk singer and good friend to so many of us. Born in Leeds, he'd left school at fourteen, and after working as a jockey, got a job as a tram conductor. It's no surprise, if you knew him, that he was voted most popular conductor by the public. He lived on honey butties and hot sweet tea, which powered him across the fells; he held the records for the Cuillin Ridge and the Welsh 3,000ers and not long before he died had run from John o'Groats to Land's End in a little over eighteen days. He always gave the impression his list of climbs was modest yet he did several tough routes in the Alps and Dolomites, like the north face of the Cima Grande.

Beardie had been a shoulder for me to lean on that New Year in Scotland.

I had provoked Jan, enough for her to spend the night dancing with a huge chap; that could have ended in a brawl had Beardie not talked me out of it. He distracted me with plans for a day out on skis and on a cold New Year's Day we walked up from Loch Morlich to the top of Cairn Gorm where we skied across the plateau to Ben Macdui and then down the Lairig Ghru back to Loch Morlich. What I remember most about that day is Beardie singing while I struggled to follow in his tracks. I never saw him again. I shall never forget him or his boundless good energy.

By 1970 I was well into writing my book about big-wall climbing. I had also taken on the editorship of the Alpine Climbing Group's bulletin. Thanks to all this, I widened my interest in world mountaineering, learning more about its history, the current scene and was giving more thought to where climbing was heading. In the Climbers' Club journal of September 1901, C.S. Ascherson and H.V. Reade opened an editorial feature titled 'British Climbing: from another point of view' with this observation: 'Every sport or pastime may be said to pass through three stages. At first it is practised in secrecy, as a kind of forbidden joy, by a few enthusiasts. Then comes the proselytising and contro-versial stage, when the original devotees endeavour to justify themselves, and to communicate their enthusiasm to others. Finally, the new thing is recognised by the world at large, and finds its place in the list of orthodox rec-reations.' This development, from simply climbing to a complex of associated activities, seemed relevant to me personally.

At first there was simply the pleasure of going out each weekend on to the crags to climb what I failed to climb before. It was enormously satisfying to discover that as my skill and strength increased so did the difficulty and quality of the routes I could master. Better still was applying my new-found abilities on harder routes that I climbed on sight, and then on routes that had never been climbed before at all. There was nothing more rewarding than sitting back after a big effort and taking in the mountain landscape with body, mind and spirit uplifted. I would go home a better man for those few hours on the rocks oblivious to everything else, absorbed in the moment of being.

These intense experiences were for me alone. Perhaps my partner on the rope, having had his own experiences, would empathise. Beyond that, only I knew what I had to do to summon up the courage, to weigh up the moves and then feel relief and pleasure from having made them. Rock climbing will always be, deep down, a very private affair.

I suppose I was, at times, smug and infuriatingly so, being given to feelings of superiority over parents and teachers who did not know what my climbing friends and I knew about the vertical world. It was, I thought, quite beyond their understanding. I became more and more consumed with the thought of climbing; the more I did the more I needed to go again, having that urge to go one step beyond, or as Royal Robbins once wrote, to have 'the wild thoughts'. I climbed without pressure, other than from within, just to see. I had my natural instinct for survival to protect me, just as when I climbed trees or up the wooden scaffolding on building sites. I found there is something good and safe in bold spontaneity, with nothing in the way of the body taking control, making the moves one after the other, without knowing exactly what the outcome will be.

Charles Evans, who led the expedition that first climbed Kangchenjunga, which impressed me so much, introduced me to a poem by Henry Wadsworth Longfellow that applies equally to climbing rocks as it does to exploring the sea:

'Helmsman! for the love of heaven,
Teach me, too, that wondrous song!'

'Wouldst thou,'– so the helmsman answered,
'Learn the secret of the sea?
Only those who brave its dangers
Comprehend its mystery!'

That comprehension seems to stay with us down the years, no matter that we err to flattery or the lure of gold.

The second evangelical stage in the onward march of climbing is 'controversial' because those who write about it become more famous than those who do not. In letting others beyond our immediate group of friends or club members know of our achievements, comparisons are made and a spirit of competition develops; others seek out harder routes to claim their own share of fame. Performance may become everything and the landscape, the setting, no longer so important, not so appreciated as it was in the beginning, during the period of discovery.

Charles Evans said in his valedictory address as president of the Alpine Club in 1970: 'To me the climbing scene seems altered in ways which deserve comment: competition is more evident than it was; so is the courting of publicity; mountaineering is more used than it was for ends not directly connected with mountains – education, the winning of prestige and the making of money through 'showbiz', chiefly film and television.' For Charles, the bond that held the Alpine Club together had little to do with 'our craft and its practice, and nothing to do with any service the Club gives its members; it depends on a common susceptibility to the atmosphere of "the wild and lonely places" … which produce in us who are of like mind the recognition of an experience shared.'

The third stage, according to Ascherson and Reade, is the end game; others arrive with a motivation far removed from climbing for its own sake. They end up subverting the original impulse by promoting climbing for wealth or fame, or to gain control. In early 1970, Dennis Gray published his memoir *Rope Boy*, expressing similar concerns that a totally amateur sport was fast disappearing under pressure from commerce and institutions. He lamented 'the serried ranks of professionals [who] stretch through climbing instruction, journalism, lecturers, equipment designers, manufacturers and retailers, and as in any boom there has been no shortage of exploiters. Mountaineers do not live in a vacuum between days on rock or hill, much as some may desire to do so. They are affected by the pressures of the society in which they live like anyone else, by the materialism and commercialisation which are the dark side of the age in which mankind has made the greatest technological discoveries and achievements in our history.'

Tony Moulam, in a favourable review of *Rope Boy*, thought Dennis was right – up to a point: 'There is much sense in the analysis of the decline of climbing aesthetics with a commercialisation and the apparent desire for regimentation and certification. However, this is for the masses. Climbing calls for the individualist who will always stand apart, poised and balanced to lead our sport forward.' This applies both on and off the rocks.

Two more influential articles appeared at this time about the traditions of mountaineering. Lito Tejada-Flores' essay 'Games Climbers Play' was published first in the Sierra Club publication *Ascent* in 1967. He explored the different disciplines within climbing and the nature of rules within those disciplines and how they lead to increasingly difficult standards. The essay was a huge influence on Ken Wilson at *Mountain* magazine. 'Margins of Safety' by Harold Drasdo was published in the *Alpine Journal* in 1969. Drasdo attempts to show that climbers organise their games in such a way as to conserve danger, much in the same way as Tejada-Flores showed that they organise their affairs in such a way as to conserve difficulty. Robin Campbell in his review of the *AJ* noted it was bad news for the safety-mongers; Drasdo's splendid conclusion that a margin of safety is 'a constant in the climber's head, rather than a variable on the soles of his boots.'

The anarchic counterculture of climbing in this period had a counterfactual: climbing in the Soviet Union. After the Second World War the only way for Russian climbers to pursue their sport was along official channels on organised climbing camps. Climbing had developed through the military during the war to help to defend the mountainous southern borders of the Soviet Union. After the war the government continued to control climbing and produced remarkably strong climbers whose motivation, style and ethical approach were radically different from the rest of the climbing world. In Russia, climbing was a team effort with much emphasis on safety; the use of fixed ropes and drilling equipment was seen to be logical. On the other hand, to get an invitation to future climbing camps meant succeeding on current objectives, engendering fierce competition.

The first actual Russian climbing competition took place in 1947 in the Caucasus. By 1955 competitions were a regular feature in the Crimea where the emphasis was on speed climbing. The first international climbing competition was staged during 1976 near the Soviet city of Gagra on the rocks of the Yupshara Gorge, now in the disputed territory of Abkhazia. Most of the Soviet Bloc countries took part as well as many European nations. Leading European climbers, such as Robert Paragot from France and Otti Wiedmann from Austria, were in favour. Then again, there is nothing sacred; everything has to be exploited – even tree climbing. The International Society of Arboriculture held their first tree climbing competition in St Louis in 1976.

In the West, public attitudes about mountaineering were greatly influenced by the post-war rush to climb the 8,000-metre peaks. In Britain, the ascent of Everest in 1953, more than any other single event, transformed climbing from something known only to its adherents into a sport talked about by everyone – at least for a time. Success on Everest, coming after so many failures, and just a few days before the coronation of Queen Elizabeth II, was suddenly in the nation's thoughts, even if I managed to ignore it. It helped promote the idea that a new Elizabethan Age had arrived, which promised to be as glorious as the first. In 1950, France was in the grip of Annapurna fever as Maurice Herzog and his team made the first ascent of a mountain over 8,000 metres. In both nations, as in Italy after K2 in 1954, climbing was a positive story after the horrors of war.

The combination of this post-war public interest and development in broadcasting technology created a step change in climbing's popularity. In the 1950s, I seemed to know most people I met on the crags, or else knew of them. During the 1960s there was a series of outside broadcasts that put climbing on television screens for the first time. Robert Paragot and Ian McNaught-Davis, rivals for the first ascent of Muztagh Tower in the Karakoram, together climbed the Eiffel Tower in Paris for a television show that was hugely popular. 'Mac' also did an outside broadcast from the Matterhorn. (According to an audience research report, viewers complained the climbers made it look too easy, and that the ascent 'became dull and lacked tension'.) Robert and Mac teamed up again with Joe Brown and Don Whillans for a climb on Cloggy that appeared on *Grandstand* between tennis and horse racing from Newbury.

There were climbs on Kilnsey and the Red Wall of Gogarth – the 'greatest show on earth', Tom Patey called it – that featured the Yosemite climber Royal Robbins. Millions of viewers watched *Coronation Street*, not the soap opera, but the route put by Chris Bonington, Tony Greenbank and Mike Thompson in Cheddar Gorge. Joe Brown became so famous from his television work that a postman delivered a letter addressed to him: The Human Fly, UK. The biggest blockbuster of all time was broadcast in 1967 from the Old Man of Hoy in the Orkneys with an all-star cast of Mac, Bonington, Patey, Brown, Dougal Haston and Pete Crew with John Cleare and Hamish MacInnes as climbing cameramen. There was even a platoon of Scots Guards to help with the logistics. Around fifteen million viewers watched as the climbers swung around on ropes and struggled up overhanging rock and listened to Mac's humorous, self-deprecating commentary. By the summer of 1970, the popularity of climbing was made evident with the screening of three TV commercials involving climbing including one depicting Chris Bonington in yellow clothing promoting Blue Band margarine on Carreg Alltrem. During the same year ITN showed clips of Chris and his expedition to the south face of Annapurna all of which helped establish him as the best-known climber in the country.

I had my own experience of this boom. In 1972 Guy Lee, Dennis Hennek and myself appeared in Leo Dickinson's BBC film *Rock Island Climb* about our ascent of the *Nose Direct* on Strone Ulladale. It was an interesting experience but the producer had no experience of climbing and insisted on cutaway shots of someone hammering rock in a quarry for a skyhook placement. Meanwhile the commentator was explaining how the climbers wanted 'to climb according to the geography of the rock and not alter it by drilling.' The film was shown on Boxing Day morning, which gave my parents immense pleasure and me too, despite the film's strange contradictions. I had the sense of suddenly being somebody. The public might have been enthralled with climbing television spectaculars but climbers themselves began to question the banality of the scripts and *Mountain* magazine complained of the 'constant portrayal of climbers as circus performers' after a programme featuring *Spider's Web* on Gogarth.

Mountain and its editor Ken Wilson had quite an influence on my climbing, especially during the late sixties and early seventies. It captured the profound changes affecting climbing at that period and Ken proved a relentless guardian of the soul of mountaineering – as he saw it. Even before he took over the Mountaineering Association's magazine *Mountain Craft*, which later became *Mountain*, he had joined the Climbers' Club and immediately started campaigning to allow women to become members, the first of many causes he took up and pursued vigorously.

In 1968 Ken took over *Mountain Craft*, which had existed since the mid-1950s as the brainchild of Jerry Wright and his Mountaineering Association. The last edition appeared in August, when Ken announced the birth of *Mountain*.

The first edition of the bimonthly magazine appeared in January 1969. *Mountain Craft* had always been popular despite its somewhat unprofessional presentation but the new magazine was something the climbing world had never seen before, with a crisp, eye-catching layout that spoke of Ken's architectural and photographic background. *Mountain* was also the first international magazine with an appeal to English-speaking climbers around the world, from Almscliff to Yosemite.

Readers often compared *Mountain* with *Newsweek* for its reporting style, and while it nominally claimed to reflect all levels of climbing in reality it concentrated on the climbers and mountains Ken thought most worthy of comment and exposure. This was not to everyone's taste. Rob Wood, who had himself contributed an article on climbing El Capitan, wrote *Mountain* a letter, with the Scottish-born ice climber Bugs McKeith, titled 'Mountain's Brave New World'. Both men were now based in Calgary, on the edge of the Rockies. Rob, like Ken, was from a middle-class background and an architect, but unlike Ken tended towards the counterculture. Rob was from Leeds and honed his climbing on gritstone and Lakeland crags; Ken was from the Midlands and concentrated on the very competitive North Wales climbing scene.

Rob and Bugs wrote: 'This is the kind of materialistic, competitive, institutionalised, indoctrination, which leads to the conformism, stagnation and suppression of individualism characteristic of our society in general. Many climbers are aware of the proximity of 1984, *Mountain*, through its *Brave New World* approach, is willingly contributing to this frightening prospect.' They also criticised *Mountain's* lack of respect for the Rock and Ice Club and Dennis Gray, who *Mountain* had accused of 'living in a world he doesn't understand.'

Rob and Bugs finished with a very pertinent question: 'Is it too late to stop mountaineering becoming a rat race – where individual spontaneity and creativity are overwhelmed by mechanistic ego-tripping rituals, sponsored by manufacturers, approved by do-good institutions and propagated by the mass-conditioning of the press media? An objective look at the North Wales scene would not inspire much optimism.' Their intervention prompted another letter from Brian Greenwood that was equally perceptive: 'to the majority of climbers climbing is still something separate from the crass materialism of everyday life, please try and keep it that way for us.'

More than forty years later, Rob wrote that with the benefit of hindsight he could now see what the 'Calgary letters' to Ken implied but failed to specify. 'Our objection wasn't so much against commercialism or institutionalism per se so much as the more insidious threat, namely the prevalent societal belief that humans are separate and superior to nature.' Mountaineering, for Rob Wood, was a way to recapture 'the euphoric satisfaction and extraordinary empowerment of reconnecting with nature and each other.'

There were some who resented Ken's combative style and bombast; every-thing seemed to him to be black or white. And there was some justification for criticising *Mountain* for promoting competition and allowing self-promo-tion. He liked league tables, and even when he was running *Mountain Craft* he produced a league table of climbers based on how many new routes they'd done at Gogarth. His penchant for lists of firsts dominated the first two editions of *Mountain*. He was always willing to correct mistakes, although one error of judgement he didn't correct was describing the 1966 Eiger Direct climb as 'probably the most difficult single climb ever accomplished'. It showed he lacked a proper understanding of how fixed ropes reduce risk.

Yet his views on bolting were considered by most to have hit the nail on the head, so to speak. Ken's relentless struggle, with the support of many others, to keep British crags largely free of bolts was a major achievement. By resisting the Continental enthusiasm for drilling every available crag in sight, he became a sort of conscience for British climbing. His main concern was always that the best traditions of British mountaineering were maintained. He was relentless in his pursuit of what he considered to be the true path. He was notoriously voluble and tenacious, which did not always go down well late in the evening at tedious committee meetings. But Ken's uncompro-mising attitude often proved justified once the rest of us had caught up with the argument.

He could change his mind about issues and sometimes gave up campaigns in the face of near-universal opposition, as he did with the use of climbing chalk. The American boulderer John Gill had used chalk in the 1950s, like gymnasts, and by the 1970s Yosemite climbers such as John Long and John Bachar were using it. Ken called young climbers using chalk the 'powder-puff kids' and bemoaned that Stanage was starting to look like 'a blackboard at school'. His headline announcing that the route *Great Wall* at Cloggy had been done free, but that John Allen had used chalk, was roundly mocked. One day, at Pex Hill, I saw Ken climbing a Hard Severe route surrounded by a cloud of chalk. I couldn't believe my eyes.

'Not you as well, Ken,' I said.

'Well everyone else is using it, so not much point in holding out,' he shouted down, sounding resigned.

He might have seemed trenchant in his views, but Ken was never consumed with self-importance. He never claimed a point of view or a line of reasoning for himself. He was happy to see others taking credit for his arguments as if they were their own. He did attack inflated egos and those on the make, although not directly. Usually he left it to those contributors with a satirical bent, like Tom Patey, Ian McNaught-Davis and the brilliant cartoonist Sheridan Anderson, to laugh the pompous out of court. *Mountain* tackled this aspect of the climbing life with some elegance, to the extent that even those mocked could see the humour in it.

Ken and his magazine matured quickly and really came of age after three years or so. Through *Mountain*, Ken, as much as anyone, helped shape the sport in a positive way. He may not have been leading from the front, in the way top climbers like Peter Crew or Martin Boysen did, but his reporting and commentary had immense impact. One issue he took very seriously was the dilemma educationalists faced in embracing outdoor pursuits generally and climbing in particular – how do you introduce kids to a risky activity safely? Ken, unsurprisingly, was determined that climbing didn't change to suit the interests of educationalists who believed you could build character through adventure. He tried to strike a balance between keeping the margins of safety satisfyingly narrow without leaving children dead or injured on the hill or crag.

Ken's great attention to detail and strong views came into their own with *Mountain*'s authoritative coverage of what became known as the Cairngorm Tragedy in 1971. Over the course of two days in November, five schoolchildren and one eighteen-year-old trainee instructor perished from hypothermia during a school winter mountaineering expedition on the Cairngorm Plateau. It is hard to recall a worse tragedy in the annals of British mountaineering. I personally found it shocking having taken so many children out on the hills in winter.

Ben Beattie, a twenty-three-year-old qualified outdoor instructor at Ainslie Park School, Edinburgh and his twenty-one-year-old girlfriend Cathy Davidson took a party of children from the school on a winter traverse of the Cairngorms. They arrived on the Friday night at the Edinburgh education authority centre at Lagganlia adventure centre in Glen Feshie. Beattie was an experienced mountaineer with a mountaineering instructor's certificate and a popular teacher who had helped form and run the school's mountaineering club. The Edinburgh authority was keen to introduce Edinburgh school children to the hills and also to white-water canoeing.

The warden at Lagganlia, John Paisley, discussed the plans Beattie had been hatching over the previous weeks and, without any objections, they set off. Beattie had split the group into a stronger and weaker party; he lead the stronger children, who ranged from fourteen to sixteen years old, over the high points of the Cairngorm plateau. Davidson would do a less demanding itinerary. Both had young assistant instructors. The weather forecast was not good, but all the children were well equipped and the leaders had contingency plans, which were later put into operation. Beattie reached the Curran bothy in good order, having scaled back his plans, but Davidson and her group, who had left the car park an hour later, did not make it. She became bogged down with the less experienced pupils in deep snow, worsening weather and stronger winds.

Davidson decided to bivouac, a recommended action before total exhaustion set in. Unfortunately, in the powdery snow it was impossible to make snow holes so they sat in their sleeping bags and polythene bivouac sacks in the swirling snow all night and the next day. Davidson tried to walk out for help but conditions were so bad she only managed a few yards before returning to spend a second night with her group out in the open. On the Monday morning, with the mountain rescue teams congregating at Glenmore Lodge, Brian Hall saw Davidson from a helicopter, stumbling through deep snow in a state of absolute exhaustion. With the weather closing in, and Davidson needing hospital, Brian and the helicopter left the scene having passed on to the rescue group the location of the children. Later that day they found only one of the seven young people were still alive; the rest had succumbed to their three-day ordeal and the terrible cold. Six teenagers should not have perished on a mountain notorious for weather that can make the area at times an extension of the Arctic. It was such a terrible waste of young life.

The fatal accident enquiry held afterwards looked into the causes of the accident and heard evidence from some of the most experienced guides working in Scotland, like Eric Langmuir and Fred Harper. The enquiry identified the main errors: Davidson should have turned back, or if not, pressed on to the bothy, or if determined to bivouac, should have found more suitable snow to dig a snow cave. Beattie was criticised for underestimating the severity of conditions on the Cairngorms in winter and in delegating large responsibility to Cathy Davidson, although it was noted she was very experienced for her age, having climbed several hard routes in the Alps and made fifteen or so winter trips into the Cairngorms. Beattie was also criticised for allowing the parties to start too late from the car park, not paying due attention to adverse weather reports and for not reuniting the two groups when the weather worsened.

The court felt that Edinburgh Education Authority and the Lagganlia centre should have known that the Cairngorms were unsuitable for school parties in winter and that Beattie's plans should have been vetted more carefully. One of the recommendations of the court was that relevant climbing authorities should look into whether or not the bothies in the Cairngorms should be removed. Fred Harper, the warden at the national training centre at Glenmore Lodge, and the man who organised the rescue, looked into whether the bothies should be closed because they were a temptation to the unwary, or leave the bothies because they have helped and will help parties in difficulty.

In an excellent article Fred wrote for *Mountain Life* he looked into both sides of the argument and decided they should be removed, not simply because they lured people into a false sense of security, but because of a third factor. He thought they should go on the grounds that the Highlands of Scotland, and the Cairngorm plateau in particular, is 'as near to a wilderness as exists in Britain' and, he thought, it was right to remove all man-made objects to keep it 'a remote, desolate, lonely, hostile beautiful place'. Eventually, the majority were for having all the bothies on the Cairngorm plateau removed. (The Corrour bothy in the Lairig Ghru continues to be maintained by the Mountain Bothies Association.)

Inevitably, the tragedy provoked a strong reaction from agencies beyond the outdoor community. One education authority decided no children could go above 1,000 feet without a certificated teacher, much to the amusement of one headteacher whose school was at 1,200 feet above sea level. The police, as always, were involved with the rescue and were as horrified at the loss of life as everyone else. Being a policeman is a difficult job at the best of times; they would prefer everyone to follow a normal pattern of behaviour. They wanted a total ban on school parties going into the Cairngorms in winter. Some police forces, local authorities and national park officials leaned towards new restrictions on climbers as well as school parties going into the mountains.

Mountain, and also *Mountain Life*, the mouthpiece for the BMC, kept the pressure on preserving the freedom to climb without interference from outside agencies; many half-baked ideas were abandoned as a consequence. Snowdonia's information officer, Rhys Edwards, wanted teachers and youth leaders to fill out an eleven-page dossier running to sixty-two questions and file it two months in advance, which the BMC described as 'a bureaucratic nightmare striking at the very basis of what mountains and mountaineering is all about in this country.'

Rhys Edwards wrote to *Climber and Rambler* magazine that 'the freedom of the hills surely has an old fashioned ring to it by now, a concept which does not bear close examination … Your readers should have realised long ago that the national park was not created for them.' Eternal vigilance is the price we have to pay for unrestricted access to the hills and to prevent others from taking responsibility for our lives in them. My friend Lyn Noble, the former principal at White Hall, was bob on when he said: 'There seems to be a need to reduce the day's walk in our hills to a hundred per cent predictable outing requiring the exercise of as little skill and judgement as possible.'

The jury at the fatal accident enquiry, under intense pressure from the grieving families' counsel, returned with a thoughtful verdict that found no one guilty of gross negligence. As *Mountain* reported: 'They stated that they did not want to discourage the spirit of adventure in children's outdoor pursuit activities but they added seven recommendations to their verdict.' None of the proposals were draconian and most of them made good sense.

While the accident enquiry was concluded in six days, the Cairngorm tragedy would have enormous repercussions throughout British climbing, having suddenly raised awareness of the potential for disaster among educational groups in the mountains. As a result the next five years were taken up with one debate after another, often confrontational, between the educationalists and the British Mountaineering Council, which represented the majority of grass roots climbers. Ken Wilson was in the thick of it and played a significant part, along with Dennis Gray, as general secretary of the BMC, in finding a reasonable way forward.

Dennis Gray told me of a BMC meeting in 1972, chaired by the kindly and reasonable Peter Ledeboer in the chair. The meeting opened with a discussion of BMC plans to take over the mountain leadership scheme. Without warning, a member of the audience leapt on to the stage and verbally attacked Peter: 'Murderers! Molesters!' Ben Beattie had been a qualified leader and the protestor believed mountain leader training was responsible for the six deaths in the Cairngorms. Too much faith had been put in certification and not enough in the value of common sense.

The BMC became increasingly involved in wrestling the Mountain Leadership Training Board from the control of the educationalists, who were led by Jack Longland. There was for a while a public clamour for more certification and tighter regulation of outdoor activities in schools. There were proposals made in Parliament that mandatory insurance should be taken out by all climbers going into the Scottish hills in winter. The BMC reluctantly involved itself in the training debate; it was thought not to do so would leave the whole of climbing exposed to all those non-climbers who sought to regulate it. Yet it will always be an uphill battle to make real mountaineering safe and convenient for anyone other than climbers.

In my experience, accidents more often happen to young students when led by an adult. When children are let loose to take responsibility for themselves they are more cautious and respond to their innate sense of survival. However, Ben Beattie was not pilloried and was recognised as a fine teacher, so much so that Fred Harper took him on as an instructor at Glenmore Lodge. This generous gesture was appreciated by most climbers and instructors who followed the inquiry. We all knew that we might also have pushed a little too hard, taking young children into the hills and causing them to suffer unnecessarily through our own ambition to succeed.

El Capitan.

YOSEMITE

Partly thanks to *Mountain*, partly because of my interest in big-wall climbing, going to America became increasingly important to me. It wasn't just the lure of Yosemite's huge granite faces. I was fascinated by the interesting cultures in American climbing that had developed through the 1960s. I'd seen the *Vulgarian Digest*, a now mythical publication put together by Joe Kelsey to capture the anarchic excess of a small group of East Coast climbers centred on the Gunks in upstate New York. The Vulgarians originated in the 1950s as a beatnik antidote to the rather straight-laced scene that prevailed at that time. As the Vulgarian Dick DuMais put it, their credo was: 'Yelling and screaming and fornicating in the woods.' The *Vulgarian Digest* ran cartoons from its inspired artistic director Sheridan Anderson, under the *nom de plume* E. Lovejoy Wolfinger III. The satirical articles and Sheridan's caricatures brought the pretentious and overblown in the climbing fraternity back down to earth. I was equally fascinated by the scene in California and began making plans for an extended visit. First, however, I had unfinished business in the Outer Hebrides.

To the right of *The Scoop* we had spotted another obvious line that had to be called *The Nose*. Since it was more or less overhanging, it might well go in winter so in the half term of February 1970 I drove north with Ray Gillies, Leo Dickinson and the rising star – and Pink Floyd enthusiast – Tony Wilmott. Despite the first 200 feet overhanging the start by about fifty feet the route was badly exposed to intense snowstorms passing across the island during what was a particularly intense winter. Since we had come all that way, we felt we had to do something. Nailing under the roof was challenging; there was a paucity of cracks that had us winding an intricate pattern wherever we could find a placement. Tony and I led the charge, while Leo took photographs of us silhouetted against the snow.

Tony was a Londoner, in his early twenties but mature for his years, now spending most of his time in and around Bristol where he had put up some audacious free and artificial routes in the Avon Gorge and Wye Valley, particularly on Wintour's Leap. His routes were memorable for being incredibly bold and having psychedelic names like *Exploding Galaxy, Pulsating Rainbow* and *Interstellar Overdrive,* indicating both his passion for Pink Floyd and his interest in substances that altered perception. Tony had also put up several significant climbs in Norway, in particular a 5,000-foot grade VI on Søndre Trolltind.

Despite the diligent efforts of Britain's two most ardent peg-men, we could only reach a point 200 feet up *The Nose* before we ran out of time. We also just missed the ferry and I had to telephone the school secretary, Mrs Robinson, from the phone box at Tarbert.

'Oh, Mrs Robinson, it's Scott here.'

'Hello Scott, where are you this time?'

'Stuck on the Outer Isles in terrible weather.'

'Oh dear, Scott, when do you expect to be back in school?'

'Could you inform the headmaster I will be two days late.'

'I will, Scott, and I shall tell him all about the weather.'

'Thank you, Mrs Robinson, Jesus loves you more than you will know.' Mrs Robinson was everyone's favourite school secretary, particularly among younger colleagues.

When I got back I immediately put in for a leave of absence so I could have four weeks at Easter to climb in Yosemite. It was a long way to go for two weeks and far too hot to go in the summer. I had thought of climbing a new route on El Capitan to the right of *The Nose,* where regular Yosemite climbers had already been at work. It was a silly idea and quite presumptuous. My regular big-wall partners, Ray, Geoff, Ted and Guy, couldn't afford time off work, so I settled for a regular rock-climbing holiday. Once again the director of education gave permission. So Jan, Tony Wilmott and I set off on the exhausting flight to San Francisco. It was the first time any of us had been in an aircraft. Jan would camp with us for a week or so and then spend two weeks checking out primary education in the Berkeley area. To that end her teacher training college had awarded her a £50 travel bursary. Thanks to Ken Wilson, we had been invited to stay with Royal Robbins, America's foremost rock climber, who would introduce us to Yosemite.

We wandered out of the airport to find a bus to Modesto and ended up in a dimly lit street, littered with beer cans. Vagrants sat in doorways. At the end of the street, at a crossroads, stood a policeman looking this way and that. He got quite agitated when we approached him.

'Don't you know this is the skid row of San Francisco? Do you know how many shootings there have been down this street?'

Royal Robbins.

Royal and his wife were wonderful hosts. Liz produced a bake from the oven with a flavour we'd never experienced before. 'Avocado,' she said when we asked. Next morning we set off for Yosemite, a place I'd been reading about since the late 1950s. I had thought the name was pronounced 'Yos-ee-mighty' and asked an American climber at the Biolay in Chamonix if he had been there.

'No sir, never heard of that place. Yos-ee-mighty. Noooo.'

'I'm surprised,' I told him. 'There's no place like it for big granite walls.'

No amount of reading or staring at photographs prepared me for that first viewing of El Capitan and the more distant Half Dome, when emerging from the road tunnel on Wawona Road. There are, among other mountain ranges, huge walls of granite, elegant rock spires, like those in Patagonia, bold pillars and buttresses in the Karakoram, glacier-striated slabs typical of Baffin Island, bald granite domes dominating the landscape around Bangalore, impressive waterfalls in Iceland and Norway, friendly meadows in the Alps surrounded by groves of stately pine trees, but only Yosemite has it all contained in one seven-mile canyon. I was struck with awe and wonder and for quite some time was simply happy at being able to spend six weeks there.

Royal was, and is, one of the most influential rock climbers in North America and the world. By 1968 he had made either the first or second ascent of all seven climbs on that mile-wide, 3,000-foot monolith El Capitan. He had also made his mark in Europe in 1962, climbing the *American Direct* with Gary Hemming on the Petit Dru's west face. Three years later he put up the more difficult *Direttissima* with John Harlin. Born in 1935 in West Virginia, his parents separated and by the time he was five he was living in Los Angeles with a stepfather who turned out to be a violent alcoholic. His mother moved out and brought Royal up on her own.

Early on, Royal learned to be self-reliant. He also got into trouble, stealing cars and breaking into houses. But after a few nights in juvenile detention, he joined the Scouts and started camping in the Sierra Nevada. Soon he was also rock climbing in the San Fernando Valley and then, aged seventeen and wearing tennis shoes, free-climbed *Open Book* at Tahquitz, the first 5.9 in North America. The following year he made the second ascent of the west face of Sentinel Rock in the Yosemite Valley, still wearing his tennis shoes. 'A maverick kid,' as Royal's biographer Pat Ament wrote, 'was unleashed on to the Yosemite scene.'

Royal shared a long and at times bitter rivalry with another Yosemite pioneer, Warren Harding, the impish devil to Royal's moral high ground. Early on they climbed together, making an attempt on the north-west face of Half Dome. Royal went on to make the first ascent of that incredible wall over five days with Jerry Gallwas and Mike Sherrick; Harding hiked the eight miles to the top to congratulate them. But Harding's ethical approach was radically different from Royal's. He took eighteen months to make the first ascent of *The Nose* of El Capitan, draping the cliff in fixed ropes, placing 675 pegs and drilling 125 bolts. The climb drew in the crowds, scoping the climbers from the valley floor, and ended in a barrage of publicity making *The Nose* the most famous climb in North America.

After completing the draft, Royal returned to Yosemite in the autumn of 1960 and set off with three companions, Joe Fitschen, Chuck Pratt and Tom Frost, to climb *The Nose*, taking food and water for ten days. The climb progressed better than their wildest dreams and after a week of continuous climbing, they topped out ahead of schedule. On the evening of 13 September 1960, they met a reception party of friends, including Yvon Chouinard and Warren Harding, to drink champagne and beer on ice. The media didn't show up this time, so they could, as Royal put it, 'honour what was sacred in obscurity.'

Having proved you could climb one of these monstrous walls in one push, Royal went on to make a series of firsts. With Chuck Pratt he climbed a new line to the left of *The Nose*, fixing ropes part way and then cutting loose. They called it the *Salathé Wall*, after Yosemite's first big-wall climber, the Swiss blacksmith John Salathé. Each time he did something new, he refined his ethics to keep the challenge fresh and make the commitment greater. He and his friends, particularly Yvon Chouinard, developed new techniques and equipment to make the climbing easier, like the pulleys Royal used to haul loads. One of the greatest achievements was the first ascent of *North America Wall* in 1964;

Warren Harding.

Royal, Yvon, Chuck Pratt and Tom Frost spent six days on El Capitan, on an area of the wall seamed with diorite shaped like America, creating the hardest aid climb in the world without fixed ropes.

Royal was still at the forefront of American rock climbing when I first went to Yosemite and not just for his routes and his enormous courage. The Lake District climber Tony Greenbank was working at Colorado Outward Bound in 1964 and met Royal at a party in Boulder. 'They said, "Wow! A Limey,"' Tony recalled. 'They thought I was Don Whillans.' Royal and Tony fixed a date to go climbing in Eldorado Canyon, Royal parking his Mercedes under the crag and sorting through his rack of pegs. Then he saw Tony's collection of slings and old car-engine nuts.

'What the hell are those?' Royal asked.

'That's what we're using in England now,' Tony said. In Joe Brown's day, British climbers had dropped pebbles into cracks and threaded a sling, then did the same with machine nuts. In 1961 John Brailsford, father of the famous cycling impresario David, developed first the Acorn and then the MOAC, a hot-forged alloy chock. It was the MOAC that really caught on, marketed in Blackpool from Peter and Maureen Gentil's Mountaineering Activities Company, hence the name. The MOAC became the most treasured piece of protection for a decade; most climbers had at least one on a long sling around their necks, along with reamed-out machine nuts on different thicknesses of hawser-laid nylon.

So Royal threw his rack of pegs back in the car and climbed their route with nuts. Those he placed on the first pitch fell out but he soon got the idea and by the time they reached the top he was sold. 'Well,' Royal said. 'That's why the British ruled the world for so long. They're so fucking cunning.' In 1966, he came to Britain, and, according to Tom Frost, 'caught the vision', learning more about British traditional climbing and acquiring some of the latest versions of wired nuts – Peck Crackers.

When he got back to America, Royal and his wife Liz had put up a new free route on Ranger Rock he called *Nutcracker Suite*, protected with nuts rather than pegs and hammer. Chouinard was sceptical at first. He climbed a route next to *Nutcracker* and called it *Cocksucker's Concerto*. But gradually it dawned on him and other Yosemite climbers the damage repeatedly nailing cracks was doing to the rock. Chouinard became a convert and adopted the clean climbing ethic as only North Americans can – full on. He closed down peg production at his Great Pacific Iron Works and switched to producing nuts he branded Stoppers. There was more to it than just saving the rock; Royal and Yvon realised that here was a new way of climbing, a new art form where climbers needed to be more creative than when simply whacking in a peg.

Being a still somewhat self-centred youth, I only came to realise later how fortunate I was to have had the chance to climb with Royal Robbins. I suppose it only came about because I had written articles on the Dru and the Cima Ovest in *Mountain* and these had given me a certain reputation. That was small fry in comparison to Royal's achievements. Royal suggested after a few short crag climbs we should join him on climbing the *Steck-Salathé* route on the west face of Sentinel Rock.

Royal had climbed the route many times and knew the approach like the back of his hand. He and Tom Frost had actually been up it in three-and-a-quarter hours, almost all free of aid except the top pitch. He later went on to climb it solo. So we were in good hands as Royal set off at a blistering pace from the car park, again in tennis shoes. Now and again he urged Tony and me to take the lead, encouraging me to climb a pitch called 'The Narrows' deep inside the cliff, a very tight and somewhat claustrophobic chimney. Royal had discovered this variation when he made the second ascent, to avoid pegging up the exposed cracks on the face taken by Salathé and Steck. I could only make progress as I breathed out and would pant shallowly after each move before the next effort. This went on for about 100 feet.

I had never before climbed with anyone so completely attuned to rock climbing who made every move count, seemingly without effort, as he moved around rhythmically from one feature to the next. No sooner were we on the top than we were haring back down towards the car park, ten hours or so after we had left it. It had been, for Tony and me, an unforgettable experience, sharing a route with a master climber at the top of his game and so solicitous of his raw recruits. Royal had the reputation in some quarters for being a cold, calculating climbing machine, aloof from other Valley climbers. I met him several times later on subsequent visits to Yosemite and always enjoyed his company. In particular I respected his integrity. He may not have achieved absolute perfection, but he made an enormously positive impact on the games climbers play.

All those years climbing in the Peak District on grit really paid off when it came to climbing in Yosemite, even if I was at the time still very much in the 'B' team. I was surprised that one-pitch routes in Derbyshire no more than sixty feet high really helped me enjoy multi-pitch crack climbing in Yosemite. The weekend before leaving for Yosemite I had enjoyed a long day at Stanage climbing as many old classics as I could. The harder routes I led, *Tower Chimney* and *The Dangler* on Stanage or *Emerald Crack* at Chatsworth, were perfect preparation. The most satisfying climb we did was the three-pitch Reed's Pinnacle; the second pitch was the finest crack I had ever put my hands into, with every jam perfectly set and every nut a sinker.

Tony and I did half a dozen short routes at the base of El Cap before we moved on to climb with others. Tony went on to climb *The Nose* of El Cap with Chris Jones, a fellow Londoner now settled in California. I got to climb the *Braille Book* on Cathedral Spire with American climbers Dennis Hennek, Don Lauria and TM Herbert. I had never experienced anyone quite like TM who from start to finish had us in stitches with outrageous stories and sudden exclamations. When I left the path to take photographs, TM yelled: 'Hey, Hennek, tell the Limey to get back in line. Scott, you could be lost for days if you lose this path. Hasn't anyone told him about the bears?' *Braille Book* turned out to be another classic Yosemite free climb. We walked up to the summit of Cathedral Rock from where there was a grand frontal view of El Capitan, that great monolith of granite spreading out left and right from *The Nose*, its south buttress, rearing up from the forest. To its left I scoped the *Salathé Wall*, by then considered the finest rock climb in the world.

My three companions invited me to join them on an attempt to climb a new five-pitch route on a minor dome-like crag, later dubbed BHOS, in Tenaya Canyon. The main virtue of the expedition was that we were climbing something new and, as far as I was concerned, in the good company of Yosemite regulars. Dennis and Don had recently made the second ascent of the very difficult and serious *North America Wall* on El Cap and TM had put up *Muir Wall* with Yvon Chouinard, a completely new route to the left of *The Nose*. The pair of them had been very committed but continued alpine-style for nine days, which really impressed Royal Robbins; it was, he wrote, 'the most adventurous ascent on rock ever accomplished by Americans.' He then promptly soloed the route in ten days.

The climb took us one and a half days up three very obvious corner cracks one after the other, followed by a scramble across to an off-width crack to finish. We all got to lead a pitch each, which we graded III, 5.7, A3. Don Lauria recalls that the crux was trying to sleep through TM Herbert's tirade on the bivouac. 'It began about midnight, during snow flurries. "Wake up, hey you guys, wake up. Hennek kick that damn Limey. Is everybody awake? I've actually been sleeping. This is the first time I've ever slept on a bivouac. Damn it, wake up and listen to me. I've been sleeping. This is incredible. Hennek, is Lauria still sleeping? Wake him up, Scott wake up, I've actually been sleeping. Hennek, kick that rotten Limey. Damn it, Scott, you don't seem to realise ... " So it went.' Don also remembered how our crag got its name. 'The next day we were back in Camp 4 and Chuck Pratt ambled up. "What did you guys do?" I described the dome and the route. He responded, "Oh you mean that big hunk of shit?" Roper [the guidebook editor] loved it, hence BHOS was named.'

Our little route was put in the shade by two Stanford University students, Chuck Kroger and Scott Davis, who made the first ascent of the *Heart Route* over nine days while we were in the valley. Jan and I had kept an eye on their progress from time to time from El Cap meadow and were there when they

Jan, Mavis Jukes – Dennis Hennek's girlfriend at the time, and Dennis in Camp 4.

came back to Camp 4. We were so impressed with their attitude and the story they told of their climb, so full of self-deprecating humour and youthful enthusiasm, in particular their description of arriving on the rim of El Cap with no one around. When valley regulars topped out, it was still the custom for a reception committee to hike up the back to welcome them. Chuck and Scott were peering behind rocks, shouting: 'Come out folks, we know you're there, quit fooling, let's break open the champagne!' It was a bit different for these two unknowns, but it was clear the era of Robbins and Harding was coming to an end.

There was a period of snowfall, so Jan and I left the valley to another area of Yosemite National Park to visit the Mariposa Grove of vast sequoia trees, the like of which we had never seen before. These are one of the few stands of redwoods in North America to escape the rapacious logging companies. Here and elsewhere in the Sierra Nevada of California, the remaining trees are safe from exploitation, including the Muir Snag, discovered by John Muir and now dead, but which lived for over 3,000 years. Nearby is the Chicago Stump, all that remains of the tallest sequoia ever found, which stood at 300 feet tall.

During an election campaign visit to Yosemite in 1966, the future governor of California Ronald Reagan was heckled from the crowd: 'What about the redwoods, governor?' To which he is said, somewhat erroneously, to have replied: 'You've seen one redwood, you've seen them all.' Reagan didn't really understand environmentalism, except when it came to the air pollution choking his voters in Los Angeles, but he did prevent a major highway being built that would have cut across the John Muir Trail. To this day the trail remains unbroken for over 200 miles all the way from Yosemite to near Mount Whitney. He also put in legislation to reduce the pollution of Lake Tahoe and prevented dam building on the Eel River, which would have flooded land sacred to the local Indian population, although he once told a reporter he didn't know where the Eel River was – when he was standing right next to it.

Reagan was governor at the time of riots over the fate of the People's Park, established on waste ground in the centre of Berkeley belonging to the University of California, but earmarked for student parking and a soccer field. Having run out of funds, the university's plans were put on hold and the site became an eyesore, filling up with rubbish and abandoned cars. Activist Stu Albert of the Yippie Party wrote an article in a radical publication saying something must be done, and soon after a hundred people showed up at the site with shrubs, flowering plants, trees and grass sods to create a park, what we would now called guerrilla gardening.

By mid-May 1969 the park was up and running; local residents loved it. There was tension with the university authorities, but meetings were planned to address the future. Reagan then intervened, sending in hundreds of police at 4.30 a.m. to pull up the plants and erect a fence. The police action provoked a riot and so the police chief sent in reinforcements armed with shotguns. 'If it takes a bloodbath, let's get it over with. No more appeasement,' Reagan said. A student called John Rector was killed by shotgun fire. Another protestor was blinded, and altogether 128 Berkeley citizens were admitted to hospital. The local Sheriff acknowledged that some of his officers, especially those who were Vietnam veterans, went after the protestors 'as though they were the Vietcong.' Jan, during her visit to Berkeley, witnessed what was left of the park, shown around by Dennis Hennek's girlfriend Mavis Jukes and Warren Harding's girlfriend Beryl Knauth. She then toured local primary schools and Berkeley University before flying home with copious notes and an illustrated book on the demise of People's Park, back to college and seven-year-old Michael.

I returned to the Valley and climbed Lost Arrow Spire with Andy Embick, and various roof climbs with Paul Sibley, having suddenly remembered I had a book to write and illustrate on artificial climbing. Kaye and Ward had given me an advance, which had just about paid for our airfares. I also did Reed's Pinnacle again, this time with the Liverpool climber, George Homer. I knew George from North Wales where he'd spent a lot of time climbing before he moved to Canada to work as a carpenter. George was the spitting image of George Harrison and equally gentle, but he made light of Yosemite's strenuous climbing; he was a craftsman on rock as well as with wood. Chouinard also introduced me to a young Austrian guide called Peter Habeler, recommending we join forces first to climb Leaning Tower, and if all went well, El Cap. Habeler, I knew, had climbed in the Andes with Reinhold Messner the year before.

The exposure on the west face of Leaning Tower was quite something but we both coped reasonably well, even where the fixed protection was a bit shaky. Some of the bolts wobbled in their holes. I felt most exposed at the very top, traversing off above the thousand-foot overhanging face, mostly because Peter took the rope off. I followed him cautiously, impressed with his confidence born from climbing regularly with friends and clients in exposed places in his native Tyrol and the nearby Dolomites. We agreed to wait a few days and then tackle El Capitan's *Salathé Wall*.

Staying at Camp 4 was a mixed blessing, but for me, being young at heart and still impressionable, unforgettable. There were two main threats to its tranquillity. The first was bears. They would come in at any time and if they could smell food in your tent, they'd rip their way in. All food had to be hauled up into the trees. Even so, the tent Royal lent Tony and me was torn to shreds; we'd cooked inside it during bad weather, and a huge brown bear couldn't resist the odours. Royal was not best pleased with our negligence. Even making dinner at the camp table, bears would shuffle into camp. I have a vivid memory of two women next to us hurling tins of food at a bear as it destroyed their evening meal.

They eventually saw it off.

The other problem was the National Park Authority's limit on camping. Park regulations were strictly enforced by rangers, some of them Vietnam veterans. One night, somewhat drunk, I got up to relieve myself against a tree when out of nowhere a voice asked: 'What do you think you are doing?' A ranger materialised from out of the darkness. 'What do you think you are doing?' he repeated. 'Ah, I'm watering this tree, officer,' I said as the ranger's hand went to his sidearm. 'Are you going to shoot me, Mr Ranger?' I said. 'I'm only an Englishman and didn't know I shouldn't pee in the forest.' 'No sir,' he said, unconvincingly, before he slipped back into the darkness.

Later that year, on Independence Day, there was a confrontation between mostly young hippies and the park authorities, known as the Stoneman Meadow Riot. There were complaints from other, more elderly visitors of loud music, public sex and drug use. The superintendent, James Olson, instructed his rangers to tighten up enforcement; they interpreted this by throwing tear gas and charging the crowds on horseback, bludgeoning young men and women with their batons. The crowd retaliated, hurling rocks and glass bottles at the rangers who beat a hasty retreat. 'There is no peace in a police state,' reported the *Berkeley Tribe*. 'There are more hippies than bears in the Yosemite National Park,' reported the *Los Angeles Times*.

It was a heady scene sitting around campfires with the likes of Royal and Liz, Dennis, Don and TM and others I had not climbed with like Chuck Pratt, Mr Cool, and the outrageous Warren Harding swigging down Californian red from a clear glass flagon. He was exercised at the time about the 'yellow peril', telling me: 'The Chinese are beautiful people but there are just too many of them. We gotta nuke them down to about seven million.' 'Don't worry,' his girlfriend, Beryl, assured me, 'he really has a heart of gold.'

While waiting to get on El Cap, I climbed the direct route on Washington Column with the East Coast climber Phil Koch. Exhausted and thirsty, I flopped in the dirt at Camp 4, my back against a tree. An old van was now parked in the spot next to mine. Loud music was blaring from inside and a young woman emerged wearing multi-coloured bell-bottom trousers and carrying a demijohn of apple cider. She put it up on her shoulder, finger hooked through the glass ring, and took a swig. Then she passed it over, saying I looked like I needed a drink. I told her it was very refreshing. She told me to have more, so I did and took another long pull. It was delicious.

'Steady now,' she said, 'it's spiked.'

'Spiked? What do you mean?'

'It's got acid in it.'

Now I was worried, expecting a sudden burning sensation in my gut. 'Why would you put acid in apple juice?' I said.

'LSD man, LSD.'

By this time Phil had gone but George Homer and his wife had arrived. We were now sharing the campsite. I told them I had been poisoned and was feeling a bit strange. George went over to talk to the girl and her hippy friends. Then he came back and tried to reassure me. 'You're going to have an LSD trip and all you can do is go with it; we'll stick around and watch out for you.'

I was suddenly totally taken by the trees around me. They now had the appearance of those stylised paintings by Henri Rousseau, but without the tigers. Then the girl came over and said in a dreamy sort of voice: 'Let's all play Frisbee.' She skimmed the Frisbee into some nearby trees but when I went to get it I stopped: the air in front of me was aglow with colour. I waved my arm up and down creating air currents that I could now see; water vapour in the air was refracting all the colours of the rainbow. I pranced around like a magician producing swirls of colour wherever the sun was shining through the trees.

George led me back to camp where I became transfixed by the sky, now a huge kaleidoscopic canopy, changing colour whenever I altered my position. The Homers seemed unfazed by my description of all this sensory splendour. The young woman's bell-bottom pants were now indescribably vivid. She came across with her Frisbee and we threw it around some more until I sat there on the grass, staring at it intently. She began giggling and sat beside me. Then we held each other, and she began talking about God and asking me if I had connected with him. I said I hadn't. She put her face right up to mine as if to kiss but I recoiled. Seeing her face close up, the pores of her skin around her nose seemed to expand, white grease protruding from them like stalks of giant black-capped mushrooms. It was as if I was looking through a powerful microscope. I told her she needed a wash.

Suddenly there was Dennis, laid back and smiling, talking to George and coming across beaming confidently. I had forgotten that he was coming to take me to TM's house for a party. I asked him if I would ever go back to seeing the world as I once had, or would I be like this forever? He reassured me. He told me he had been in and out of nine such LSD trips, and that I shouldn't panic, just relax and go with it. We set off in Dennis's truck but then I remembered I was going to climb *Salathé Wall* next day with Peter.

Dennis drove over to where Peter was camping. He had just prepared a stew and offered a few spoonsful on a cob of bread. I looked at it in my hand, quite taken by the variety of ingredients that slid off on to the ground as I twisted the bread round to see more of it. Peter rushed forward asking what I was doing, concerned I was ill. Dennis took him to one side and explained that I would be out for the count for at least eight hours and perhaps it would be best postpone our climb for a day. Peter wished me well as I climbed back into Dennis's car.

He now had another passenger and I found I couldn't stop farting. I kept apologising profusely and Dennis and his friend kept saying: 'Oh no! There he goes again!' Dennis then threw me a karabiner to explore. It immediately melted into my hands. I could feel the atomic structure of the aluminium as it flowed through my hand. Flesh and metal had become one.

'You have to see the granite cloud,' Dennis said, meaning El Cap. It was now bathed in evening light and to me at least had become vast and dominant. He sat me down near El Capitan meadow where the wall morphed into a giant Egyptian fresco with every pictograph fitting into the geography of the cliff as if it had been set in stone forever. I turned away in disbelief only to find it was still there; all I could now see was El Cap. *North America Wall*, in particular, I thought, should be renamed the Egyptian Wall; there were painted men with plant pot hats with angular faces and Pharaonic beards and every other image of ancient Egypt, all slotting together on the rock like a giant jigsaw.

We continued on to TM's house where the intensity of my new state of mind began to ease off. Even so, I was still tripping. There was a full moon shining on the leaves of an almond tree that shimmered like silver as every droplet of moisture refracted a moonbeam. Beryl Knauth came to see how I was coping and I couldn't help but reach out and touch her cheek since it was also shining in the moon with every droplet of perspiration on her face refracting the light. I tried some food and it exploded off every taste bud in my mouth with such intensity that I ate very little. Guests at TM's were sympathetic I hadn't been warned; some were quite angry I'd been sandbagged. I told them it wasn't a problem; it had been, and still was, an amazing experience. In any case, I had given up passing judgement on others, at least for the time being. I was in a state of universal benevolence.

The consensus was I was lucky my trip had happened in the Valley with good friends around and that my personality could cope with this sudden opening of the doors of perception. They cited friends who after numerous LSD trips simply could not function, could not concentrate long enough to hold down a job, who became depressed and sometimes manic, even ending up in care. It took me quite some time to get off to sleep that night. I felt unusually tired and emotionally drained in the morning. Then I began to pick up and reflected on this, my first and only experience of LSD. I was left understanding the interconnectedness of all things – the rock, the trees and the water vapour in the air as well as my new-found friends. The net result was to dispel some of the feelings I had of my own self-importance. In this way I shed some of the heavy burden I had been carrying all those years.

The following day Peter and I packed all our gear, food and five gallons of water into one giant kitbag weighing 100 pounds. We hauled it up the first three pitches of the *Salathé Wall*, tied it off then abseiled back down for a

Peter Habeler on the *Salathé Wall*.

final night on the ground before our great adventure. We were excited, especially as this would be the first ascent by a non-American party. Above all, we knew the route was going to test us; it was far higher and harder than either of us had climbed before. During the previous weeks I had often looked up from the base of El Cap, simply staggered by the sheer vastness of the rock above me, so compact and overhanging at the top. The only possible way to cope with something which was obviously going to take us several days was to break it down into daily climbs, picking a feature such as a flake or a tower some eight or nine pitches up and aiming for that, not thinking beyond it. I knew that by nibbling away at it, the adventure would start to solve itself.

To start with, Peter and I did not get on well, probably because we were both projecting our fears of this huge undertaking on to each other. I was a bit put out discovering Peter had arbitrarily put our salt tablets, brought to stop us developing cramps, into the water bottles. Every time we went to slake our thirst it was with very salty water. We were so easily niggled, I think, because we barely knew each other, foreigners from very different backgrounds and quite different in character too.

Like many Austrians I had met on my travels in Europe, Peter kept his own counsel, did not get too involved and was not at all extrovert and certainly not flamboyant. In many ways he was similar to Royal Robbins, especially in the measured way he climbed and took everything in his stride, without complaint, that is until it came to hauling the haul sack. Peter found it very frustrating weighting the pulley system because he was so light. Being so light, and a brilliant rock climber, he was very fast, much faster than me and he became impatient with my slow progress. He would goad me into climbing faster by suggesting I come down so he could take over. I think we both found the climbing harder than expected, especially on the final pitch up to Heart Ledge, which was very thin; I wondered how Robbins, Frost and Pratt had managed to stand there, drilling holes for bolt protection.

On the second day we came together more harmoniously and became even more so the higher we got and the more committed we became. Of course it helped that we ate and drank away the weight of the sack. Sack hauling also became literally less of a drag as the route steepened to vertical, even overhanging. At our second bivouac on top of El Cap Spire we ate and drank in true communion, chatting over the route and our reactions to it. At the start I had let my irrational fears of the route build up into a shell of self-pity as a sort of defence mechanism, which I then projected on to my partner. This was completely irrational; I could not have had a better partner. A wave of contentment swept through my tired mind and body as I lay in a rocky hollow looking up at the clouds scudding across the night sky and feeling the blood oozing around my worn-out finger ends.

Next day we climbed another ten pitches, and the wear and tear on our hands became excruciating. We both climbed as carefully as time would allow so we didn't cut our flesh on the many sharp burrs on our hardware. Sitting quietly, slowly paying out the rope as Peter pegged his way up the crack above, I saw a frog. It hopped down a crack at the back of my ledge. It set me wondering how ever could it survive in this vertical desert and just how many more were there on this huge wall. I had been warned to look out for rattlesnakes and rats but I had never heard tell of frogs. I felt good up there because of that frog; he seemed to know that we were all in it together – not just the El Cap scene but the whole business of being alive.

Eventually we reached the third bivouac known as Sous le Toit ledge. It was something of a disappointment after the previous two very spacious bivouacs. With only room for one backside on the ledge, and preferring to lie out flat, I made a cocoon for myself out of the ropes. It was like a makeshift hammock that hung out over the cliff next to the ledge. There was a vast gulf below my back, and I slept fitfully, the morning's climbing across the vast roof above preying on my mind.

Peter belayed under the roof, hanging from angles and bongs poking out of shallow pockets. I was glad to leave him and place more pegs between us. Then I set out across it. I soon found myself looking down vertically on to the trees, now 2,500 feet below. I had never been so exposed and found it quite harrowing despite all the previous overhangs I had climbed in Britain and the Dolomites. I kept eyeing the pegs and the rope that no longer seemed quite so thick, but took some comfort by reminding myself how I had used an old climbing rope for towing a car out of a ditch without it snapping. We were completely committed; there was no way we were going to reverse this part of the route. Having got around the overhang, Peter led on through in good order up flared cracks in the headwall. I felt with mounting excitement we had not far to go. That evening of the fourth day we pulled over on to the rim of El Cap, walking into the forest like sailors reaching land after weeks at sea.

It had been an amazing four days, not eating too much, hardly drinking, deprived of sleep, always uncomfortable and always the fear of getting it wrong and falling. Yet on that last day of climbing it had been a real joy; I felt I could have gone on for quite a few more days yet; I had suddenly become so attuned to being there that everything else was of no concern. In those hours of concentrated effort very little of the world beyond the bit of rock in front of us crossed my mind so much so that being on El Cap had become my world. The weather had been good, as had the rock and Peter proved a superb companion. I did not want for anything more as we crunched across the pine cones looking for a place to spend the night. I noticed the subtle variety of colour in the forest, green upon green and then the smell of pine, so pungent, fresh and new. I was like a child again, reborn with my perceptions enhanced in the calm of the evening. The whole landscape appeared vibrant and stayed that way for quite a few days afterwards, as did my inner tranquillity. I was now completely at peace with myself.

Local Eskimo children in Pangnirtung.

BAFFIN

Back in Nottingham, Jan was angry and resentful at missing out on fun and 'experiences' while she was studying and looking after Michael. She was particularly annoyed I had been through an LSD trip without her being there to share it. Tony had impressed Jan with his free-and-easy lifestyle and the insights he shared with her of his own experiments with mind-expanding substances. She told me that Tony was more her kind of man. I didn't know what to make of that; but I understood Jan was on the profundity trail, spreading her wings after a strict childhood. She, like me, knew in an ill-defined way what Bob Dylan meant when he wrote that if you're not busy being born you're busy dying. We struggled on.

If things were difficult at home, it was good to be back climbing with my friends from the Nottingham Climbers' Club again. In the summer, thanks to Brian Royal, a climbing friend at what is now the Sport and Recreation Alliance, and Eric Laws, Nottingham's sympathetic director of museums, the NCC was given permission to climb on Nottingham's 130-foot Castle Rock during July as part of the Nottingham Festival. Normally the rock was completely off limits. There had been an attempt to climb the Rock in 1931 by members of the old Nottingham Mountaineering Club; Don Brown and G.W. Seymour went off early one morning in secret and got within ten feet of the top where they were stopped by difficult, overhanging rock and loose earth. Requests to climb on it had otherwise been met with firm refusal.

Now, as the *Nottingham Post* reported, and Gina (Madgett) Holmes recorded for Radio Nottingham, the authorities had allowed my 'childhood dream to come true'. Altogether we unearthed twelve routes, of which half were probably worth repeating. The best we called *Balcony Buttress* at HVS with two pegs for aid, which ended just below the castle wall. The rock was soft sandstone, not very stable and covered with city grime from factory chimneys and car exhausts.

If permission were ever granted again then a good clean from an abseil rope would improve things. As it was, we cleaned as we climbed and then came down 'Mortimer's Hole', the secret passage which led the supporters of Edward III to the bedroom of the regents Isabella of France and her lover Roger Mortimer. He didn't die well.

Having climbed the highest cliff in Nottingham, the NCC now planned to climb the highest cliff in Europe, the Troll Wall near Åndalsnes in Norway. Yosemite had put me in debt, since I was on unpaid leave, so to cover domestic expenditure while I was in Norway I had somehow to raise £100. Bob Holmes who worked in the local planning office came to my rescue and kindly printed up thirty or so black and white photos I had taken in the Dolomites and Yosemite on the council's giant copier. They were a bit grainy, being poster size, but looked presentable stuck on hardboard. A few days before leaving for Norway I set off in the minivan to sell the prints to various climbing shops, first in Leicester then Birmingham, Stafford, Liverpool, Manchester and Sheffield. Late that night I arrived home exhausted but with £75 in my pocket.

Four days later, at the campsite outside Åndalsnes, peg hammer in hand, I was beating dents out of Ned Newton's Austin van. Ted Wells and I had scrounged a lift from Bergen with Ned and I'd offered to take a shift of driving to relieve him. Unhappily, on a twisty mountain road, I met a bus hurtling around a bend. With a steep rock wall to the right, and a void to the left, I only had one option, slam on the brakes and slam into the front of the bus. The girder-like bumper of the bus was unscathed but Ned's car got a bit crumpled, hot water steaming out of the radiator. I hitched a lift to a nearby town, located a scrapyard with, unbelievably, several Austin vans, hitched back with a radiator, installed it and drove on to Åndalsnes.

The weather in Norway that summer was mostly dismal but there was a lively crowd on the campsite from all parts of Britain and around the world. The first ascent of Troll Wall by Tony Howard, Bill Tweedale and John Amatt from the Rimmon Club had made this corner of Norway as highly fashionable among the world's elite climbers as the Dolomites or even Yosemite. Ed Ward-Drummond and Ben Campbell-Kelly were trying a new route on Troll Wall as a group of us walked up for a reconnaissance. We started finding little stuff sacks still full of gear strewn over the slope under the cliff. They were each clearly labelled with their contents: bolts, drills, leepers, RURPs, matches, packets of soup. 'Boy Scouts,' someone said. The pair had abandoned their route in heavy rain and climbed an escape route, tossing their haul bag, which had burst open on impact. We collected everything we could find and took it back to the campsite.

In between storms, I put up a new route, about 500 metres long, on Adelsfjell with Ted Wells. Then, with Terry Bolger, I climbed *Hoibakk's Chimney* on

Being interviewed by Gina Madgett for Radio Nottingham.
Photo: Bob Holmes.

Climbing Castle Rock. **Photo**: Bob Holmes.

The tallest big wall in Europe, the Troll Wall in Romsdal, Norway.

Søndre Trolltind. The chimney is a natural drain for the mountain – the *Alpine Journal* warned 'there would be a risk of drowning' if you got caught there in bad weather – but I enjoyed climbing with 'Bolge'. He was a big strong lad who worked at the Stanton and Staveley ironworks and while Bolge had not been on too many long routes, he never flinched, curious to see what came next and how we might cope. Ours was the third ascent. Guy Lee and Neil Lockwood had made the second ascent a few days before. The route seemed to tunnel through the mountain at times, with all manner of features: grassy amphitheatres with flowers and ferns, luminous in the dark interior, giant chockstones and steep cracks to jam within the chimney itself. We reached the top at nightfall as it started to rain so we bivouacked between two boulders with our anoraks stretched across while we huddled underneath, miserable and soaked. Next morning we abseiled back down the route; we'd been told it was 2,500 feet but it was clearly no more than 1,500 feet, although that didn't detract from what was a classic climb.

We were now fit and, with the weather set fair, four of us, Ted, Jeff Upton, Guy Lee and I, packed our sacks for the Troll Wall and the *Rimmon* route. We walked up from Fiva Farm through the birch woods and started up the highest rock wall in Europe, steadily on the initial slimy slabs, and then kicking up long patches of snow, before short, steep rock steps took us to the first bivouac – and for us the last. Next morning we were in great form, and the weather was excellent. It's around 5,000 feet from the first bivouac to the top of the wall up a series of features – the Great Cracks, the Great Wall, Flake Crack, Narrow Slab – on a route that is wonderfully varied, and thanks to our fitness and the fact we'd been on big walls together before, we were able to climb a lot of the route free. Where we did use aid, we found that the pegs were in place. In just thirteen hours we were through the Exit Chimneys and into the summit gully. The climb had progressed better than we had dared hope and faster than any previous ascent by about a day.

Tony Howard had written a guidebook to Romsdal with several contributors, including the veteran local Arne Randers Heen and Ralph Høibakk from Trondheim. I met them both, and they helped me with the Norway section of my book, as did the other great Norwegian climber Arne Næss, father of deep ecology and the author of many routes in Norway and leader of the successful Norwegian Hindu Kush expedition to Tirich Mir. I could see why Tony and his Lancashire mates had taken to Norway; they stayed there for a few years, despite the high cost of living. Beer was three times the price as in England. But the land and the people were a revelation, such beautiful landscapes and so few people living in them. Most of those we got to know were thoughtful and hospitable to strangers.

Despite its isolation and space, Norway had been through a similar process

Jeff Upton on the Narrow Slab on the Troll Wall.

of rapid development that I'd seen in the rest of the world. A post-war boom in hydroelectricity had seen many of its most beautiful rivers dammed and by the end of the 1960s Norwegians were no longer taking their magnificent landscape for granted. As in America, several of the leading wild land advocates were mountaineers, like Sigmund Kvaløy Setreng, who instigated the Ecopolitical Ring of Co-operation that became increasingly active as one after the other of Norway's dramatic waterfalls were tamed, in particular the 2,000-foot Mardalsfossen, among the ten highest in Europe. Despite support from environmentalists all over Norway and beyond, and non-violent demonstrations involving Setreng, Arne Næss and hundreds of demonstrators, the hydroelectric scheme went ahead in 1970. The magnificent falls disappeared underground for most of the year. Only in summer is a small amount allowed to flow to please the tourists.

Norwegian environmentalists struggled to understand why their campaign had failed. Their demonstrations failed to stir local people who thought they were getting jobs and had a conservative respect for the law. Norway has a long tradition of communitarian tolerance when it comes to the land, captured in the law around *allemannsretten*, the freedom to roam. You can even camp on someone's property for a night, as long as you're 500 feet from any buildings and are polite. The Norwegian mountaineer Nils Faarlund has spent much of his life trying to reawaken the old concept of *friluftsliv*, a word coined by Henrik Ibsen that loosely translates as 'open-air life' and is pronounced 'free-loofs-leaf'. 'It can be a guide towards the future, a way home,' Faarlund writes. 'A joyous encounter with free nature can be a turning point for both the individual and society. No force is stronger than joy. Thus there is hope!'

A similar sentiment comes from the great pioneering Norwegian mountaineer, Carl Rubenson, who set the world altitude record back in 1907 on Kabru in the Himalaya, and refers back in time to when men lived together in nature. Rubenson noted: 'In every healthy human being there is the deep need to feel at home in nature, to show himself that his mind has roots, roots that haven't yet lost their grip in the earth. It is that need that drives us city folk out to sea, into the forest, and up into the mountains.' That was how I also felt.

I had taken over the ACG bulletin from Colin Taylor, a stalwart Alpine Club member, and aiming to emulate his high standards published an article by Toni Hiebeler on Reinhold Messner. It gave a complete list of his incredible climbs, as well as detailing the strict ethic by which he climbed. With this article, and previous notes in *Mountain*, British climbers were now becoming aware of the Messner phenomenon. He had climbed some of the hardest routes in the Alps in incredible times and sometimes solo, like the fourth ascent of the north face of Les Droites which he did in just eight hours; the previous fastest time had been two days.

During late December, Ken and three of us from the NCC, myself, Bob Wilson and Ken Moseley, drove to Italy to interview Reinhold for *Mountain* magazine. We stopped in Austria on the way to do some skiing and met a friendly team from Salzburg. Since we didn't know how good Reinhold's English was, we recruited one of them, a buxom lass called Edith wearing traditional Austrian dress, to help translate. We met Reinhold in a pub just over the Brenner Pass. Like me, he was at the time a teacher, while also running his own guiding school. He was obviously fit. I remember what impressed me the most on our first meeting was his single-minded dedication to climbing; it was like meeting a top Olympic athlete. He said his training regime was to run a thousand metres up a hillside near his family home at Villnöss before breakfast carrying varying weights in his rucksack and then again in the evening before dinner. I could not think of a single British climber who had that degree of dedication. He answered all our questions, was not at all guarded and struck me as a young man who was confident of his chosen path if somewhat haunted by some inner demons.

The interview was duly published in *Mountain* alongside Reinhold's polemic on drilling expansion bolts. 'Murder of the Impossible' continued the debate from where Walter Bonatti had left off in his memoir *On The Heights*: 'With the use of expansion bolts … The sense of the unforeseen almost entirely disappears and so the challenge of the climb itself and the meaning of the word impossible.' Walter is often considered to have been the world's finest alpinist, certainly of his generation, but his words were not heeded and so as more and more climbers resorted to the drill, Reinhold Messner repeated Walter's message ten years later: 'Today's climber doesn't want to cut himself off from the possibility of retreat: he carries his courage in his rucksack, in the form of bolts and … by methodical manual labour.' He cast derision on those who said they carried drilling equipment for emergencies. The essay put Reinhold Messner at the vanguard of the climbing ethics debate and earned him the opprobrium of lesser mortals.

I had long understood the value of properly researched information to exploratory climbers. In 1959, my parents had given me *Mountain World*, a compendium of mountaineering and exploration published by the Swiss Foundation for Alpine Research. I devoured the contents and hunted down the whole series, which began publication in 1946. The edition for 1954 had photographs of Mount Asgard and other fabulous peaks right up on the Arctic Circle on Baffin Island. Having climbed the Tre Cime di Lavaredo north faces and the *Bonatti Pillar* on the Dru, I wondered how I might get over to Baffin Island and a route like those somewhere entirely new. Not long after this notion took root, I was in the Cairngorms celebrating the start of 1969 and ran into Rob Wood, who had recently made the first British ascent of *The Nose* with Mick Burke. We kept in touch while Rob completed his architectural training and I gained more big-wall experience in Norway and Yosemite.

At the time, the magazines were reporting on big, siege-style expeditions, like the Japanese attempt on the south-west face of Everest when eight Sherpas were killed, and the bad-tempered German ascent of Nanga Parbat's Rupal Face that included Reinhold Messner and his brother Günther and ended in a Munich court. These expeditions seemed to me, and especially to Rob, to be the antithesis of what climbing was all about. Expeditions involving months of planning often gave the participants little opportunity for actually climbing. They were often fraught affairs yet the participants became household names as much from exposure on the television and in advertisements as for the climbing they achieved.

Rob and I grandly decided our Baffin Island expedition would be different, more like the Nottingham Climbers' Club trips to Kurdistan and Afghanistan. We wanted to create a spontaneous atmosphere for climbing more like the Biolay in Chamonix or Camp 4 in Yosemite, a light-hearted, joyous venture, an abundance of routes, dependent only on mood and weather. We invited our friends, Steve 'Sid' Smith, Guy Lee and Ray Gillies, and from America, Dennis Hennek and Phil Koch, who I knew from Yosemite. In the end our Baffin Island adventure turned out to be a scaled-down version of the Himalaya blockbuster expeditions after all, albeit without a leader. We compromised in the face of mounting costs we couldn't afford. Rob planned a winter food and fuel drop by ski-plane, but with that and the flights from Montreal to Frobisher Bay and on to Pangnirtung on Baffin, along with all the food and fuel, we were looking at a personal contribution of £500 for each team member.

While Rob organised the logistics, I worked as fundraiser and submitted an application to the Mount Everest Foundation. That got us £100: good for credibility but a drop in the ocean in terms of costs. So I appealed to Nottingham firms. John Player and Sons offered £500, unlimited cigarettes and funds to shoot a film. It all seemed too good to be true, especially when Mick Burke, the sorcerer who had led his apprentice Rob Wood up El Cap, agreed to be cameraman. The fact the film would help improve the image of what was already seen as a rather dubious product did not bother any of us that much, least of all Mick, the only smoker among us.

The main area of climbing activity on Baffin Island was at the centre of the Cumberland Peninsula, around Pangnirtung Pass and Summit Lake, thanks to the explorations of Pat Baird and his friends in 1953. Pat was born in 1913 and brought up in the north of Scotland on a huge estate in Caithness; the laird became a remarkable explorer and expedition leader. He took to rock climbing early in life, as a member of the Scottish Mountaineering Club and at Cambridge, and in 1934 joined the famous Antarctic explorer James Wordie on his boat-based expedition to Greenland and north-east Baffin Island as both climber and geologist. On Greenland he climbed the Devil's Thumb with the Himalayan veteran Tom Longstaff.

From that first visit, Pat began a lifelong passion for Baffin Island; he returned numerous times on scientific and mountaineering expeditions. In 1936 he was a member of the British Canadian Arctic expedition, which explored the Southampton Island area in the Northern Territories by boat, and continued when forced to abandon the boat. In 1938 he accomplished a remarkable journey in the north of Baffin Island after his companion, Reynold Bray, was blown out to sea in his canoe and lost. During the war Pat joined the Canadian Army and married Bray's widow, Jill. He trained mountain troops and for a time was under the command of the Everest veteran Frank Smythe. Pat ended the war a lieutenant colonel.

From the army, he joined McGill University, becoming director of the Arctic Institute in Montreal. More expeditions to Baffin followed, and in 1953 came the trip to the Cumberland Peninsula. The team included a contingent from the Swiss Foundation for Alpine Research, in particular the Swiss guide Jürg Marmet, who went on to make the second ascent of Mount Everest in 1956. It was this expedition that appeared in my 1954 edition of *Mountain World*. Pat Baird, wrote Angus Erskine in his obituary, 'was an old-style explorer, a master of all trades. As a scientist he was a geologist, glaciologist and meteorologist, also a surveyor and knowledgeable observer of wildlife; he was mountaineer, long-distance walker, cross-country skier.' When I wrote to Pat for information, he let me know he would like to go again. What could have been better than having on our team someone who knew the way, was said never to have criticised anyone and could walk non-stop for fifty miles on a bar of chocolate.

With our preparations for Baffin well underway, in the spring of 1971 I travelled with Jan and Michael and friends from the Nottingham Climbers' Club to the Ordesa National Park in the Spanish Pyrenees, somewhere we'd visited in 1963. The ancient walled village of Torla is set against spectacular red walls and buttresses a thousand metres high, the most impressive being Tozal del Mallo, a triangular wedge of orange and red limestone towering 1,500 feet above the forested valley of the Rio Arazas. Tozal is an outlier of the region's highest mountain of Mondarruego and even now is little known among British climbers. We had to buy a guidebook in Spanish and it's possible we made the first British ascent. Local climbers seemed surprised to find foreigners there, but warmly welcomed us. Ray Gillies, Dave Marriott and I climbed the route put by the great Catalonian climber Josep Anglada with Francisco Guillamón. Snow on the route slowed us down but we found a convenient ledge with dead wood and bivouacked by a small fire.

The ancient walled village of Torla in the Ordesa National Park, Spain.

Mid-afternoon on the second day, we climbed through the summit cornice and scuttled down easier rock and stone couloirs to arrive back at our bivouac at the base of the route to find bears had been at our food with granola scattered all over the snow.

Home from Spain, I discovered my application for leave of absence to go to Baffin for two months had been rejected. The director of education sent me an amicable letter suggesting that perhaps it was time for me to decide whether I should leave teaching and climb full time. I resigned with some reluctance. I knew the satisfaction I got from teaching was proportional to the time and effort I put into it, but now more than ever I spent more time pondering visits to the mountains and not so much the children in a classroom.

It was, to a certain extent, a step into the unknown. How would I now support my family? Jan had begun teaching and said she would help; she also knew that I'd be able to generate enough income. I overheard some friends in the pub talking about an exorbitant estimate for some straightforward building work. I said I'd do the job for half the estimate. So it was my younger brother Garry and I became S & S Builders. Garry was now at Nottingham University studying civil engineering so between us we had some idea of what construction work involved. We did the job in two days, carting away all the rubble to a nearby dump in the back of my minivan and I ended up with the equivalent of a month's teaching wage for just two days' work. Before leaving for Baffin I had jobs lined up for when I returned.

We flew over the vast tundra of northern Quebec, over the ice floes of Ungava Bay, and swapped the jet for a Twin Otter at Frobisher. Within a few hours of leaving Montreal we were on the last lap of our journey to Pangnirtung Fjord into the mountains of Baffin Island. Cloud lay loosely over the range but the pilot was able to point out Summit Lake Pass for he had often flown above it on his way to Broughton Island. We badgered him for his impressions of the mountains and he came up with answers we wanted to hear: 'Big flat-topped mountains, like sawn-off chimney stacks,' he yelled over the roar of the engine. That, we thought, would be Mount Asgard. Now we could see individual peaks, rising up from sea level to six or seven thousand feet, Alpine in proportion and Alpine in character. We circled and then descended into Pangnirtung. After the dust settled over the dirt strip, we clambered out into the sun to find a semi-circle of young Eskimos[1] standing around in striped, flared trousers and shoulder-length hair. We erected our tents near the runway and set off to explore the town.

---

1 In 1971 everyone we met referred to the indigenous population as Eskimos. From the mid-1970s, 'Inuit' replaced 'Eskimo' in Canada, where it is seen as derogatory. In Alaska, where the indigenous population speak Yupik and not Inukitut, as they do on Baffin, the word Eskimo is still in use. For the purposes of historical context, I've used Eskimo throughout.

Tozal del Mallo.

An Eskimo boy eating raw seal steaks in Pangnirtung.

Pangnirtung began as a trading post for the Hudson's Bay Company in 1921, but grew significantly only in the early 1960s when an outbreak of distemper killed most of the sled dogs around Cumberland Sound. The Canadian government was also taking a closer interest in Arctic affairs as the region's strategic importance grew during the Cold War. Pangnirtung offered modern amenities, particularly healthcare, which reduced high infant mortality rates, but also prefabricated, centrally heated houses, a well-stocked and expanding Hudson's Bay store and a modern school, staffed by Welshmen. Pangnirtung grew from a settlement of a few families grouped around the original Hudson's Bay post and an old whale-processing plant to a thriving community of more than 800 souls.

We arrived with romantic ideas of meeting sturdy Eskimos striding across the tundra, clothed in seal-skins, paddling kayaks or else surrounded by yelping husky dogs. The Eskimos we met over the next seven weeks were in all outward appearances entirely westernised, wearing fashionable winter clothes you'd see in any Alpine resort. They had long ago preferred motorised canoes and skidoos to kayaks and dog sleds. The only kayak we saw was hanging up in the local museum. There seemed little remarkable about the Eskimos we met, but as we spent more time with them we realised their outward appearances were deceiving. They would make a lasting impression on all of us.

Ray and I had travelled together among the Tibbu of Chad and Afghan tribesmen in the Hindu Kush. They lived simple lives in harsh environments

Eskimo children in Pangnirtung. **Photo:** Dennis Hennek.

yet they received us in a spirit of true hospitality. We admired them for their natural good humour in the face of adversity. Their uncomplicated lives and obvious contentment caused us to question our own. It happened again as we became more familiar with the Eskimo. They too had a cathartic effect on us; for a time we purged ourselves psychologically of our frenetic, materialistic, cluttered lifestyles.

Jonah was twelve years old and the undisputed leader of the gang of friends he brought to sit around our campfire down by the airstrip. They must have been curious. Most visitors from the south stayed at the local hotel, but at $40 a night, that wasn't possible on our tight budget. If we lacked creature comforts we did have the pleasure of their company. The boys came each night to listen to Sid and Dennis playing their mouth organs, join in the singing and share our drinking chocolate. It was incredible how much respect they had for each other. How often when the smallest member of the gang spoke the rest of them turned to listen. They never became so excited and egocentric that they tried to shout each other down. After the person speaking had finished having his say, there was this sing-song murmur in response, demonstrating the group's attention, a far cry from the urban children I was used to teaching where the one that shouted loudest tended to receive the most attention.

Towards the end of our stay we came to know some of the older people. We met senior school children back home from Frobisher Bay and schools in the south. Although the prospect of regular employment in Pangnirtung was remote, they had no intention of leaving the settlement, or so they said. Naturally the extended family grouping would attract them home again. The climate and pace of life in the south would take some acclimatisation and adjustment but perhaps also the incomparable majesty and haunting beauty of the fjord had something to do with their reluctance to leave. There is something magical about being up in the Arctic; it may have something to do with the quality of light being bluer than elsewhere. Our spirits were lifted just being there.

We often sat watching two old men down by the shoreline, chipping away at whalebone and rubbing down soapstone into primitive depictions of local objects. Their work demonstrated a capacity to reach below the surface for that streak of mysticism many primitive peoples seem to possess. Local craftsmen had organised themselves in a co-operative, which has in the intervening years made Pangnirtung a centre for the arts. The elegant simplicity of these carvings is now immensely popular with tourists and dealers in the south, one of the reasons the settlement has prospered in the forty years since we first went there. When we came to leave Pangnirtung what we did not sell we used to barter for beautiful soapstone and bone carvings.

Rob and I visited the homes of several Eskimo families and found the old people happily absorbed into an extended family scene just as they always had been in their old igloos and tents. Rob cast his critical architect's eye over the prefabs. After seeing the remains of several houses destroyed by winter winds and knowing the Eskimos were more or less given a modern home in return for a nominal rent, Rob suggested that they could be encouraged to build their own stone cottages from the granite hillsides. He talked of returning the next summer with the approval of the settlement manager to develop this idea. It would save on future deliveries of prefabricated parts, provide employment and give the Eskimo the satisfaction of having built his own home. We also noticed hundreds of rotting seal carcasses littering the shoreline and felt that they were a waste of a valuable fuel source. Canadian taxpayers were paying for oil deliveries to heat homes and provide electricity from generators.

As the tide turned in the fjord, a crowd of men and women gathered, standing on boulders casting lines for Arctic char. When we visited this was a neglected industry, one that we thought might eventually provide a great many more Eskimos with employment. Now a small port has been built and as well as char, the people of Pangnirtung are exporting turbot. In 1971 the locals were forced to rely heavily on subsidies and welfare. We hoped the inevitable increase in government support would be tempered with respect for the old ways and that the struggle down the generations against the inhospitable Arctic would not be in vain. For them to be completely swamped and absorbed into the North American way of life would be a rather tragic loss for everybody.

Dennis Hennek rowing one of our canoes on Summit Lake below Base Camp, with the magnificent
Freya Peak directly ahead.

There was apparently very little, if any, crime in Pangnirtung, as with people living close together in the back-to-back terraced houses of Nottingham there was very little trouble on account of the self-policing afforded by the close proximity of neighbours, friends and relatives. This all changed when families were moved out to distant estates, breaking down the extended family support system, isolated in their new homes and tiny gardens.

Two years from conceiving the expedition, we were labouring along Pangnirtung Fjord, some of us on foot and some by canoe, steering it around ice floes as we headed for Weasel Valley and the mountains. Dennis and I were transfixed by the skill of an Eskimo hunter known as Killabuk who joined us on the walk in. Towards the head of the fjord we watched him leave our canoe and stalk a seal we could not see, across the pack ice, inching his way forward behind a little screen of plywood, painted white. Eventually a shot rang out and Killabuk reappeared, pulling the seal across the ice, now with a neat hold through the front of its head, just above the eyes, and behind a bloody cavity.

We didn't make it all the way to the head of the fjord. Just six miles from the village, at a constriction, the water became choked with ice so we were forced on to land, carrying heavy loads of 100 pounds. At least a helicopter based at Pangnirtung for the summer had already flown in our heavy camera gear and Base Camp tent. Thanks to Pat Baird's connections we were able to procure its services at a rate we couldn't resist. Turning one headland after another, hoping that the next one would be the last, we finally staggered into the Weasel Valley to camp beneath Crater Lake, trusting its moraine walls wouldn't collapse while we were under them.

Freed of our heavy loads, we were able to take in the incredible scenery in the perpetual twilight of the Arctic night. Mount Ulu stood sentinel, guarding the approach to the valley. It was the first of many unclimbed granite mountains we were to admire over the coming weeks. We continued up this valley, turned a corner and there before us was the unforgettable 5,000-foot west face of Mount Thor. We passed under the snout of the retreating Fork Beard Glacier, the tundra stretching up to striated slabs of rock so recently vacated by ice.

The tangle of lichens and mosses were peppered with purple saxifrage, the yellow Arctic poppies, white heather, willow herb and Baffin Island's tallest tree, the Arctic willow now sprouting woolly catkins as it straggled along the ground. This mantle of vegetation supports a wide variety of bird and animal life; we saw snowy owls and occasionally a peregrine falcon, as well as lemmings, Arctic fox and hare now in its summer garb romping across the tundra. We also found caribou moss, still contaminated by atomic weapon testing in the Arctic in the 1950s and 1960s. Health workers were warning Eskimo women not to breast feed their children since their milk was contaminated from consuming caribou livers, a great delicacy among the locals.

The team at Summit Lake, Baffin Island, in 1971. L–R: Steve Smith, Ray Gillies, Dennis Hennek, Guy Lee, Phil Koch, me and Rob Wood.

We took great care to be roped crossing the streams, recalling how John Fleming had perished in the Hindu Kush, and after walking twenty miles averaging just one mile per hour we arrived at Base Camp shattered. Pat Baird had gone ahead to our cache of food with the helicopter and set up some of the tents. When he landed, Pat realised the food, deposited by ski-plane during the winter, was five miles away from where he had recommended and so Pat had busied himself ferrying the huge pile to his preferred campsite above Summit Lake.

Despite his fifty-eight years, Pat was still fit enough to climb a virgin summit every year or so and this is what we did in our first week. Pat, Rob and Steve climbed twin summits overlooking Base Camp and Summit Lake while Dennis and I climbed two 6,000-foot peaks south of Mount Asgard. Ray, Guy and Phil climbed a peak at the head of Baldur Glacier. The weather was perfect throughout those first few days. Only the mosquitoes troubled us. With five summits climbed we were considerably fitter than on our walk in and felt ready to tackle the big walls of Asgard.

Food and equipment were laid out on the tundra in eight neat piles. The small tents were taken down and we all moved into our big Stormhaven tent ready for an early start next morning. Then ominous high-flying cirrus moved in and before long the sky was full of thick grey cloud bringing rain and wet snow. By morning the tent was lashed by a ferocious gale. We went out to secure the guy lines and pack away the food in polythene sheeting. The hillside was

The north buttress of Breidablik.

virtually a sheet of water with every stream overflowing its banks. Visibility dropped to a few yards and we had difficulty in standing in the force-10 winds. We rescued wind-tossed cans from the stream and topped up our supply of water ready for a long stretch inside the tent. At least the mosquitoes had gone to earth. After digging drainage channels around the flysheet, we ducked back inside the tent where the weather kept us pinned down for the next two weeks.

We read everything we had: Hermann Hesse, *The Hobbit*, Tolstoy's *War and Peace* and even the advertisements on our food packaging. We argued, discussing and solving most of the world's problems and purging ourselves of a multitude of sins, from professionalism to ego-tripping in articles. Rob had brought Charles Reich's *The Greening of America*, and its countercultural ideas of a more ecologically conscious world. Like *Silent Spring*, it had challenged the underlying philosophy and impact of modern industrial society. With the use of Agent Orange in Vietnam, environmental degradation had become a weapon of war and the role of companies that made it, like Monsanto, a hot topic. A million people in Vietnam were disabled by it. We split the book into pieces so we could all read it at once, and we debated its ideas, everything from personal attachment to fame and fortune and living an alternative lifestyle closer to the natural world.

'Almost always, men have lived subject to rigid custom, to religion, to an economic theory or political ideology,' Reich argued. As the rain lashed against the tent, we discussed his ideas about a new kind of consciousness, particularly Rob, who saw in the book a way of life that was more in tune with nature, with a more fluid and intuitive understanding of reality, more concerned with quality of life and a direct grasp of happiness than prestige or material possessions. It was, above all else, Vietnam that caused young and old to question the brutality of the corporate state and awaken what Reich called 'Consciousness III', which he describes as a 'search for meaning, for community, for liberation'.

Man, it says, is not part of a machine, not a robot, not a being meant to starve, or be killed in war, or be driven like a beast, not an enemy to his own kind and to all other kinds, not a creature to be controlled, regulated, administered, trained, clipped, coated, anaesthetised. His true nature is expressed in loving and trusting his own kind, being a part of nature and his nature, developing, growing, giving as fully as he can, using to the full his unique gift, perhaps unique in the universe, of conscious life. Consciousness III seems the closest to valuing life for its own sake. Almost always, men have lived subject to rigid custom, to religion, to an economic theory or political ideology. Consciousness III seeks freedom from all of these.

Discussions did get heated at times. Rob had taken part in the demonstrations outside the US Embassy in London and had also taken up the cause of homeless

The 3,000-foot-tall east face of Freya Peak (main), with Steve Smith on Point Killabuk (inset).
He refused to go right to the end of the slabs!

families in the slum areas of London. He had recently completed his thesis on the alienation of the modern city and how urban life in general was destroying the environment. He would later buy into a commune on an island off the coast of British Columbia. We missed Pat's calm, authoritative presence. He left during the storm for Montreal, under pressure from his publisher to revise his textbook *The Polar World*.

After two weeks, a patch of blue sky appeared through the swirling morning mist. By the afternoon the sun was out and we were being bitten by a thousand ravenous mosquitoes. Given the loss of time, we decided to concentrate on two big walls near camp. So far, exploration on Baffin, such as it was, had focused on exploring and making first ascents by easy routes. We now hoped to do something never before attempted in Arctic Canada and climb one of the big granite faces around us. Guy and Phil set off that same afternoon for the elegant 2,000-foot north buttress of Breidablik.

The rest of us also took advantage of this respite from the weather. The east face of Freya Peak reared up for 3,000 feet in slabs and a headwall to a point easily seen from our camp. We named the point Killabuk, since the main summit of Freya was set well back towards Asgard. We regretted not making an earlier start since the slabs were at 5.7 a bit harder than expected and required a rope. The headwall was also more difficult than we bargained and with very little food and no bivvy gear we debated whether it would be prudent to retreat. We sat around undecided until Dennis said, 'Well, why don't we just go up and have ourselves an adventure.' As one came the reply: 'Yeah!' And so we went for it.

Towards evening we were on the headwall but the crack system we were following ended abruptly. We could neither free climb or peg our way up and so the only solution was to arrange a pendulum and try to reach another line of cracks away to the right across a hundred feet of blank rock dripping with water. From a peg placed as high as possible we fixed a rope and slid 150 feet down it. One after the other we swung backwards and forwards, gathering momentum and distance until we could clamber into the new crack. After this exhilarating manoeuvre we made good progress to a ledge suitable for a miserably cold, wet bivouac. Winter was obviously drawing nearer for there were now a few hours of dark. We were only 600 feet from the top but the headwall overhung its base by fifty feet and we found the climbing strenuous.

Next morning, as the crack we had gained was now overhanging and full of loose flakes, we followed a ramp round to yet another crack system, crawling along as the ramp narrowed alarmingly. Right at the end it was just possible to stand precariously in balance and reach for a ledge. I tried not to notice the thousand-foot void below. From the ledge I stepped round a corner into sunlight as the sun rose, each of us warming our cold bodies and numb fingers as we flopped down on a large ledge.

Above, the mountain was cleft by chimneys set at right angles to one another. We wriggled and pushed, getting good friction from the rough red rock. Shafts of sunlight pierced the dark recesses of the mountain now full of the sound of heavy breathing and clanking pegs. After 200 feet we were disgorged on to a wide terrace below the final wall. In two more pitches of hard pegging and pleasant free climbing we arrived on the summit twenty hours after leaving camp.

We felt elated to be there, looking down on our tents and across at the peaks stretching out in all directions, still covered in fresh snow from the storms. It is always a good feeling to arrive on the top of an unclimbed summit. We lay out in the sun among the weathered rocks scattered about the flat summit. I took photographs of Steve venturing out on a block of granite jutting out for twenty feet above the slabs 1,200 feet below. Having been cooped up for so long in the tents we were doubly elated at having carved out a fine route involving a variety of problems and difficult route finding.

Hurrying down the back of the mountain, we made six long abseils to eventually reach the Caribou Glacier. We arrived back at Base Camp a few hours before Guy and Phil. They came steaming in from their long walk home from Breidablik and quietly described the great climbing they had found and how, after eighteen long pitches of pegging and hard free climbing, with a bivouac in hammocks, they had reached the summit. Over the next few days Guy, Phil and Steve climbed a prominent unclimbed peak beyond Breidablik but the weather was bad and Mick, still gathering material for his film, was lucky to find a window in the cloud just as their three bright red anoraks arrived at the summit. To make sure we had a film of a climb in the can, Rob, Dennis and myself repeated Guy and Phil's excellent route on Breidablik while Mick filmed us.

We had ten days left. Having climbed eight peaks, including the rock faces of Killabuk and Breidablik, and having the film in the can, we could be reasonably contented the expedition had been a success and our sponsors would be satisfied. Yet at a personal level we were far from satisfied and never would be until we had climbed Asgard. The peak has twin summits, north and south. The Swiss team had climbed to the north summit in 1953 from the relatively easy east side, as reported in *Mountain World*. Guy, Phil and Rob now set off to climb the south summit by its south ridge. Dennis and I had walked right round Asgard a few weeks earlier with the 'film crew' helping carry 300 pounds of equipment. We considered climbing the west face of the south peak but eventually settled for a sweeping 2,000-foot dihedral on the north peak. To reach it we would have to negotiate a thousand feet of easier-angled mixed ground.

For a second time we moved into our lonely tent pitched on the glacier below the west face. The day after our arrival was overcast and cold but we

Mount Asgard, viewed from the air.

went up to the foot of the dihedral and stashed all the heavy gear and food. We returned to the tent after ten hours' climbing to await a settled period of good weather for our ascent which we thought could take up to seven days. During the night bad weather blew in and the temperature dropped to -10° Celsius. Snow piled up against the tent and we settled in to sit out yet another storm.

The wind blew in gusts of over a hundred miles per hour and pummelled our tunnel tent violently. It was a daft place to be testing a prototype but fortunately it survived. Wind whistled through the external poles like a flute while ice hammered into the tent walls with the sound of cymbals being brushed, reaching a crescendo. Every so often the end wall of the tent boomed loudly like a huge drum. Then it would be dead calm and we would wait, tensed, for the wind to come whistling back and slam into the tent, which flexed and shuddered at the new onslaught.

It felt good to be so close to the harsh environment lying in warm sleeping bags, a private world seven feet long and four feet wide where everything was orange. It played strange tricks on the eyes when we looked outside; Asgard had a blue haze, a cold Arctic blue, and was plastered in snow. With frozen water beneath us and frozen water masking our mountain, we talked of California's sun-soaked mountains and surfing off Ventura. The only liquid in this frozen land was produced on our stove with its little ring of flame.

We slept, re-read Hermann Hesse and slept again. Still the storm continued. One morning a shaft of sunlight broke through and lit up the notch below the south ridge of Asgard and then reached the tent. The snow around us sparkled like a million diamonds until the wild grey sky closed in. We had managed to curb our frustrations up to now but we both knew time was running out and winter might have arrived. It had never been so cold. We packed up and, shouldering huge loads, walked out to the big tent at Summit Lake where we devoured a large quantity of chocolate bars from the mountain of food remaining. We sat around playing over and again Crosby, Stills, Nash and Young's 1971 live album *4 Way Street* and in particular Graham Nash's classic 'Teach Your Children'. We also wore out a copy of Bob Dylan's *Bringing It All Back Home* and its brilliant questioning of society's loss of direction; the line about the president of the US sometimes having to stand naked was particularly relevant as Richard Nixon's chickens came home to roost.

Climbing had started off so well but seemed to be turning out all wrong, as Melanie Safka sang in 'Look What They've Done To My Song'. Dylan's album was really an indictment of unbridled capitalism and consumerism; to me Dylan is a genius and a prophet without preaching.

Phil, Rob and Guy had gone around to King's Parade Glacier on the east side and climbed the south ridge to the unclimbed South Peak of Asgard. The front that scuppered our attempt on the west face of North Peak caught them on the summit after twelve pitches of superb free climbing and just a little easy aid. The descent became an epic as light snow flurries turned into a full-blown blizzard. They were lucky to get off the mountain without frostbite. We both felt a little left out of this success but admired their effort. Climbing Asgard had added considerably to the success of the expedition as a whole.

We prepared to strike camp and walk out but faced with our mountain of filming equipment and camping gear, Rob, Ray and I volunteered to run the fifty miles back to Pangnirtung. The helicopter was still based there for another two days and we decided to hire it rather than make several journeys up and down Weasel Valley ferrying kit. We set off light, knowing we had a food cache on a prominent boulder not far from the fjord head but to our dismay we arrived there shattered and hungry to find it had gone. A lone trekker thought it abandoned and took it. We did have brewing gear but only one tin of corned beef to last the next twenty-five miles down the side of the fjord to town. Rob took the can and prepared to cut it into three. I said: 'Cutter gets the last slice.' Rob was incensed but eventually forgave me. But he never forgot.

The unforgettable west face of Mount Thor.

Don Whillans.

DON

Back in Montreal we sat around the airport on a huge mound of luggage, as early morning commuters flowed round us on their way to work. After weeks in the Arctic, it felt like a crowd scene from a Buster Keaton movie, with everybody walking unnaturally fast. We tried to hire a car, but they wouldn't take cash and no one had a credit card, so we caught a bus to Hudson Heights to stay with Pat and Jill. They took one look at our emaciated faces and fed us huge steaks and new potatoes lathered in butter. Jill insisted that should we ever return to Baffin we must stay with her. I told her that could be sooner rather than later.

From Montreal we took a Greyhound down to Burlington in Vermont to stay with Phil and his mother. Again we received that full-on traditional North American hospitality. There was, curiously, in the hallway of their house, the Stars and Stripes emblazoned on a polished marching pole – it made me think what a relatively new country the USA is. We then hitchhiked south to New Paltz to climb at the Shawangunks. Arriving in a tropical thunderstorm as the streams and gutters were overflowing, Ray and I were driven into town, appropriately enough, in a van full of canoes and canoeists. We had agreed to meet Guy and Dennis at Emil's bar but we ended up in Charlie's bar, listening to a bluegrass band who had attracted a huge crowd, including Guy and Dennis, with whom we drank late into the night before staggering out to sleep in a barn.

Next morning we climbed on the wonderful quartzite rock of the Shawangunks. Despite the summer storm, it was incredibly hot and felt more so as our bodies were still attuned to the Arctic. I climbed in my underpants and stuck to the shade. Dennis was friends with several of the Vulgarians, that loose and spontaneous band for whom climbing and dissipation went hand in hand, including Dick Williams who ran the local climbing store, Rock and Snow, and also Elaine Matthews and Dick DuMais.

Guy Lee on our second attempt at *The Nose* of Strone Ulladale, June 1971.

Their generosity and enthusiasm for showing a few Brits around made me very grateful. Jim McCarthy, one of the leading lights at the Gunks, arrived at the crag and pointed out some of the classics like *High Exposure* and *Shockley's Ceiling*. The latter route had featured on the cover of the *Vulgarian Digest* with its editor, Joe Kelsey, climbing naked. Jim then pointed out some of the harder routes he and Dick Williams had put up recently. As he was doing so John Stannard turned up. Stannard had been doing even harder climbs; in 1967 he had made the first ascent of the famous Gunks route *Foops*, one of the first 5.11s in America. Like Jim, he was a very strong and precise face climber.

After a few days staying with Jim and Dick, we caught the bus to New York. Guy had become fed up with the pair of caribou antlers he had carried all the way from Baffin so he left them in the forest below the Shawangunks, smiling at the thought of zoologists pondering over their origins. In New York we stayed with another Vulgarian, the diminutive psychiatrist Bert Angris. He had a fridge full of pills for any psychological eventuality and had us cracked up with laughter recalling all the outrageous behaviour of the Vulgarians. Looking back on those few days at the Gunks, it was so reminiscent of the climbing scenes in North Wales, the Lake District or Derbyshire where, after days on the crag, climbers congregated in the local pub or cafe, like the Padarn in Wales, or the Lover's Leap caff in Stoney Middleton. It struck me that to have a wholesome climbing scene, a pub is an essential ingredient, which made the Gunks particularly attractive since they had two. We took Dennis home with us to introduce him to colder climes and climbs, and warm beer.

We also took him to the Strone. For Guy Lee and me it was our seventh visit to the lonely Glen Ulladale. The last climb I did before going to Baffin Island was on the Strone with Guy. In June, in an almost evening cloud of midges, we climbed a route well to the right of *The Scoop* we called *Sidewinder*. We managed to climb it in three days without bolts and with far more free climbing than on *The Scoop*. We led through, had one bivvy en route and, apart from the midges, found it a more enjoyable climb than *The Scoop*. We also attempted to climb *The Nose*, for me the third time having been there with Tony Wilmott and later Steve Read and again this time we were not successful although we did get higher. We crossed under a ten-foot roof, but neither of us could find the means to climb the exceedingly blank rock above. Except for an incipient crack where the wall of a shallow corner came together, that would not take a peg, there was nothing for the next twenty feet and, since I had put all thoughts of ever bolting again behind me, we returned home.

This time all three of us were match fit from our efforts on Baffin Island and we came armed with a BBC film crew including Leo Dickinson and a BBC producer, Derek Smith, who hoped to make a half-hour documentary about climbing the *The Nose*. We re-climbed the initial 200 feet of overhanging rock to reach a ledge below the ten-foot roof that had stopped us before and settled in for the night. It was a big temptation to drop down to the ground for a good night's sleep and then prussik back up the ropes next morning. That would have turned the climb into a siege, and every time we bale from a route we lose contact with the rock emotionally. The spell that is holding us there, driving us on, is suddenly broken. Any relief is temporary and soon dissipates to be replaced with a sense of failure. Knowing all this, we stayed where we were, sleeping in hammocks last used on Baffin Island.

This time on *The Nose*, we had the benefit of Dennis's aid-climbing experience and equipment he brought from America: more RURPs, crack tacks and copperheads and bashees that turned out to be the secret weapon we needed in our armoury. In the morning I was allowed first go at the next pitch, having been thwarted twice before. I easily managed the ten-foot roof and, a few feet above, began fiddling my way up with these new gadgets for hour after hour, oblivious to everything except the little patch of rock just above my head, trusting my weight to skyhooks hung from nubbins of rock, a copperhead tapped into an incipient crack; another, hammered harder, until it smeared itself into the rock's grain. I stopped breathing, stepping up, not at all sure it would stay put. I felt the same with the next three, each one tested and finally accepted, clipped, the ladders attached, and then stepping up, my thirteen stones hanging on those little blobs of copper.

I breathed a little easier after placing a RURP the size of a large postage stamp hammered a full half-inch into the crack. From that I could place another skyhook, then a bashee, a blob of aluminium that I hammered in which somehow held. That got me to a crack, and I nailed in two Leepers, side by side. They bottomed out after an inch, so I tied them off with a loop of cord to stop them levering out. I heard nothing except my own breathing and the rush of blood in my ears, thought of nothing else except the next move, until, reaching a wider crack, I made good progress and reached a ledge 150 feet above Guy and Dennis, some ten hours after leaving them.

I took stock of our situation. Guy and Dennis had been incredibly patient. Dennis remarked that in ten hours we could have climbed ten regular pitches on El Cap. It was too late to complete the route so Guy and Dennis remained where they were and I hauled up my sleeping bag and hammock and arranged it above an eighteen-inch-wide ledge. Dennis had designed the hammocks to be totally waterproof and they got tested to the limit as it began to rain hard. I discovered I'd set my hammock in the course of a waterfall that was now cascading over me, yet I stayed dry apart from a little condensation. Then the wind began to blow and the hammock started swinging around. I ate a tin of sardines in oil and followed that with marmalade butties, which Guy had made and put in the haul sack. I actually felt quite good up there in the hammock, just a thin cocoon a millimetre thick against the wind and rain. I was, I suppose, elated at having negotiated the blank section of rock below, third time lucky. Down below the film team went chasing after our tents as they blew away across the rock and heather. Next day Leo was filming as the three of us completed the route. When we got back to the car we found the estate's gillies had let our tyres down.

Dennis caught his flight to Los Angeles and I went back to my new life as a jobbing builder. We had bought a new house, a three-storey semi-detached villa on Raleigh Street not far from where the original bicycle factory had stood and among rows of back-to-back terraced houses, now earmarked for demolition. It was in a disgusting state, not fit for human habitation. The previous inhabitants, a large extended family, had preferred to put their garbage in the cellar than use the dustbins. It took three days to clear it out, even with the help of friends, and then I discovered that the cellar's beams were rotten and needed replacing. I went on the dole for six months while I did the renovation, managing to find timbers from the nearby slum clearances that were about to be burned. As I worked on the house, I also got involved with building an adventure playground being built on the waste ground, and an urban garden, planting rows of runner beans where workers at the Raleigh factory had once lived.

While I was lying in the bath one morning in February, Don Whillans rang to see if I wanted to go to Everest with him and Hamish as part of a

German expedition. I told him I did and asked him when. 'In a few weeks,' he said, and then added that we had to do some fundraising and organise the oxygen equipment from a firm in Nottingham. I don't suppose, if I had remained a schoolteacher, Don would have asked me along. He knew I was no longer tied down to a regular job. It showed me that unless I took a few risks now and then, I couldn't expect to give myself any extra possibilities in life.

I had never before considered going to Everest, let alone the south-west face. Of course, I had heard all about it; it had been so often in the news over the last three years. The face was the next logical step in the exploration of the mountain. The first ascent of Everest in 1953 by Tenzing and Hillary had followed the south-east ridge attempted the year before by Tenzing and the Swiss Raymond Lambert. The 1953 expedition had been a great team effort brilliantly led by John Hunt. They were able to take advantage of improved equipment and clothing, and able to rehydrate high on the mountain using improved pressure stoves. Griffith Pugh, the expedition physiologist, gave the climbers a better understanding of what was required physically to reach the top. Had it not been for a failure of oxygen apparatus at the south summit, Charles Evans and Tom Bourdillon would have made it on 27 May and become the household names themselves. That became the fate of Tenzing Norgay and Ed Hillary. There is so much luck as to which expedition climbs a mountain first and who gets to go to the summit.

Following on from this original and naturally least difficult route, Chinese and Tibetans ascended the north ridge in 1960, completing the climb that George Mallory and others pioneered in the 1920s. In 1963 the Americans Tom Hornbein and Willi Unsoeld climbed the much steeper west ridge, committing themselves to traversing the mountain by descending the original route. Climbing on Everest thus progressed as it does on all mountains, from the easiest ridge to the hardest and then on to the steep faces in between the ridges. The south-west face was the prime candidate, given that it was for political reasons the only one available to non-Chinese climbers. The Nepali government had lifted their ban on climbing and it was Japanese climbers who, in the spring of 1969, first took up the challenge.

Although mountains have always been sacred landscapes to the Japanese, before the war the chance to indulge in modern mountaineering was confined to the privileged elite, particularly when it came to climbing abroad. Japan was still a very feudal and relatively poor country. There was one notable pre-war Japanese Himalayan expedition in 1931 when a Rikkyo University team from Tokyo climbed Nanda Kot in the Garhwal Himalaya. The war in the Pacific put everyone's Himalayan ambitions on hold but by the end of the American occupation in 1952, Japan had embraced democracy in all spheres of life so that activities once only possible for the privileged few were now open to everyone.

That included mountaineering. Suddenly, masses of people had access to crags and mountains as outlet for their supressed energy and the frustrations of wartime privation. During the following thirteen years, sixty-four Japanese expeditions went off to the Himalaya accounting for twenty-two unclimbed summits. Japanese mountaineers were therefore well-placed to take advantage when the Nepalis lifted their ban on climbing and well-placed to take their next logical step on the south-west face of Everest.

In March during the pre-monsoon season of 1969 the Japanese Alpine Club sent out a small party to ascertain if it was worth sending a larger reconnaissance group in the autumn. The Japanese returned hopeful that a route could be found and so came back a few months later with a much larger group. The autumn weather was perfect with very little wind and even good, firm snow conditions on the lower slopes of the face. All through October they pushed on up the central couloir, establishing three camps with their Camp 5 at 25,600 feet. From here the lead climbers, Naomi Uemura, Masatsugu Konishi, Hiroshi Nakajima and Shigeru Satoh, pushed the route to just below the base of the rock band on 31 October. They had gained valuable information about the route and the difficulty of erecting tents at the top of the couloir where snow cover was sparse. For their next attempt in the spring of 1970 they brought specially designed tent platforms.

The 1970 Japanese expedition couldn't resist the temptation to have a go at the original route as well as the south-west face and thus make the first Japanese ascent. So they brought thirty-nine climbers, doctors and journalists and employed seventy-seven Sherpas, who would work together until Advance Base Camp had been established in the Western Cwm. There the expedition would split. Hiromi Ohtsuka was in overall charge, while the south-west face team were led by Masatsugu Konishi and the south-east ridge team by Teruo Matsuura. The leaders decided unilaterally which climbers would go on which route – a decision that caused a degree of unrest. The expedition was also devastated by the deaths of seven Sherpas, six of them in one avalanche, one of the worst accidents in the mountain's history. Then a team member called Kiyoshi Narita died of a heart attack.

Ohtsuka changed his mind several times, wanting to concentrate his resources on the ordinary route but under pressure from those anxious to climb a new route. This was reminiscent of 1963 when the Americans, Hornbein and Unsoeld, battled to have their attempt on the west ridge of Everest kept on the agenda. Naomi Uemura and Matsuura reached the summit on 11 May followed by Katsutoshi Hirabayashi and Sherpa Chotare the next day. Hirabayashi checked out the upper part of the south-west face by climbing down a short distance from the south summit. He thought it looked very difficult and so it proved: winter winds had stripped the face almost bare of snow.

The much smaller south-west face team, without Uemura, who had been on the previous two recces, still made good progress. On 10 May, Takashi Kano and Hiroshi Sagano with support from two Sherpas climbed past 8,000 metres, taking off their crampons to climb bare rock for 400 feet to the left-hand side of the rock band. From their high point they could see an obvious ramp leading up left towards the west ridge. Above the start of the ramp a narrow cleft forked right, cleaving through the rock band leading up to the broad band of snow above it. They knew climbing the gully would not be easy but thought it possible. They dropped back down full of optimism for a well-earned rest at Advance Base. Unfortunately, on the way down Kano was struck on his back by a falling rock. Ohtsuka called off the attempt on the face because of the danger of rock fall and because he calculated the rock band could not be climbed before the arrival of the monsoon. He chose instead to make further attempts on the original route but bad weather came in and the expedition was called off on 20 May.

In the spring of 1971, Norman Dyhrenfurth, leader of the successful 1963 American team, and Jimmy Roberts were co-leaders of an international expedition to tackle not only the south-west face but also the west ridge direct. There were nine climbers earmarked for the face and ten for the ridge. Roberts, a former Gurkha officer, co-ordinated the Sherpas at Base Camp while Dyhrenfurth took control of events on the mountain. The two teams of climbers were allowed to choose their objective. All went reasonably well until the death of an Indian member of the west ridge party, Harsh Bahuguna, and in the most awful circumstances, caught on a fixed rope retreating down from the ridge in a worsening storm. Don Whillans mounted a rescue attempt but in vain. For ten days Harsh remained hanging down the snow slope not far from Advance Base Camp. His brother Jai would also die on Everest, fourteen years later.

After the storm ended, depression set in and many of the team contracted a debilitating virus. Food supplies proved inadequate and it became apparent there were not enough Sherpas to cover both the south-west face and the long and difficult west face direct. The ridge was abandoned in favour of the original route to allow a better chance for the summit. Following the cremation of Bahuguna at Gorak Shep, Jimmy Roberts proposed abandoning the original route to concentrate resources on the south-west face. There simply weren't enough resources to do both. Dyhrenfurth, in his democratic way, put this proposal to a vote, a foregone conclusion given that he included the Sherpas, and two Swiss members, Michel and Yvette Vaucher, at the time in the icefall, were unable to vote. Only the Italian Carlo Mauri and the famous French alpinist and politician Pierre Mazeaud voted for the South Col route. The Sherpas naturally preferred the shorter, more straightforward snow slopes of the face rather than the long flog up the Western Cwm.

Yvette Vaucher was hoping to make the first ascent by a woman, and so she and her husband, along with Mauri and Mazeaud, regarded the vote as an Anglo-Saxon plot to get the British up the south-west face at all costs. Mazeaud called Dyhrenfurth a *salaud* and threw snowballs at him. 'There was talk of cowardice, dictatorship, lies, drunkenness, insults to France and Italy, bad organisation, weak leadership and other niceties,' Norman recalled. 'Yvette threw stones at my tent.' After much debate, much of it emotional, these four elected to go home, but not before a parting shot from Mazeaud, broadcast to the world's media: 'They expect me, Pierre Mazeaud, member of the French Assembly, aged forty-two, to work as a Sherpa for Anglo-Saxons and Japanese. Never! This is not me but France they have insulted!' In 1978 he became the first Frenchman to reach the summit and was later a senior French jurist with whom I became good friends.

Toni Hiebeler also left the expedition but through sickness, followed later by Dyhrenfurth, almost completely immobilised by a viral infection. Jimmy Roberts took on the leadership of the expedition and since the American climber, John Evans, was incapacitated at Base Camp, Don Whillans was promoted to climbing leader. Only Don, Dougal Haston, Reizo Ito, Naomi Uemura and the two Austrians Wolfgang Axt and Leo Schlömmer were fit. They all returned to the face at the end of April and to the campsites and platforms established by the Japanese the year before. Here they pitched sturdy box tents designed by Whillans.

On 5 May, the teams established Camp 5 at 26,000 feet from where Don and Dougal first inspected the left-hand break through the rock band. They were less impressed than the Japanese in 1970, considering it too steep and technical and with no obvious campsite. They turned their attention to the possibilities of finding a break on the right side of the rock band, heading off up snowfields and ledges where they were easily able to establish Camp 6 at 27,200 feet. Whillans could see a practicable route leading out to the south-east ridge but it was hardly taking the challenge of the face itself, even if a dash to the summit would have constituted some kind of success.

Whillans and Haston remained out front for three weeks without returning to Advance Base Camp. They were criticised by some of the others, particularly the Austrian Schlömmer who offered to go out front if a Sherpa came down to carry up his personal gear. Whillans flatly refused this, having already written off Schlömmer as lazy. Both Austrians departed the expedition, adding to the notion that the whole thing was a British plot from start to finish to put Whillans and Haston on the top. The two Japanese, Reizo Ito and Naomi Uemura, gave continuous and loyal support, without concern as to who completed the route.

All this was the background to Don's invitation. Reining in my excitement I asked for more details.

Dr Karl Maria Herrligkoffer.

'Ah should tell you, Doug,' Don said, 'it's being run by Dr Karl Herrligkoffer.' I already knew about Dr Herrligkoffer from reading Herman Buhl's account of his ascent of Nanga Parbat and the subsequent court actions. I knew also that he and Reinhold Messner were currently locked in combat in the courts over Herrligkoffer's latest Nanga Parbat expedition to the Rupal side.

'How are we going to cope with him, Don?'

'You can leave the doctor to me,' said Don, 'I can handle him.' I had no doubt that Don could do just that. I was always in awe of Don, a little man but incredibly strong and such a gifted and courageous climber, with a natural agility and sense of balance. The only thing he'd been interested in at school, he told me, was gymnastics. He seemed to like people who were either his own height, or much taller, and more powerfully built. Perhaps with these two preferences he knew where he stood. There was no ambivalence.

Hamish had been to Everest before, almost twenty years ago, on quite a different kind of expedition. He told me how he and Johnny Cunningham, after hitchhiking out from New Zealand, had arrived at Everest Base Camp in 1953 intent on climbing Everest by making use of camps the Swiss had abandoned the year before. Skint, illegal and ultimately thwarted by Hillary and Tenzing, they had to ask their remaining Sherpa to leave, which he sadly did. He walked away but suddenly turned back and held out his hand clutching a spoon. It was the only spoon they had between them. 'Please sahib, you have the spoon.'

Don's invitation came right out of the blue. I'd never thought much about climbing Everest or even of going on a big expedition. But after putting the phone down I was in a state of uncontrollable excitement. 'Why me?' I wondered. He had muttered something about needing a good man for the rock band but that was up at 26,000 feet and I'd only been to 22,500 feet before on Bandaka. Those worries evaporated as I contemplated the prospect of becoming Doug Scott – Everest climber. I wasn't expecting much of myself but it would be a good opportunity to check out really high-altitude climbing. Just to go through the icefall and into the fabulous Western Cwm, to see for myself Kathmandu and the Sherpas of Nepal – that would be quite something.

Dr Karl Maria Herrligkoffer's expedition was initially German and Austrian but later included climbers from Italy, Switzerland, Czechoslovakia, Iran and Britain: Don, myself and Hamish. Although he was not a climber, Herrligkoffer had built up a reputation and a lot of experience organising expeditions. Although he forced climbers to sign notoriously restrictive contracts, which he enforced through the courts if necessary, he nevertheless did give many young German and Austrian climbers their first opportunity to visit the Himalaya, including Reinhold Messner.

As it turned out, Herrligkoffer's main interest in having a British contingent was to tap the British media market for finance. Chris Bonington and Dougal Haston had earlier considered joining the expedition and Chris had gone over with his agent, George Greenfield, to Munich. However, verbal agreements given by Herrligkoffer over media rights were broken and along with their impression that Herrligkoffer had little idea of what climbing the south-west face of Everest was about, both he and Dougal withdrew.

As our departure drew near, several incidents suggested our international Everest expedition was not going to fare any better than the last one. Don went over to Munich to brief the doctor but Herrligkoffer was almost continuously busy, either in court with Reinhold Messner, or signing postcards to old ladies who supported his expeditions. I drove out with a lot of the equipment we had organised in Britain: tents from Blacks, oxygen equipment from Nottingham and special tent platforms that Hamish had designed and manufactured. There was also clothing Don had designed including one-piece down suits, neoprene over-boots and harnesses of Don's design manufactured by Troll. The Germans didn't seem interested in this equipment and turned up at Everest dressed for the Alps. Within a short space of time Don's ideas about equipment had universal approval. His harness in particular was a useful innovation for Himalayan climbing; when caught short you could quickly free yourself up without having to untie.

I managed to get in a few days' skiing and to meet up again with Edith, our interpreter. The doctor did not take to me, writing me off as a hippy and superfluous to requirements. He told Don he didn't want me, but Don said 'No Doug, no Don,' and the doctor relented. As money came in from *The Observer* and television contracts Hamish had organised, the doctor told Hamish that he didn't want either Don or myself and offered Hamish a special deal. Hamish replied: 'No Don or Doug, no Hamish.' Following this experience, Hamish christened him Sterlingskoffer. (Don would take credit for this soubriquet, not the first time climbers assumed that pithy witticisms were necessarily Don's.) Right up to departure the trip for the British contingent was on, off, on and finally off again. As Don was having a goodbye celebration in his local pub in Lancashire, he still didn't know if we were wanted. Since we had bought our tickets, we set off for Kathmandu anyway and after talking to the doctor in our hotel, Herrligkoffer decided we could come along after all.

The approach to Base Camp was full of bizarre incidents and mishaps. We were all presented with a supermarket plastic bag full of medicines including opium pellets. Herrligkoffer advised me to take them to help overcome the diarrhoea I had picked up in Kathmandu. I did so just at Phakding after landing at Lukla and promptly fell asleep for four hours. Don's advice was to throw the bag of medicine away; his stock cure was a tin of Vaseline, which he applied regularly to all his orifices. Expedition members each had their own approach to preparing for the face. The Czech-born German Peter Bednar told us he had been circuit training twice a day for months and on the walk in frequently ran up and down hillsides to keep fit.

Resting up after reaching the mountain, a very irate Iranian called Mischa Saleki walked into Base Camp clutching his ice axe, asking for Herrligkoffer and promising to put the pick in the doctor's head. Don took him to one side and sat him down and later brought him over to Hamish and myself, now in a somewhat calmer state. He told us that the doctor had invited him to join the expedition and raise funds in Iran, which he had done only to be crossed off the list. Mischa had not taken this humiliation lightly. Hitchhiking across Europe and Asia, he walked alone up the valleys into Base Camp with revenge in his heart. Don told him that his story was similar to ours and to calm down and take it easy. He was here now and could join with us and make a foursome.

Peter Bednar now arrived and promptly collapsed. 'Ah, dud Czech,' said Don unkindly, but you had to smile. There appeared to be very little concern for acclimatisation. We had walked straight through to Base Camp without pausing. The Base Camp manager, a Professor Edelwald Hüttl, didn't actually reach Base Camp but had to retire en route with altitude sickness. His replacement, Horst Vitt from the German Embassy did reach Base Camp, only to die from pulmonary oedema. Alice von Hobe, a pharmacist friend of Herrligkoffer's, took up the task of managing Base Camp, which she did reasonably well considering her inexperience.

Members of the expedition, L–R: Adi Huber, Leo Breitenberger, Felix Kuen and Werner Haim.

During the first part of the expedition Don's old problem of vertigo surfaced. He suffered headaches, pangs of nausea and was laid up in his tent. This didn't go down well with the Germans, who accused him of being lazy. Don didn't help matters after discovering that the aluminium box he was sat on contained beer, and he proceeded to drink them all. Sepp Maag, a veteran Austrian alpinist and stonemason, couldn't resist building a fireplace and shelf space of baronial proportions on to the gable end of our Base Camp shelter. Don watched Sepp with interest, day after day, as the old man manoeuvred moraine rocks into place, although not so interested that he actually lent a hand.

'You know, Doug,' he said as we watched Sepp, 'give me a bloke who can work with his hands any day.' And with that observation Don dipped into the box he was sitting on and opened another beer.

We then had trouble with the Sherpas, who weren't at all satisfied with the inadequate equipment provided. There were not enough sleeping bags or duvets to go round and they were not prepared to make do with blankets and sweaters. Dr Herrligkoffer had to helicopter out and fly home to Munich for more supplies, leaving a very large expedition without its original leader. The position was handed over to Felix Kuen, an Austrian army lad while Don was designated climbing leader. There was always tension between some of the Austrians and Don. We later discovered that this was a consequence of a pre-expedition briefing from Leo Schlömmer from the previous year's international expedition that Don hogged the lead.

Hamish MacInnes (left), Felix Kuen (second left), Don Whillans (right) and other members of the spring 1972 Everest south-west face expedition.

Hamish and I had spent quite a bit of time in the icefall, a place I found beautiful, especially in the mornings when the sun first skimmed the frosty surface of the ice blocks and séracs. I'd worked away with a few of the German lads – people like Horst Schneider and Adi Weissensteiner and found them good companions on the hill. There was, however, definitely an element in the team that was suspicious of Don and probably Hamish and myself; this didn't augur well for sharing the hardships ahead.

Don recovered from his vertigo and was able to make several carries into the Western Cwm and up to Camp 3 on the face. Then in late April a storm rolled in and everyone came back down to Camp 1 on top of the icefall, sheltering in a big green Stormhaven tent. We passed the time listening to All India Radio and one of the Germans turned it up as they read out the football results for the first leg of the UEFA European Championship quarter finals. Germany had soundly beaten England 3-1 – and at Wembley too. Felix Kuen, who in particular had a morbid fear of Whillans, turned in triumph to Don: 'Ah, so we have beaten you at your national game, *nein*?' Don's eyes narrowed as he glared at Felix, and with perfect timing told him: 'Aye, but we've beaten you at your national game – twice now isn't it?' It wasn't a very happy trip and not the best example of international co-operation, although the German lads who spoke English were actually quite amused at Don's banter.

The expedition continued and eventually Don, Hamish and I reached Camp 4 where we erected Hamish's platforms and Don's box tents with some difficulty.

Whillans box tents on MacInnes platforms at Camp 4 on Everest in the spring of 1972.

The slope was almost all fractured rock and frozen shale. While we were there, I pushed on alone, up the remnants of old fixed ropes, some of them cut and missing that I replaced, to reach the old Camp 5 site. I had a scary moment pulling up on an old piece of rope when it snapped, leaving me teetering on my crampon points for a split second, about to tumble 4,000 feet down the face. I lashed out at the ice with my axe and the pick caught, allowing me to keep my balance.

The three of us spent over two weeks on the face, establishing camps 4 and 5, digging out snow platforms and erecting Hamish's ingenious aluminium constructions. Just as things were looking good and the build-up was gaining momentum, Herrligkoffer returned and invited everyone down to a party. We resisted the lure of Base Camp, staying up in the Western Cwm to avoid losing time during reasonable weather. There were all kinds of problems, a lot of illness and some danger. Rocks would periodically come down the face, piercing the box tents while we were in them. Schneider and Weissensteiner did a lot of hard work but then Adi caught a rock on his knee that put him out of action for some time. The face was particularly bare of snow that spring with far more rock than ice. Leo Breitenberger succumbed to cerebral oedema and had to be lowered down the face from Camp 3.

The main problem for us was that Felix Kuen was determined that Don and therefore all of us should relinquish the lead well before Camp 6. All kinds of deals were struck and struck again as the situation changed. All this fell on Don's shoulders, wearing him and us down when we should have been conserving energy. I learnt a lot from Don about saving energy. On one occasion I rushed up to Camp 5 having become more acclimatised and feeling good. As soon as I arrived, I started digging furiously into the old Camp 5 site, looking for loot left by the international brigade from 1971, and then, like an archaeological dig, right down to the earlier level of Japanese equipment from the year before. I found an assortment of interesting goodies: walkie-talkies, chains of karabiners, packets of mysterious Japanese freeze-dried food but as I sat down to rest I realised I had done too much. I was getting double vision. I looked at the bunch of karabiners and saw that they were melding into each other. I mentioned this to Don.

'Now, you've got to stop rushing about up 'ere, Scottie, you've got to take it easy. Come on, we'd better get you down.' So I threaded my figure of eight and abseiled down the ropes and as I did so recovered my composure. Soon after I was having a brew with Hamish at Camp 4.

It was an interesting experience sharing a tent with Don, which I did for most of the expedition. He was not one for camp chores, and spent most of his time in the tent sleeping, thinking or tinkering with equipment. His latest obsession was modifying a prototype oxygen mask, which covered the whole of his head like a diving helmet, making it lighter by trimming off pieces of rubber and various straps with his penknife. Every day above Base Camp I would put on the early morning brew and cook the evening meals too, not easy in a tent on the side of a mountain. I never minded too much; ever since camping with the Scouts I had quite enjoyed cooking. But on the day of my big solo effort up to Camp 5 I came back down the ropes yelling 'Get a brew on!' only to arrive at the tent to find Don still tinkering around with his equipment. Not only was there no brew, he had drunk all the water I had melted earlier that morning. I brought in more snow and eventually passed a brew around, then prepared the evening meal: mashed potatoes, tinned sausages and peas. When I handed a plate to Don, I said: 'I'm not your mother you know Don.' He looked at me with a strained expression: 'You're not one of those people who moans about a bit of cooking?' He was so outrageous I had to chuckle to myself.

I didn't mind really, he was such good value in other ways. I learned a lot from Don and admired his composure in the face of mounting, unjustified criticism from Felix Kuen. Despite a determined effort by other members of the expedition, the equipment and food needed for this style of climbing was simply not moving up the face. It all seemed rather hopeless and unlikely the expedition would get higher than Don's high point of the year before. For us the crunch came in the middle of May when the German and Austrian contingent gave Don an ultimatum: either he went down or they would abandon the climb. Don, by this time, decided enough was enough and said he was going home. Other members of the expedition said they hoped Hamish and I would continue but apart from the dispiriting lack of progress we remained loyal to Don and left Base Camp with him.

Within a day or so, Kuen radioed down from the face that it was too cold at 'Lager Sechs' and descended. The whole expedition left Base Camp within a few days of us. Ken Wilson at *Mountain* looked into the reasons for this 'lamentable failure. Poor leadership seems to have been the biggest single weakness: Herrligkoffer played very little part in the proceedings, while Kuen seemed bent on leading from the front, studiously avoiding any consultation with Whillans on tactics … Whillans' attempts to maintain a sensible tactical plan to avoid the starvation of supplies and manpower that stopped last year's expedition were constantly frustrated by the Austrians, who seemed to believe that he was trying to get into the front and snatch the summit for himself.'

For me it had been a fantastic experience; I really enjoyed being with Hamish and Don and with many of the German and Austrian climbers too. I certainly found it interesting to be on Everest. I found I could cope with the altitude and the intense cold. All of us who go into the mountains have experienced cold in Scotland and the Alps in winter but up at 26,000 feet, where there is only one

Signing expedition postcards. L–R: Don Whillans, me, Michael Anderl, Dr Herrligkoffer and Alice von Hobe.
Photo: Hamish MacInnes.

third of the oxygen, it gets really cold but without the fuel you need to create heat. In other situations I knew when it was time to stop and warm up frozen fingers before they became frostbitten, but up there, high in the thin, cold air of Everest, I found I had to act a lot faster than usual or I would end up having my digits chopped off. I had used oxygen at times and at others I climbed without; it didn't seem to make a lot of difference towards the end of the expedition when I had fully acclimatised. My horizons had been considerably widened.

I had coped reasonably well with homesickness despite all the inter-team acrimony. It's in that kind of situation that the lure of home and the support of family and friends are strongest. The one benefit from all the arrivals and departures on this rather chaotic trip was the number of letters received and delivered, keeping me in touch with home and Jan, whom I was thinking about a great deal. In a letter written from the Western Cwm, I told her: 'I miss you and think about you on every occasion, walking, puffing along with loads up and jogging back down, dry as a bone, lying here from dark to sleep and then again in the morning I remembered you today going off to school in your long coat and with laughing eyes and red cheeks poking above your long white scarf, waving goodbye as I am getting Mike to clean his shoes for school. I do want to be with you both sharing the daily round. I know you will be coping but I am wanting to be part of it all again.' It was the old conundrum: when I was at home I yearned to be out with the boys again on some distant mountain; after a few weeks abroad, I would be longing to be back home again.

Just after I got back from Everest in early June I heard Chris Bonington had permission to go to Everest that autumn and that he was taking a small group of his old climbing friends to tackle the ordinary route. I didn't think too much about it. All my thoughts were focused on going to Baffin Island with Dennis and also two new recruits, Paul Nunn and Paul Braithwaite. It was quite a surprise when I got a call from Chris inviting me to join him, Hamish, Dougal Haston, Nick Estcourt and the rest of his team on the south-west face. I accepted without hesitating or discussing it with Jan who I knew would understand that I had to go.

A few weeks later, at an Alpine Climbing Group meeting in North Wales, we had a chance to talk about the trip. Most of the team were there for the evening meal and drinking session. The main item of conversation was the exclusion of Don. Hamish and myself both voiced our opinion that Don should be going; no one knew the face better than he. Other friends such as Tom Hurly from the ACG who were not involved with Everest but were friends of Don told me how bad Don felt at being excluded. We put more pressure on Chris but he was adamant; he could not function as leader with Don on the expedition. He had made his mind up and there was no way he was going to change it.

It was a bitter pill for Don to swallow. That evening he sank over twenty pints, most of them bought by sympathetic well-wishers. I suppose that was Don's way to hide from the lowering of his self-esteem, that yet another of his climbing ambitions had been thwarted. He had missed out on the first British ascent of the Eiger's north face after repeated attempts with Chris, who had grabbed that prize with Ian Clough instead. In the Karakoram Don narrowly missed reaching the summit of Masherbrum when his partner became dangerously exhausted near the summit. He missed out on the summit of Trivor on Wilf Noyce's expedition after a mystery virus laid him low. Now, after two attempts at the south-west face, it was not going to be third time lucky.

I couldn't blame Chris. Don had written a self-indulgent *Mountain* article after the 1970 Annapurna expedition that criticised the Bonington style: 'Chris has developed from an easy-going, generous, haphazard lieutenant in the army to a high-powered, materialistic photojournalist, to all outward appearances motivated only by money.' Chris wrote later about his decision: 'Don was a superb mountaineer, there's no shadow of doubt about that, but he is also quite a prickly kind of customer. He just didn't fit in to the 1972 team. This wasn't just a personal decision of my own; it was one that was felt by several team members many of whom are close friends of Don's and of course I had been a close friend of Don as well.' In fact both Dougal and Mick Burke were supportive of Chris's decision. Chris didn't 'feel that Don would fit into the team that I had chosen.'

It slowly dawned on me that Dougal was not in favour of Don's inclusion so I put it to him that we both owed Don our support by getting him on to the expedition. Dougal practically spat out his reply: 'I owe that man nothing.' Dougal thought clinically and had come to the conclusion it was time for Don to step aside. I was beginning to see that Don would not have slotted easily into the sort of expedition this was becoming or any kind of expedition, for that matter. I nevertheless felt a deep regret that we were not to have the benefit of Don's sound common sense and his ability to see so clearly into all kinds of problems that arise on big mountaineering expeditions. I would also miss his ability to see through pretentiousness and pompous self-importance. Don had the ability to cut people down to size – his size. But while that ability might be useful in the pub on a Saturday night, it wasn't so welcome high on the mountain. I also knew that my efforts to persuade Chris to include Don were partly because I felt grateful to Don for asking me along to Everest in the spring.

The south-west face of Everest.

EVEREST AGAIN

In late June 1972, I was checking in at Montreal airport for the flight to Frobisher Bay dressed in all my climbing clothes, wearing my harness with pegs and karabiners attached, a cagoule over everything and a rope across each shoulder.

'Why are you wearing ropes?' the woman behind the desk said, looking confused.

'Because we are climbers,' I said. 'Is the flight on time?'

'Yeah, I think so,' she said, handing over our boarding passes. We staggered on to the aircraft having saved ourselves excess baggage charges equivalent to our transatlantic fares.

Dennis Hennek and I were heading back to Baffin, this time with Paul Nunn and Paul 'Tut' Braithwaite. We left Pangnirtung in a boat on a sled pulled by Jok Polliollok's skidoo and within two or three hours had reached the head of the fjord, which was this year still completely frozen. There we shouldered monstrous sacks weighing in at 130 pounds each. We could only manage a few hundred yards before backing up to a convenient boulder to rest. After two days of slushy spring snow and wading the many braided rivers, we reached our old Base Camp above Summit Lake.

It had not been such a bad walk, just the four of us camping out on the tundra in two lightweight tents. I told the others about my bizarre visit to Everest and the strangeness of big expeditions. Paul wrote after our climb that 'little expeditions are more likely to be good expeditions, even at their most extended; and I could think of few places more suitable than Baffin for such an approach. Anyway, the battle of Everest seemed to me to have undermined the very term "expedition", which now implies multiple forms of exploitation and rigid organisation for which the only compensation for many individual climbers is pretentiousness. The alienation of heart, combined with the extreme graft involved, seems to me to be the complete antithesis of what mountaineering is all about.

Our 1973 Baffin team. **L–R**: Ray Gillies, Dave Cracknell, Dan Meadows, Rob Wark, Mick Webster, Steve Read, Clive Davies, Rob Wood, Dave Bathgate and Paul 'Tut' Braithwaite.

A small group, friendly, intimate, motivated but not utterly achievement-orientated, promised to get away from all that … especially with Dennis who proved to be anything but the lean, rock-drilling technocrat that I half expected. Instead he was a muscular, blond, fun and pleasure-loving character who seemed to enjoy the occasional discipline of climbing and to do it well. Within a few hours we seemed like a team.'

We split the loads at Summit Lake and in two carries made camp under Asgard by a glacial lake. Six days after leaving Montreal, we were ready to go. We humped gear up the thousand feet of mixed ground to the base of the wall and, while the newcomers dug out a big snow cave, Dennis and I set off up the open corners above, climbing free and pegging where we couldn't. Then Dennis arrived at a blank section – no more cracks. There was nothing for sixty feet, just a water streak. It was hard to take, but Paul and Tut took it well as we went into reverse, abandoning the snow hole to consider our options. We opted instead for the east side and a 4,000-foot pillar and headwall to the flat summit of Asgard North Peak.

We led about a quarter each, half a dozen pitches at a time, over the finest granite a climber could wish for, but the climbing always had an edge to it since we had no idea whether we could overcome the final 500 feet, which reared over us. Dennis got the crux, a squeeze chimney for which he stripped down to his vest and pants. Dennis, used to such features from all those months he spent in Yosemite, thought it was 5.9, but modern guidebooks say it's 5.11.

Dennis Hennek leading the squeeze chimney on the East Pillar of Mount Asgard in 1972. The pitch was later dumbed down when seven bolts were placed up the side of the fissure.

Someone repeating our route sometime later added seven bolts alongside it, a pathetic act of vandalism.

The last pitch, a solid hand-jam crack, was mine and I pulled over the top after thirty hours of continuous climbing. We were snoozing on the summit when Dennis announced he could see our tents by the lake were now in the lake. The spring snow was melting fast. It took a whole day to descend because of soft snow in the basin below the saddle of Asgard's twin summits, wading downhill chest deep, sometimes disappearing completely, until we recovered our snowshoes on King's Parade Glacier. The last two miles to the lake took less than an hour. Recovering our tents from the lake, we were relieved to find our sleeping bags were merely damp.

We ambled the fifty miles back down Weasel Valley and alongside the fjord over five days, finishing the last of our food as went. On the last day a team of Italian climbers flew over our heads in a helicopter on their way to Base Camp. We felt quite superior walking all the way back out to Pangnirtung under our own steam, quite forgetting that the year before we would have paid any price for a seat in a helicopter. Pangnirtung was busy with tourists when we got back. Ross Peyton's prefabricated hotel – Peyton's Place, we dubbed it – was being extended; the wonderful, unspoilt wilderness had become a well-advertised national park.

Dennis had driven to Montreal from California and I planned to drive back with him, having collected Jan, Michael and a college friend Ann Gerty from the airport, for a holiday before going to Everest. We took a route around Lake Superior to Montana and Wyoming where Michael watched fascinated as the geyser Old Faithful erupted at Yellowstone. Dennis and I climbed the Devil's Tower having run the gauntlet of several rangers. We stayed at the Climbers' Ranch not far from Grand Teton where Chuck Pratt was custodian. Jan went for a swim one evening and got into difficulties. Michael, who was now quite a strong swimmer, pushed a floating log towards Jan that she managed to grasp just in time. Michael may well have saved his mother's life.

We visited Arches National Park and Canyonlands, but Jan had been feeling queasy for most of the trip, especially in the mornings, so we headed for the Red Cloud Ranch in Colorado where Dez Hadlum and his wife Ann were working. After fishing for trout in beautiful mountain lakes, Dennis left for California and the three of us flew home from Denver leaving Ann on the ranch. Or should I say, four of us, since Jan discovered she was pregnant just before I flew out to Nepal to join Chris Bonington and the rest of the expedition in the last week of August.

For the second time in 1972, Hamish and I were back in Nepal heading for Everest, but now with an all-British team, all good lads and one good woman, our expedition nurse and Dr Barney Rosedale's assistant, Beth Burke.

56 The south-west face of Everest seen from Nuptse in the evening light, autumn 1979.
57 The Mani Rimdu Festival at Thame, spring 1972.
58 Dr Karl Herrligkoffer perplexed that all the Sherpas went on strike demanding sleeping bags and duvets.
59 Climbing through the icefall during the spring 1972 Everest expedition.

60 Carrying sections of the tent platform up to Camp 4 during the spring 1972 attempt.
61 Don carrying a load to Camp 3.

62

62 Everest, autumn 1972. L–R: me, Hamish and Don at Camp 1, wearing the custom down suits and rubber overboots that Don had developed for Annapurna 1970 and Everest 1971.

63 Sherpas and members of the autumn 1972 expedition retreating to Base Camp from Camp 1. Just after taking this photograph the séracs above collapsed over the ladder killing Tony Tighe, a young Australian who had helped run Base Camp.

64

65

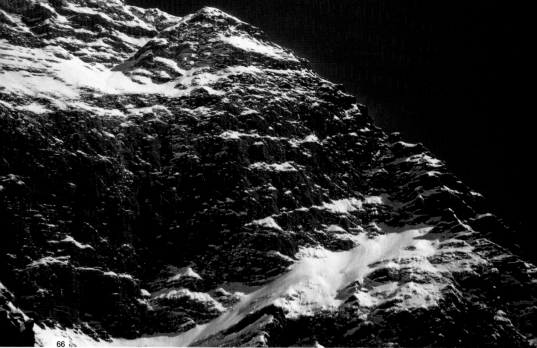

66

64 Dougal at the highest point, 27,300 feet, on 14 November 1972 and from where we decided to retreat.

65 The gully through the rock band, reported to be full of snow and comparatively easy by Dougal, who had looked up it in 1971. In 1972 we found it blown clear of snow and a formidable problem.

66 A detailed image of the 1,500-foot rock band sandwiched between the upper and lower snowfields. The gully through the rock band, attempted by previous expeditions and which proved to be a cul-de-sac, is visible on the right-hand side. The south summit is towards the top of the image.

67 Chris Bonington sitting at Kala Pattar, reflecting on our recent climb up the south-west face of Everest, October 1975.
68 A team shot at Base Camp, October 1975.

69 Chris and Dave Clark working on logistics at Camp 2, September 1975.
70 Nick and Tut who pioneered the route through the rock band.
71 Pertemba Sherpa, our brilliant sirdar. **Photo**: Chris Bonington.
72 Mick Burke.
73 Dougal Haston in the icefall.

74 At the foot of the gully.
75 Dougal climbing out of the gully to Camp 6.
76 The team followed our progress across the upper slopes using telephoto lenses. **Photo**: Nick Estcourt.

77 Dougal moving across the face above Camp 6 towards the south summit couloir.
78 Dougal on the 1,000 feet of fixed rope we put in from Camp 6 across the upper snowfield above the rock band.

79 Dougal Haston on the Hillary Step. The summit is the sunlit snow on the right.

80

South West Face

SN⁰ 016

British Everest Expedition 1975

MESSAGE FORM

ORIGINATOR'S No. ℛ./.11

MOST URGENT

TO: PARARASTRA MANTRALAYA AAROHAN SAKHA DATE: 2032/6/9

FROM: L O B E E   TIME: 1200 hrs

MESSAGE: DOUGAL HASTON RA DOUG ⊗ SCOTT YEHI
ASWIN 8 GATE BELUKI 1800 BAJE SAGARMATHA
KO CHUCHURA PUGNU BHAYO (.) NIJA HARU GATA
RATI SOUTH SUMMIT MA BIVOUAC LAGAI
BASE RA AJA BIHAN ASWIN 9 GATE 0845
BJE MATRA CAMP 6 MA AAI PUGI CHUCHURA
PUGE KO SAMACHAR BATAYE (.) NIJA HARU DIN KO
1400 BAJE MATRA CAMP 2 MA AAI PUGNE BHAYE KO
HUNDA PURNA BIBARAN THAHA HUN SAKE KO
CHHAINA (.) DAL LE CHUCHURA JAN DOSRO
PRAYETNA PANI GARNE BEHORA ANUROD/

25 / voice
1205 / 8L

SIGNED

80 Dougal on the summit of Everest, at 7.00 p.m. on 24 September 1975.

81 Our LO's telegram reporting the news of our successful summit. It reads:

To: FOREIGN MINISTRY EXPEDITION DEPARTMENT

From: L.O. B.E.E.

Time: 1200 hrs

Message: Dougal Haston and Doug Scott has reached to top of the Everest in the evening of 24 September (8 Aswin B.S.) at 1800 hours. Last night they have built camp at South Summit and stay there and today in the morning of (9 Aswin B.S.) 25 September A.D. at 0845 hours they returned to camp 6 and told us they summited the Everest. They have said that they will only be arriving at camp 2 at 1400 hours today so we can't give you a full report until then. The rest of the group intend to make 2nd attempt to the summit.

Message sent at 1205 hours. Signed by L.O.

82 On our way out from Everest in October 1975, Dougal and I were congratulated by Tenzing Norgay.

83 I am sitting by the memorial to Mick Burke at Gorak Shep. **Photo:** Jan Scott.

84 Returning to Heathrow. Photo: Air India.
85 With Chris at the *Daily Express* 'Men of the Year' event. Photo: *Daily Express*.

The British Everest south-west face expedition departing London in August 1972. Front, L–R: me, Beth Burke, Dougal Haston and Chris Bonington; back, L–R: Nick Estcourt, Graham Tiso, Hamish MacInnes and Dr Barney Rosedale. **Photo:** BOAC.

Her husband Mick was held up at customs again, extricating film equipment, as he had been on Baffin Island the previous year. Before leaving Kathmandu, we went for a last meal at a restaurant called The Garden of Eden. Kathmandu had been a magnet for hippies taking advantage of its lax drugs laws, but now that was coming to an end. Since the spring, cannabis had been made illegal and many of the hippies had been put on planes home. Yet many of the restaurants and guesthouses continued to sell hash cakes, which most of the team sampled.

The cake I ate had a rather hard, chewy centre that in retrospect I really should have left. The next thing I knew I was waking up at the Hotel Shanker unable to move. My arms and legs seemed glued to the bed. This was particularly upsetting for our leader, Chris, who was anxious we all left immediately on waiting jeeps for the village of Lamosangu and the start of the long hike to Base Camp. I managed, through numb lips, to tell Chris it would all work out and not to worry. Barney confirmed that in a day or two the patient would be fit to travel. When Mick returned from his day's struggle at the airport, he was highly amused at my predicament and we set off with Beth soon after to catch up with the others.

When we got to Khumbu, I visited Dorji Lama at a little *gompa* on the far side of the Dudh Kosi from Phakding. Dorji had been employed on the Herrligkoffer expedition in the spring and had asked to purchase a whole pile of clothing and climbing equipment from me. We agreed a price and he told me I was to collect the rupees from his *gompa* on the way out. When I got there, his family told me, with a smirk on their faces, that Dorji was on a religious retreat. Dorji looked very surprised when I knocked on his door three months later. After a long discussion about honouring one's commitments, he paid up and we remained on good terms thereafter, often sharing a pot of Tibetan tea.

Having seen so many locals walking the trails barefoot, even across the moraine to Base Camp, I had a mad impulse that I too would walk barefoot and build up a thick callous of skin to protect my feet from the cold of Everest. So from Lamosangu onwards I'd gone without shoes and socks. Each day was less painful than the last and my skin did harden as I felt the grain of the land change beneath my feet all the way to Base Camp. A few days later, carrying a load up to Camp 1 through the icefall and then returning to Base Camp, I removed my toasty double boots and peeled off my socks, only to find that a quarter inch of thick skin from my soles had come off with them. That cost me a couple more days.

The Sherpas were already putting up the Base Camp tents and kitchen shelters when we arrived and I recognised some of them from the spring. Jimmy Roberts, our Base Camp manager, introduced us to the newcomers. Jimmy was credited as having started the first trekking business in the 1960s and as a colonel in the Gurkhas was very much respected. Sitting around on boxes and barrels in a very crowded mess tent one evening, Jimmy said to his loyal deputy: 'Ang Phu, the mustard.' Since Ang Phu was sat around the other side of the tent, I moved to pass the mustard to Jimmy myself. 'Thank you, Doug,' Jimmy said, holding his hand up like a policeman stopping traffic. 'Ang Phu, the mustard.' So Ang Phu had to make his way around some twenty people to pick up the mustard and, with a beaming smile, passed it over to Jimmy with both hands as if making an offering to the gods.

Soon we were back in the Western Cwm with our leader throwing one team after another at the south-west face, tilting at that great windmill in the sky, but all his efforts and ours came to nought. The westerly winds hammered the mountain that autumn. Kelvin Kent's hands were badly frostbitten hauling himself and a heavy load up the fixed ropes to Camp 4. Towards the end of October rockfall sliced open Graham Tiso's head while he was cooking inside a box tent at Camp 4. Our doctor, Barney, despite having cracked his ribs from coughing, stitched up the wound. He was called on again when a gas cylinder came bounding down from Camp 4 and smashed into Ang Dawa's face. Within a week Ang Dawa was back carrying loads.

The wind made the intense cold that much worse and its debilitating effect caused mistakes when fumbling with gear. Both Dave Bathgate and Nick Estcourt dropped their rucksacks at different times. Mick and I were paired together and we worked really hard into the night to re-establish Camp 4 after it had been destroyed in a severe storm. The next day we carried loads up to a site for Camp 5 at 26,000 feet. While Mick was digging a tent platform, I moved to one side to take his photograph but in an effort to get more of the surrounding mountainside in the frame, I stepped over the edge and disappeared down the fifty-degree slope towards a vertical drop of 2,000 feet. I clawed with my bare hands at the snow and rock and somehow stopped myself before I was airborne. From my new position I had a unique view of Camp 4 so I took a photograph and clambered back to Mick. I told him how I'd fallen and nearly been killed. He didn't look up from his digging: 'Ah, I wondered where you'd been.'

Chris was conducting operations from the 'stalls' as he put it, down at Camp 2 in the Western Cwm. He knew from all the logistical information he had gathered that time was running out. He was naturally anxious to see Mick and me start breaking trail for a site at Camp 6. Unfortunately, that night, in an effort to get to sleep in the intense cold of -40° Celsius, and after a week of hard work up high, I had followed Mick's advice and taken a sleeping tablet and missed the early morning call on the two-way radios. It was the first time I had used 'sleepers' and when I finally came to after ten hours spark out, I decided it would be my last. We stayed put all day, since Mick had bad piles and a hacking cough; in any case we were both worn out from putting up two camps in high winds late into the night. The inside of our tent began to resemble a butcher's shop as Mick kept clearing his raw throat with his fingers and wiping them on the frosty fabric. It was all rather ghastly really.

I told Chris in a slurred voice we needed to come down for a rest before we could tackle the rock band; this was a task Mick and I had been earmarked for two months before. So it came as a bit of a disappointment to hear Chris tell us on the radio that he had revised his plans. Dougal and Hamish were to come up and lead the rock band from Camp 6. Could we therefore stay up and establish Camp 6 for them? On Annapurna two years before, Chris had done something similar, deciding to send Dougal and Don up when he felt Mick was flagging. Now Mick got on to the radio: 'Up to your old tricks is it then, Chris?'

Nick Estcourt and Dave Bathgate moved up to join us at Camp 5. I couldn't resist a wry smile when Mick and I heard Nick on the radio telling Chris: 'It really is cold up here, you can have no idea how cold it is.' Graham Tiso, down at Camp 4, had measured -38° that morning. Next day Nick and I set off up the face with Mick filming while Dave secured the camp. We swung leads right up to the base of the rock band, fixing 1,200 feet of rope to an altitude of 26,700 feet up rock, ice and powdery snow. Then I headed down with Mick all the way to Camp 2 to find out what our leader had in store for us.

This was the first time in my life that I'd been told where and when to climb – and without much consultation. I found that hard to accept, as did Mick. I told Chris he was being manipulative, just like Herrligkoffer, without any thought for his team members. Comparing Chris to Herligkoffer was the ultimate insult and Chris countered by telling me that if I didn't agree with his decisions then I should pack up and go home. With Barney acting as mediator we calmed down and Mick and I both agreed to support Hamish and Dougal in their attempt on the rock band.

Chris may at times have displayed a lack of empathy in his decision-making, as Herrligkoffer usually did, but any similarities ended there. Chris, unlike the doctor, was a climber, one of the most experienced in Britain, in the Alps and out here in the Himalaya. He had already reached the summit of Annapurna II and Nuptse. In 1970 it was thanks to Chris's organisation that his team succeeded on Annapurna up the most technically difficult face yet attempted on an 8,000-metre peak. That expedition secured Chris's reputation as an expedition organiser.

Unlike John Hunt, Chris was frequently lampooned in the climbing press particularly in *Mountain* where Ian McNaught-Davis satirised him as Cassius Bonafide, the conqueror of Annaplus. He was accused of chasing fame and fortune. I would have found that kind of mockery hard to take and no doubt it was painful for Chris, all the more so because he really was a bona fide climber of the first rank. I admired him for taking such criticism on the chin and carrying on regardless. The climbing world has always been suspicious of the commercialisation of the sport. Chris, with his appearances in advertisements in national magazines and on television, seemed to be leading the charge in that direction.

His background was more complicated than many knew. He certainly didn't have an easy childhood. His father, having refused to work, left Chris and his mother, Helen, for pastures new when Chris was only a year old. Brought up mostly by his grandmother while his mother went out to work, Chris lived in rented accommodation and money was always tight, right up to the time he joined the army. As an only child from a one-parent family with frequent changes of school during wartime, Chris never developed a settled peer group, as I had in Nottingham. He only had himself to rely on. He never seemed to get homesick and while establishing a settled family life was important to him, he was always the last to want to terminate an expedition. He would be pushing to go that extra mile when most of the rest of us were eager for home.

Climbing up to the rock band from Camp 5 with Nick Estcourt.

Despite his upbringing, Chris was seen as posh with his plummy accent at a time when many successful climbers were from the working classes. As a consequence, he was subject to varying degrees of inverted snobbery, envy and the usual British habit of attacking those who are successful. There were times when Chris didn't strike the right balance in his fundraising and public appearances. He modelled the clothes he wore for lecturing in *Vogue*, and appeared in television advertisements, neither of which went down well either among the rank and file in the Padarn or the Alpine Club establishment.

On 14 November, after sterling supply work from the Sherpas – especially Ang Phurba and Pertemba, and Chris, Dave and Nick, Dougal and Hamish set off from Camp 5 to establish Camp 6. Mick and I followed in support under a cloudless blue sky but in a biting wind. Hamish had to retreat when his oxygen apparatus completely froze. I caught up with Dougal at the site of Camp 6, taking photographs of him and all the peaks now visible beyond the corniced ridge between Nuptse and Lhotse. Mick shot some film and I looked around for the line through the rocks. I couldn't see that much through the spindrift other than a steep corner-crack in the rocks leading up 200 feet to the right hand-edge of the face.

I could see no direct way up to the snowfields above the rock band and was a little baffled that we had come this way rather than aim for the gully to the left of Camp 5 the Japanese had approached two years earlier. I asked Dougal where Don had got to in 1971. He pointed up the ill-defined walls and terraces above. I shrugged and made no further comment; ordinary conversation was impossible over the wind and I didn't want to waste any more energy screaming into each other's ears. Dougal had already decided he was going down and I merely concurred. It was definitely too late in the year to be climbing steep rock at 27,000 feet, especially without any obvious way through it.

There was relief all round that the decision to give up had been made. There was also a good feeling among us all, back down safely in the Western Cwm. One result of the shared suffering and exposure to danger over the previous six weeks had been to bring us closer together. One thing was obvious: whoever came back to Everest post-monsoon would have to come earlier in the year. On the descent I took quite a few photographs from various angles of the gully on the left side of the rock band. Just before Camp 5, Dougal and I stopped where we could see right into it. There seemed to be a continuous line of snow all the way up it, which looked encouraging. Where there is snow a human can go, providing it doesn't avalanche.

I never understood why two experienced hands like Dougal and Don could have been lured towards the right-hand corner of the rock band twice. Not only did it look difficult to climb, Don had demonstrated in 1971 that it could be avoided by exiting the face to the right. The corner I saw and photographed

The upper section of the south-west face. Our initial attempts took a line to the right-hand side of the large rock band running across the centre of the face. **Photo**: Ang Zangbu.

did not even lead on to the upper snowfields and would likely have been just another escape route off the face, albeit a bit higher than the one Don discovered in 1971. On the left there was no such easy escape. All in all, by tackling the rock band on the left the route would be as logical and committing as the original route on the Eiger's north face. The other advantage was that the technical difficulties were lower down than on the right and more sheltered from the westerly winds that made climbing quite impossible for us in the autumn of 1972.

As we went down through the ice wall I met Tony Tighe, a young Australian friend of Dougal's who had helped Beth and Jimmy run Base Camp. As a reward, and at our insistence, Chris had agreed Tony could take a quick trip into the legendary Western Cwm before we left. We never saw Tony again. As he passed under the largest and most precarious séracs in the icefall, one of them collapsed on top of him, burying Tony under hundreds of tons of ice. He was a super guy whose company we all valued and his death was a shock for everyone; Dougal and Chris took it especially hard, since it was so reminiscent of the death of Ian Clough right at the end of the Annapurna expedition, who also perished under a collapsing sérac.

Chris expected problems with Nepali tourism officials since Tony didn't have a permit to go beyond Base Camp. I suggested to Chris we should all shoulder the blame, seeing as we all lobbied for Tony to go into the icefall. Chris was adamant that as leader he must take the consequences, which might include a ban from climbing in Nepal. Fortunately it didn't come to that, but it was typical of Chris not to shirk responsibility. He might have been a top-down leader but that is what is required on big, siege-style expeditions. The Sherpas particularly want to know who to take orders from and address their problems to. The climbers were all strong individuals, and it helped having someone equally strong to keep them in line, motivated and focused on the same goal. Chris as leader had little time to rest from the daily logistical planning and carrying his share of the loads, which he did right up to Camp 6.

It was wonderful to be walking out over the close-cropped yak pastures and along the gentle trails of Khumbu, past Tengboche monastery and on down through the villages to Lukla and a flight to Kathmandu. When I got off the plane, I was in for a lovely surprise on discovering Michael waiting to greet me. A Nottingham poultry farmer had offered to fly Jan and Michael to Nepal, but with Jan pregnant he came out with Maggie Bathgate. He had got rather bored waiting for a week, but we made up for lost time exploring Kathmandu on foot and by rickshaw, visiting the monkey temple, Durbar Square and the busy streets of Thamel with its stalls of Buddhist bronzes and sculptures in wood, stone and bone. Most of it looked genuinely old. Michael's constant question was: 'How much?' and he revealed himself to be an excellent haggler.

Little by little he asked me about the climb, which he had followed closely with Jan; he knew all about the rock band and the rockfall, the high winds and intense cold. Most of his information came from the excellent reports sent back by Chris Brasher who had been right up to Camp 2 in the Western Cwm. Jan had felt that the regular bulletins were a real comfort keeping her in touch with our climbing and helped to stave off desperate feelings of loneliness and being abandoned.

Chris Brasher had been good company but sometimes after a hard day spent humping loads up the face his questioning became a bit tedious. Towards the end, with food stocks low and the mess tent horribly cold and squalid, Chris approached Barney concerned about the tingling in his lower limbs. Barney warned him it could be phlebitis. Chris was off down to Base Camp that same afternoon, so afraid of a blood clot that he never looked back. Of course, said Barney later, with a wry smile, what he didn't tell Chris was that his pins and needles could have been the result of sitting for hours on the boxes at Camp 2.

The year after our attempt, in the autumn of 1973, the Japanese returned and again divided their resources between the face and the original route. The expedition came out earlier but despite having previously thought it possible to climb through the gully on the left in 1970 and after three failed attempts on the right, they too incredibly decided to attempt to break through on the right side of the rock band.

There was a bizarre incident during the expedition, giving the lie to the notion that fist fights on Everest are a new phenomenon. Some of the climbers overheard a conversation between the leader and a TV producer who was reluctant to return without having gone to the summit. The climbers leapt to the assumption that the TV crew would be going to the summit in place of themselves. A heated discussion took place in the Western Cwm, ending in punches at midnight at 22,000 feet.

The Japanese established Camp 6 on the face but gave up in the face of bad weather. Two climbers, however, went all the way from the South Col up the original route to the summit on 26 October. The Japanese were thus the first expedition to climb Everest in the post-monsoon season. This was interesting information for the future and helped lower the psychological barrier against climbing the south-west face in the post-monsoon season.

Early in March 1973 I was back home in Nottingham being briefed by Jan's midwife, a homely woman but recovering from a slipped disc. Jan had gone into labour and the midwife needed me in pole position to receive the baby. I will never forget the crown of the baby's head appearing, and then there she was, our daughter Martha, quickly exercising her powerful lungs. As the midwife was dealing with the umbilical cord, blood gushed out from between Jan's legs and all over our bed. The midwife rushed to the bathroom for more towels while I stood there horrified, wondering what I would do if it didn't stop.

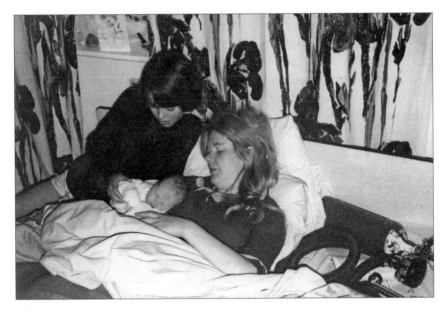

Jan and Michael with Martha, 1973.

'Burst fibroid,' the midwife said, but she looked worried too and we debated calling an ambulance. Luckily all was well, but I don't remember a more frightening moment in my life, made worse by not having a clue what to do.

I was home with the family for the following month, helping Jan with Martha, changing nappies, shopping, going for walks sometimes with Michael and the Nottingham Climbers' Club into Derbyshire. After Easter, having been offered the chance to lecture in America about Everest and needing to do more interviews for my book, I returned to the States, this time with Ken Wilson who was eager to gather information for *Mountain*. So Ken and I arrived in Yosemite where Ken was in his journalistic element, stoking everyone up with a combination of flattery and hard-hitting questions. He was quite taken by the beautiful Beverly Johnson.

'Beverly,' Ken said, 'how many 5.10 climbs have you led?'

'That's not the question you should be asking,' Beverly replied. 'The question is how many 5.10 climbers have I laid?' Ken was stunned into silence. (It was rare to see Ken stuck for words. He had trekked up to Everest Base Camp in the autumn to report on our climb, and after two weeks with a porter who spoke no English made up for lost time by talking non-stop for the rest of the expedition.)

Beverly was a good climber by anyone's standards, having climbed the north-west face of Half Dome and the *Steck-Salathé* on Sentinel. Over eight days in the autumn of 1973 Beverly and Sibylle Hetchel made the first all-female

Australian Rick White, who I would climb with in Yosemite in 1973.

ascent of El Cap, climbing the *Triple Direct*, a combination of the *Salathé*, *Muir Wall* and *The Nose*. Later Beverly became the first woman to solo a route on El Cap, when she climbed the very difficult *Dihedral Wall* alone. She was also the first woman to lead a fire crew in Yosemite.

While climbing and working in the Valley, I met Rick White, an Australian in his mid twenties who had made his name climbing hard new routes in his native Queensland, or the 'banana republic' as he called it. Rick had climbed the hardest route in Australia at the time at Mt Maroon and added scores of climbs to another of his discoveries, Frog Buttress. He was tall and strong, the quintessential Aussie, down to earth and ready to give anything a go. We teamed up to climb *The Nose* as free as possible, taking five gallons of water so we could spend as long as necessary, but compromised with a hammer and a few pegs as well as a huge rack of nuts.

The first three pitches were hard, especially the third, but where we resorted to aid it was mainly on nuts. Gradually we got into the swing of the climbing and after a night on Sickle Ledge we completed the King Swing and gained the Stove Leg cracks, mostly perfect hand jams. It was grand to be climbing on such a spectacular route free of aid for a thousand feet up the cracks, slotting nuts in every now and then for protection, swinging leads, pitch after pitch with our hands deep in the mountain and acres of sunlit, rippling granite stretching out right and left. We complemented each other perfectly, in harmony even when the weather turned. Standing on El Cap Tower, looking out at the sky, some white flakes of snow floated by, not at first settling on the rock. Rick looked puzzled.

'What's all that then Doug? Pollen?' I told him it was snow. 'Ah, we don't get much snow in Queensland.'

We were told ours was the first ascent in 1973 and we were rewarded with the chance to quench our thirst from globe-like cacti growing in the cracks, providing a welcome addition to our water bottles. Apart from using the *in situ* bolt ladders and bolts for the pendulum swings, as well as the odd fixed peg, we only placed fifteen pegs ourselves. All the rest of the climb we protected or aided on nuts. We managed more than half the route free and we weren't aware of anyone having climbed it with less aid. Later in the year Bruce Carson and Yvon Chouinard made a 'hammerless' ascent of *The Nose*, while over on Half Dome, Dennis Hennek, Doug Robinson and Galen Rowell made a completely clean ascent of the north-west face. Galen later wrote an article about it for *National Geographic*, thus bringing the concept of clean climbing into popular climbing culture.

As Rick and I were nearing the end of the climb, approaching the rim of El Cap, we started to hear voices. It came as quite a surprise to be taken out of the little world we had created for ourselves. We were even more surprised when, from out of the hazy cloud formed around the rim, a man appeared. He stood there, looking down at us.

'Have you just climbed El Cap?' I asked.

'For sure,' he replied. By the time we were all on top, we had discovered the tall man was Hugh Burton, who had, with his fellow Canadian Steve Sutton, just climbed a variation to *Dawn Wall*. The year before, at only twenty years old, they had put up *Magic Mushroom*. Later that year they came back with Chris Nelson and the legendary Charlie Porter to put up another new route, *Mescalito*. We spent the night together, savouring the aftermath of so many days focused on fine climbing. Steve and Hugh, for lads so young, seemed remarkably attuned to living on big walls. They were able to sit out long periods of bad weather in their hammocks or just lie in if not in the mood for climbing. They had even brought a library of hardback books of esoteric literature to read. They asked me about Baffin and climbing big walls in the Himalaya and what a good idea it would be for us all to go off and climb in the Karakoram.

Inevitably, the Valley scene featured a great deal in my book on big wall climbing. I was fortunate to be in Yosemite at a transitional stage; things were moving on from the formative years of Robbins, Harding and Chouinard. Old aid routes were starting to go free and nut protection was making peg hammers obsolete. Rock climbing in the States had, by the early 1970s, developed from an eccentric, fringe activity for a few often middle-class kids dropping out under the influence of Kerouac and the beat culture. Climbing was increasingly popular and

El Capitan. *The Nose* takes a line roughly at the point where light meets shadow.

Rick White on the bolt ladder between the Texas Flake and the Boot Flake on *The Nose*.

had settled down in the increasingly regulated environment imposed by the National Park Authority. Climbers themselves were starting businesses and guiding schools which brought their own discipline.

I met up with Royal again, who had since I saw him last refined his climbing philosophy and set it all out in the popular and influential book *Basic Rockcraft* and was about to publish *Advanced Rockcraft*. Within a few years, 400, 000 copies of these two books had been sold. In *Basic Rockcraft*, under the heading 'Values', Royal had written: 'A first ascent is a creation in the same sense as is a painting or a song.' The choice of route is 'an act of brilliant creativity'. Introducing modern technology is of 'enormous importance like a single word in a poem it can affect the entire composition.' In Royal's opinion the less use made of artificial aids the more likely the climb would conform to his artistic ideal.

That hadn't stopped Royal placing 110 bolts on *Tis-sa-ack*, his fourth route on Half Dome, climbed in 1969 with Don Peterson. Royal seemed determined to dominate the exploration of the north-west face. In 1970, twelve years after he had climbed El Cap, Harding also returned, this time to climb *The Wall of the Early Morning Light*, now simply called *Dawn Wall*. His route took twenty-seven days and he placed 330 bolts. For Harding, it was just an extension of his usual ethic. For Robbins, despite *Tis-sa-ack*, it was an abomination. He decided to erase Harding's route, and set off with Don Lauria, intending to chop every single bolt. They ended up making the second ascent, this time in six days, after Lauria decided chopping bolts was boring and that the route was a lot harder than they had assumed. Robbins would admit his double standards, and acknowledge his respect for Harding. In Glen Denny's magnificent book of black and white photographs of Yosemite and Yosemite climbers, there is a photograph of Royal after the first ascent of *Tis-sa-ack* and one of Warren after *Dawn Wall*. They both have sacks on their backs, both look shattered from their ordeals. Their exhaustion isn't tempered with the usual relief and joy from a dream achieved. Neither looks happy with what they have done.

Ken and I drove to Estes Park in Colorado to stay with the climber Steve Komito. Steve was a correspondent for *Mountain* and ran a boot repair service. He also provided a base for the guide Michael Covington. Michael was a fine climber and his Fantasy Ridge guiding service hired some of America's best, from Billy Westbay and Doug Snively to Yosemite pioneers Jim Bridwell and John Bachar. Michael was brought up in Idyllwild in California where he played with Apache kids and learned to climb at Tahquitz. He also had a musical bent and was on the verge of signing a contract with Paul Simon's brother Eddie until Art Garfunkel suggested that perhaps the cut and thrust of the music industry would take him away from ski racing and climbing.

He turned his back on music and took up a guiding concession that had become available in the Rocky Mountain National Park, but not before Joni

Mitchell had written a song about him, *Michael from Mountains*. Michael and I seemed to hit it off; he was always cheerful and optimistic with an easy, generous disposition that Jan also found attractive. We got to do quite a lot of climbing together on Lumpy Ridge and later on the Diamond and in the Himalaya.

Steve Komito had been an engineering student but gave that up after two years to become a climbing store manager in Boulder where he climbed with some of the pioneers in the area including Duncan Ferguson and Layton Kor, making the first free ascent of *Naked Edge* and *Outer Space* in the days before harnesses. Steve was always known affectionately as Komito and there was no one more generous. His hospitality brought itinerant climbers from all over the States. Here too, in Colorado, climbing was in transition. I was taken up some fine, classic crack climbs on Twin Owls by Doug Snively and Billy Westbay, two outstanding climbers who nevertheless still carried their hammers, just in case. Two years later Doug and Billy would again take me climbing but by then their hammers had been relegated to the tool shed.

Ken and I would hang on Komito's tales of climbing in Colorado. He'd once been carried out of a party by Layton Kor tied to a door because Layton had spent the whole night hunting a climbing partner and didn't want to lose this one. Komito also yarned away about a CIA operation in the Himalaya in the mid-1960s when leading American climbers were taken to India to place a nuclear-powered sensor on the summit of Nanda Devi, India's second-highest mountain. Both Ken and I had heard whispers of these operations before. With China testing its new atomic weapons, competing powers wanted to know what was going on.

Komito told us how, in 1965, American and Indian climbers working for their respective intelligence agencies had carried a plutonium-powered generator to within 500 metres of Nanda Devi's summit. Heavy snowfall that October forced the expedition to abandon the ascent and the equipment was left tied to a rock step on the side of the mountain on the orders of Captain M.S. Kohli. In 1966 an Indian team discovered the device had been avalanched and there was no sign of it. The CIA sent the climbers back with new recruits to help scan the Nanda Devi sanctuary but it was never found. An atomic device had been lost in the headwaters of the Ganges.

A year later, in 1967, at Kohli's suggestion, the CIA placed a similar device on the peak of Nanda Kot near Nanda Devi. It provided the required information: no, the Chinese did not have long-range missiles. After three months the device stopped transmitting after heavy snowfall but it was eventually recovered. It had melted out the ice and snow around it. Several leading American climbers had been involved, including Tom Frost and Robert Schaller. There may have been health consequences. Jim McCarthy discovered he had testicular cancer in 1971, but recovered. The Sherpas involved were not so lucky.

All of them had carried and slept alongside the device; all, we were told, erroneously as it turned out, had now died from varying forms of cancer. Sonam Gyatso, a good friend of Captain Kohli, died of liver cancer in 1968.

After a lecture at Gary Neptune's new climbing shop in Boulder, Ken and I left for Seattle where I was due to lecture to the American Alpine Club. We were staying with Clark Gerhardt; Clark later loaned me his clapboard cabin by one of the many lakes outside Seattle, where I spent a week in beautiful seclusion sifting through his large climbing library and putting the finishing touches to my book. We also planned to go climbing with him and his friends from the Swallow's Nest climbing store.

As though it were scripted, we found ourselves sitting in a restaurant with Robert Schaller, top surgeon, Himalayan mountaineer and, so we had learned, CIA operative. He very quickly let Ken know that if he ever wanted to come back to the States, he should not write about Nanda Devi. At that moment a woman at the next table stood up and took our photograph. Ken never did reveal all the information we had learned, although the well-known American columnist Jack Anderson did, and several books and magazine articles have since been published, causing consternation in India.

Robert Schaller, it turned out, had climbed Nanda Devi solo in September 1966. He had set out with Tom Frost but Tom was not so well and Schaller pressed on in perfect weather. He pioneered a rocky variation to the original 1936 route and had this been known he would undoubtedly have been lionised in the climbing world. As it was all of his notes and photographs were confiscated. 'I climbed everything in sight whenever we had a few days off,' he said. He was also awarded the Intelligence Medal of Merit, which was promptly taken off him and kept at Langley.

Ken and I spent a lot of time hanging out in the Swallow's Nest, Bill Sumner and Mike Heath's climbing store located in an old barber's shop under a freeway in Seattle. Bill, a nuclear physicist, designed a brilliant ice axe called The Thunderbird with a blue fibreglass handle and a dropped pick, quite the best Himalayan axe I ever used. We'd sit on old sofas around the potbellied stove chewing roasted peanuts washed down with a can of beer late into the night, after a lecture at some nearby hall or university or after climbing up the steep granite cracks of Index, on the odd occasion it wasn't raining.

Ken and I had started to get on each other's nerves. His magazine had a growing international reputation and I resented that he was becoming rather imperious, even pompous. When a car arrived to take us to my lecture, he insisted he sit in the front seat, telling me it was his turn. I told him journalists should sit in the back; the front was reserved for climbers. He stood there, frothing with anger. I told the driver to leave. 'Leave Ken behind?' 'Yes, drive on,' I said, and turned up the music to end the discussion. I didn't feel good about that either.

The east ridge of Changabang, with Kalanka behind.

CHANGABANG

Five weeks after leaving North America I was back on Baffin with the Nottingham Climbers' Club and other friends for further exploration of the Cumberland Peninsula. The fjord was still frozen so we took snowmobiles right up to the top of the inlet. Rob Wood was back with us, keen to revisit Summit Lake with some newcomers to Baffin Island, Steve Read and Dave Bathgate among them. I went off with Tut, Clive Davies and the doctor Mick Webster to an area south of Mount Turnweather where we walked and scrambled over a dozen peaks which we left unnamed and unmarked having decided – temporarily – to step out of the usual publicity game. Later in the trip a group of us attempted the central pillar of Mount Overlord. We made good progress until I hauled up a sack with an ice axe attached that plucked a fair-sized rock from out of a crack and sent it like a guided missile on to Mick Webster's head. He was the only member of the expedition wearing a crash helmet and the force of the blow depressed the helmet's fibreglass into Mick's skull leaving him concussed and needing stitches. Mick supervised his own recovery. Friends from Newcastle, Ken Rawlinson and Steve Blake, completed the climb, all forty-two pitches of it, two years later. Clive, Tut and I then checked out the north face of Mount Turnweather and its two magnificent buttresses about 2,500 feet high. They looked too difficult for us with loose flakes overhanging possible routes at critical points. We left them for another day.

We met a lone hiker on Baffin that year; we knew him only as *En Solitaire*, and he later wrote an article about our encounter that I happened to read. It's always instructive to see yourself through the eyes of others. He first met us at the campsite at Pangnirtung as we were getting a lecture from a Mountie about the prohibition on selling gear to Eskimos:

'I don't think the Mountie had really planned to press the issue. In any event, he backed off. I'd met the Englishmen when I'd first got off the plane and I was delighted to have them as companions while waiting for transport to the outside. They'd been on Baffin for better than a month, climbing steadily. I knew about half of them by virtue of their reputations but they dismissed any accomplishment with less than a word and took a great interest in my activities. *En Solitaire* they called me. How fine that sounded, but I knew that it was nothing to be especially proud of. These fellows were the real adventurers. In all likelihood, most of them had quit the jobs that had supplied the money to get over here across the ocean to the ends of the earth. And now that it was ending they were selling sleeping bags and laughing at it, as much at ease as any diplomat at a cocktail party. And right then, I would have traded places with any of them in an instant ...

'Six of us had supper at the Pangnirtung Lodge. Dish after dish disappeared as if by magic. But it was a healthy sort of gluttony. Laughter sprouted round the table and the waitress, a pretty girl from Ontario, was obviously enchanted with these disarming gentlemen.

"Coffee, Mr Bathgate?" she asked.

"Are you sure Mr Bathgate isn't seated across the table?"

"I thought that was Mr Braithwaite. Which one is Bathgate?"

"Perhaps who you think is Braithwaite is actually Bathgate?"

"I'm not sure who I think is Mr Braithwaite."

"Why don't you ask Bathgate?"

'I just like to hear Englishmen talk. I could have listened a lot longer but Nordair came and dumped us in Frobisher Bay.'

During the spring of 1974 Chris asked me if I fancied joining a team he was putting together for the first ascent of Changabang in the Indian Himalaya. I immediately accepted and congratulated him on managing to get permission. Changabang in the Garhwal was within the 'Inner Line' the Indian government had drawn to keep foreigners well away from the Chinese border. The Indians were still smarting from the humiliating incursion by the Chinese on their northern frontier in 1962. Chris had been over in India the year before and had mooted the idea of a joint expedition with the Indian Mountaineering Foundation. The IMF had suggested four Indians join up with four Brits to attempt Changabang.

While scanning books and periodicals for suitable big-wall objectives at altitude, Changabang had already registered in my mind as a suitable candidate. Tom Longstaff, quoted in Arnold Mumm's *Five Months in the Himalaya*, said that: 'Changabang is the most superbly beautiful mountain that I have ever seen; its north-west face, a sheer precipice of over 5,000 feet, being composed of such pale granite that it is at first taken for snow lying on the cliffs at an impossibly steep angle.' There was a photograph of the west side of Changabang as seen from the Bagini Pass. I had read others too who had been moved to

On the Rhamani Glacier, looking towards Changabang. We realised we were in the wrong valley and had to cross over the Shipton Col into the Nanda Devi Sanctuary in order to climb Changabang from the south.

express their delight at first seeing the granite shark's tooth of Changabang. During the Scottish Himalayan Expedition in the early 1950s Bill Murray, on sighting Changabang, was moved to write: 'one's pulse leapt and the heart gave thanks – that this mountain should be as it is.' My namesake, the mountain photographer Douglas Scott, has a colour photograph in Murray's book of Changabang that was captioned: 'The shark's tooth in the centre is not a snow peak but milk white granite with some snow on the very tip.'

So yes, I was definitely interested in going to Changabang: as somewhere revered by Hindus, a place restricted to foreigners and a peak not only unclimbed but also never attempted. I was in the fortunate position of being able to accept such impromptu invitations. It had been a risk leaving a steady job when I had no idea at all of how I was going to earn a living. The point was being made to me again that only by taking such risks do interesting things happen: first Everest, now Changabang.

The climbing of Changabang proved to be relatively easy and without any major incident for a change. There were of course all the usual frustrations on the walk in. At one time there were porters scattered all over the hills of the Garhwal bogged down in snow under huge loads; it had been very difficult to hire porters in the first place. I did have a short altercation with Chris, objecting to him playing the tank commander that he once was, deploying his troops without consultation but that was soon cleared up and left me wondering why I got so worked up about these things. It was in reality a marvellous trip; Chris was far more relaxed than when taking responsibility for a big siege-style campaign.

In fact, I enjoyed everyone's company. Alan Hankinson had come along to record events for an expedition book. 'Hank' was the ITN obituary man, often appearing alongside Alastair Burnet and Reginald Bosanquet. 'Yes my dear,' Hank said, 'I have you on file along with Dougal Haston, Martin Boysen and of course Chris.' I'd known Martin off and on for years and although we'd never climbed together I'd spent a week in the Chalet Austria with him near Montenvers, sitting out bad weather in 1959. He was the arch-festerer, quite content to bide his time while I was jumping about worrying my holiday would be over before it'd even started. He always seemed the detached cynic but on this expedition we struck up a sound relationship, which I hoped would continue into the future. I was impressed with his vast knowledge of wild plants and animal life. I was most astounded at Martin's ability to climb steep rock on sight, like a giant sloth, making move after move on boulders up to thirty feet high during the walk in.

We did quite a bit of climbing together early on; we arrived in the wrong valley and had to cross over very steep ground via the Shipton Col to the south-east side of the mountain. We also climbed Bagini Peak, probably making the second ascent after the Swiss climber André Roch who had left a cairn there. It had been the perfect day out, starting with tea at 3 a.m., climbing towards the rising sun, skimming the frosty snow crystals right up to the summit where we rested for a bite to eat. But then the hiccup; I had brought what I thought were two small tins of juice, except the labels had fallen off and what seemed liquid in the heat of the day turned out to be spicy potatoes. I devoured them but Martin hurled his can off the summit. We'd already made the same mistake climbing Shipton Col and he wasn't happy.

I mentioned to Martin that I had brought my big-wall rack just in case we got the chance to climb on Changabang's granite walls. Martin thought my ideas about the west face were pie in the sky, which they were on this expedition since we had an obligation to include at least some of the four Indians on the first ascent. It made sense to take the easiest logical way up the mountain and that proved to be from the east up a knife-edged arête. All four of the British contingent went to the summit and also Balwant Sandhu, the leader of the Indian contingent, and Tashi Chewang. On the ascent I climbed mostly with Dougal Haston, the fourth member of our climbing team, not saying much, not giving much, but not taking anything either.

It was quite a privilege to be climbing with the man who had made the second British ascent of the Eiger's north face, the first ascent of the *Eiger Direct* and the south face of Annapurna, and had come away from the ill-fated international expedition to Everest's south-west face with his reputation not only intact but enhanced, unlike those of most others involved. It surprised me that though we were quite different characters there were similarities in our early lives and in our introduction to climbing. Dougal was brought up with easy access to open country by a railway with two equally adventurous friends and was steered away from anti-social activities, in his case, through a youth club rather than, as in my case, the Scouts. Dougal's youth club had been founded by Alick Buchanan-Smith, later secretary of state for Scotland, just as I was helped along by Bob Pettigrew and Geoff Sutton during my formative years.

At school he was a 400-yards champion at about the same time I was running middle distance for my county. We were both built for endurance and to cope reasonably well with high altitude. There were, however, significant differences, as Chris observed: 'Doug: undisciplined, warm-hearted and emotional, full of a vast restless energy, Dougal: cool, analytical and taciturn. Yet both had in common a huge appetite for hard climbing and exceptional endurance and a love for the mountains.'

For once, the 'joint' aspect of the expedition was a marvellous success, thanks to the Indian contingent. Balwant, known as Balu, was particularly urbane and well read, often quoting from modern Western classics. He had no illusions about the standard of Indian climbing: 'Okay, so we've climbed Everest, put nine on top, but we have still much to learn from you Western climbers, certainly about the alpine-style approach to the hills. We hardly know anything at all about technical climbing; we just don't get the chance. Our boys just can't afford to go out every weekend or for long holidays. If they could, they'd find it hard to locate the equipment.'

Balwant was hoping our expedition would be a springboard for a few Indian climbers to learn more about modern techniques in mountaineering. It was obvious that in India the structure was still very hierarchical and Balwant was very much the leader, but he was a leader in the best tradition: always calm, cool and collected. I never once saw him lose his temper, not even when performing a balancing act down the knife-edged corniced ridge on the descent from Changabang while I screamed at him: 'We don't want another Harsh Bahuguna on this trip.'

Balwant's second-in-command was Captain Kiran Kumar, who had done a tremendous job in sorting out all the permits and paperwork, making all the expedition's purchases, arranging transport and getting all the loads up to Base Camp in a very difficult area. He could flare up at the porters, screeching at them with an angry grimace on his face, which soon turned to smiles. Then he would banter with them good-humouredly and thus goad them a little further to Base Camp.

Kiran was unfortunate in being the only casualty on the expedition. During our attempt to cross the Shipton Col, Kiran had, on impulse, decided to follow

Martin and me. He set out alone traversing a steep snow and ice slope until he dropped his ice axe. He then took off a crampon to use as a claw but could neither move on nor retreat. He told me that at that point he remembered his parachute training, 'So I put my chin on my chest and as I jumped I put my knees to my chest and went down like a little ball.' In fact, the little ball went several hundred feet down steep ice and snow, bounced over rocks and got away with a twisted shoulder. Sadly, after all the hard work he had put into the expedition, more than anyone else, his accident cost him his chance to reach the summit.

The other members of the Indian contingent were both instructors at the Himalayan Mountaineering Institute in Darjeeling. Ujagar Singh did not speak English, was more self-contained than even Dougal, and by the end of the expedition I had hardly got to know him at all. We appreciated the hard work he had put into the expedition helping Kiran but unfortunately he never acclimatised to join us on the summit push. The other climbing member was Tashi Chewang Sherpa, who could speak many languages, including English, and so we got to know him quite well. He was an experienced climber and particularly good on rock as well as high up in the Himalaya where, he said, he had almost summited Nanda Devi. In conversation he mentioned Tom Frost whom I had recently seen in Yosemite. Had he, by chance, been involved in the covert mission on Nanda Devi? He told me how he and other Sherpas had climbed with Tom and other foreigners putting the sensor up on Nanda Devi. He had actually carried the 'SNAP' reactor on the mountain. I asked him what it was like. 'Oh, very good, sahib! Very heavy but it kept me warm and went bleep-bleep, bleep-bleep.' Here at least was one Sherpa who had survived to tell the tale, although Tashi sadly passed away a few years ago from cancer.

There was another Sherpa on the expedition who I got to know called Norbu. He became for me a link with the past. Tashi acted as interpreter as Norbu told me about all the well-known expeditions he had worked for before the war, like Hugh Ruttledge's 1936 Everest expedition, when he was just a kitchen boy, and even earlier in 1930 on Kangchenjunga with Norman Dyhrenfurth's dad Günther. Of all the foreigners he had met, none impressed him more than Bill Tilman. This is how I reported it for the expedition book: 'According to Norbu, Tilman was always away first in the morning shouldering a large amount of food and equipment, in excess of the standard Sherpa load. He always arrived first at the day's destination having sometimes run along parts of the route. He would have tea brewing by the time the rest of them caught up with him, and then he'd praise those who'd made good time and yell and scream at those he thought had been lazy or lacking in some way. On at least one rest day he made all his Sherpas a cake. Tashi, who was translating all this for me, was made to repeat this fact several times. Tilman was always

On the Changabang Glacier just before setting out for the climb.
L–R: me, Martin Boysen, Tashi Chewang Sherpa and Dougal Haston.

the first to cross turbulent streams, pass difficult rocky sections, and shoulder awkward loads. He was obviously a born leader and Norbu, at any rate, was still very impressed.'

Tilman was not a man to waste too much time in planning an expedition menu. He and his regular climbing companion Eric Shipton were happy living off the land. He recognised it was difficult to satisfy every expedition member's culinary requirement, and it was therefore 'all the more important to get this job of provisioning done before any other members of the party arrived to further darken counsel by urging the claims of their pet foods.' While crossing an unknown pass in the Badrinath region not far from Changabang, their staple diet, Shipton wrote, 'was bamboo shoots ... except where hungry bears had forestalled us, it was fairly easy to collect a potful of the little green cylinders which, boiled, constituted our evening meal.'

Tilman and Shipton's attitude and style have entered the folklore of mountain exploration: their days of total silence because there was nothing worth saying that had not been said before; the schism between them over whether to take one shirt or two on a three-month journey. It is tempting to run away with romantic notions that the pre-war men were more 'pushy' or hardier than today's explorers. Norbu was full of admiration for our effort on Changabang, where, when it came to the crunch, we disappeared for five days carrying all our own equipment and food up very hard and steep terrain, harder, perhaps, than pre-war expeditions would tackle.

In reality it's a continuous process. We were able to go for steeper objectives because our equipment was better and lighter. We had efficient gas stoves and freeze-dried foods that weighed a fraction of pre-war rations. We had prior knowledge of the area from readily available maps and photographs. We also had more understanding of the debilitating effects of altitude and dehydration. All this gave us enormous confidence. Then there was perhaps the most important advantage, that we have seen others reach comparable standards elsewhere, breaking down psychological barriers enabling us to push on further.

Getting to the east ridge of Changabang was complicated and time consuming. We had to transfer our camp and supplies from the Rhamani Glacier over the Shipton Col to the Changabang Glacier where we camped below the south face. Bad weather had us tent-bound for three days but just as we were running out of food the weather improved. A full moon allowed us to set off at 10 p.m. on 2 June for the ridge. It was bitterly cold, especially waiting around while the six of us queued up to climb several steep ice walls. By 8 a.m. we were camped on a snow terrace in a safe place below a solid ice cliff at around 21,000 feet. We rested all day and then at 2 a.m. next morning, on 4 June, we climbed up to the ridge and, after some twenty rope lengths up the steep and corniced snow arête, were at the first of two summits by 4 p.m. All the way we had fantastic views towards Nanda Devi, Trisul and the other incredible peaks of the Garhwal.

I wrote in my diary about our descent from the summit: 'Having knocked off what may have been the marginally higher second summit, Dougal and I hurtled back down the ridge on the heels of the others. The mist evaporated from our mountain while all above was a blanket of grey clouds. The mountains of the Garhwal had lost their sparkle and looked exceedingly sombre. Over in secret Tibet, however, the sky was a pale, watery blue and the sun lit up a patchwork of rolling pastures between purple mountain ranges. Now I can recall that startling scene more than any other on the whole trip. I gazed out from the Changabang snow arête totally absorbed. There was none of the usual habit of relating this scene to others I remembered because I had never seen anything quite like this before. I was too tired to consider that none of the peaks out there had important names, that I might write about them, or that here was the forbidden, mysterious land of Tibet, for I was seeing the scene as a child might, lost among it. For once I was not a separate performer, geographer, mountaineer, admirer or whatever, using the mountains, but felt actually part of them. The feeling did not last long, for soon the dark closed in and we were left to stumble and curse, groping for our previous footsteps.'

We had permission to climb Kalanka but Changabang was enough for the season and we all departed, me earlier than the rest, because I had to get back quickly to go off on my next trip – to the Pamirs in Russia. I left with a porter

Nanda Devi, viewed from Changabang.

for the three-day walk out, staying with him and his friends in the forest, eating their food and smoking their beedis, the first cigarettes I had smoked since I was twelve years old camping on Exmoor. Later I stayed at his village of Lata. Walking out it occurred to me it was the first time I had actually spent much time out of the company of other Westerners, despite having been to the big mountains of Asia four times now. One thing I noticed immediately, as in my old hitchhiking days in Europe and North Africa, was just how much more approachable one seems to be when alone; all kinds of interesting things happen that wouldn't in a crowd.

Back at Joshimath I got talking to a towering Sikh army major who suggested I accompany him to Badrinath. I couldn't believe what I was hearing. As far as I knew almost no foreigners had visited Badrinath since the British left in 1947. He took me up in his army jeep, passing hundreds of pilgrims making their way to one of the most holy places in India. Long ago Indian sages had established four abodes of God, Jagannath at Puri, Rameswaram in Tamil Nadu, Dwarka in Gujarat and Badrinath, situated at the four corners of the country. To this day there are pilgrims who travel great distances, undergoing every kind of hardship, to visit these four sacred places – the *char dham* or 'four abodes'. Badrinath however is just one of the religious places pilgrims include in their itinerary in the north of India; there are several tributary streams that make up Mother Ganga, the most holy river in India, not just the Alaknanda which flows past Badrinath, but also Gangotri on the Bhagirathi,

Kedarnath, the home of Shiva, on the Mandakini and Yamunotri on the Yamuna. These four together are known as the *chota char dham*.

After a few hours exploring Badrinath and its environs, two secret service policemen took me to the local jail for questioning. Fortunately I had just changed the film in all of my three cameras and those they confiscated were unused. They seemed very surprised to find a Westerner wandering about and said I was the first they'd seen in the region. Ironically, on the walk in, Dougal had mentioned that the military attaché at the British Embassy in Delhi had asked him if he would take notes and photographs of all the military installations in the area of our approach to the road head for Changabang. It's an indication of how restricted this area was at the time. I asked Dougal whether he would do his duty for queen and country. He replied that as far as he was concerned, he had served his dues and they 'are not getting anything more from me.' It was a reference to the sixty days he had spent in Barlinnie prison for running down James Orr in a van when Dougal was drunk. I never got to see the hot springs nor much of the mountains because the cloud was down. I think the place meant more to the pilgrims than it did to me. It has from very ancient times been considered of religious significance, featuring as it does in the *Mahabharata*.

I left Badrinath on a local bus that was bursting at the seams; a beggar woman, presumably untouchable, with a baby in her arms, stood in the gangway with more of her children pressed against her. I gave up my seat for her, much to the dismay of the well-dressed chap in the next seat, but then asked myself: 'Why bother with my Western ideas and morals. Why not just sit and watch?'

At Haridwar, waiting for a bus back to Delhi, I saw an old man keel over on his seat just in front of me. He didn't get up, and after a few minutes two men arrived and examined him. Then they went off and returned with a door, gently placed the body on the door, covered it up with a cotton sheet, raised the door on to their heads and quietly marched out, in step, with no fuss at all. It was as though nothing had happened and the man had never been there.

Next day I flew back to Europe.

A pilgrim at Badrinath.

КОМИТЕТ

по физической культуре и спорту

при Совете Министров Узбекской ССР

Свидетельство

ВРУЧАЕТСЯ

СКОТТ ДУОГУ

за восхождение на пик Ленина (7134 м.) в Заалайском хребте совершенному _3 . августа_ 1974 г, в составе команды _Великобритании (Англии)_

по маршруту _английскому варианту_

Жетон „Пик Ленина" № I395

Зам. председателя комитета Ю. ЕГОРОВ

Председатель федерации альпинизма Узбекистана В. РАЦЕК

9 . августа 1975 г.

гор. Ташкент

СССР

МАСТЕР СПОРТА

The certificate to show our summit of Pik Lenin was official. I had been certified for the first time in my climbing career.

TRAGEDY IN THE PAMIRS

While preparing to leave for Changabang, Dennis Gray, now general secretary at the British Mountaineering Council, rang to tell me about an invitation he had received from the Soviet Sports Federation to send a team of six English climbers to an international camp below Pik Lenin in the Pamir Mountains of Central Asia. He had been asking around but hadn't found anybody. As it happened, six of us were planning to go to Baffin Island: Tut Braithwaite, Guy Lee, Paul Nunn, now lecturing in economic history at Sheffield Polytechnic, Clive Rowland and Gordon 'Speedy' Smith of the Rock and Ice and Rolls-Royce's engineering design department. Since most of us had already been to Baffin Island, and since we were curious about the Soviet Union, we agreed to take up Dennis's invitation and go to the Pamirs instead.

We set off to Moscow overland by train from the Hook of Holland, across Western Europe and then through the Iron Curtain into East Germany and beyond in sealed carriages. There was a seemingly endless stream of forms to fill in, not just at national borders but at internal boundaries too. Things were particularly bad in East Germany. When the train guard reappeared, carrying yet more forms for us to complete and flanked by two soldiers in great coats shouldering rifles. 'More forms for filing', said Tut. Clive opened the carriage window and with Guy's help we tossed the new forms out of the window; they swirled into the night and we sat down again. Clive had bought a laughing box from a joke shop, and deemed this the perfect moment to set it off. The train guard stared at us, incredulous, then turned on his heel and walked off, followed by his bodyguards and the sound of laughter. We didn't see him again.

At Brest, on the border between Poland and Belarus, we stopped in a gigantic vaulted hall where the coaches were lifted up into the air, ready to be dropped on to bogies of a narrower gauge. Huge men with thick arms and massive naked shoulders glistening with sweat swung sledgehammers at the undercarriage.

By now we had discovered that the pick of our ice axes fitted exactly into the door's lock so we were able to escape the carriage for the first time and roam around. It was like Dante's Inferno, with flames and sparks from welding torches lighting the gloom and steam hissing from engine boilers – and the unrelenting cacophony of metal striking metal. When the operation was completed, we chugged on, hour after hour, through the taiga, endless miles of pine and spruce sandwiched between the steppe and the tundra of the frozen north.

At the Hotel Sputnik in Moscow, we and the other groups of climbers gathered from around the world were greeted by the most famous of Soviet mountaineers, Vitaly Abalakov, a veteran of many first ascents, some of them in winter judging by the number of digits he had missing. He gave a speech along the lines of whoever dared to climb with him in the past had to be incredibly fit, able to run mile after mile, walk up hill after hill and always with a huge sack on their back. They must be capable of performing a hundred press-ups and scores of pull-ups. Growing tired of this, Clive, who had given up scrubbing out boilers at Tinsley Steelworks for forestry work up in the Highlands, interjected: 'And lose all their fingers?' Vitaly was not amused.

The hotel manager offered us some advice on how to make our dollars go further. In Moscow there were shops where tourists could spend their hard currency; we should go there and buy as many Marlboro cigarettes as we could afford and then sell them on to locals for twice the price in roubles. This way we would get twice the exchange rate available at the bank. Lacking dollars, we persuaded our American cousins to join the venture, since they seemed to have an inexhaustible supply. As it turned out, it was much harder to shift the cigarettes than we were told, and the Americans started getting anxious. Luckily, just before departure, we found a buyer for the lot and handed the Americans their cash, less, of course, our commission.

Not being able to speak Russian was a problem. We learned a few words, but essentially used just one: 'horosho', meaning 'good'. Armed with this, after a night on the town with two young women, we somehow ended up in the room I was sharing. They were, they explained, out of work ballet dancers from the Kirov who hoped we would help them out financially. They seemed a little too broad in the beam to be pirouetting across a stage and in the end we had to let them go without having got to know them beyond their heavy-duty corsets and their few words of English. We were constantly in trouble for the most trifling things. Walking barefoot across an area of grass in central Moscow, a group of outraged Muscovites approached us with rolled-up newspapers, telling us to keep off. John Roskelley, one of the star alpinists from the American group, was almost arrested for crossing the road without waiting for the lights to change.

The opening ceremony at Base Camp in the Achik-Tash valley.

We flew on a rickety Ilyushin jet to Osh in Kyrgyzstan. We knew about Aeroflot's doubtful reputation – they lost 200 aircraft in the 1970s – but someone said, 'Don't worry lads, it's just an Ilyushin.' A smaller aircraft took us to Daraut Kurgan where schoolgirls presented us with roses, and then we climbed on to a truck for several bumpy hours to Base Camp in the Achik-Tash valley. Over 200 other climbers and trekkers had gathered there at 12,000 feet from twelve different nations. The six of us were camped between eighteen Americans and four French from Paris. In the line of tents opposite were a Japanese group and Helmut Voelk with some jolly, beer-drinking Bavarians. There were some Scots and numerous Austrians in two groups, one of six climbers led by the very experienced Wolfgang Axt, who had been on Everest in 1971; he had already heard about our ascent of Changabang the month before. The other Austrians, in reality a commercial tour group, numbered fifty-three, all of them hillwalkers except for the leader, who was none other than Marcus Schmuck who, with Fritz Wintersteller in 1957, had led most of the way up Broad Peak when making the first ascent with Hermann Buhl and Kurt Diemberger.

We had problems from the start adapting to the peculiar demands made by our Russian hosts. The organiser, an urbane Soviet 'master of sport' called Eugene Gippenreiter, told us: 'Send us your leader to raise your flag at the opening ceremony.' We didn't have a leader and there was flagging enthusiasm for erections of this kind and no enthusiasm at all for nationalistic ceremonies.

'What about your changing of the guard at Buckingham Palace?' Eugene asked.

'That's for the tourist trade and has nothing to do with mountaineering,' we replied. The problem was solved when a member of the Scottish team remembered it was his flag too and hauled it up alongside the others. The Union Jack was later mysteriously replaced with a pair of frilly knickers belonging to one of an independent women's group that turned up. The Russians took that one badly. There were soon more demands for a leader, this time to attend a meeting of leaders. We worked out a compromise and decided to take it in turns to be leader. At the meeting, our leader of the day reported that sinister noises had been made with regard to upgrading international meets such as ours into a full Olympic event. At these moments Clive's laughing box was turned on and the idea laughed out of court until the officials, scurrying around, homed in on the box. Clive turned it off and put it in his pocket before it was confiscated.

'Eugene, what about mountaineers competing in the Olympics?' we asked.

'We are split in the USSR,' he admitted, 'between those like myself who oppose the idea on aesthetic grounds and those officials who seek status, power and a higher salary from such a move.' It was reassuring to know there were climbers in Russia like Eugene. We did try to talk to the Russian climbers about their views on climbing being upgraded to an Olympic sport but it was very difficult to talk to them beyond sharing a few pleasantries; they would become uneasy, pointing out they were being watched or quickly shuffle off back to their friends. Even up here at 12,000 feet there were apparently KGB men looking on.

Eugene asked us why we refused to take radios to keep in contact with rescue parties. 'They won't work from where we're going on the south side of Pik Lenin,' we told him. We told him we felt they took away some of the adventure that comes from sorting out your own problems in isolation. We also knew that radio contact might lull a team into a false sense of security. The radio might not work and the rescue team might not be in a position to help, especially if it's bad weather causing problems in the first place.

'Why do you go over the Krylenko? Why can't you climb the Lipkin route or climb a new spur on the north side – like the French climbers?'

'We like the look of the south-east face and we certainly don't relish ploughing up a furrow with sixty Austrians and dozens of others.'

That's how it went on – friendly skirmishing – until we took off over the 19,000-foot Krylenko Pass up a 5,000-foot, forty-degree, north-facing snow slope. That was hard work. The soft crust gave way to soft powder underneath. Every step up the unbroken snow was a struggle, especially as we had only been in the mountains a week and weren't acclimatised. Several American groups followed our steps a day later and we met them as we dropped down to bring our last load over the pass.

Molly Higgins was one of the youngest, and shortest, of the Americans, and the most vocal: 'Why do you guys take such fucking big strides?'

After three days' work, we had packed up our top camp at a big crevasse at 17,400 feet and taken all our gear over the pass to camp three miles down the Saukdara Glacier on the south side of Lenin. We hoped to climb a new route on the 4,000-foot south-east face to the left of the route Toni Hiebeler and Michael Schneider climbed with two Leningrad climbers in 1969. A strong American team had the same idea and arrived the day after to cache gear by our camp and then return to camp at the crevasse on the Krylenko face. Clive and I went to check out the approach to our intended climb but without warning I fell through the snow into a crevasse.

Instantly I entered another world. One moment I was plodding across a broad undulating expanse of snow, the next I was plummeting through a cavern of glittering crystals and icicles that tinkled down around me as I came to a stop on a shelf some twenty feet down with the rope tight above me. I clambered out with Clive's help and told him how pretty it was down there. We then noticed five tiny dots moving up the 1969 route; just before dark three Estonian climbers arrived out of the gathering dusk to tell us it was five of their party. They were most insistent on being called Estonian and not Russian. They went back to their camp after a brew and a chat, their huge clinkered boots crunching across the frozen snow.

The good weather ended with three days of heavy snow. Two of our group were sick with the altitude, forcing us to leave the tents and make for Base Camp. It was an epic journey back up to Krylenko with visibility down to a few yards and the soft snow bogging us down with every stride. Paul Nunn and Speedy were in bad shape and deteriorating fast as we regained the high pass. It should have been a two-hour climb but with Clive taking Paul's weight and the rest of us stopping for Speedy and shouldering his gear, it took seven.

At the pass, the mist cleared, blown away by the strengthening wind, to reveal nine or ten climbers high up the east ridge of Lenin; they were presumably Estonians going to help their friends on the 1969 route. We had problems of our own; it was now 4 p.m. and we were at 19,000 feet with no tent or food. Peering over the pass we were horrified to see that the whole of the Krylenko face had avalanched. We had no choice but to slither down the avalanche scars, riding small avalanches of our own making and rolling clear when they grew too large for comfort. As we started this dangerous descent, we passed the site of the American camp at a big crevasse. Ominous black crows were pecking in the snow.

We dug frantically but found only abandoned food, equipment and Molly Higgins' diary. They had certainly left in a hurry; we could only hope they were not buried in the jumbled blocks of snow that had swept over the camp

Avalanche scars and debris on the Krylenko face.

Pik Lenin. Our new route climbed the prominent left–right diagonal ridge.

down to the Lenin Glacier. It was an oppressive place and we were glad to move on, hurrying down the dangerous slope. Pausing for breath, looking around, we realised we were one short. No Speedy. Tut turned around and climbed back up the slope and eventually found him sitting on a ledge, tossing snowballs in the air. 'You'll never find me,' Speedy said. The altitude had left him rather unhinged.

By dark we reached our tent on the moraine and found the American Jeff Lowe in another tent, laid up with an injured knee. He told us how some of the Americans had been swept down the face but had narrowly escaped with minor injuries. The Americans, together with a large Japanese party who were also avalanched, had lost most of their equipment. On Peak 19, 6,852 metres high, or to give the mountain its full title, Peak Nineteenth Party Congress, avalanches had hit a separate American team attempting steep snow slopes on the north side. Gary Ullin was killed, suffocated in his tent. Bob Craig, his tent companion, was luckier; John Roskelley and John Marts pulled him out alive. Over cups of tea we discovered several rescue parties were out helping stranded teams all over the north side of Lenin. The remaining three Americans on Peak 19, marooned on the north face, could be seen through telescopes from Base Camp. A helicopter dropped food and equipment lost in the avalanche. They eventually returned to Base Camp with the support of several nationalities.

Our own struggle seemed insignificant in comparison to these events. After squatting in various foreign tents for the night, we broke trail for six miles back to Base Camp where we were a five-minute centre of attention before the prospect of fresh fruit, caviar and smoked salmon overwhelmed any desire to recount the horrors of Krylenko to 200 curious climbers and walkers. Base Camp, with hot food, hot showers, film nights and football matches was certainly well organised; that side of the show could hardly have been better. But with the death of Gary Ullin and the grief of his companions there was a noticeable shift in the mood of the whole camp to something much more friendly and supportive.

The weather now improved and we tried to persuade the camp commandant, a psychiatrist called Michael Monastyrski, to help us around to the south side of Pik Lenin either in trucks or by helicopter. He told us it was strictly out of bounds to foreigners, why exactly he would not say. So we moved back up to our camp on the moraine, intending to return over the Krylenko Pass. Next morning we developed avalanche paranoia; the slopes beneath the pass were on the move again.

Although the Russian climbers had achieved some amazing climbs in these mountains and elsewhere in the Caucasus and Tien Shan, making long multi-day, even multi-week, traverses here on Pik Lenin, very little new had been done. There were still several obvious lines that had never been attempted. We therefore decided to abandon all our expensive equipment, cameras and personal gear below the south-east face along with our ambitions for a new route on Pik Lenin in favour of a long ridge climb up the north-east side from the Lenin Glacier. The French lads had already climbed one elegant spur on the north side and we decided to try another.

At the end of July we set off up the well-defined north-east ridge, five of us with three members of the Scottish contingent, Bruce Barclay, Greg Strange and their doctor Alan North following along with Speedy, who took advantage of their extra tent space. Having lost so much gear on the other side of the mountain, ours was limited. The route was awkward to start; the base of the ridge had been truncated by the glacier and was consequently steeper rock and soft snow, but the weather was beautiful. Once we'd overcome that obstacle, we made good progress up the snow arête above, although the snow was often knee-deep, even thigh-deep at times, and we rotated leads frequently between the five of us to avoid fatigue. We quickly overcame a rock step, although it was loose and soaked with melting snow, and made camp by a cave in an ice cliff a little way below a subsidiary summit at 18,200 feet. That night we fed well on fresh smoked salmon, caviar, wholesome bread, a jar of jam and fresh fruit.

Early next morning of 1 August, we traversed this rocky subsidiary with Paul Nunn in the lead but had to descend a good way after that, wading slowly through

Our new route on Pik Lenin.

wet snow before rising again towards the north ridge. Again we rotated the effort, but we were a tired bunch by the time we joined the Lipkin route above Camp 3. We hunkered down at about 20,000 feet alongside the French who had spare capacity and kindly accommodated Guy. Paul Nunn suffered badly that night and decided to descend the Lipkin so now we were four, plodding on up to about 22,000 feet where we camped again, spending a restless night, head to toe, packed in like sardines in a two-man tunnel tent. Speedy and the Scots remained some way down the north ridge, out of sight.

The next day the snow was hard and wind-blown and we had to cut steps with our axes. Having been forced to abandon our gear on the far side of the Krylenko Pass, we didn't have crampons and shared one rope between us, which we only brought out on the rocky sections. Ours might well have been the first and probably only ascent of Pik Lenin in Vibram-soled boots. It had not been a very technical climb, merely long, but always with superb views, especially the higher we got, looking east towards Xinjiang and Kashgar in China. Guy surprised us all on the summit when he unzipped his anorak and pulled out the front page of his local Nottingham paper with the headline: 'It's The Tops!' I took his photograph next to a large bust of Lenin. Tut held it up to his face and looked the bust in the eye, squaring up to Lenin at 23,406 feet.

We left the summit at 3 p.m., down the steep wind-blown snow, facing inward to the slope. A group of Russian women watched us as we descended, shaking their heads in concern as every so often the toes of our boots bounced off the hard surface. One of them said we ought to wear crampons. She pointed to hers telling us that they were made in Russia from titanium. Tut told her in a sad voice that they weren't available in England, which made the Russians feel rather sorry for us. We told the women we thought the weather was changing; it had been very windy up there on the summit. They seemed to be going well and told us they intended to camp soon. In the morning they would make the first all-female ascent of Pik Lenin and then the first all-female traverse of the mountain by coming down the normal Razdelnaya route.

In the gathering darkness we came across Dr North who was looking for his team and looking a bit befuddled. We suggested he came back down with us but he didn't like that idea and plodded up as we continued down, eventually coming across the rest of Dr North's party. Speedy was not well, having suffered nausea all night. His two companions were also a little despondent and so they all elected to turn around and descend to their tents, a little distance below ours. It was another bad night and we were packed up by 7 a.m., reaching the Scottish camp at 8 a.m. Dr North was still out by himself; his companions said they would wait to make certain he was safe before continuing down to Base Camp.

Guy Lee on the summit of Pik Lenin, next to the large bust of Lenin.

Visibility was poor descending to Camp 3 on the Lipkin as the bad weather continued and we were glad of a kind offer of tea and coffee from Jock Glidden, Christopher Wren and Al Steck, the great Yosemite pioneer. Al looked his age but was still determined, despite cracked ribs he'd suffered in the avalanche on the Krylenko face. There was no shortage of food since several parties had abandoned theirs; the French nougat was especially popular.

Now we had lost some altitude, we slept brilliantly and woke only when the Americans left for the summit. Heading down, we gathered news from other climbers, learning that our Scottish friends Graham Tiso, Ronnie Richards and Ian Fulton had made it up Pik Lenin by the Razdelnaya route. We also heard that Dr North had survived his bivouac and reached the summit, and although he suffered frostbite in his toes, he had found his companions. Apart from that, all the other teams seemed to be progressing well.

We reached Base Camp pleased with our route but I don't think any of us ever thought of returning to this range. The low-angled, humpy topography didn't offer much technical interest for alpinists; the rotten snow and crumbling rock, combined with regular earth tremors, weren't that appealing. We discovered at Base Camp that an earthquake had triggered the avalanches that killed Gary Ullin on Peak 19 and, as it turned out, the five Estonians we had seen attempting the Hiebeler route. We might have suffered the same fate had Paul and Speedy been in better shape.

Over on Peak 19, with John Marts in support, Jeff Lowe and John Roskelley paid their respects to Gary and then completed their new route up the north face in his memory. Base Camp was also grieving the death of Eva Eisenschmidt, a young Swiss girl who succumbed to hypothermia in the vicious storm that blew in as we returned from the north-east ridge. There had been a valiant rescue attempt by two French climbers from Grenoble, François Valla and Michel Vincent, but Eva died anyway. They did succeed in rescuing her companions, Heidi Ludi and the Bavarian model, Anya, both of them badly frostbitten.

The day after our return to Base Camp, we heard more terrible news from the radio tent. One of the Russian women we had met on the upper part of the Lipkin route was dead and the remaining seven were in desperate trouble. They had persevered with their plan but the weather was appalling and they were horribly exposed in their inadequate cotton tents, with no snow shovels to dig holes. A group of us – French, American and British – formed a rescue group and requested a helicopter to take us at least as far as the base of the Lipkin route and, if possible, some way up it. No helicopters were available. Eventually, the American Jeff Lowe, Tut, Guy and I, along with the four French climbers from Paris, climbed up to the ice cave camp on the Lipkin where we found two masters of sport, both strong climbers, Boris and Kostya.

It was obvious, being 5,000 feet below the women and with the storm raging worse than ever, that the situation was hopeless. Most of them were now dead. Before we left Base Camp, we had heard a heartbreaking radio call from their leader, Elvira Shatayev: 'What will happen to us? What will happen to the children? It's not fair, we did everything right.' She had begun weeping. Abalakov sat by the transmitter trying to console Elvira. 'My dear, beautiful girl, you have been very brave, all of you, please hold on, we are trying to reach you.' Elvira came back on the radio later: 'We are sorry, we have failed you. We tried so hard, now we are so cold.' Abalakov pleaded with Elvira to stay awake and told her that Kostya and Boris and others were trying to reach her.

The atmosphere in the cave was sombre as we listened to Elvira's last transmissions at the conclusion of our forlorn attempt to reach her and her companions. Jeff Lowe described the scene: 'For the benefit of Doug, Tut and me, Boris translates the message that is crackling through the radio: from the camp of the Russian women on the summit we hear the news that "the others are all dead – I am too weak to push the button on the radio any longer – this is my last transmission – goodbye." So, our efforts have been in vain – we knew they were useless when we left Base Camp, but this is too much. The last woman is dying tonight, several thousand feet above us. She is dying and we are powerless to help her. Boris tells us that his (and our) comrade in the cave, Kostya, was engaged to be married to one of those poor women. When I look into Kostya's eyes across the candlelit cave, our lack of a common language is no barrier to communication. The anguish is evident … Almost as if he had prepared for this moment Tut produces a bottle of Scotch from nowhere. A toast to the Russian ladies. The toast has words, but they are forgettable. What won't be forgotten by those who were there that night on Peak Lenin was the ambiance that developed under those desperate and melancholy conditions … We got to know each other that night in some very important ways. We walked together on paths that are normally closed to strangers. We all felt the common bond of the human condition. I was glad to have these particular people to share this dark situation with. I saw the light in the souls of a few strong individuals shining through a rent in the clouds of a thunderstorm.'

Al Steck, Christopher Wren and Jock Glidden had also been high on Lenin, out of radio contact and hunkered down in their tent with no idea of the drama taking place above them during those protracted two days. Released from the storm, they continued to the summit with a group of Japanese. As they climbed along the ridge, they discovered first one, and then another and finally seven of the dead women. Jock described it thus: 'At the base of the last 800-foot east snow slope our party merged with the Japanese and soon afterwards we discovered the first body lying alone on the snow. Allen Steck radioed our discovery and position to base with the operable Japanese radio. As we ascended the slope we discovered two more bodies lying on exposed levels each about 150 feet apart, then three more uncovered bodies huddled together in a hollow, which was probably a tent platform. Finally, near the summit, a seventh was found leaning over the remains of a shredded Soviet tent and a rappel rope was anchored near-by.' The eighth body, Elvira's, was not discovered until a week later when Vladimir, her husband, went up with a support party, discovering Elvira wrapped up in the ruins of the tent under the bodies of her comrades.

We all descended to Base Camp for the closing ceremonies, which were already underway with white tablecloths spread out on the grass and visiting dignitaries who, we quickly realised, had been flown in by helicopter. Our mood changed from sadness to anger; we had requested helicopters to take us to the foot of the north face of Lenin perhaps saving two days; two days in which we might just have got to the women and brought at least some of them down alive.

We finally left the Achik-Tash grasslands and Base Camp with my reputation under a cloud. Drunk on Bulgarian wine, angry at recent events, I made a protest by trying to overturn a Russian police car. At least we got a good route out of our five weeks in Russia and we made a lot of new friends. The Russians weren't so put out by our attitudes. Michael Monastyrski, the camp commandant, told me: 'First, I hate you [because of our appearance], then I respect you [for putting up a new route] and now I like you [for assisting in the rescue]. You are good boys, fine alpinists.'

'We know this Michael.'

'Ah, there you go again. What can I say?' he said, beating the air with his fists in mock frustration.

There were aspects of life in the Soviet Union that seemed wrong and cynical. The stamps we put on our envelopes to post home had a whale on them and were labelled 'Save the whale year', and yet this was one of the few countries killing whales at that time. The worst aspect, as far as I was concerned, was the way all Russian lives were regimented. For example, we learned it was impossible for an ordinary Russian to leave their town without a permit. Just down the road on the outskirts of town he would have to show that permit at a checkpoint. To go climbing spontaneously was difficult; it was always done through trade union groups or sports committees. At one time climbing had been much as it was in Britain and other Western countries in the best traditions of the sport but all that changed with the advent of communism.

When they got home, the four lads from Paris wrote honestly about their visit to the Pamirs saying they had spent most of their time rescuing people. In response to their understandably negative view, an article appeared in *Pravda* saying the French were cowards and they refused to go out to rescue Russian women whereas the British, although hippy in appearance, were very brave to have attempted to bring them down. This was absolute nonsense of course as the entire French contingent had actually instigated the rescue and done all they could, not only to rescue the eight women, but also in supporting the evacuation of Peak 19 and helping rescue Eva and Anya. French pride was offended. The famous French alpinist Pierre Mazeaud, late of the international Everest expedition and now a politician in the ministry of education, asked me through an intermediary if I would write a statement giving a true account of those events, which of course I did.

Curiously, despite the language differences, we found that we socialised more with the climbers from Paris – Bernard Germain, Benoit Renard, Michel Berquet and Yves Morin – than the Americans, who were on a sort of diplomatic mission as ambassadors for America in the wake of Richard Nixon's visit to Moscow in 1972. They'd been told they were expected to put on a good show, demonstrating the American way of life to the Russians and this they did, keeping themselves to themselves and having almost as many meetings as the Russians. The Americans even had a meeting on their day off to decide what they were going to do with it. Even so, we strengthened old friendships and made new ones among a formidably strong group of climbers.

Perhaps because there were so many different accidents and deaths, we never heard any more about high-altitude climbing becoming an Olympic event. It certainly didn't get much support from the Western nations represented at the camp. The Soviet attitude to mountaineering certainly suffered a severe setback with the death of the eight Russian women. Tragically they lacked the experience and necessary equipment to weather such a terrible storm at 23,000 feet. They were also, it seemed to me, blinded to the build-up of danger by their overwhelming ambition to succeed. They were locked into an itinerary and determined to achieve their targets, factors which prevented them changing direction as conditions dictated.

With the Soviet state controlling the nature of climbing there, Russian mountaineering culture tended towards the collective, something which became engrained in the subconsciousness of subsequent generations – the cornerstone of their approach. There is in such dogma an admirable, even noble, purpose of supporting one another, the strong supporting the weak. It may well also have been the main reason all eight Russian women perished on Lenin.

Arlene Blum, an American biochemist climbing with Heidi and Eva rather than as part of the American group, has written powerfully about the Pamirs tragedy. Arlene, who would become a successful Himalayan climber herself, reported a conversation that she had with the leader of the women's team, Elvira Shatayev, just before their departure. Clearly Elvira and her team were extremely ambitious to make the first all-female ascent of Lenin and they definitely did not want to join forces with Arlene's group of foreign women climbers. Arlene felt strongly that the Russian women wanted to get there first. It seems nationalism drove them as much as the prestige of a first female ascent. They had faith in the Soviet system of climbing. Elvira was proud to tell Arlene that, 'our group is very strong, we have strong collective spirit and will stay together no matter what happens.' And so the women died, including Elvira, like the captain of a sinking ship staying with her gallant crew.

The Russians' confidence had an impact on Arlene Blum, as did the number of people on the mountain. 'Elvira's team is climbing in spite of the forecast,' she thought to herself. 'I guess we can.' The safety net of guides out on patrol with radios and the presence of helicopters in the area may also have induced a false sense of security. Events on Pik Lenin laid bare, for all to see, the dangers of external organisation and regulation subverting a small group from taking responsibility for their own lives with self-reliance and cautious decision-making.

To balance the books, there had, according to the camp commandant, been only two deaths on Lenin during the 1,300 ascents since the first in 1928. Of the fifteen climbers that perished there in 1974 during the international camp, Gary Ullin and the five Estonians were unlucky to have been climbing when an earthquake triggered the avalanches that killed them. The women, too, were unlucky; the storm that blew in was particularly ferocious. It is also true that the nine women who died were warned of the imminent approach of the storm and that it would be particularly severe; they chose to ignore advice to descend immediately.

Early on the morning we left the Pamirs, there was another earthquake. I thought Tut was pulling my sleeping mat from under me to wake me up and he thought I was doing the same. We leapt out of our tent along with all the other confused campers. Standing there, comparing notes, we rode another wave passing through the earth that continued on up the valley and through the mountain, triggering snow and ice to fall from Krylenko and Peak 19. My final memory of the Pamirs was standing on the meadow with Tut, Guy and Clive and the Americans to join Ullin's parents in remembering their son. Chet and Phyllis Ullin had travelled 12,000 miles to pay their final respects to Gary. Bob Craig, in his excellent book about that terrible summer, *Storm and Sorrow*, described those final moments of the expedition:

'A final memorial was held at the great rock attended only by the Americans and four Englishmen to whom we had grown close. We formed a circle and held hands as Phyllis Ullin requested. The twenty-third psalm was read from the Bible we had borrowed from our friends from Grenoble, and Chet Ullin, tears streaming down his face, sang one of Gary's favourite boyhood songs, 'I Want to Wake up in the Mountains'. The Ullins pulled apart from the circle, went to the rock, and, still holding hands, wept before the inscription to Gary. There was little emotion left in any of us. We simply wanted to leave the Pamirs and return home.'

The Ogre, viewed from the Biafo Glacier.

STRATEGY AND TACTICS

Late in 1973, Chris Bonington heard that a Canadian expedition to Everest planned for the post-monsoon season of 1975 had fallen through, and he immediately applied for the permit. In those days, of course, there was only one permit issued per season, something that helped preserve the mountain's mystique and made opportunities to climb Everest highly desirable. In Delhi, on our way to Changabang, Chris got a telegram confirming that he had been successful in his application.

I didn't have a lifelong yearning to climb Everest; as far as I can recall I never gave it a second thought and didn't feel left out when other British climbers went in 1971. I certainly never felt motivated to organise my own Everest expedition. All that had changed by the end of 1972 after attempting the south-west face twice. The upper part of the route had captivated me; I was consumed with curiosity as to how to climb through the rock band and survive the long haul beyond to the summit – and back.

I had been in Vancouver in the late summer of 1973 and first heard then that the Canadians might not be going to Everest because of financial problems. When I got home, I wrote to the expedition leader, Hans Gmoser, the Austrian-born Canadian skiing guide. The letter outlines much of my thinking about climbing in general and the south-west face of Everest in particular. I suggested to Gmoser a Commonwealth expedition, which would broaden the opportunities for raising finance, made up of half a dozen Canadians, half a dozen British climbers, one or two from Australia and two or three from New Zealand. I wanted climbers who were prepared to make a co-operative effort and carry loads alongside the Sherpas, an Everest expedition that was less hierarchical than I'd experienced hitherto.

'Steve Sutton and Hugh Burton,' I wrote, 'have not been high before but they are made of the stuff that gets you high. Rob Wood rarely talks about climbing in the Rockies without mentioning Brian Greenwood as a very competent, all-round mountaineer. Then there is John Amatt who has shown drive and organising ability in the past, particularly in Norway. A few suggestions thrown in to support your own.' Gmoser had already selected half a dozen climbers, including Greenwood, but not the others. I also suggested Rick White from Australia, like Steve and Hugh, another friend from Yosemite days, and the New Zealand doctor Lindsey Strang, who had been working at Ed Hillary's Kunde Hospital in Khumbu and shown incredible stamina.

Before writing to Gmoser I'd been in touch with Jimmy Roberts in Kathmandu and we'd shared ideas about Sherpa support on the mountain. 'We should try to encourage the high-altitude Sherpas all we can by making them full members and indeed feeling like full members by asking their advice at every opportunity, eating and sleeping with them, using identical equipment and by climbing with them.' I had an idea for teams of six working together, two of them Sherpas, taking it in turns to fix the route up to the rock band where the climbing was not so difficult.

Some of my British choices for the climbing team were predictable: Dougal Haston, for example, and Tut Braithwaite, who I described to Gmoser as being Britain's most prolific alpinist. I also recommended Barney Rosedale, the doctor from the autumn 1972 expedition who also spoke fluent Nepali. I also included Mick Burke, who had won ITN Sports Cameraman of the Year in 1972 for his film about that expedition, made, as I told Gmoser, 'practically singlehanded.'

'The big question,' I told Gmoser, 'would be whether to include Don Whillans or Chris Bonington, or both, or neither. Their experience on high mountains is second to none, particularly Don's, but they do have their own personal antagonisms. They would be an asset to fundraising but then Everest raises its own funds. Really it rather depends on their willingness to adjust to the spirit of such an expedition. Personally I have found great pleasure in climbing with both of them.'

The style and nature of leadership was something I'd thought a lot about: 'The Sherpas expect a leader figure and would need one to sort out the inevitable squabbles that arise over gear, etc. Second, the vast logistics on Everest require someone to make decisions quickly, to deploy materials and climbers effectively and fairly – committee meetings do not seem to work so well, as shown in 1971.

'This does not mean the leader has to be heavy-handed, rather he should play the role of chief logistician, a background figure who comes to the fore in the face of Sherpa strikes and steps in by virtue of his experience and his personality to mediate, encourage and sympathise … I cannot see how any leader, who stands to gain large financial rewards and who is likely to attract an inordinate amount of publicity to himself, can hope to win the deep respect of the rest of the team upon whose efforts he is so dependent. Perhaps Charles Evans struck the right balance on Kangchenjunga for he was never hampered nor encouraged by commercial considerations in that he did not have to earn a living from the proceeds.

'It might lead to a freer exchange of ideas and a less inhibited atmosphere if the leader did not take it into his head to write the expedition book. That should come from well edited transcript, letters home, diaries, as well as reflected comment, all of which would give immediacy to the event and at the same time be fair to all members. I'll leave the leadership question to your further comment and perhaps ultimately to discussion with Don, Chris and the rest of the team.'

Beyond personnel and leadership, I outlined my ideas about tactics on the mountain. For me, going as early as late July was important. The climbers needed to spend at least five weeks acclimatising on the walk in, with a sojourn around Namche Bazaar and ferrying loads through the icefall as conditions allowed, so that we would be in a good position to make use of the settled weather between the monsoon, which usually ended in the second half of September, and before the cold, strong winter winds blew in from Central Asia. I explained to Gmoser my idea about the left-hand gully in the rock-band; I'd recently written an article about this for *Mountain*.

It was fortunate that Gmoser never answered my letter as my ideas would probably have ended up as badly as the 1971 Internationale. Interestingly, according to Chic Scott's history of Canadian climbing, it was Canada's foreign affairs ministry that cancelled the permit, having heard that the expedition was struggling for finance, to save embarrassment. It's a mysterious affair. Raising sufficient funds was always a challenge. After the pressure of raising enough finance for a well-equipped and supplied expedition to the south-west face in 1972, Chris was reluctant to go back on the route. He had an idea of climbing the regular south-east ridge with a lightweight team.

During our climb of Changabang, with the support of Martin and Dougal, I managed to convince Chris it would be a pointless exercise to go all the way to Nepal simply to repeat a route that was now over twenty years old, even if he was going to do it without Sherpa support. 'You couldn't just walk past the south-west face,' Dougal said. To be honest, Chris didn't need much persuading that going where no man had gone before was the right thing to do. As a consequence, Dougal and I had one of the most fantastic experiences of our lives, right up to the summit of Everest.

Most of the invited team gathered in Chamonix during December for the chance to climb together and try out the latest clothing and equipment we'd be taking to Everest. We had a mass ascent of the Aiguille Verte, via the *Couturier Couloir*, and then on Christmas Eve Tut and I went for a winter rock climb on the Aiguille du Midi. We set off up the Rébuffat route but found it slow-going; the steep granite was iced up and then a storm moved in. A hurricane was blowing by the time we finished and we dived through the door of the cable car station just before we completely froze. Outside there was a maelstrom; inside was eerily calm.

The last car had gone, so we were stuck for the festivities. Looking around for somewhere to sleep we found a room full of winter coats hanging on pegs belonging to the cable car workforce who were now all down in Chamonix and about to celebrate Christmas. We spent two nights in that hut while the storm raged outside and on Boxing Day the cable car returned full of excited skiers and the workforce, who found us still fast asleep under a pile of their coats. At least it amused the rest of the team when we finally reappeared having missed out on the festivities.

My big wall book was finally published and sold well, receiving reasonably good reviews, particularly from Walt Unsworth, the editor of *Climber and Rambler*, who immediately shot up in my estimation: 'I would rank it as the most important contribution to British climbing literature in the last decade,' he wrote. 'Nobody who had a deep concern for the sport can afford to be without it.' It's subsequently been picked out as an influential book, and featured among the writer Jill Neate's fifty most important mountaineering books. That is not to say the book didn't have its faults. Paul Nunn, reviewing it for the *Fell and Rock Journal*, thought it 'a good book' but 'it seems to me that to write a book which describes technical aids and big wall rock climbing is not really striking a blow for free rock climbing standards.'

Its publication prompted invitations to do some lectures, including one for the Scottish Mountaineering Club; their preferred choice, Reinhold Messner, had been forced to cancel, unexpectedly called back to court in Munich for that mountaineering equivalent of Jarndyce and Jarndyce, Messner and Herrligkoffer. I followed that up in March with lectures in North America, starting in Boston and the next day lecturing to the New York branch of the American Alpine Club. I then flew to Denver for a lecture organised by the *Mountain Gazette*, staying with Dez and Ann Hadlum who had recently left Nottingham to settle in North America.

In Colorado I met up again with Molly Higgins, who I'd met in the Pamirs. All of us in the English contingent had admired her for overcoming the prejudice she faced from some of those in her own party who were sceptical about her ability. She proved them wrong by making the first ascent of Pik Lenin by an American woman. After the Pamirs trip, Molly came over to the UK and climbed in Derbyshire and the Lake District and we developed an attraction for each other. My relationship with Jan was at its lowest ebb, hardly surprising given that I was away climbing most of the time and leaving her behind with the children. I struggled with her changing moods; she suffered badly with pre- and post-menstrual tension. I would never know how she would be when she woke up in the morning, which I found wearing. We talked about it, but I wasn't able to offer her the support she needed.

Molly and I spent three days in a cabin in Eldorado Canyon while outside a snowstorm blew through. Then we climbed a snowed-up gully in the freezing cold, our hands sticking to the karabiners. I was concerned at being seen around Boulder with Molly; a few folk from Nottingham were now living in Colorado, as well as mutual friends we'd made out there, and I didn't want Jan finding out I was spending time with Molly while she was stuck at home with the children. So we parted, planning to meet later in Yosemite. Molly was sad and hurt about that. She headed to Yosemite to climb with friends, agreeing to see me there later.

I went to Estes Park to see Steve Komito and Michael Covington, keen to climb the Diamond on Longs Peak. The winds were hammering the mountain, as they often do, and it was far too fierce for steep face climbing. So we settled instead for the softer option – and soft snows – of Taylor Peak with Michael and Doug Snively. By the time we had got ourselves organised the weather had improved and so we skied up to Taylor's east face under a cloudless blue Colorado sky to take a look. The spring snow was pretty appalling but we were determined to do something so climbed a line just left of a prominent ridge that dominates the centre of the face. A right-leaning ramp took us to a large snowfield but in the warm sun balconies of heavy wet snow were tumbling off towards us, so we headed to a rock band for better belay protection. Half a dozen pitches later we were on the summit, stretched out in the sun, enjoying the long mountain views.

On my way to Yosemite, I climbed in the Eastern Sierra, making an attempt to climb a new route on the Keeler Needle, near Mount Whitney, with Dennis Hennek and Rick Ridgeway whose idea it was. Rick was pegging away above an overhang when the peg he was hanging off came out and he fell, unzipping all the pegs below. He hurtled out into space and then swung under the overhang where the lip's sharp edge half-cut through both ropes. We retired to regroup but bad weather blew in and I took off for more lectures in San Francisco, Berkeley and Palo Alto where I stayed with Arlene Blum who I had met in the Pamirs. Although Arlene hadn't been part of the official American group, she had become close to one of their group, a talented all-round climber called Bruce Carson. Arlene herself had led the first all-female team to Denali, and would do the same on Annapurna a few years later. Bruce was part of the new wave of Yosemite climbers, making a solo ascent of the Chouinard-Herbert route on Sentinel, not only his first grade-VI climb but done without a hammer. At the time, it was considered a hugely inspiring ascent. Bruce was, as Royal Robbins said, 'what a man should be ... strong, gentle, good.' Tragically for Arlene, Bruce died later that year, falling through a cornice on Trisul in the Indian Himalaya.

Finished with lecturing for a while, I met up with Molly in Yosemite to stay at Camp 4 and climb on the lower crags of the Valley. It felt great to be back; Molly was overflowing with high spirits. I seemed particularly fired up on this trip, probably because of her, and we climbed well together, starting with *Midterm* – a typically strenuous Chuck Pratt creation on Arch Rock – and *Anathema* on Cookie Cliff, both demanding climbs which I felt strong climbing. Romance and the mountains are a powerful combination, conspiring to override my concern for Jan. It seemed I was growing fonder of Molly with every route. I was reading a newly published book, *Centennial* by James Michener, which included the saga of a pioneering Coloradan family. Some of the characters reminded me of Molly: a resourceful, tough, big-hearted, passionate woman who told it as she saw it. Later that year she would make the first all-female ascent of the Diamond, along with Steph Atwood and Rob's wife, Laurie Wood.

One evening we drove down to El Portal, a small town downstream in the Merced Valley, to dance the night away to a rhythm and blues band. I had teased her about only ever wearing outdoor clothing, and she'd put on a little blue dress over her strong, athletic body, which was now making all the right moves to really good music. We ended up, at midnight, lying on the dew-soaked grass under a fall moon, making love until I was interrupted, startled by a warm wet tongue travelling up my spine from bottom to head. I turned round to see a horse looking down curiously at us from over a fence which had us convulsed in fits of laughter.

We went down to the Cookie area with Rik Rieder, a very steady and bold climber, one of the best of that era in Yosemite, to climb the newly climbed classic *Outer Limits*. It's one of the best short routes in the Valley, but Molly recalls I was feeling melancholy and weak so we sat on a rock while Rik led the first pitch of awkward jamming but I perked up and lead through across the hand traverse to finish. Molly took both pitches in her stride, as she did on most of the routes we climbed together. I felt privileged also to have been climbing with Rik; as Jim Bridwell wrote, 'he was one of the most talented climbers to come along in many years and proved to have amazing confidence and calm on long runouts.' Later that year Rik was climbing *Pacific Ocean Wall* on El Cap when a rock hit him on the head and he had to have emergency brain surgery, from which he eventually recovered.

Still anxious that Jan would find out about our affair, I told Molly we should not climb exclusively together, worried again that people would consider us to be in a permanent relationship. So I ended up on the most strenuous and

Molly Higgins on *Outer Limits*, The Cookie Cliff, Yosemite. Rik Rieder belaying.

gruelling climb I did that spring with strong man John Long, already a veteran of the Valley, albeit a young one. John, one of the greatest chroniclers of American climbing, said he had just the route for me knowing how I loved gritstone. It was, he told me, called *Meat Grinder*. So it proved. I arrived at the top of a 100-foot corner-crack exhausted, my hands ground down and blood-ied despite years of gritstone wear and tear.

Jim Bridwell then pointed me at the hardest climb I led in the Valley, *Little Wing* in the Ribbon Falls area, recently put up by Charlie Porter, Mark Chapman and Bruce Pollock. The name was taken from the Jimi Hendrix song, all about his ideal woman 'riding the wind'. It was said to be 5.11, a grade I hadn't climbed before, at least on sight. It turned out to be a committing line, up the edge of a steep buttress and pulling up around a corner, reaching up for holds at full stretch not knowing if I could make the move, but making it anyway. Time stretched, but there was no doubt in my mind and I was at the top almost without realising it. That's a route I've never forgotten.

I reluctantly left Molly and Yosemite to lecture for Royal Robbins in Modesto and Fresno, and then in Ventura at Yvon Chouinard's Great Pacific Iron Works. Once out of the cloistered climbing world, I came across a different kind of American life, or at least Californian life. All went well travelling to Modesto and Fresno, where Royal rewarded me richly for the presentations he organ-ised. I then set off hitchhiking from Fresno mid-morning needing to be in Ventura, some 200 miles away just north of Los Angeles, to start my talk at 7.30 p.m. that evening.

Things went really well at first. A rep pulled over who said he needed company to keep him awake after a heavy night out on the town. Then I got a lift with a vast Mexican lady who worked her way through a joint and as she did so began to keel over against me in the car. Luckily she stopped to do some shopping so I took the chance to extricate myself. My next ride was with a podgy black man in a smart blue short-sleeved shirt who angled the conversation around to the bathhouses in San Francisco. Had I any experience in that direction, he asked, as he threw another empty beer can out of the car. We had a frank discussion about litter, and I was back where I started on the side of the road.

A rather inoffensive little man now pulled up promising to take me most of the way. Not only did he have prominent front teeth like Bugs Bunny, he actually spoke like him. After a few pleasantries, he got on to the subject of his infertility and the fact that he and his wife sadly could not have children. His doctor, he said, had recently given him a useful suggestion. I made the mistake of asking what that might be. He pulled off the highway, reached into the glove compartment and pulled out a polystyrene cup. What he really needed, he said, was some 'sperms' from an anonymous donor. He asked me if

I would be that donor, to my acute embarrassment, until he mentioned that if I did put a contribution of my 'sperms' in the cup he would give me $5. I told him my 'sperms' were worth far more than that and we parted company.

I was now stuck in the middle of the freeway, so I had a long wait for the next lift. Eventually, a young woman stopped in a VW Beetle who was going down to Edwards Air Force Base not so far from Los Angeles. Things began well, but with every joint she smoked, the journey grew more erratic and her stops became more frequent. With only two hours to go before the lecture she got out of the car and disappeared, skipping through the scrub towards the horizon. I set off in hot pursuit to find her impersonating an aeroplane, arms outstretched and howling like a jet engine as she weaved through the bushes. She was divorcing her husband, who was an air force pilot, so that might have had something to do with it.

After coaxing her back to the car I sat her in the passenger seat and told her I was now driving. Luckily, she soon fell asleep, finally waking up as we arrived at Chouinard's shop in Ventura, five minutes before the lecture. She ended up sitting on the front row alongside Dennis Hennek and friends, listening to me saying how it was on Everest in 1972. Tom Frost came up to me afterwards, congratulating me on mimicking an accent identical to that of Mick Burke and Don Whillans, who he remembered so well from Annapurna.

I went on to lecture in Flagstaff, Laramie and Albuquerque, repeating my mantra to each host that it would be best if I were picked up at the airport, taken to the nearest crag and pointed at classic routes, where I would remain until it was time for the lecture. This worked out well and helped me overcome the loneliness of the one-night stand. From New Mexico I flew north to Salt Lake City, Boise and then Vancouver for a few days to catch up with Rob Wood and the numerous other Brits who had moved to British Columbia. Rob and I were headed for the Karakoram later in the summer, so we had a lot to talk about.

After a welcome break, I headed south to Portland where I told the audience, rather grandly, that I had never taken a flag up a mountain as climbing was beyond nationalism. Near the front of the auditorium, Willi Unsoeld, who had reached the summit of Everest in 1963, stood up with both his hands in the air, like a born-again preacher, shouting 'Yeah!' followed by a whole row of his students. 'Yeah!' I then travelled east, stopping off for lectures in Minneapolis, New York and North Conway for Dick Williams before flying home in early May.

On the plane I suddenly wanted to be home with Jan and the family again. I had enjoyed being with Molly and looked forward to seeing her again; the strength of my feelings for her had overridden the anxiety I felt at upsetting Jan and the children as well as disrupting my life in Nottingham. I suppose, as a man, it was easy for me to compartmentalise my relationships without too much anguish or soul-searching. When I was with Molly I was with Molly; when I was with Jan, which was for the majority of the time, I was with Jan and the family. Our relationship had been a fairly open one, and there were other affairs. I didn't think I was being so unreasonable, especially as for half the month I had to cope with her frequent mood swings. In retrospect, I really struggled with my frequently angst-ridden behaviour and I was consumed with guilt during the half of the month that things were going well. Nevertheless, there was a steady deterioration in our relationship – love grew cold and lurve hardly happened.

With funds in short supply our British Karakoram Expedition flew out on Afghan Air to Kabul from where we took buses through the Khyber Pass to Rawalpindi in Pakistan. With me were Rob Wood, Tony Watts, Bob Wilson and Clive Rowland. Ronnie Richards, who I had got to know in the Pamirs the year before, would be joining us later, having just helped deliver equipment and supplies for the Everest expedition that autumn overland to Nepal.

Contacts at the British Embassy suggested we stay at the home of Colonel Eric 'Buster' Goodwin, who lived in a rather rundown house on The Mall with his adopted Pathan family. Buster, who was rather frail by the mid-1970s, had been a political agent and loyal colonial servant who had stayed on after partition since he had no one in Britain. I remember he had a craving for cheese; we thought at first it was mice nibbling away at our supplies during the night but it turned out to be our host instead. We left this charming relic of Empire with a whole round of Long Clawson blue Stilton when we left.

The Pakistan government had only decided to open up their mountains to tourism two years earlier. Unfortunately the infrastructure wasn't really yet developed to deal with visitors; delays on flights in the mountains ran into weeks and there was an acute shortage of porters, resulting in a huge hike in costs. The locals knew their value. They took advantage of the situation, frequently stopping to renegotiate their rates of pay. All the expeditions to the Karakoram in 1975 experienced these problems with most failing to achieve their objectives, including us.

We had hoped to climb Sosbun Brakk, a peak of 21,040 feet situated just west of the mighty Biafo Glacier. We had to sit around for two weeks before we could fly into Skardu and organise jeeps up to the roadhead at Dusso. From there, after six days' walking past the village of Askole and along the ablation valley alongside the Biafo Glacier, we ran into heavy spring snow, deep and wet. For two days we waded through this up to our waists before giving up on our objective. We decided instead on making a reconnaissance of The Ogre from the Uzun Brakk Glacier; perhaps we could attempt some of the smaller peaks in the area.

It had been a most frustrating trip so far, not helped by most of us suffering from acute diarrhoea. It was so bad that those affected were naked from the waist down once we'd passed Askole, so we weren't caught short. A few weeks before, some friends of Clive from Sheffield had been in these parts with the intention of climbing The Ogre, but had given up when their porters refused to carry much beyond Askole. They had left behind a hidden cache of gear and given Clive directions. The porters from Askole must have had an inkling that we planned to retrieve it. They shot off ahead with uncharacteristic speed when we were about half a mile from the prominent pile of rocks marking its location. Buried treasure! Through our binoculars we watched the Baltis scrambling among the rocks and then hiding chains of karabiners and other loot inside their shalwar kameez.

When we caught up with them, they were sitting around relaxing as though butter wouldn't melt in their mouths. The cache was almost empty; just a few tins of food were left but little else. We asked the porters where the climbing gear and medicines had gone. One small, dark-skinned cleric with a long black beard dropped on to his knees and started wailing, clutching both hands together before raising them towards me in supplication as I asked him again, this time more sternly, where the gear had gone.

The others sheepishly lowered their heads, so as not to catch my eye, but I spotted a karabiner peeking out from the tunic of the son of Haji Mehdi, Askole's headman. I grabbed it, and like a magic string of handkerchiefs, pulled out over twenty all clipped together, and then recovered packets of antibiotics and other medicines. In no time at all the other porters were adding to the pile of looted supplies. We told the cleric he was a bad Muslim and a bad example to his people. This produced more wailing. I solemnly punched Haji Mehdi's son on the nose. He promptly burst into tears. After a long discussion about how they'd let down themselves, their village and Pakistan in general, we concluded the meeting amicably, having agreed to keep quiet about the theft, much to the relief of the porters and in particular the cleric, who prostrated himself on the sandy ground by way of thanks.

After a week wading through soft snow on the lower flanks of mountains, we gave up trying to reach any summits but we did get splendid views of The Ogre. Feeling inspired, Clive and I decided to mount an expedition there for 1977, although we couldn't make up our minds as to the most attractive route. Clive tended towards a long, alpine-looking ridge with interesting rock steps leading to the final tower and the main summit of The Ogre. I was quite attracted by a prominent, 3,000-foot prow of granite, being still enamoured of big-wall climbing; the idea of climbing steep rock at altitude appealed to me.

Bob and Tony were now out of time, so went into reverse, descending quickly with our now compliant, hard-working porters. On the way out we were treated like royalty in Askole, sitting down for tea, dates and dried apricots. The headman's son was especially attentive. We were asked to attend to various ailments and once again our medical box won us many friends. I was to see a lot more of Askole in the coming years.

Home from the Karakoram, I spent a few weeks at home in Nottingham with Jan and the children preparing for Everest. During this period, Dougal, who had separated from his wife Annie, dropped in with his Swiss girlfriend Ariane Giobellina. It was one of the few occasions when we met socially outside of climbing events or expeditions; I was pleasantly surprised to find Dougal far more relaxed and at peace with himself than before. He had an exciting but always turbulent life with Annie. It seemed to me that in Ariane he had met a kindred spirit who kept her own counsel, exercised self-control over feeling, was a keen observer and, through this mutual understanding, they both grew in stature. Dougal even found time to play with two-year-old Martha in her 'house': a huge cardboard box under the kitchen table.

At the end of July I caught the train to London and met with most of the rest of the team at the Tower Hotel on the north bank of the Thames. We flew out the following day and arrived in Kathmandu on 31 July.

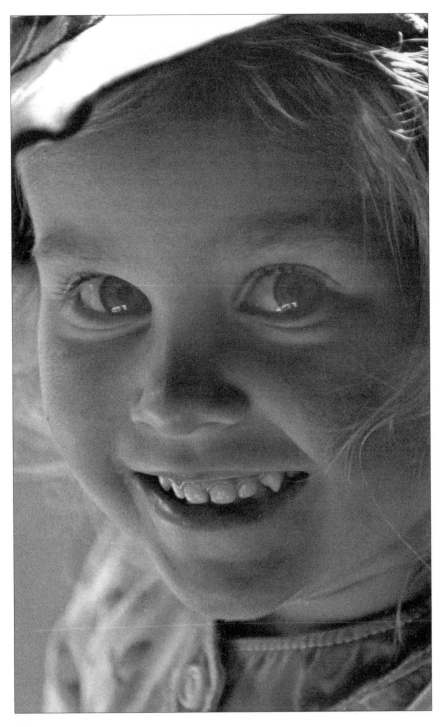

Martha.

On the summit of Everest at 6:35 p.m. on 24 September 1975. **Photo**: Dougal Haston.

EVEREST REGAINED

No matter how much we might try to convince ourselves that Everest is just another mountain, reaching its summit changes everyone who does it, in one way or another. It's the peak with the most history, the greatest height, the thinnest air, the lowest temperatures and the wildest storms. Standing there with Dougal Haston between 6 p.m. and 7 p.m. on 24 September 1975, watching the valleys of Nepal fill with evening cloud and the light catching the summits of the mountains poking up from Tibet's purple plateau, making out in a sweep of 400 miles the perfect curve of the earth, feeling fulfilled, confident, on top of the game – I was not humbled, exactly, but aware of something much bigger than myself, of which I was merely a part. I was again a child lost in wonder.

Our success remained uncertain from beginning to end. The pundits back home had written us off since all five previous attempts on the south-west face had failed spectacularly below the rock band, some 2,000 feet short of the summit. During the early planning stages there were negative comments from climbers and non-climbers alike, centring on the value of spending so much cash on one climb at a time of economic and industrial gloom. Even Ken Wilson, whom Chris Bonington dubbed 'the weathercock of climbing opinion', in a letter to Dougal, felt, 'this trip offers little hope for optimism and I fear that you and the climbing world will be the object of counter-productive publicity if the project fails.'

It was only in hindsight that we realised we'd actually had more going for us than we thought. Six of us had been on the face before: Chris Bonington, Mick Burke, Nick Estcourt, Dougal Haston, Hamish MacInnes and myself. Three of us – Dougal, Hamish and I – had been there twice. By now, Chris had honed the art of large expedition planning to perfection. He worked long into the night, poring over his computer printouts, and yet he was one of the first away next morning, either pushing out the route or humping loads up the ropes.

We were also well funded enough to afford all the latest equipment for twelve climbers, sixty Sherpas and their talented sirdar, Pertemba, known as 'PT'. As with the six 'sahibs', many of the Sherpas had been on the south-west face before. PT had been right up at Camp 6 in support of Don and Dougal back in 1971. You could argue that our ascent demonstrated once and for all that if enough experienced climbers and high-altitude Sherpas are put to work on a big face, with good leaders, and with oxygen, fixed ropes, and reasonable weather, then one can more or less guarantee success on any big face in the Himalaya. Yet we still couldn't be sure, not even after all the camps from 1 to 5 were stocked, not even after Paul Braithwaite and Nick Estcourt had put in a brilliant day's climbing up and through the left-hand gully of the rock band, opening the way to Camp 6.

Everest in 1975 almost ended for me before it began, with the death of a young, mute Sherpa boy. The Sherpas do not talk down to their children as we sometimes do in the West; they treat them with the same deference as they would adults. Early in June 1972, Don Whillans, Hamish MacInnes and myself stayed with a Sherpa family at the small *kharka* at Pheriche, on the trail to Base Camp, where we saw another side to Sherpa culture. Two of the children, aged about twelve and eighteen, were deaf and dumb; these two children were not treated as equals but as contemptible, pushed and kicked by their father around the house and outside in the fields. We naturally befriended the lads and gave them carrying jobs, paying them well and supplying them with food.

The next time I saw them was in 1975 at Kunde. I came across Mingma, the eldest of the brothers, and his blank face lit up in recognition, his bright smile displaying his brilliant white teeth. Being unable to speak he used his face to show his emotions to good effect. I located PT who was embroiled in distributing loads to our porters. I suggested Mingma should have a job and he told me that he had already sorted out a load for him. Over the next few days, walking in with Tut, we both saw quite a lot of Mingma, as did Mick Burke who named him 'Easy Rider' since he always wore a leather jacket.

At Gorak Shep, Tut and I decided to camp on the nearby hill of Kala Pattar so we could better acclimatise and take photographs of Everest at dusk and dawn. We arranged with Ang Phu and Adrian Gordon to take Mingma up with us to help carry some of the heavy camera equipment and a tent. After our night out, Mingma came up to help us down with the equipment. He was well pleased as it meant extra work. We had also seen his father the day before who had been driving yaks carrying our gear up to Base Camp and he was quite jubilant to see his son in gainful employment. It took Mingma a little less than an hour to get down, and then he set off for Base Camp, another two hours or so up the trail, which was busy with yaks and porters coming and going.

Next day Tut and I arrived at Base Camp having covered the distance in just over an hour from Gorak Shep, but there was no sign of Mingma. Chris organised a search party after consulting with our Sherpa liaison officer, Mike Cheney. While everyone was getting ready, Chris became quite angry, telling me that although I had shown great compassion in hiring Mingma, I had disrupted the Sherpas' routine and could have caused a death; his rebuke was based I think on Mike Cheney's fears that he would carry the can for my whim. But as I explained, Mingma was already working for us; I'd just given him a little extra work. Chris unreservedly withdrew his comments and apologised.

Jim Duff, one of our two expedition doctors, ever empathic, poured oil on troubled waters but I still felt upset at Chris's attitude. Everyone took a sector and fanned out down the valley, all in radio contact with Base Camp. I felt very much alone with my three Sherpas, anxious that the lad couldn't shout if he was trapped under moraine debris or fallen ice. While we searched, I made the decision to leave the expedition. I couldn't shake off the accusation and possibility that I might have caused the death of a lad so young and disadvantaged. I needed to get away from that kind of accusation.

Scrambling around like a madman, I heard Adrian Gordon, our Base Camp manager, report that he'd sighted clothing and then a body in a stream. I hurried over and climbed down to him and saw Mingma lying there in the fast-moving water. I lifted him gently out and laid him on the gritty bank. He must have tripped and fallen, banging his head and becoming unconscious. His face was just like it was when he was around camp, set firm, withdrawn into his silent world. I sobbed uncontrollably for him and, I suppose, for me. Chris appeared having run the two miles from Base and put his arms around me and wept and spoke of his son Conrad, who had drowned in a stream as a toddler.

Chris showed great sympathy and dispelled the lingering tension of our argument a few hours before. He also dispelled the notion of fault; this had been an accident, pure and simple. Adrian too was incredibly kind, reminding me that all I had tried to do was make Mingma's life better. Mick Burke, with typical pragmatism, pointed out the Sherpas were not unduly troubled; his time had come and he had gone on to a better life. I hoped I could accept it that way but for a while I not only gave up all ambition to climb Everest, I was all set to return home.

Taking part in a siege-style expedition has many similarities with working for a big organisation. As an employee, we are most concerned with the role we've been given, want promotion and appreciate praise from those in positions of power. From conversations between the lads it was obvious that every decision Chris made from start to finish was being scrutinised minutely. This was only natural in such a close-knit bunch where everyone would be affected in one way or another. On a big mountaineering expedition, especially to Everest, there is both luck and design in who gets to climb high and eventually reaches the top. This was very apparent on the first ascent of Everest; John Hunt chose Charles Evans and Tom Bourdillon for the first summit team, and but for a faulty oxygen system they would have been the household names forever associated with the first ascent. As it was, a day later, the lives of Ed Hillary and Tenzing Norgay were changed forever.

On 25 August Chris came over to my tent and asked if I would go up into the icefall next morning with Dougal. I rushed around camp getting my gear together, suddenly excited at the prospect of some climbing. Although it had been a fabulous walk through the foothills, once we reached Khumbu and began walking past so many fine peaks, like Ama Dablam and Cholatse, the urge to climb had grown stronger in all of us. I also hoped that once embroiled in the climb the raw memory of Mingma's death would fade a little.

Pairing me with Dougal also made me think. I was conscious that I was with someone special, for everyone knew that Dougal was summit material; what did my friend Tut think of this arrangement? I had only just spoken to Tut about a hint from Chris that he wanted me to lead the rock band. On the strength of that, I had asked Tut if he fancied doing it with me. Now, here I was, out of the blue, paired with the star of our show. All I could do was go along with the flow and see what turned up next. There was no telling against the double dictates of unpredictable mountain weather and the problems of the route.

After a 4 a.m. breakfast, I clattered across the moraine, following marker flags alongside the snowy path that wound up into the icefall. I noticed I was breathing heavily, and felt concern, but took comfort from knowing I was in better shape than at the same stage in 1972. Even so, I had a way to go before I was fully acclimatised; there would be a bit of suffering yet. Dougal passed by, gliding along the trail as though on rails, as I sweated and stumbled in his wake. Perhaps in a week's time I would be moving with the same economy.

We rested at the avalanche debris that had scoured the route Nick Estcourt had led earlier and then took it in turns out front, through virgin snow, to the base of a 200-foot ice cliff. I lead up to half height and Dougal came through to lead the steeper top section. By now Pumori was lit up behind us in a spectacular white burst of light, a complete contrast to the gloomy, freezing icefall. As Dougal led up he had to chop off slender icicles that tinkled down past my stance; then he traversed on hands and knees along an ice shelf just below the top cornice.

Our concentration was interrupted by shouts from below. Mick Burke and Arthur Chesterman, Mick's soundman, had arrived to film us and capture the sounds of the icefall as it shifted downhill. It wasn't the place for Dougal to hang around, so he continued inching his way across and up through the

Dougal Haston (top) and me on Everest in 1975. Bottom: Chris Bonington Picture Library.

cornice, much to Mick's annoyance as he had no chance to set up his camera gear. Dougal disappeared to belay safely back from the edge of the cliff and then I scrambled after him.

'Why did you let him lead it?' Mick shouted up.

'Because he's better than me.' I was gasping too hard to come up with a better answer.

'You're not going very well, are you?' he said as I squirmed my way along the gangway and out on to the top.

'Cheeky little sod,' I said to Dougal. He was oblivious to such jibes. I yelled to Mick: 'Seeing as how you're too late to film you may as well make yourself useful and ladder this position.'

We left Mick, Arthur and their Sherpas to the difficult task of anchoring ladders to the vertical ice cliff. The sun was now skimming across the snow, bringing life and colour to that desolate place. Mushrooms of fresh snow sparkled like sequinned cushions. Light glinted from scalloped walls of ice and refracted through the icicles that hung everywhere we went. It was good to be back. We moved faster, knowing that later in the day the snow would turn to mush, and by 10 a.m. we had scrambled across the last of the crevasses and up the remaining snow slope to the top of the icefall. We stood at the entrance to the Western Cwm. As luck would have it, we had popped out at the perfect place for Camp 1. It was a flattish area completely surrounded by crevasses that would absorb even the biggest avalanches thundering down from Nuptse on the right and Everest on the left. We fixed our rope here and slid down to meet the climbers and Sherpas at work all through the icefall securing ladders up the route.

In the debilitating heat of afternoon, a group of us put up our tents and settled in for the night at Camp 1. None of us seemed to be having any problems with the altitude and we slept soundly – too soundly perhaps, because we didn't wake until 6 a.m. After breakfast, Dougal and I wandered off looking for a safe route up the Western Cwm. Hamish, Allen Fyffe, Mick and Arthur opted for construction work with the Sherpas, and we left them building the first and largest bridge only a few yards away from camp. We took a number of wrong turns and had to retrace our steps frequently. It seemed impossible this year to avoid making huge zigzags around yawning lateral crevasses, cutting across the cwm from one side to the other. The number one consideration, however, was safety; this would be the main supply route for Sherpas and climbers doing hundreds of carries. It was essential not to go too far under the walls of the cwm, which were dangerously avalanche prone.

Even so, we kept finding ourselves pushed against the 5,000-foot wall of Nuptse, its ice flutings iridescent in the sun. From time to time, small avalanches would tumble down its couloirs. It wasn't a safe place and we grew alarmed at

Dougal Haston in the icefall.

the amount of avalanche debris. But we could find no way to cross the crevasses in the centre of the glacier. At 2 p.m. we were far enough up the cwm to see the rest of the way up to the bottom of the south-west face and returned to camp confident that on our third day we would have completed the route there.

Next day, Ang Phu and Ang Phurba followed us up the cwm, leaving marker wands along the route as they went. During the night a huge avalanche had cut across some of our tracks to the cwm's narrows. A team of Sherpas could easily have been wiped out or suffocated under a slide that big. It was essential we brought Hamish up to somehow bridge the wide crevasses in the centre of the glacier. After prospecting for crossing places, we continued making the route up to Camp 2, now on the final easy leg of our journey.

It was good to be back in that incomparable valley, the highest in the world. I looked round at the famous landmarks: Lhotse's summit, the Geneva Spur to the South Col, the south-west face of Everest and the rock band high above. There was so much more snow on the face this year that we thought we might be a more direct route to Camp 4 from Camp 2. With a final burst of energy we pushed on to a campsite suitable for Camp 2 – our Advance Base. It was more or less the same site we had used post-monsoon in 1972, apparently safe from avalanches, being on top of a slight bulge in the ice. We turned back just as Ang Phu and Ang Phurba were arriving having done a first-rate job marking the track every sixty yards or so. The following day we descended down to Base Camp, well pleased with our efforts.

A few days later, I was back at Camp 2 with Mick, Allen Fyffe and Ronnie Richards. It had been a gruelling day. We'd sweated up there with big loads and now snow was falling on a miserably cold afternoon. Mick and I had shared the trail breaking and had put in more wands along the route. It was still early days and the altitude had left us very tired. Mick had started to put on a brew and was just changing gas cylinders when Nick arrived. He had come up to help Chris make a decision about the alternative route we'd discussed.

I must admit that I thought this slightly odd and Mick said so, for he was a bit touchy about this sort of thing; he never really seemed to come to terms with his dual roles of cameraman and climber. It seemed to me he still felt very much a climber and very much resented not being consulted on matters of mountaineering. Nick made a jibe at Mick's expense; Mick responded by throwing snow, which upset the stove. Once Mick had dealt with that, he threw a punch at Nick, who retreated, embarrassed, back down the cwm. Mick later sent down a note with one of the Sherpas apologising. It was strange how these moments of drama could flare up and then almost immediately burn out. None of us wanted to look like the bad guy in the expedition book. Charlie Clarke wrote in his diary: 'No splits, no factions, no nastiness, but it's all there in their hearts.'

Chris Bonington sorting out logistics at Camp 2.

Chris decided unexpectedly to stay on at Camp 2 and give more thought to the alternative route. So he joined the four of us as we put up the first of the Advance Base Camp tents. I could see the huge stress Chris was under. He had been wholly committed to this expedition, nursing it along every step of the way. He was taking total responsibility. He faced all the worry of the Sherpas passing through the narrows at the entrance to the cwm, the monsoon snow clearing from the south-west face, avalanching over the rock band. Now there was an alternative route to think about. As Nick had pointed out on the way up, he seemed particularly jumpy, living on his nerves. Perhaps it wasn't surprising with so much sponsored funding at stake. It was understandable that he blew his top occasionally, as he did now, flaring up at Mick for having a holdall in his personal kit that he shouldn't have. Mick tried to explain Hamish had given it him, but Chris was adamant: 'I don't want to discuss this any further, Mick, it must go back into the stores.'

Next day we put up more tents at Camp 2 while watching the face and the path taken by avalanches. Nick had come back up from Camp 1 and, having seen the face from a different perspective, was wholly committed to the old route. The rest of us kept an open mind, knowing that it would be far less effort if we could find a more direct way to Camp 4. The discussion went on all day, an ebb and flow of opinion, until suddenly Chris ended the debate: 'We'll go the old way, I've made my decision.' It wasn't exactly democratic but it worked. He had listened to us rather like a prime minister might consult cabinet colleagues before making a decision. We all agreed it was a relief that a decision had been made and that the route would be one we knew from 1972.

That evening Allen Fyffe and I marked the route up to the foot of the face in readiness for the next day fixing the start of the route, but now Chris asked if he could join us in going up to Camp 3 and mentioned also that Nick would be coming as well. I was a bit put out by this. Mick and I had been tasked with pushing on to Camp 3 and given there was so little opportunity to be out in front, when it came our way it was something to savour. I recalled how in 1972 Chris had sometimes panicked and called lead climbers back prematurely because progress wasn't fast enough, not fully understanding the problems of the team out front, as I'd experienced at Camp 5. I began to feel uneasy about my role on this expedition but kept this all to myself. Chris was already wound up with more important matters. Mick had labelled Chris the 'mercurial mad Mahdi' on account of his frequent changes of mind. That was a bit harsh; we all change our minds as circumstances alter. With everyone waiting and watching, if the leader has second thoughts the impact is amplified. I continued to hope, quietly, that the weather, route and individual fitness would determine everyone's role and that we weren't simply dependent on the last person to influence Chris.

In the end, Nick decided not to go up to Camp 3 but rest instead; Chris said he merely fancied a day out load-carrying in support. I felt really mean for having been so possessive about our stint in front. Chris just needed to be on the mountain, helping make the route, to clear his head of all the problems he was juggling. It was great to have him with us, carrying a load to the foot of the face, where he left us to get on with fixing the first 1,200 feet up the face to the site for Camp 3. We discovered the snow was neither so deep nor so dangerous as it had appeared from below, certainly on these more moderate slopes low down, and we arrived without trouble. Mick even had some film in the can.

Over the next week or so the expedition established and stocked camps 4 and 5, working away like a well-oiled machine. Even so, we suffered a casualty. While Hamish was on the fixed ropes between camps 4 and 5, a huge amount of powder snow poured down the face and immersed him in spindrift for quite some time, forcing its way into his lungs. Thereafter, sadly, Hamish was confined to Camp 2 with a series of chest problems.

Above Camp 5 we faced the crux of the route: getting through the rock band, some 500 feet high at its left-hand end. Chris, Ronnie Richards and I fixed a rope up to its base, just to the right of the gully that Dougal and I had discussed. From there Tut led leftwards across steep, fractured rock covered in powder snow, a pitch I thought was the hardest on the climb and certainly equal in difficulty to Nick's magnificent lead out of the gully, from where it was possible to access the upper snowfield. After five previous expeditions had stalled at this point, the two of them had managed to solve the problem of the rock band in a single day.

All my fears about missing out were behind me now. Dougal and I were the lucky lads Chris had chosen to move up to Camp 5 where he and various Sherpas had been supporting the climbers on the rock band. Next day we took off up the ropes to put in Camp 6 and hopefully reach the summit.

'I'm not sure that we can keep you supplied,' Chris said in a forlorn voice as I was preparing to set off after Dougal up the fixed ropes. Chris explained that his back end was collapsing. I thought: nasty that, haemorrhoids up here. His problems were rather more significant than that, and unfortunately involved us. He had too many fit climbers, all strong characters, looking for the ultimate satisfaction of the summit. Some were disgruntled with how Chris had planned the next few attempts and were talking about quitting. Our other doctor, Charlie Clarke, suggested Chris should return for a rest, having been up high for so long, and deal with the problems at Camp 2.

By the time Chris had made it down to Camp 2, Hamish, feeling superfluous to requirements, had left the expedition; having devoted considerable time and energy before the expedition to improving our equipment he must have been so disappointed. Seeing his deputy leader walking out on the expedition

Dougal Haston climbing up to the site of Camp 6.

must have been hard for Chris to take, especially as Hamish was one of his oldest friends.

When I caught up with Dougal in the gully, he cursed the indiscipline of those below. 'We'll manage, youth, it'll be all right,' I said, without knowing how. I continued up the cleft, leaving Dougal to fiddle around with his crampons, which kept coming adrift from his sponge overboots. The last information I'd had from Nick was a warning to watch out on the fixed ropes because he hadn't managed to secure them that well.

So I just clipped on to the ropes as a safety line and climbed the snow in the gully and the snow-covered rocks across to the exit ramp and the end of his rope, where I put in extra anchors and belayed. From there, I was able to fully appreciate the great job Nick had done climbing this gangway of fractured rock with only a thin covering of snow, the rock above impeding his movement, and all this wearing a framed rucksack and without oxygen; his cylinder had emptied down in the gully.

Ang Phurba now came up, carrying our tent for Camp 6. This splendid Sherpa belayed my rope as I went up new ground for thirty feet including a ten-foot vertical corner and belayed again. I was bringing up Ang Phurba as Dougal came into view with his crampons swinging from his waist. I continued on up, running out 250 feet of rope on steep snow until I found myself looking across the upper snowfield towards the south summit couloir. I just had to pause and take it all in. After so many years of thinking about being here, I had actually made it.

We pitched camp, chopping a ledge for the tent in a rib of snow, as Chris, Mick and Mike Thompson arrived after a magnificent carry, all with vital loads of food, rope and oxygen. They descended with our thanks; Mike shouted back: 'Just get up, that's all the thanks I need.'

That evening we nearly blew it, literally. When changing oxygen cylinders, gas escaped and the flame from the little gas stove enveloped the pan and threatened to engulf the tent and burn it down. It might have done so had I not thrown the oxygen bottle out into the snow as Dougal turned the stove off. Disaster averted. Next morning we ran another thousand feet of fixed rope across the snowfield and came back for a second night at Camp 6.

We lay in our down bags that night, listening to the wind buffeting the final pyramid of Everest and rocking our little canvas box. I had no real doubts, just nagging little thoughts about how vulnerable we were, how much we were at the mercy of the weather, how lucky we should be if we reached the summit. Then towards dawn the wind faded and we were off, into double boots, crampons, windsuits and harnesses, downing a cup of tea and off along the ropes, jumar clamps sliding on their icy sheaths. It took only a quarter of the time to reach our high point of the day before and then we were on to virgin slopes.

Dougal Haston above the Yellow Band.

As one doubt was resolved, another took hold. Past the umbilical cord of fixed rope, Dougal's oxygen set packed up. He was all for going back, but I unscrewed the jubilee clips to find the pipes gunged up with ice.

'You must dribble more than me,' I told him as I worked with my penknife and then flailed the pipes and mask against the rock. The ice came pouring out and Dougal could breathe again.

Now we had to tackle a short thirty-foot step barring entry into the south summit couloir. It took some effort climbing steep limestone at 27,500 feet. I managed to put in three pegs all in a cluster in a shallow groove in the rock and then continued more confidently to the top and beyond to belay and change oxygen bottles, leaving one tied off with one of our two ropes to use on our return.

Then yet another doubt arose as Dougal lead through up the couloir, where he found himself wading through unconsolidated snow; thigh deep became waist deep, and finally, with me pushing from behind, chest deep. We didn't reach the south summit until 3.30 p.m. I dug a hollow in the soft snow bank on the far side of the ridge, the Tibetan side since we were now on the frontier. I needed to get out of the bitter wind, blowing at forty miles per hour, while Dougal got inside his bivouac sack to melt water on the stove. In a rasping voice from a painfully sore throat, he suggested we stop now and go for the top early next day. I didn't relish a bivouac, not having a down suit or sleeping bag, and knew I would probably want to go down next morning.

Dougal, and others, suggested later I had left Camp 6 intending to bivouac, perhaps because I packed a stove and cooking pot. That wasn't the case. I often carried a stove rather than bottles of water, since water tended to freeze up high and there was a weight advantage by melting snow as I went. I had no intention at all of bivouacking. I had left my down suit at Camp 6; it was tight round the knees, restricting my movement every time I lifted my leg. Without it, dressed in silk, cashmere and nylon pile, I knew I'd be terribly exposed if we stopped for the night.

Suddenly restless, I got to my feet and asked Dougal to mind the rope while I checked the snow conditions further along the ridge. If it was firmer than the couloir below, I suggested, we should carry on. Traversing the frontier ridge was a wonderful experience; I paused to look around beyond the confines of the Western Cwm. Now I could see the mountains and the rolling brown landscape to the north. Even better, the snow seemed firmer, and with the boost we got from that reviving drink, we made good progress along the ridge, swinging leads, keeping well left of the cornice overhanging the 9,000-foot Kangshung face.

Dougal led up the Hillary Step in short order despite the snow here having the consistency of sugar. We weren't stopping now. Dougal simply swept away the surface snow to reach the more solid stuff beneath. Meanwhile, I changed the film in my camera, sitting precariously astride a snow arête with one foot

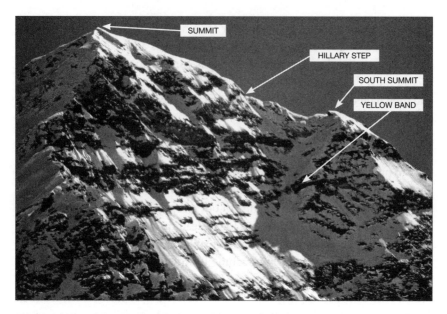

SUMMIT

HILLARY STEP

SOUTH SUMMIT

YELLOW BAND

The upper section of the south-west face, with the key features highlighted.

in Tibet and the other in Nepal. I slipped my bare hand out of my woollen mitt, wound up the film and looked in my rucksack for a new cartridge, fairly certain I didn't have one. I wasn't too bothered about running out; no more bloody cameras. Right at the bottom of my sack, not in a container, I found an unused reel but the film was frozen and kept snapping off as I tried to feed it on to the spool. Then I'd have to tear it down so I can try again, all this with the rope in my teeth. If I hadn't succeeded the picture I took of Dougal on the Hillary Step would have been my last.

The step itself was buried in snow and much easier than when Hillary and Tenzing first climbed it. I led through, nearing the limit of my endurance. Perhaps my oxygen had run out, because I became aware of a complete shift in perspective. My mind had parted company from my body and I was looking down on myself from about fifteen feet above my left shoulder. From this new angle I began directing operations, offering myself advice on how to make progress. I watched myself stumbling through the crusty snow and suggested I got a better rhythm going or I would never make it. I then watched as my physical self slowed down and adopted a steadier guide's pace; I then instructed myself to move to a safer line up the ridge, away from the cornices. It all seemed so natural at the time.

At 6 p.m., we found ourselves walking side by side on to the summit. Dougal, usually a reticent fellow, had a huge smile on his face and then gave me a hug. After so much effort, and on a perfect late summer evening, we were there.

With the shadows beginning to lengthen, Dougal Haston approaches the summit of Everest on the evening of 24 September 1975.

The wind had dropped, and the early evening was perfectly still. We didn't say much to each other, only to point out distant mountains. The photographs I took, that I've shown so often since, dominate my memories of the summit, although sometimes the elation of that moment breaks through and I remember how it was. An hour later, having watched the sun filtering through the layered clouds to produce the finest sunset I've ever seen, we thought we'd better go down too. By the time we reached the top of the Hillary Step it was dark and our head torches were failing fast. I hurriedly fixed a 'deadman' aluminium plate for the abseil down the step. At the bottom, now in total darkness, we tried to pull the rope down but it unexpectedly stopped. We had carelessly left a knot at the end of the rope, which had jammed in the deadman's wire loop. I reached up and cut the rope as high as possible and continued back along the ridge.

Our head torches had gone out on the Hillary Step and the wind was blowing snow into our tracks, so we decided it prudent to bivouac at the south summit. Without sleeping bags or canned oxygen, we dug into a snow bank and sat on our rucksacks for the next nine hours. Since no one had spent a night out this high without oxygen, we were not certain as to what would actually happen. Dougal had a long and involved conversation about the relative merits of various sleeping bags with Dave Clark, our equipment officer, who was in Base Camp at the time. Not having a sleeping bag was obviously very much on Dougal's mind; I thought he was losing the plot and must have cerebral oedema.

Before long however I too found myself drifting in and out of a conversation with my feet, which had become two separate, conscious entities sharing our cave. I told the right foot that the left foot was just not warming up. The left foot was clearly resentful, telling me I never used it. I asked the left foot what it meant by that: 'Well when you kick a rugby ball, you always kick with your right foot.' It slowly dawned on me that I should pay the left foot more attention and when I took off my boot and sock, I found my left foot was seriously cold and turning wooden with frost. It took a full hour of pummelling and rubbing my foot before I could get any heat into it and it started to revive. Dougal kindly opened up the front of his down suit to let me put my bare toes under his armpit. Then, to keep warm and not nod off to sleep, I continued to enlarge the cave.

In the event, we were pleasantly surprised to survive without oxygen, sleeping bags or, as it turned out, suffering any frostbite. Afterwards, I felt I could risk an unplanned bivouac anywhere – that is anywhere there was enough snow to dig a cave. One night at 28,700 feet had broadened the range of what and how I would climb in the future. I knew from then on I would never again burden myself with oxygen bottles. Yet despite what I and others have said about how all the support of men and materials on these big expeditions widens the margin of safety so much as to leave adventure climbers unsatisfied, our great friend Mick Burke did not come back from his ascent.

Chris had despatched a second team the day after our ascent. Peter Boardman and Pertemba reached the summit in cloud and with a storm blowing in. As they left the summit, Mick Burke appeared and went on up towards the top to film for the BBC. I'd passed him as we descended and he was coming up. He congratulated me, but seemed tired and rather subdued; I think the burden of filming had worn him down. Mick's partner, Martin Boysen, had turned back from their summit bid having lost a crampon and with his oxygen malfunctioning. Peter and Pertemba waited two hours at the south summit in whiteout conditions as the weather deteriorated but Mick never appeared. We agreed it most likely that he walked through the cornice hanging over the Kangshung face. His companions, Peter and Pertemba, only just made Camp 6 after stumbling about in zero visibility, unable to distinguish snow in the air from snow on the ground.

Down at Camp 2 in the Western Cwm, while we waited to discover Mick's fate, a huge cornice broke off Nuptse and swept through our midst, breaking ribs and blacking eyes, a final close call that we all survived. We were sleeping side by side when suddenly the tent fabric was pressing down on us; I realised my arms were pinned tight against my sides. I actually used my teeth to tear the tent fabric to let in some fresh air. With just a little more snow, Dougal and I would have suffocated, just like Gary Ullin on Peak 19 in the Pamirs. Eventually, Charlie Clarke and the Sherpas pulled us out. Charlie's sense of humour came to the fore when he jokingly told us he had woken our leader, who told him to 'shoot the looters' and went straight back to sleep.

During the descent to Base Camp I had more time to reflect on what we had accomplished, particularly on our summit day and in the cave. Once again I was made aware that in going to the limits of endurance, regions of my being that are normally hidden reveal themselves and it is possible to find help within. Most people seem to attribute such psychological revelations to chemical changes induced by extreme exercise or hypoxia. On the other hand it could be a consequence of tapping into morphic fields or the universal consciousness. It might be that a passage in Isaiah has relevance: 'And thine ears shall hear a word behind thee, saying, "This is the way; walk ye in it," when ye turn to the right hand, and when ye turn to the left.' There have been so many essentially similar accounts from Polar explorers, sailors, mountaineers and survivors at the end of their tether – of getting into conversation with a presence that has often proved useful, if not vital, to survival – that, far from the phenomena being dismissed as hallucination, it continues to intrigue psychologists and all of us that have had first-hand experience of the 'Third Man', as it has been called.

I began to understand that until I was totally committed, completely fixed on going forward, then there was always prevarication, doubt and energy all over the place. Only when my energy was totally channelled towards the goal did I stop dithering. From the moment I decided to go for it, unexpected forces came into play to help me get to where I wanted to be. This became apparent to me for the first time when pushing up the south face of Koh-i-Bandaka in the Hindu Kush. I was encouraged by observing, deep inside, a calm prescience that all I had to do was to keep on keeping on, and all obstacles, one after another, would be overcome. This calm prescience or faith that all will be well only comes about when everything is right; in mountaineering, I have patiently prepared for the moment and gained the necessary experience, I have served my apprenticeship, and waited for conditions on the mountain and the weather to be favourable. Most importantly, my partner and I are entirely compatible. I write this in the light of many climbs, although none awoke my understanding more than climbing Everest with Dougal.

Looking back, I can see there was an important corollary to all of this – the requirement, at some point, to give up all ambition to achieve a particular mountaineering goal. It might have been illness, bad weather, technical problems, or poor team dynamics that caused me to write off my ambition. But the moment I totally let go events began to change the situation, as if by magic, right on cue, to allow me to continue: the weather improved, we found a solution to the technical problems, we recovered from sickness, the team suddenly began working harmoniously. So we pack up and go again but now more humbly than before and more in touch with ourselves and each other and the world around us. If we continue to make progress and reach the summit, then now it comes as a gift.

The view from the summit of Everest. Ama Dablam is poking out of the clouds in the centre, while the Nuptse–Lhotse ridge is partially shaded in the foreground. I carried two cameras to the top: one with colour film, one black and white.

Jan and her class receive the news. **Photo:** Nottingham Post.

EPILOGUE

It wasn't only my life that Everest changed. Jan was sitting in the staffroom at school when the news came through. Everyone thought she'd gone mad when she started leaping up and down. She went straight into the classroom to tell her children the news and they cheered and cried. She would often tell them what I was up to. She also used to tell them that she was trying to alter my image so that I'd look just like John Lennon. The reality was that my round NHS specs fitted better under snow goggles; she was always more of a hippy than I was. My hair was long mostly because it was a nuisance to get it cut. But she liked that image, and she liked the fact I was getting public recognition for what I'd achieved.

Before long there were television crews in school filming the papier mâché model the children had made of Everest and reporters asking her questions about how it felt. Two days later, Jan and Michael were flying to Kathmandu to meet me courtesy of the *Daily Mail* who sent Bob and Gina Holmes along to photograph and report on our reunion. Bad weather had settled on Khumbu, and they had to spend five days in Kathmandu waiting for a flight to Lukla. Rushing up into the mountains from the airstrip was a trial for Jan, given she wasn't acclimatised, but Michael chivvied her along. 'Come on Mum, we're nearly there, Dad will be waiting.' In her rucksack she'd packed a John Lennon tape, photographs of Martha, some flapjack from her mother and lots of messages, including one from the Sheriff of Nottingham. When she passed some Sherpas wearing expedition t-shirts, she asked about me. 'Oh,' they said, 'the lama.' My long hair and glasses had made an impression. 'He's in the pub.'

She was walking up the trail below Namche Bazaar when we met, and I can see her now, with a big straw hat over her long blond hair, walking up the path hugging a gaggle of children clutching the skirts of the blue Sherpa *chuba*

Jan and Michael were flown out to meet me courtesy of the *Daily Mail*. **Photos**: Bob Holmes.

she was wearing, and all of them singing. We were soon hugging and kissing, as she did with the rest of the team who always enjoyed her company.

We spent the next few days trekking in Khumbu, with Chris, Alan Tritton from Barclays, and Chris's agent George Greenfield, a lovely man, who entertained Michael by playing Scrabble. Michael and Jan wanted to see the summit of Everest, so we walked up to Tengboche. The sky was overcast as we toiled up the slope but the clouds parted just as we arrived to reveal the top of the mountain. I told her aboutthe climb and surviving the bivouac. Then we went back to Kunde to meet up with the rest of the expedition for a party with the Sherpas. Michael played football with some of the pupils from the Hillary School and seemed quiteunaffected despite the altitude of 13,000 feet. A yak was slaughtered and cooked for a day and a half by Purna the cook, and we washed it down with copious amounts of chang and raksi.

There were more parties, of the diplomatic variety, in Kathmandu and Delhi and then we were back at Heathrow where a horde of well-wishers and journalists were waiting. I spotted Martha sitting on Dad's shoulders. My parents were both really excited, especially my father. Ever since he'd given up boxing to take care of his family, he'd taken a keen interest in whatever I did, and as I became better known as a climber and articles started appearing in the newspapers, he would faithfully cut them out and stick them in his scrapbooks; there are seven of them overall, and the one with the cuttings from Everest had an image of me standing on the summit chiselled in gold on the binder. A few years later, not so long before he died, I went down to London with Dad to collect my CBE at Buckingham Palace. He said to me: 'Thank God I lived to see this day.'

No one could have predicted what a big thing our climb became in the media and that it would enter the public consciousness. It was a gloomy time in the UK, with economic woes, frequent strikes and IRA bombings. Suddenly, here was a success story and the media took it to heart. We were all affected by the ascent of the south-west face, especially Jan who became even more outgoing. Dougal and I had disappeared off the radar for a day so when we reappeared unscathed her relief was immense; she enjoyed the success.

Jan had a lovely smile and was always good for a sensible quote so she often appeared in the newspapers and on TV and radio. She was, in fact, quite a good ambassador for climbing; she had a genuine appreciation of the sport and of the qualities of independence of mind and spirit that climbers often have. Jan was naturally sympathetic, giving more than she took, loyal to family and friends, tender with children and particularly good when helping grieving wives and mothers overcoming the loss of those climbers who did not make it back from the mountains.

Little more than a year after climbing Everest, I was struggling up the steps of the cemetery in the Swiss resort of Leysin holding one end of Dougal's coffin; his oldest schoolmate, 'Big Eley' Moriarty, was at the other. He'd been killed in an avalanche while skiing. It was a dismal day, dank and cold; there was snow on the ground, and we'd had a few, so it was hard to stay on our feet. Other deaths upset me more, particularly those of Georges Bettembourg and Roger Baxter-Jones; my memory of Dougal's death is one of anger that he wouldn't be there. We had planned a lot of climbs together.

As I said, no one who climbs Everest is ever quite the same. In my own experience, I returned home far more aware, stronger and with an inner peace that lasted quite some time before it dissipated and I left home for more such transformative experiences to Denali, K2, The Ogre, Nuptse and Kangchenjunga. My experience on Everest put me in a good position to tackle bigger challenges in the mountains. All my life I had fought against inertia. Every time I overcame the desire to have just one more cup of coffee, read the paper, watch TV, talk on the telephone, I gained strength to act – to push on with the line of study, to follow up leads – to take the next step.

Rumi, centuries ago, reflected that 'what you seek is seeking you.' Letting go to go for it never seemed to happen for me when I was consumed with my own self-importance. That is why it always seemed to me that the most important lessons took place in the playground where a few well-chosen words could puncture pretentious views and self-indulgent actions in a moment. For that reason, I will always be grateful not only to my parents and Jan for providing a stable home but also to my schools, the Scouts, the Moderns Rugby Club and, above all, the Nottingham Climbers' Club. These were where I learned the necessary lessons to climb Everest and many more high mountains thereafter.

There is in Bill Murray's book on the Scottish Himalayan expedition of 1951, a passage on the subject of making things happen. 'Until one is committed there is hesitancy, the chance to draw back, always ineffectiveness. Concerning all acts of initiative (and creation), there is one elementary truth, the ignorance of which kills countless ideas and splendid plans: that the moment one definitely commits oneself, then providence moves too. All sorts of things occur to help one that would never otherwise have occurred. A whole stream of events issues from the decision, raising in one's favour all manner of unforeseen incidents and meetings and material assistance, which no man could have dreamt would have come his way.'

Like Murray, I have learned a deep respect for one of Goethe's couplets, freely translated by John Anster:

> Whatever you can do or dream you can, begin it.
> Boldness has genius, power and magic in it!

ACKNOWLEDGEMENTS

My grateful thanks to my wife Trish for creating an environment conducive to thinking and writing, and also for listening and commenting as I read to her each chapter as I wrote it.

To Ruth Moore, who has run my office and that of CAN since 1998 and has typed up this book from my handwritten scrawl or, as more often than not, as I read it out to her. And to Anne Manger who helped with the typing since 25 April, the day the earthquake struck Nepal, an event which has dominated our lives ever since.

My brothers, Brian and Garry, for elaborating on events and offering numerous helpful suggestions after reading the relevant chapters. And my uncle Roy Gregory and 'auntie' Vera Smith for recalling my mother's early life.

For Frank Earp, for tales of Halfway House and Nottingham Canal, and Honorary Councillor Bill Bradbury, Jennifer Walker (née Lowe) and David Summers for memories of Charlbury Road.

To Clive Davies, Mick Garside, Wes Hayden, Dez Hadlum, Molly Higgins, Guy Lee, Lyn Noble, Bob Pettigrew, Steve Smith, Graham Spooner, Geoff Stroud, Peter Thompson, Di Stubbs, Rob Wood and Phil Lee: all of whom supplied copious notes on our early climbs together and/or later found time to check the relevant chapters.

I must also thank Jan's sister, Tena, and college friend Ann Gertie for helping to date events in our lives together.

My editor, Ed Douglas, has been invaluable in making this tome less tedious and silly; John Coefield, my picture editor, has done a good job in the book's presentation. And finally, a big thank you to Jon Barton the MD of Vertebrate for including me in his growing list of climbing authors.

NB Ever since climbing Everest I have attempted to write an autobiography; during the last forty years I have had help first from Jan, then editorial assistance from Margaret Body and also Jenny McLeod for typing support. Although *Up and About* is vastly different from earlier versions I am sure it has benefitted from the input of Jan, Maggie and Jenny.

BIBLIOGRAPHY

Abbey, Edward, *Desert Solitaire: A season in the wilderness* (New York, 1968).

Abbot, A.E., *The Number Seven* (London, 1962).

Adams, Douglas, *The Hitchhiker's Guide to the Galaxy* (London, 1979).

Afford, A.B., *The Story of White Hall Open Country Pursuits Centre* (Buxton, 1978).

Ament, Pat, *Royal Robbins: Spirit of the Age* (Lincoln, 1992).

Amos, Dr Denise, 'World War Two in Nottinghamshire' on *The Nottinghamshire Heritage Gateway* [website] <http://www.nottsheritagegateway.org.uk/events/ww2.htm>

Angell, Shirley, *The Pinnacle Club: A History of Women Climbing* (Glasgow, 1988), 179.

Anon., 'California: Postscript to People's Park', *Time*, Vol. 95, No.7 (16 Feb. 1970).

— *Nottingham Journal* (August 1942).

— *Outside* (April 1978).

— *The British Empire* (BBC TV Time-Life Books), No.48 (1972).

— *The British Empire* (BBC TV Time-Life Books), No.70 (1972), 1959.

— 'The "Swinging Sixties"' on *The Socialist Party of Great Britain* [website] <http://www.worldsocialism.org/spgb/socialism-or-your-money-back/swinging-sixties>

Bachman, B.B., 'Baffin' in *Mountain Gazette*, No.26 (Oct. 1974), 10–15.

Bailey, Dan, 'Stanage Causeway Resurfacing Furore' on *UKClimbing.com* (April 2013) [website] <http://www.ukclimbing.com/news/item.php?id=68011>

Barford, J.E.Q. ed., *Climbing in Britain* (Harmondsworth, 1946).

Boardman, Terry, 'The Drive Towards a New World Order in the 1990s', *New View*, No.1 (1999).

Bonatti, Walter, *On The Heights*, trans. Edwards, Lovett F. (London, 1964), 88.

Bonington, Chris, *Everest South West Face* (London, 1973).

Borlee, Jacques, *De Freyr à l'Himâlaya: les grandes heures de l'alpinisme Belge* (Brussels, 1987), 96–97.

Bridwell, Jim, 'Brave New World' in *Mountain*, No.31 (January, 1974).

Brooke, Richard, 'Notes 1973: Polar Regions' in Pyatt, Edward, ed., *The Alpine Journal*, Vol.79 (London, 1974), 260.

Buchman, Frank N.D., *Remaking the World: The speeches of Frank N.D. Buchman* (London, 1955), 46.

Byne, Eric and Sutton, Geoffrey, *High Peak: The story of walking and climbing in the Peak District* (London, 1966), 187–192.

Campbell, Robin, in *Scottish Mountaineering Club Journal* (May 1970), 339.

Carpenter, Humphrey, *That Was Satire that Was* (London, 2000).

Cleare, John, 'Joe Brown at Eighty' in *The Climbers' Club Journal* (2011), 60–66.

Craig, Robert W., *Storm & Sorrow in the High Pamirs* (Seattle, 1977), 209–210.

Denny, Glen, *Yosemite in the Sixties* (Santa Barbara, 2007), 122, 123.

Drasdo, Harold, 'Margins of Safety' in Blackshaw, Alan, ed., *The Alpine Journal*, Vol.74 (London, 1969), 159–168.

— *The Ordinary Route* (Glasgow, 1997), 156.

Earp, Frank E., *Nottingham Hidden History Team* [website] <https://nottinghamhiddenhistoryteam.wordpress.com>

— *The A-Z of Curious Nottinghamshire* (Stroud, 2014), 36–38.

— 'The Old Stones of Nottinghamshire' *in The A–Z of Curious Nottinghamshire* (Stroud, 2014), 92.

Earp, Joe, *Nottingham Hidden History Team* [website] <https://nottinghamhiddenhistoryteam.wordpress.com>

Ellis, Derek, 'Equipment and Technique: 1972' in Pyatt, Edward, ed., *The Alpine Journal*, Vol.78 (London, 1973), 256.

Erskine, Angus, in *Scottish Mountaineering Club Journal*, No.175 (1984), 91–94.

Evans, Charles, 'Valedictory Address' in Pyatt, Edward, ed., *The Alpine Journal*, Vol.76 (London, 1971), 7–17.

French, Patrick, *Younghusband: The Last Great Imperial Adventurer* (London, 1994), 252.

Frison-Roche, Roger, and Jouty, Sylvain, *A History of Mountain Climbing* (New York, 1996), 9.

Goldsmith, Edward, Allen, Robert, and others, *A Blueprint for Survival* (Harmondsworth, 1972).

Gray, Dennis, 'In memoriam: Eric Beard' in Blackshaw, Alan, ed., *The Alpine Journal*, Vol.75 (London, 1970), 339–341.

— *Rope Boy* (London, 1970), 304–316.

Greenwood, Brian, in *Mountain*, No.15 (May 1971), 39.

Gurnham, Richard, *A History of Nottingham* (Andover, 2010), 80, 159.

Hankinson, Alan, in Bonington, Chris, Boysen, Martin, Hankinson, Alan, Haston, Dougal, Sandhu, Balwant, and Scott, Doug, *Changabang* (London, 1975), 83–87.

Harding, Warren, *Downward Bound: A mad! guide to rock climbing* (Englewood Cliffs, 1975).

Harper, Fred, in *Mountain Life*, No.9 (Aug/Sept 1973), 6–7.

Harwood, A.C., *The Recovery of Man in Childhood*, (London, 1958).

Hastings, Max, *All Hell Let Loose: The World at War 1939–1945* (London, 2011), 124.

Jones, Chris, *Climbing in North America* (Berkeley, 1976).

Kelly, Phil, Hoey, Graham, Barker, Giles, *Peak Rock* (Sheffield, 2013), 146.

Kohli, M.S., and Conboy, Kenneth, *Spies in the Himalayas: Secret Missions and Perilous Climbs* (Lawrence, 2003).

Lauria, Don, in *American Alpine Journal* (1971), 362.

Lear, Linda, *Rachel Carson: Witness for Nature* (New York, 1997).

Lee, Martin, and Shlain, Bruce, *Acid Dreams: The Complete Social History of LSD: The CIA, the Sixties and Beyond* (New York, 1985).

Lee, Peter, 'Making a Billion Hindus Glow in the Dark', *CounterPunch* (June 2008).

Liedloff, Jean, *The Continuum Concept* (rev. edn, London, 1986).

Loynes, Chris, and Higgins, Peter, 'Safety and Risk in Outdoor Education' in Higgins, Peter, Loynes, Chris, and Crowther, Neville, eds., *A Guide for Outdoor Educators in Scotland* (Penrith, 1997), 26–29.

Mackinder, Halford J., *Democratic Ideals and Reality: A Study in the Politics of Reconstruction* (London, 1919), 186.

MacNaught-Davis, Ian, in *Mountain*, No.15 (May, 1971), 33.

Miles, Barry, *The Beat Hotel: Ginsberg, Burroughs and Corso in Paris*, 1957–1963 (New York, 2001).

Moritz, Carl Philip, *Journeys of a German in England: A Walking Tour of England in 1782* (new edn, London, 2009), 176–177.

Moulam, A.J.T., in *Mountaineering*, Vol.VI, No.1 (1971), 17.

Mumm, A.L., *Five Months in the Himalaya* (London, 1909), 83.

Murray, W.H., *The Scottish Himalayan Expedition* (London, 1951), 6–7, 98.

Needham, David, *Battle of the Flames: Nottinghamshire's Fight for Survival in WWII* (Ashbourne, 2009), 50, 78.

Noyce, Wilfrid, *To the Unknown Mountain: the ascent of Trivor* (London, 1962).

Nunn, Paul, 'Asgard Outing', *Mountain*, No.26 (March 1973), 33–35.

Oldfield, Geoffrey, *The Illustrated History of Nottingham's Suburbs* (2nd rev. edn, Nottingham, 2009), 88–89.

Orwell, George, *Keep the Aspidistra Flying* (new edn, London, 2012).

Perrin, Jim, *The Villain: The life of Don Whillans* (London, 2005).

Pretty, Harry, ed., *Oread Mountaineering Club: 50th Anniversary Journal 1949–1999* (Derby, 1999), 174.

Pryor, Francis, *The Making of the British Landscape: How We Have Transformed the Land, from Prehistory to Today* (London, 2011), 579–585.

Rebuffat, Gaston, *Starlight and Storm*, trans. Hunt, John, and Noyce, Wilfrid (London, 1956), 29–50.

Redfield, James, *The Celestine Prophecy* (London, 1994).

Reed, Peter, and Rottenberg, David, eds., *Wisdom in the Open Air: The Norwegian Roots of Deep Ecology* (Minneapolis, 1995), 24–25, 158.

Reich, Charles A., *The Greening of America* (New York, 1970), 326.

Roberts, David, *Moments of Doubt and other mountaineering writings* (Seattle, 1986), 214.

Robbins, Royal, in *Mountain Gazette*, No.33 (May 1975), 24–25.

— *Basic Rockcraft* (Glendale, 1971).

Roper, Steve, *Camp 4: Recollections of a Yosemite Rockclimber* (Seattle, 1994), 223–225.

Russell, Jean, ed., *Climb if You Will: A Commentary on Geoff Hayes and His Club, the Oread Mountaineering Club* (Ashbourne, 1974), 71–74.

Scott, Doug, *Big Wall Climbing* (Oxford, 1974), 140–168.

— *Mountain*, No.3 (May, 1969).

— *Mountain*, No.22 (July, 1972), 20–25.

— *Mountain Craft*, No.60 (Summer, 1963).

— *Mountain Craft*, No.71, (Spring, 1966).

— *Mountain Craft*, No.75, (Spring, 1967).

— 'On the Profundity Trail', *Mountain*, No.50 (May, 1971), 12–17.

Sheldon, William, *Atlas of Men: A Guide for Somatotyping the Adult Male of All Ages* (New York, 1954).

Sillitoe, Alan, *Life Without Armour* (London, 1995).

— *Raw Material* (London, 1972).

Smith, Carol, 'Spy Robert Schaller's life of secrecy, betrayal and regrets' on *Seattlepi.com* (2007) [website] <*http://www.seattlepi.com/local/article/Spy-Robert-Schaller-s-life-of-secrecy-betrayal-1232285.php*>

Speck, Frank G., *Naskapi: The Savage Hunters of the Labrador Peninsula* (Norman, 1935).

Steiner, Rudolf, *World History In The Light Of Anthroposophy* (London, 1950).

Strong, Roy, *The Spirit of Britain: A Narrative History of the Arts* (London, 1999), 644 onwards.

Sutton, Geoffrey and Noyce, Wilfrid, *Samson: The Life and Writing of Menlove Edwards* (Stockport, 1961).

Synnott, Mark, 'The Russian Way' on *Climbing* [website] <*http://www.climbing.com/climber/the-russian-way*>

Takeda, Pete, 'The Secret of Nanda Devi', *Rock & Ice* (Feb. 2012). <*http://www.rockandice.com/lates-news/the-secret-of-nanda-devi*>

Tejada-Flores, Lito, 'Games Climbers Play' in Cox, A.D.M., ed., *The Alpine Journal*, Vol.73 (London, 1968), 46–52.

Terray, Lionel, *Conquistadors of the Useless*, trans. Sutton, Geoffrey (London, 1963).

Tranter, Philip, and Tranter, Nigel ed., *No Tigers in the Hindu Kush* (London, 1968).

Watson, Adam, *A zoologist on Baffin Island, 1953* (Rothersthorpe, 2011), 229–234.

Weger, Ulrich, 'The Initiation of Action and the Weakness of the Will', *New View*, No.59 (2011), 58–60.

Wells, Colin, ed., 'Jerry Wright' in *Who's Who in British Climbing* (Buxton, 2008), 534–535.

Whillans, Don, 'Appendix A: Solo by Motor Bicycle from Rawlpindi to Lancashire', in Noyce, Wilfrid, *To the Unknown Mountain: the ascent of Trivor* (London, 1962).

Whillans, Don and Ormerod, Alick, *Don Whillans: Portrait of a Mountaineer* (London, 1971), 52–53, 178–179.

Whitworth, Douglas, *Nottingham: Life in the Postwar Years* (Stroud, 2006), 40.

— *Nottingham in the 1960s and 70s* (Stroud, 2009).

Williams, John L., *America's Mistress: Eartha Kitt, Her Life and Times* (London, 2013).

Wilson, Ken, 'GUEST EDITORIAL: Ken Wilson on the BMC Presidential Election' on *UKClimbing.com* (April 2009) [website] <*http://www.ukclimbing.com/articles/page.php?id=1787*>

— 'The Cairngorm Tragedy', *Mountain*, No.20 (March, 1972), 29–33.

— 'Royal Robbins Interview', *Mountain*, No.18 (November, 1971), 27–35.

Wilson, Ken, ed., 'Recent Dirty Tricks', *Mountain*, No.31 (January, 1974), 12.

Winthrop Young, Geoffrey, Sutton, Geoffrey and Noyce, Wilfrid, *Snowdon Biography* (London, 1957).

Wood, Rob, *Towards the Unknown Mountains* (Campbell River, 1991), 35, 37–38.

Wood, Rob, and McKeith, Alistair 'Bugs', in *Mountain*, No.13 (January, 1971), 35.

Woodforde, James, *The Diary of a Country Parson 1758–1802* (new edn, Norwich, 2011).

INDEX